Sign: Akan National Park, Hot Springs

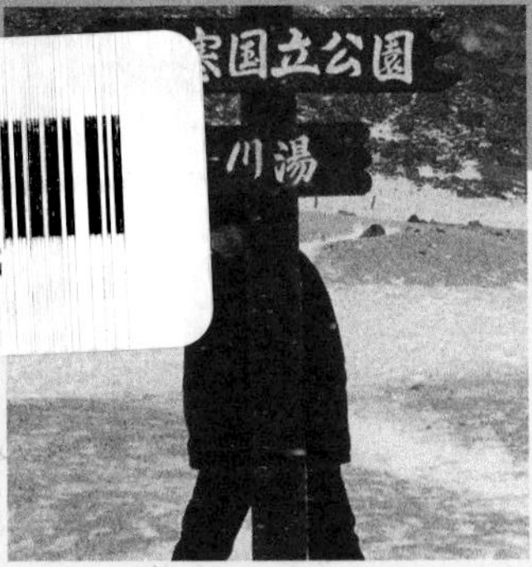
寒国立公園
川湯

冨樫義博

I'll do my best.

Yoshihiro Togashi

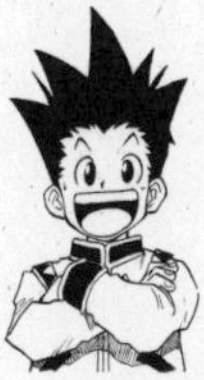

Yoshihiro Togashi's manga career began in 1986 at the age of 20, when he won the coveted Osamu Tezuka Award for new manga artists. He debuted in the Japanese **Weekly Shonen Jump** magazine in 1989 with the romantic comedy **Tende Shôwaru Cupid**. From 1990 to 1994 he wrote and drew the hit manga **YuYu Hakusho**, which was followed by the dark comedy science-fiction series **Level E**, and finally this adventure series, **Hunter x Hunter**, available from VIZ Media's SHONEN JUMP Advanced imprint. In 1999 he married the manga artist Naoko Takeuchi.

HUNTER X HUNTER Volume 25
The SHONEN JUMP ADVANCED Manga Edition

STORY AND ART BY
YOSHIHIRO TOGASHI

English Adaptation & Translation/Lillian Olsen
Touch-up Art & Lettering/Mark McMurray
Design/Matt Hinrichs
Editor/Yuki Murashige

Editor in Chief, Books/Alvin Lu
Editor in Chief, Magazines/Marc Weidenbaum
VP, Publishing Licensing/Rika Inouye
VP, Sales & Product Marketing/Gonzalo Ferreyra
VP, Creative/Linda Espinosa
Publisher/Hyoe Narita

Printed in the U.S.A.

Published by VIZ Media, LLC
P.O. Box 77010
San Francisco, CA 94107

SHONEN JUMP ADVANCED Manga Edition
10 9 8 7 6 5 4 3 2 1
First printing, March 2009

www.viz.com

THE WORLD'S MOST
CUTTING-EDGE MANGA
SHONEN JUMP ADVANCED
www.shonenjump.com

SHONEN JUMP ADVANCED MANGA

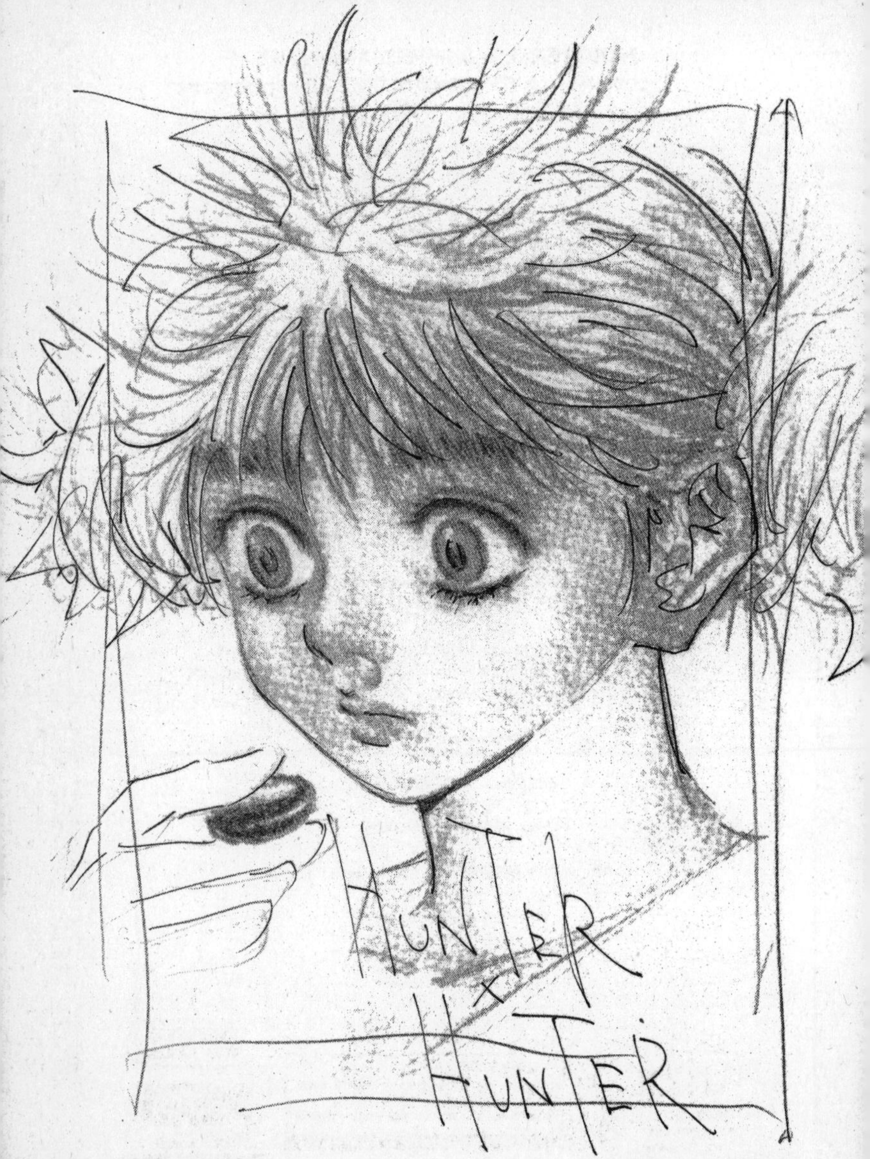
HUNTER
×
HUNTER

Story & Art by
Yoshihiro Togashi

Volume 25

Gon

OUR EAGER HERO. NOW A HUNTER, HE'S ON A SEARCH TO REUNITE WITH HIS FATHER!

The Story Thus Far

GON DREAMS OF BEING A HUNTER LIKE THE FATHER HE BARELY REMEMBERS, THE GREAT GING FREECSS. HE PASSES THE HIGHLY SELECTIVE LICENSING EXAM, BUT FINDING GING WILL BE EVEN HARDER.

GON AND KILLUA ESCAPE AN ENCOUNTER WITH THE FORMIDABLE NEFERPITOU IN EXCHANGE FOR KITE'S CAPTURE. FINALLY, THE KING ANT IS BORN—A VICIOUS CREATURE WHO WOULD EVEN EAT HIS OWN KIND. THE KING LEAVES THE NEST BEHIND AND TAKES OVER THE REPUBLIC OF EAST GORTEAU. KITE IS EVENTUALLY RECOVERED BY THE HUNTERS, BUT HE IS NO LONGER THE MAN HE USED TO BE... AND GON VOWS TO TURN HIM BACK.

OUR HEROES SNEAK INTO THE CAPITAL OF EAST GORTEAU, BIDING THEIR TIME UNTIL THEY STORM THE PALACE WHERE THE KING AND HIS ROYAL GUARDS ARE. THE DAY FOR "SORTING" IS ALMOST AT HAND...

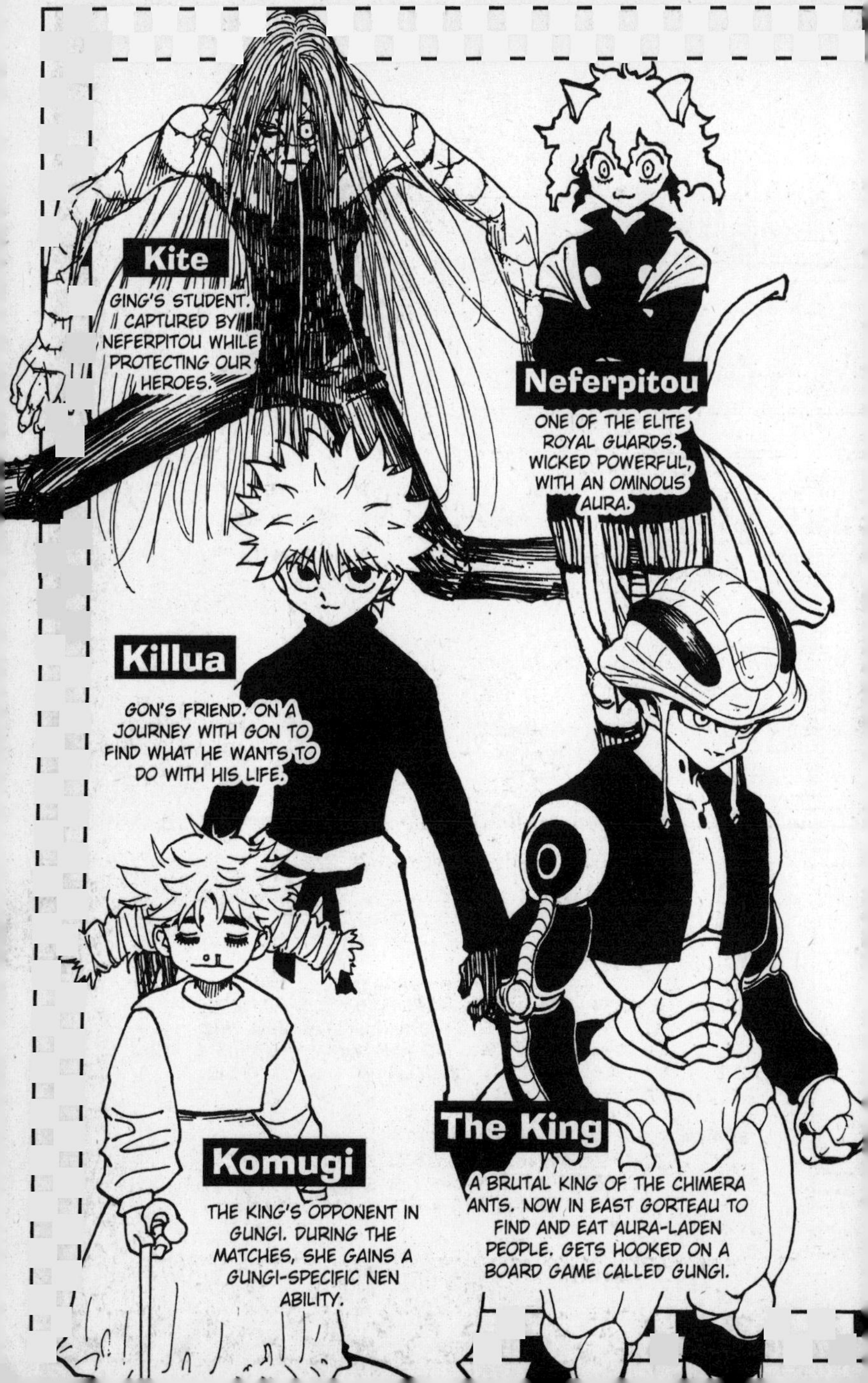

Kite
GING'S STUDENT. CAPTURED BY NEFERPITOU WHILE PROTECTING OUR HEROES.
Neferpitou
ONE OF THE ELITE ROYAL GUARDS. WICKED POWERFUL, WITH AN OMINOUS AURA.
Killua
GON'S FRIEND. ON A JOURNEY WITH GON TO FIND WHAT HE WANTS TO DO WITH HIS LIFE.
The King
A BRUTAL KING OF THE CHIMERA ANTS. NOW IN EAST GORTEAU TO FIND AND EAT AURA-LADEN PEOPLE. GETS HOOKED ON A BOARD GAME CALLED GUNGI.
Komugi
THE KING'S OPPONENT IN GUNGI. DURING THE MATCHES, SHE GAINS A GUNGI-SPECIFIC NEN ABILITY.

HUNTER × HUNTER

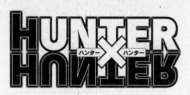

Volume 25

CONTENTS

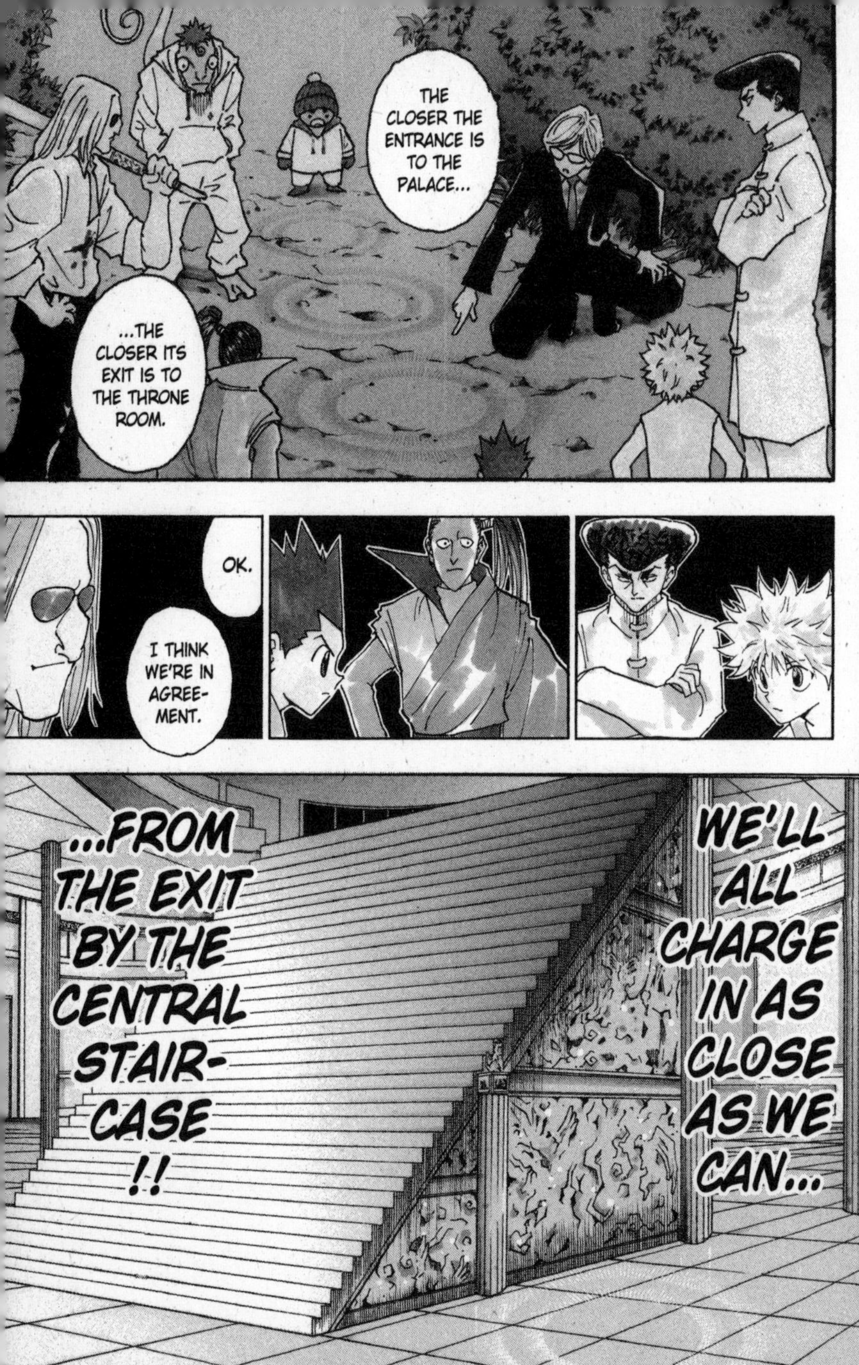
THE CLOSER THE ENTRANCE IS TO THE PALACE...
...THE CLOSER ITS EXIT IS TO THE THRONE ROOM.
OK.
I THINK WE'RE IN AGREE-MENT.
WE'LL ALL CHARGE IN AS CLOSE AS WE CAN...
...FROM THE EXIT BY THE CENTRAL STAIR-CASE!!

Chapter 261: Charge: Part 1

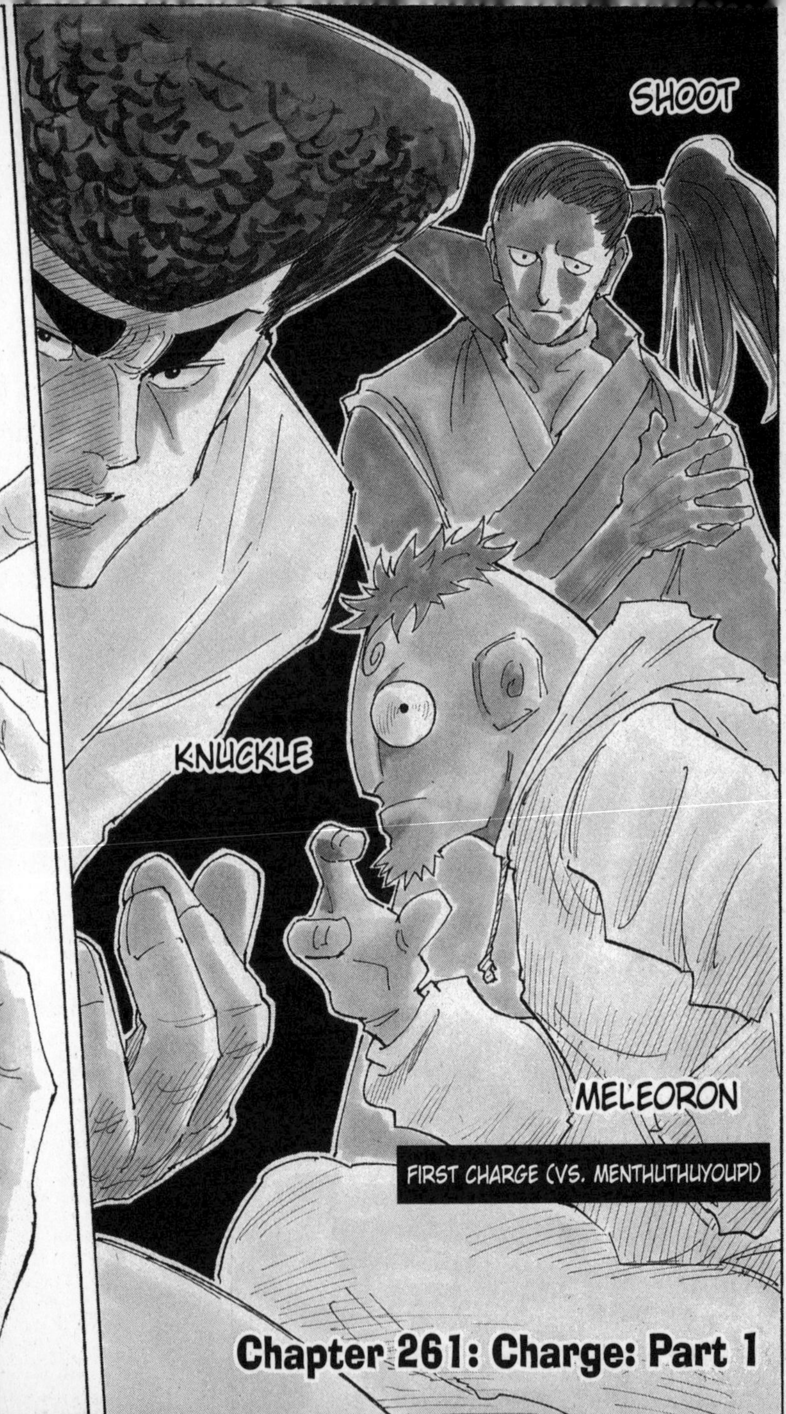
SHOOT
KNUCKLE
MELEORON
FIRST CHARGE (VS. MENTHUTHUYOUPI)

Chapter 261: Charge: Part 1

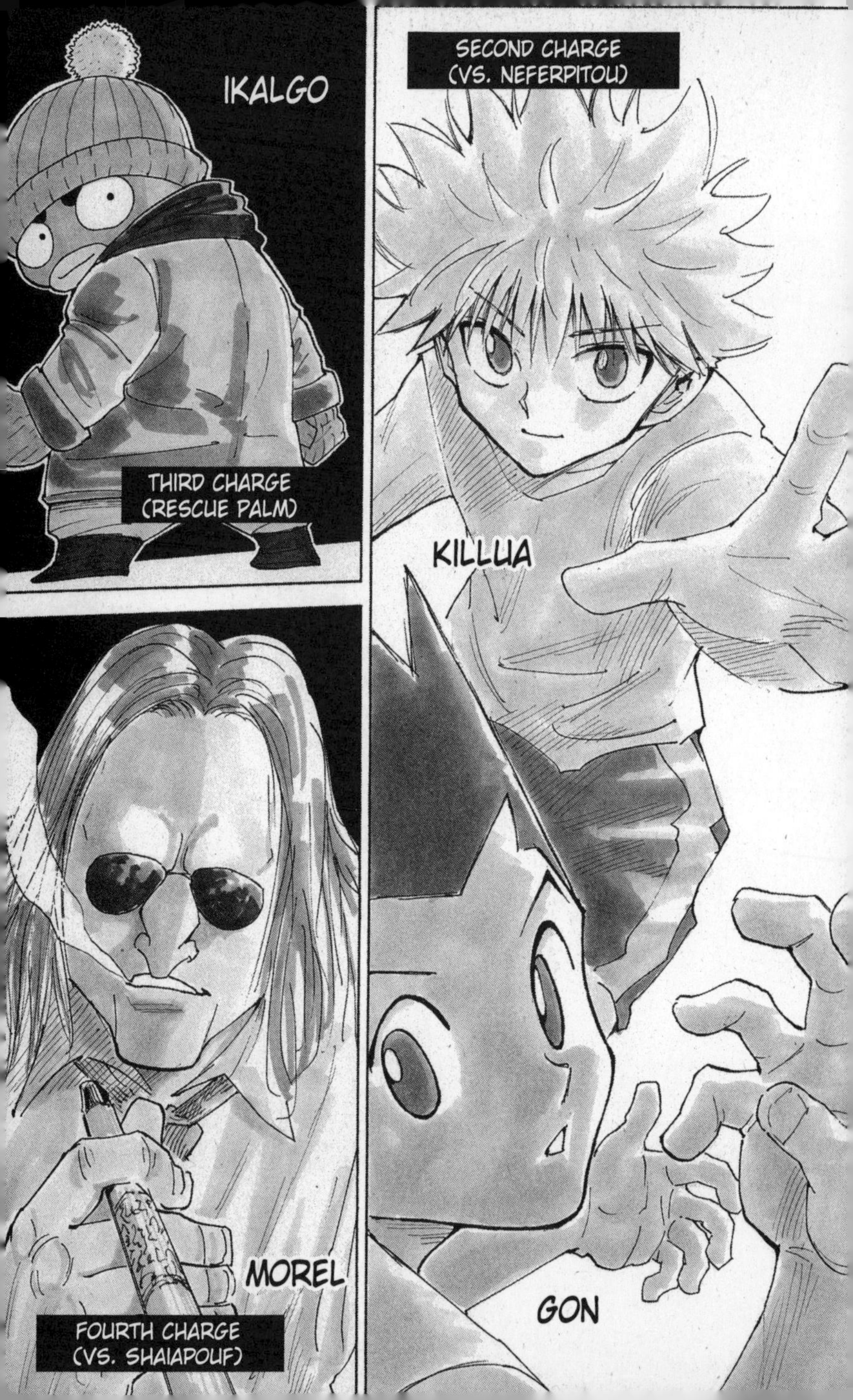
SECOND CHARGE (VS. NEFERPITOU)
KILLUA
GON
IKALGO
THIRD CHARGE (RESCUE PALM)
MOREL
FOURTH CHARGE (VS. SHAIAPOUF)

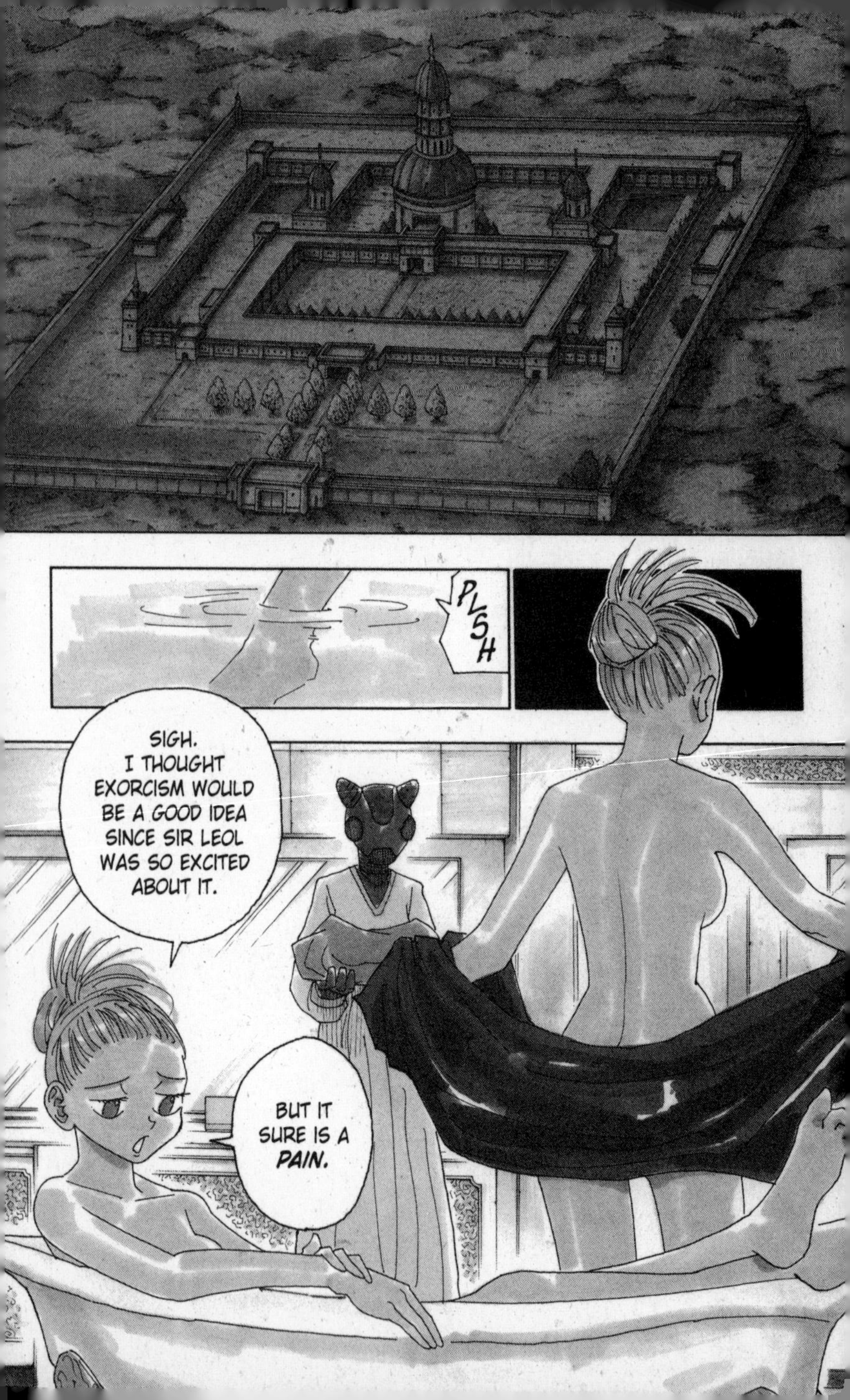
PLSH
SIGH. I THOUGHT EXORCISM WOULD BE A GOOD IDEA SINCE SIR LEOL WAS SO EXCITED ABOUT IT.
BUT IT SURE IS A *PAIN.*

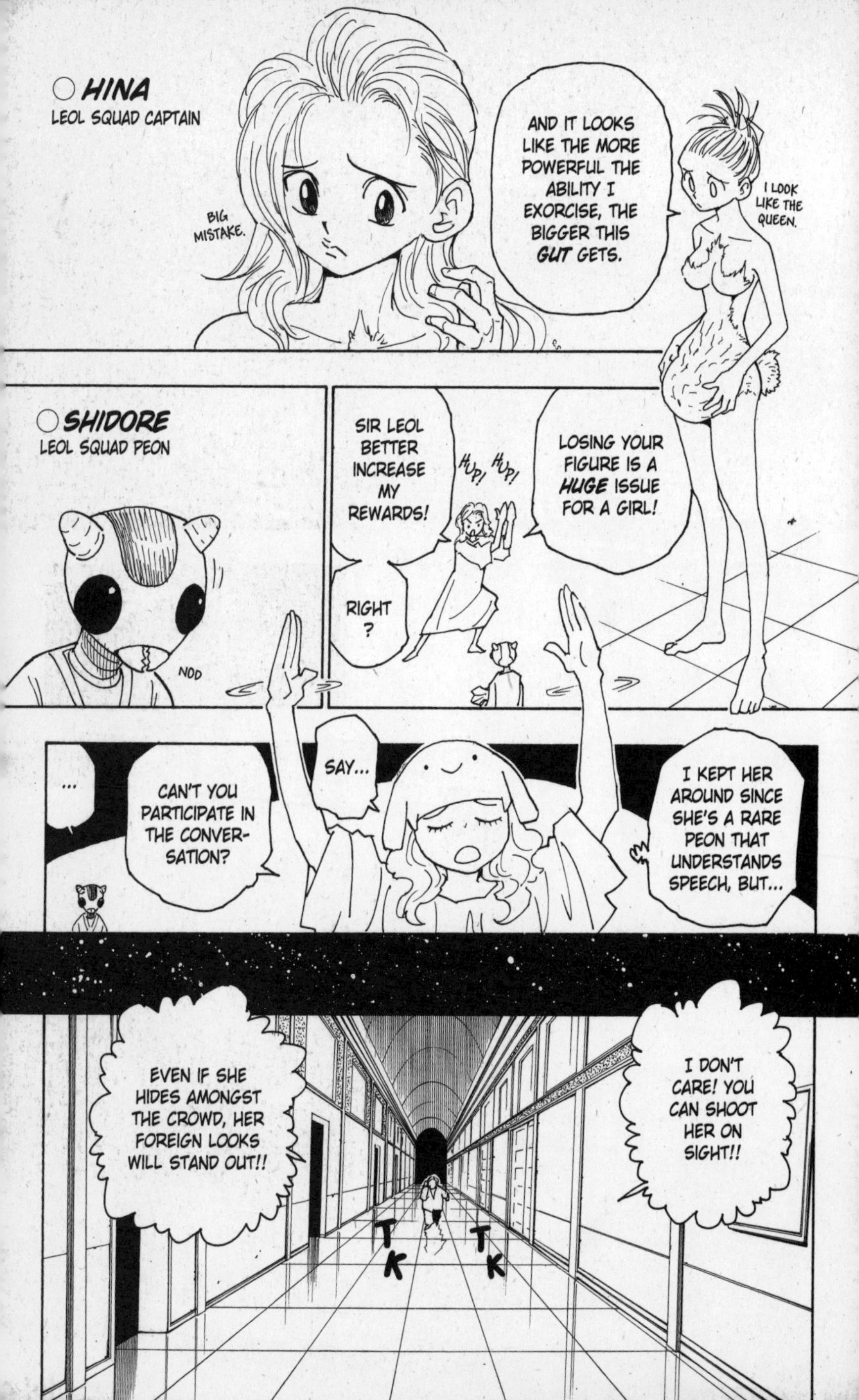
I LOOK LIKE THE QUEEN.
AND IT LOOKS LIKE THE MORE POWERFUL THE ABILITY I EXORCISE, THE BIGGER THIS GUT GETS.
BIG MISTAKE.
HINA
LEOL SQUAD CAPTAIN
LOSING YOUR FIGURE IS A HUGE ISSUE FOR A GIRL!
HUP! HUP!
SIR LEOL BETTER INCREASE MY REWARDS!
RIGHT?
SHIDORE
LEOL SQUAD PEON
NOD
I KEPT HER AROUND SINCE SHE'S A RARE PEON THAT UNDERSTANDS SPEECH, BUT...
SAY...
CAN'T YOU PARTICIPATE IN THE CONVER-SATION?
...
I DON'T CARE! YOU CAN SHOOT HER ON SIGHT!!
EVEN IF SHE HIDES AMONGST THE CROWD, HER FOREIGN LOOKS WILL STAND OUT!!
TK
TK

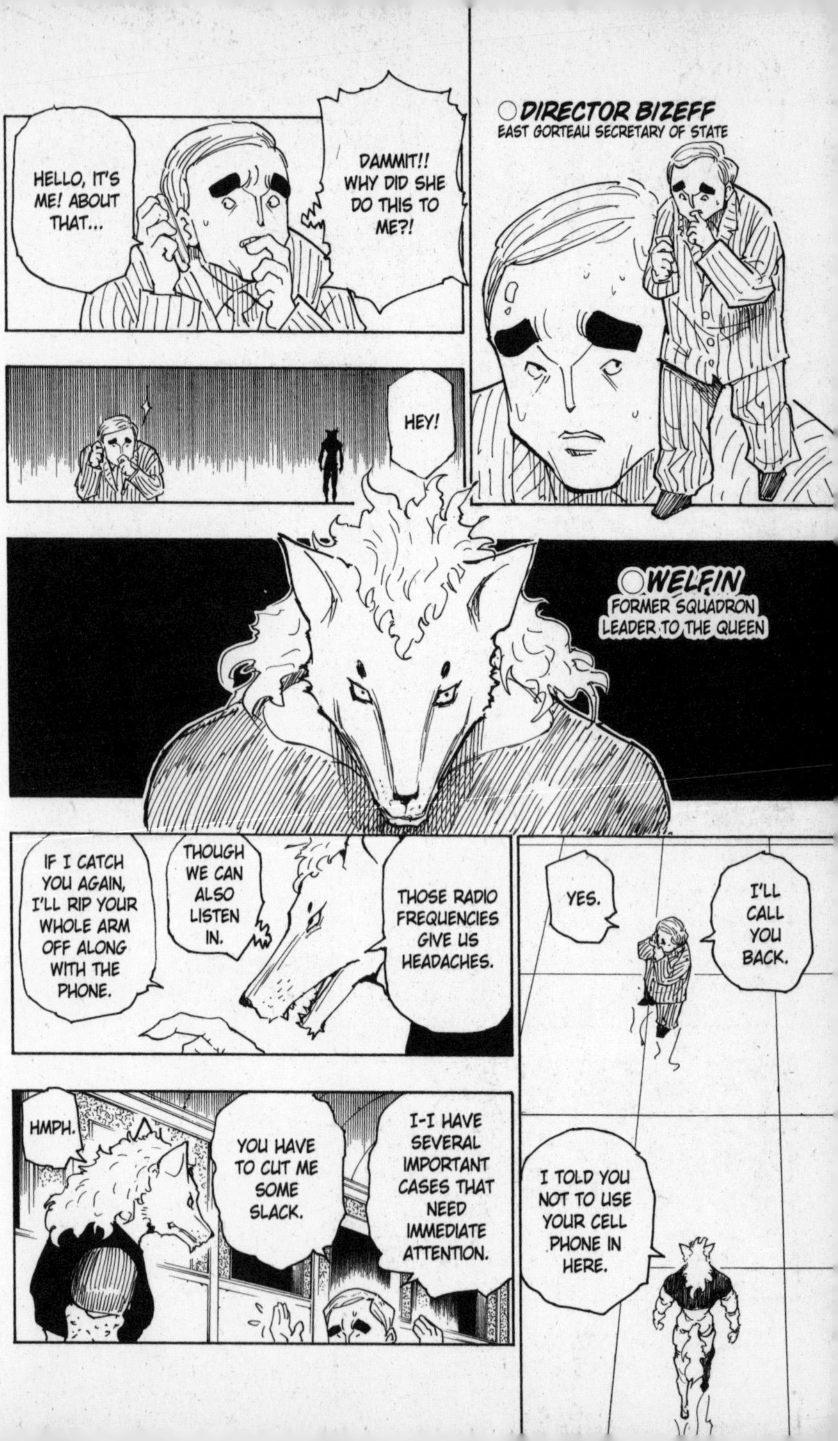

○DIRECTOR BIZEFF
EAST GORTEAU SECRETARY OF STATE
DAMMIT!! WHY DID SHE DO THIS TO ME?!
HELLO, IT'S ME! ABOUT THAT...
HEY!
○WELFIN
FORMER SQUADRON LEADER TO THE QUEEN
I'LL CALL YOU BACK.
YES.
I TOLD YOU NOT TO USE YOUR CELL PHONE IN HERE.
THOSE RADIO FREQUENCIES GIVE US HEADACHES.
THOUGH WE CAN ALSO LISTEN IN.
IF I CATCH YOU AGAIN, I'LL RIP YOUR WHOLE ARM OFF ALONG WITH THE PHONE.
I-I HAVE SEVERAL IMPORTANT CASES THAT NEED IMMEDIATE ATTENTION.
YOU HAVE TO CUT ME SOME SLACK.
HMPH.

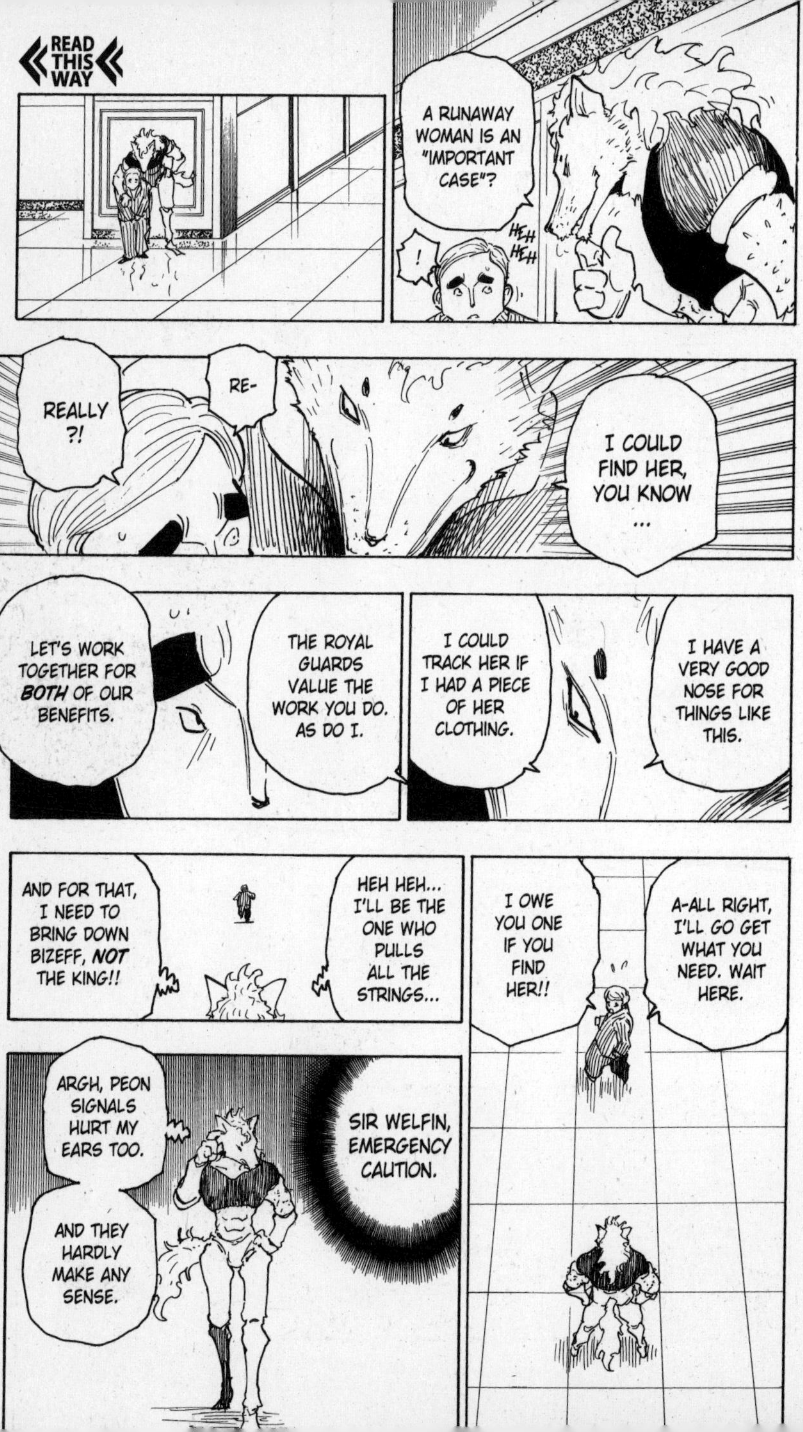
READ THIS WAY
A RUNAWAY WOMAN IS AN "IMPORTANT CASE"?
HEH HEH
!
I COULD FIND HER, YOU KNOW ...
RE-
REALLY ?!
I HAVE A VERY GOOD NOSE FOR THINGS LIKE THIS.
I COULD TRACK HER IF I HAD A PIECE OF HER CLOTHING.
THE ROYAL GUARDS VALUE THE WORK YOU DO. AS DO I.
LET'S WORK TOGETHER FOR BOTH OF OUR BENEFITS.
A-ALL RIGHT, I'LL GO GET WHAT YOU NEED. WAIT HERE.
I OWE YOU ONE IF YOU FIND HER!!
HEH HEH... I'LL BE THE ONE WHO PULLS ALL THE STRINGS...
AND FOR THAT, I NEED TO BRING DOWN BIZEFF, NOT THE KING!!
SIR WELFIN, EMERGENCY CAUTION.
ARGH, PEON SIGNALS HURT MY EARS TOO.
AND THEY HARDLY MAKE ANY SENSE.

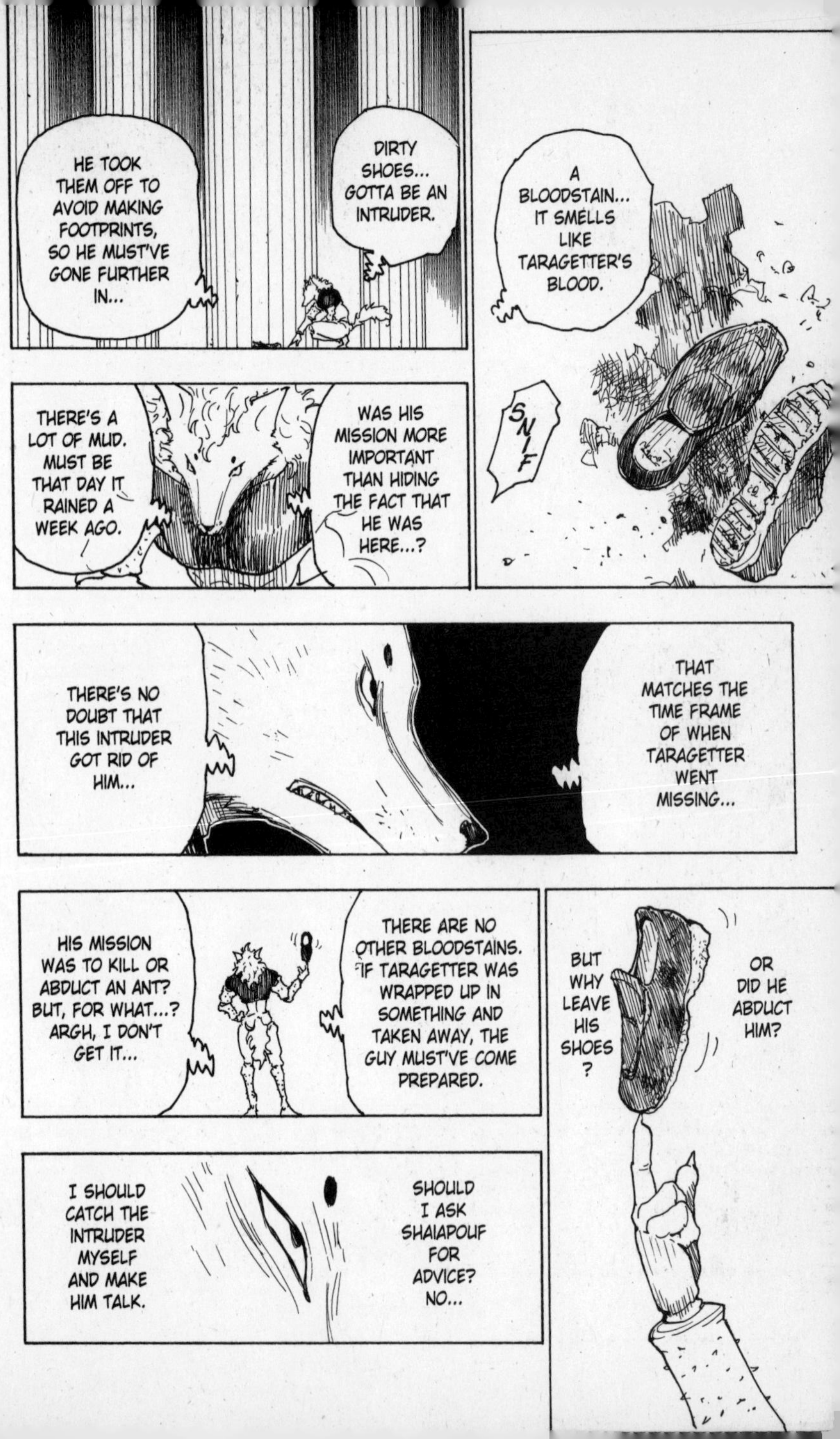
A BLOODSTAIN... IT SMELLS LIKE TARAGETTER'S BLOOD.
SNIF
DIRTY SHOES... GOTTA BE AN INTRUDER.
HE TOOK THEM OFF TO AVOID MAKING FOOTPRINTS, SO HE MUST'VE GONE FURTHER IN...
WAS HIS MISSION MORE IMPORTANT THAN HIDING THE FACT THAT HE WAS HERE...?
THERE'S A LOT OF MUD. MUST BE THAT DAY IT RAINED A WEEK AGO.
THAT MATCHES THE TIME FRAME OF WHEN TARAGETTER WENT MISSING...
THERE'S NO DOUBT THAT THIS INTRUDER GOT RID OF HIM...
OR DID HE ABDUCT HIM?
BUT WHY LEAVE HIS SHOES?
THERE ARE NO OTHER BLOODSTAINS. IF TARAGETTER WAS WRAPPED UP IN SOMETHING AND TAKEN AWAY, THE GUY MUST'VE COME PREPARED.
HIS MISSION WAS TO KILL OR ABDUCT AN ANT? BUT, FOR WHAT...? ARGH, I DON'T GET IT...
SHOULD I ASK SHAIAPOUF FOR ADVICE? NO...
I SHOULD CATCH THE INTRUDER MYSELF AND MAKE HIM TALK.

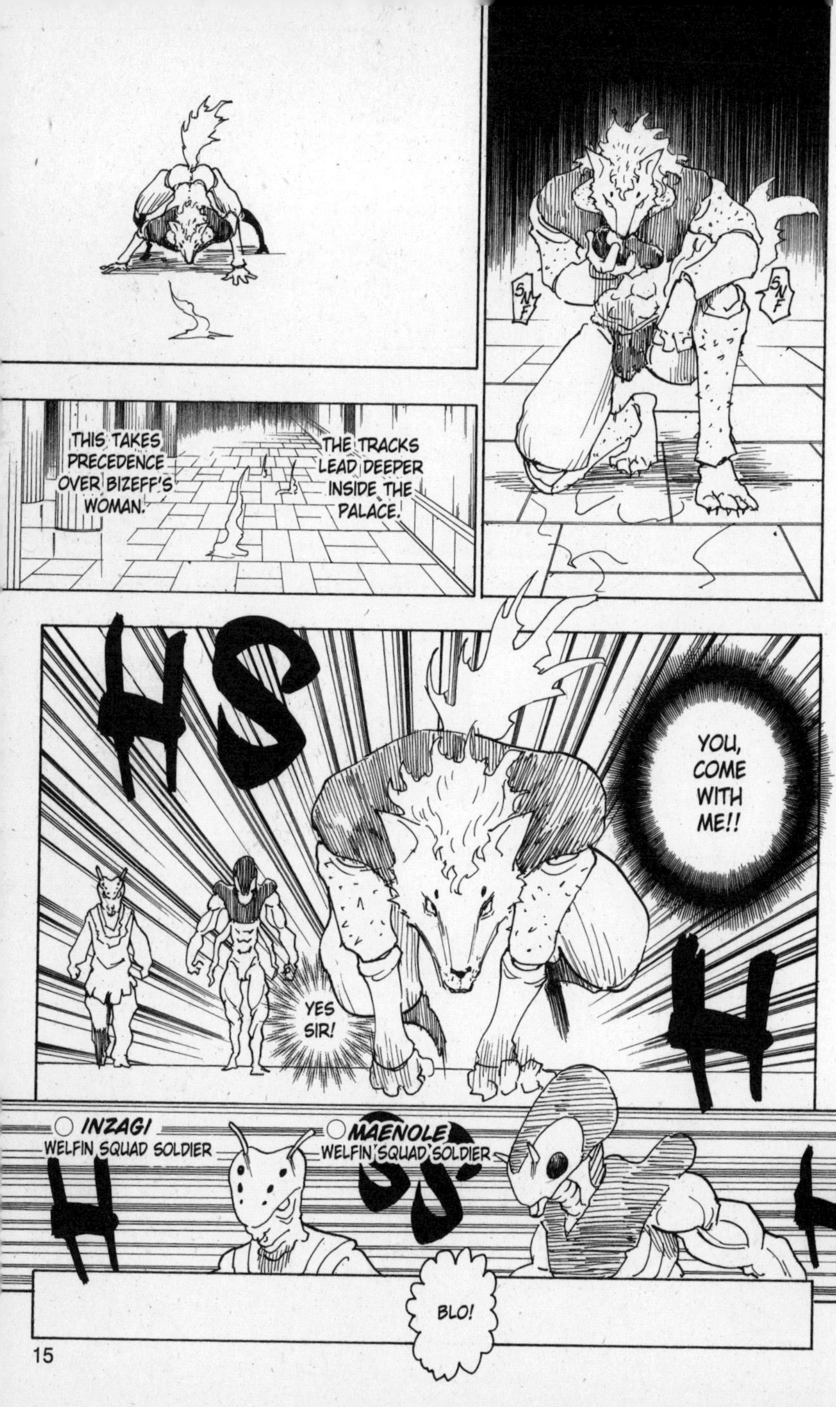
SNF
SNF
THE TRACKS LEAD DEEPER INSIDE THE PALACE.
THIS TAKES PRECEDENCE OVER BIZEFF'S WOMAN.
YOU, COME WITH ME!!
HS
H
YES SIR!
H
MAENOLE
WELFIN SQUAD SOLDIER
INZAGI
WELFIN SQUAD SOLDIER
H
BLO!

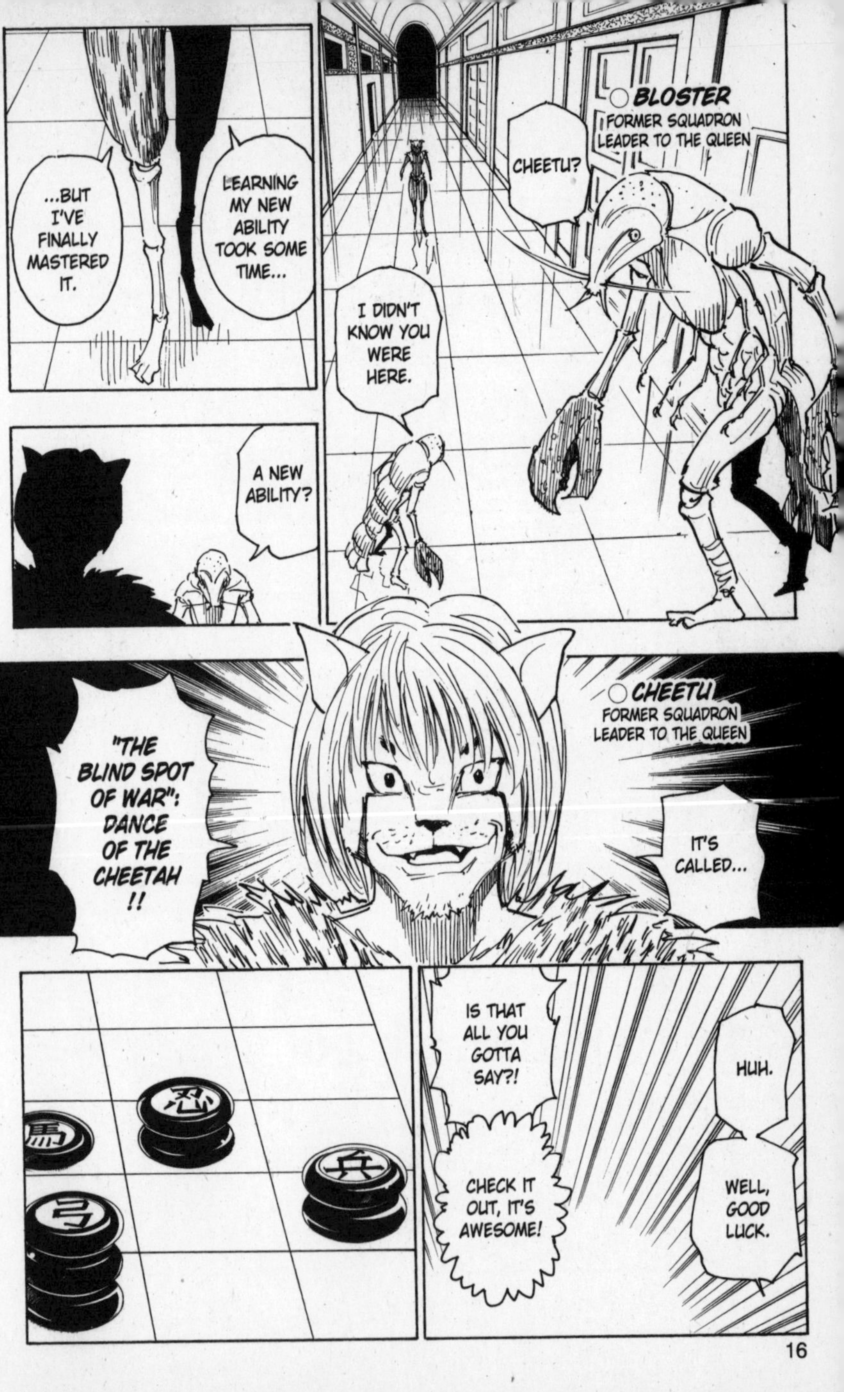
BLOSTER
FORMER SQUADRON LEADER TO THE QUEEN
CHEETU?
I DIDN'T KNOW YOU WERE HERE.
LEARNING MY NEW ABILITY TOOK SOME TIME...
...BUT I'VE FINALLY MASTERED IT.
A NEW ABILITY?
CHEETU
FORMER SQUADRON LEADER TO THE QUEEN
IT'S CALLED...
"THE BLIND SPOT OF WAR": DANCE OF THE CHEETAH !!
HUH.
IS THAT ALL YOU GOTTA SAY?!
WELL, GOOD LUCK.
CHECK IT OUT, IT'S AWESOME!
兵
忍
馬
弓

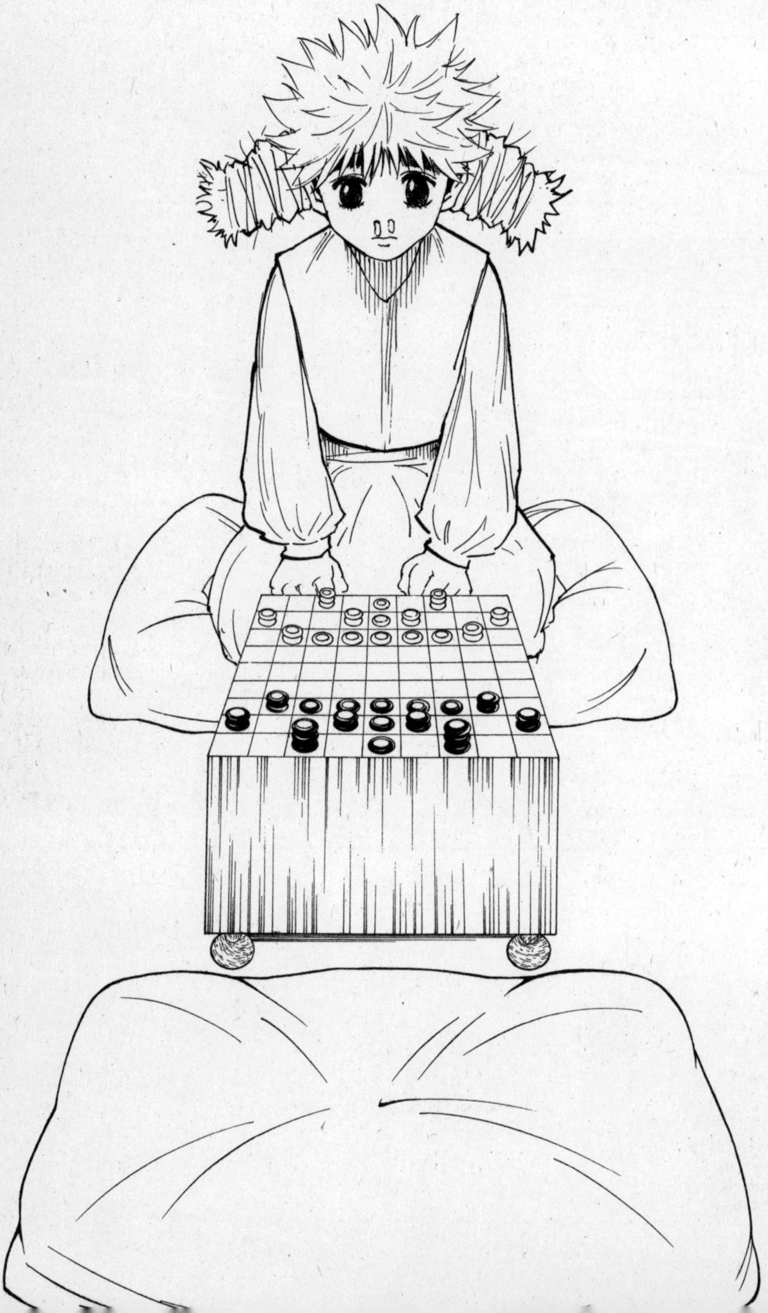

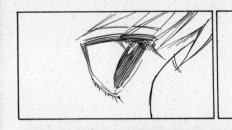

I ASKED HIM HIS NAME...

AND HE WOULDN'T TELL ME ...

I WANT TO PLAY...

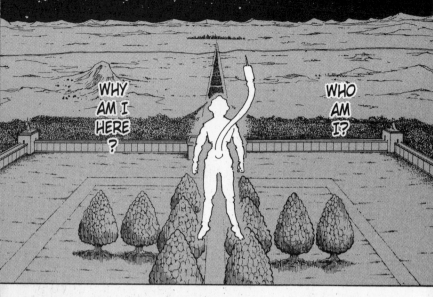

WHO AM I?
WHY AM I HERE?
A KING WITH NO NAME.
A BORROWED CASTLE.
MY SUBJECTS...
...ARE MINDLESS DRONES.
HEH.
HEH HEH.
IF THIS...
...IS THE MANDATE OF HEAVEN I HAVE BEEN GIVEN...
I FEAR...

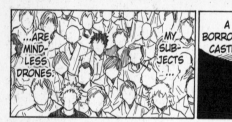

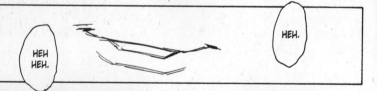

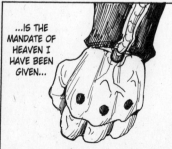

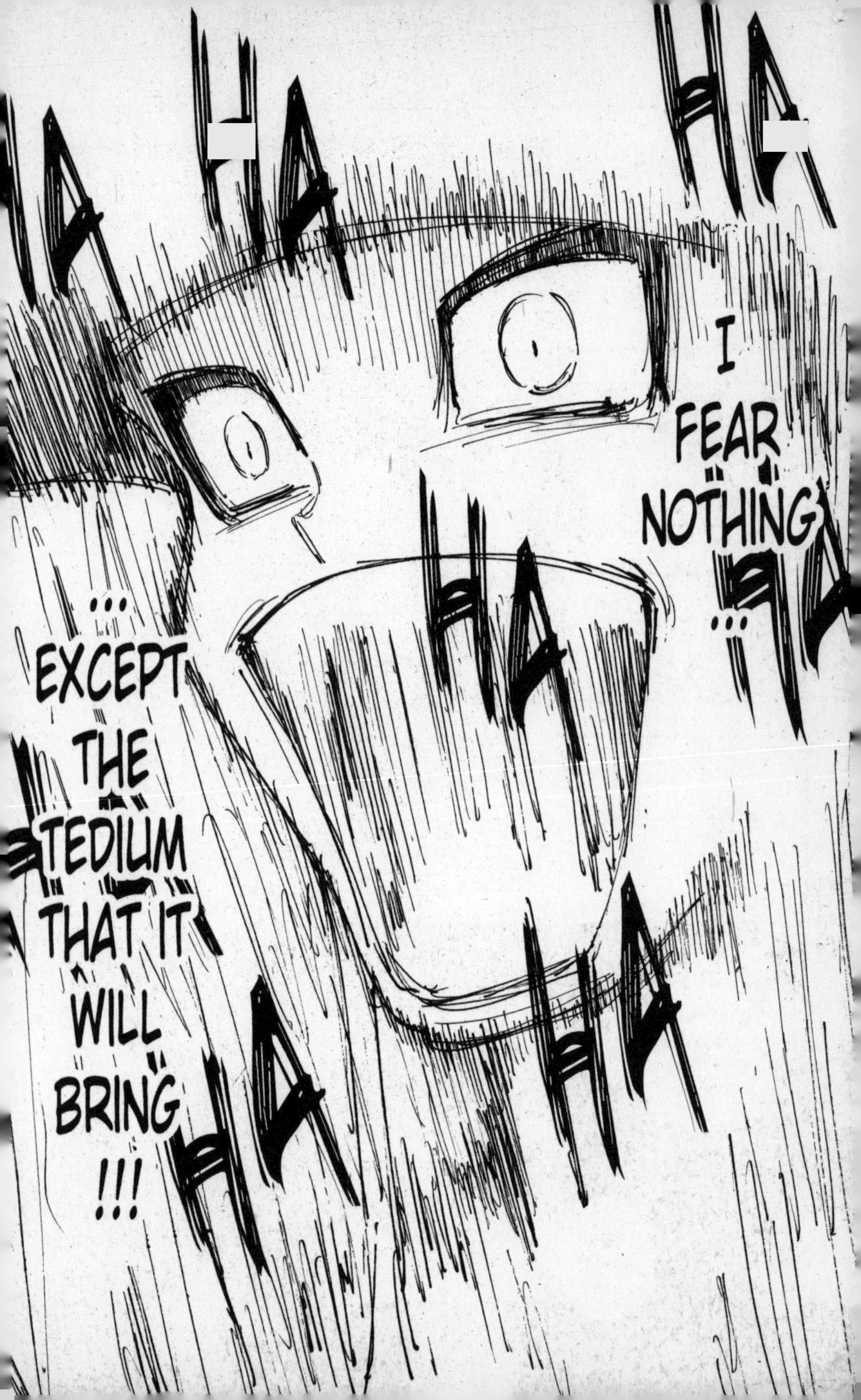
HA HA
HA HA
I FEAR NOTHING ...!!
HA HA
...EXCEPT THE TEDIUM THAT IT WILL BRING!!!
HA HA
HA

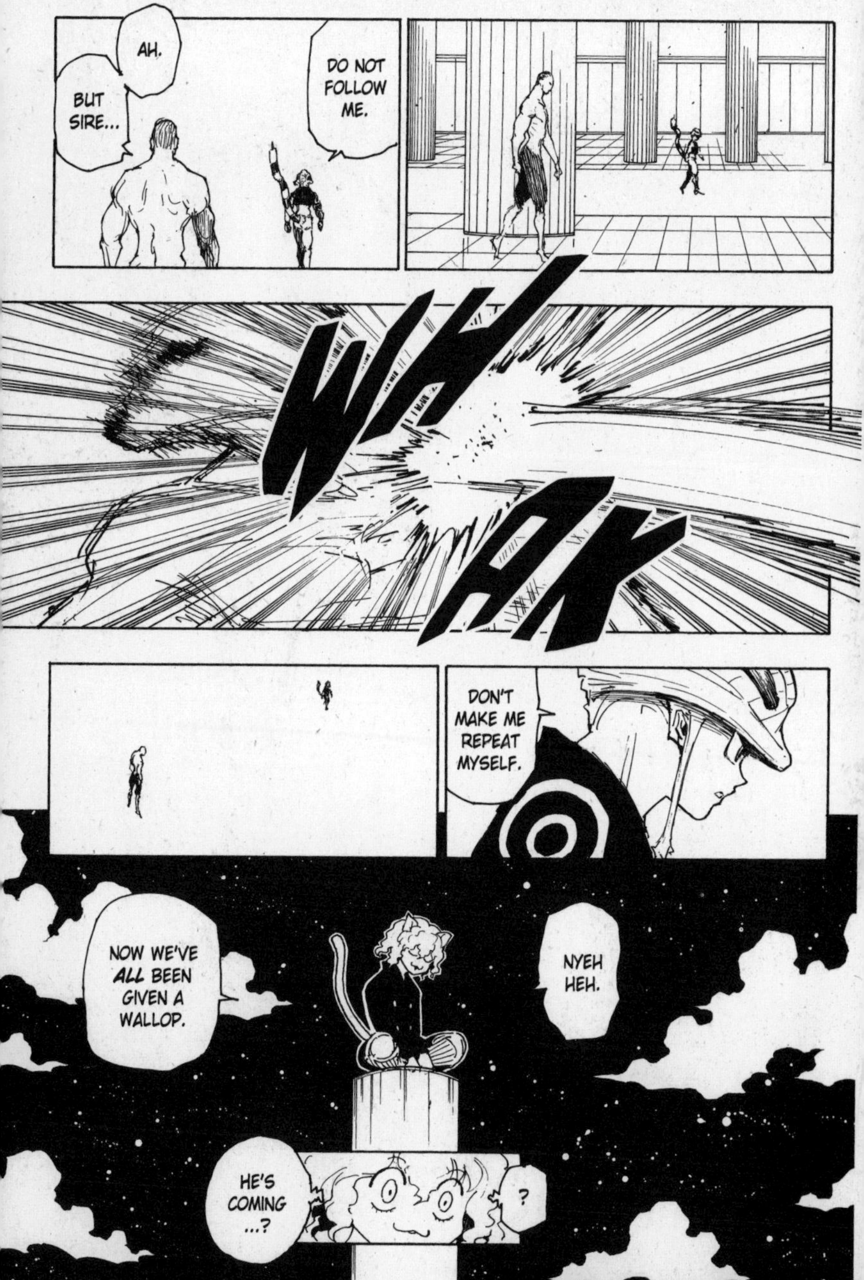
DO NOT FOLLOW ME.
AH.
BUT SIRE...
WHAK
DON'T MAKE ME REPEAT MYSELF.
NYEH HEH.
NOW WE'VE ALL BEEN GIVEN A WALLOP.
?
HE'S COMING ...?

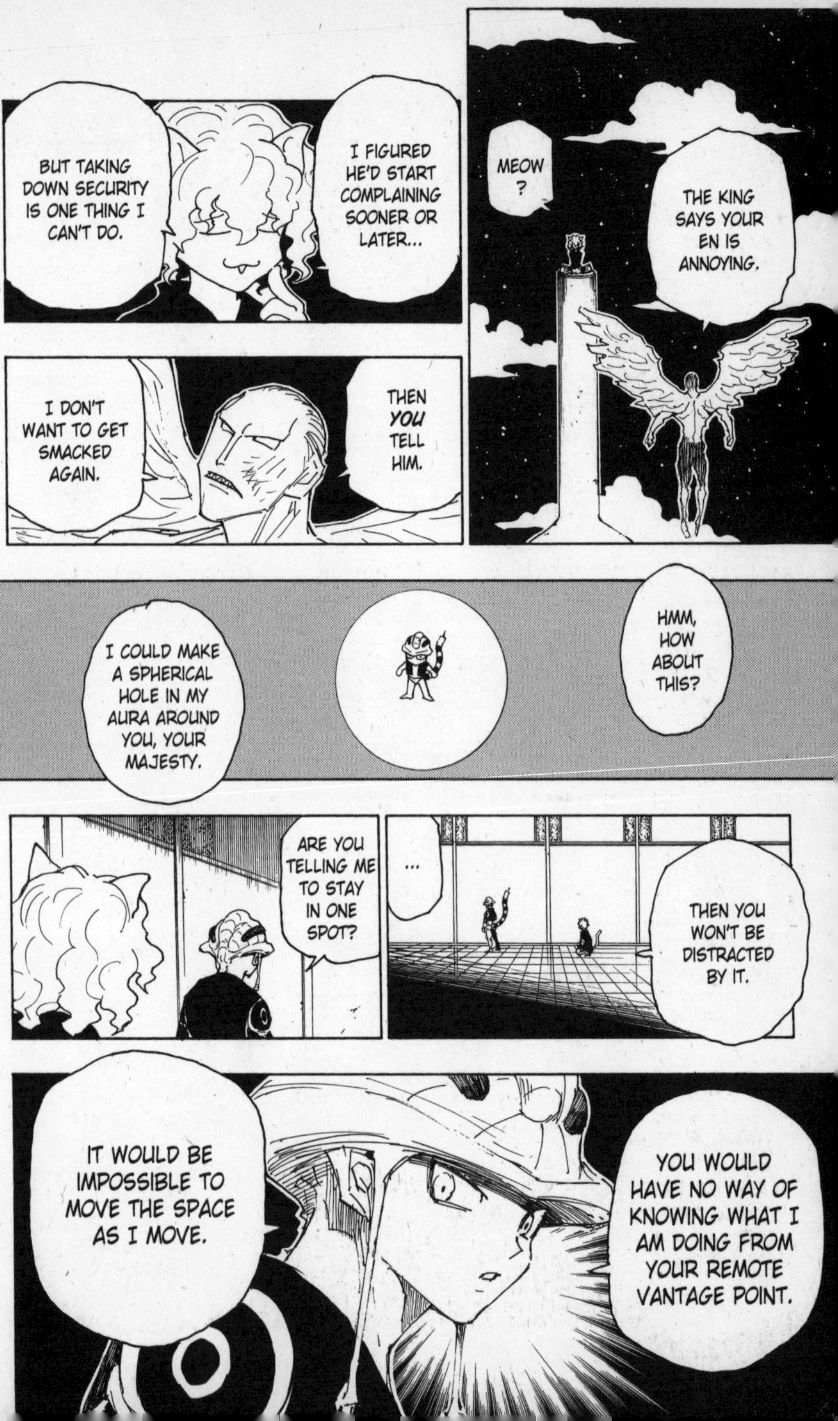
THE KING SAYS YOUR EN IS ANNOYING.
MEOW ?
I FIGURED HE'D START COMPLAINING SOONER OR LATER...
BUT TAKING DOWN SECURITY IS ONE THING I CAN'T DO.
THEN *YOU* TELL HIM.
I DON'T WANT TO GET SMACKED AGAIN.
HMM, HOW ABOUT THIS?
I COULD MAKE A SPHERICAL HOLE IN MY AURA AROUND YOU, YOUR MAJESTY.
THEN YOU WON'T BE DISTRACTED BY IT.
...
ARE YOU TELLING ME TO STAY IN ONE SPOT?
YOU WOULD HAVE NO WAY OF KNOWING WHAT I AM DOING FROM YOUR REMOTE VANTAGE POINT.
IT WOULD BE IMPOSSIBLE TO MOVE THE SPACE AS I MOVE.

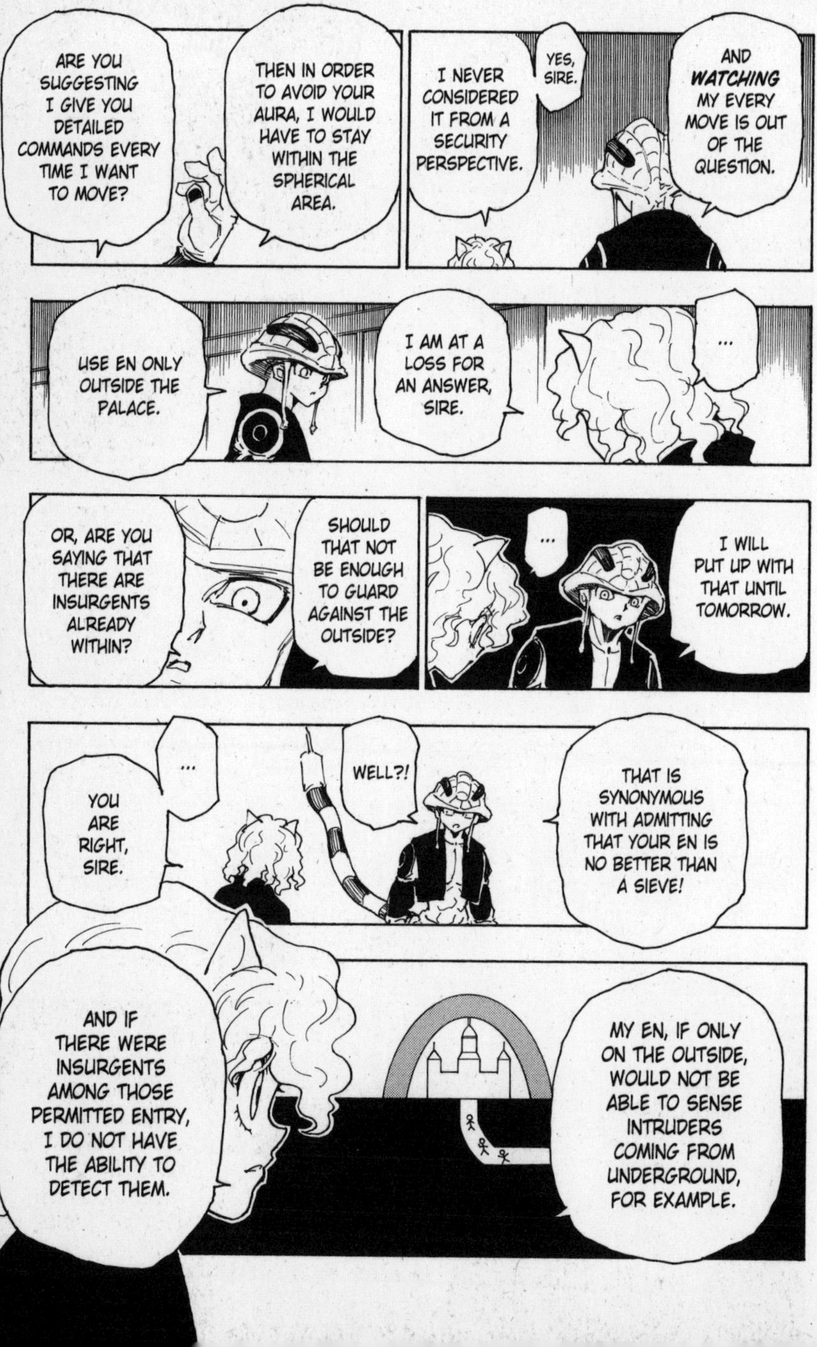
AND WATCHING MY EVERY MOVE IS OUT OF THE QUESTION.
YES, SIRE.
I NEVER CONSIDERED IT FROM A SECURITY PERSPECTIVE.
THEN IN ORDER TO AVOID YOUR AURA, I WOULD HAVE TO STAY WITHIN THE SPHERICAL AREA.
ARE YOU SUGGESTING I GIVE YOU DETAILED COMMANDS EVERY TIME I WANT TO MOVE?
...
I AM AT A LOSS FOR AN ANSWER, SIRE.
USE EN ONLY OUTSIDE THE PALACE.
I WILL PUT UP WITH THAT UNTIL TOMORROW.
...
SHOULD THAT NOT BE ENOUGH TO GUARD AGAINST THE OUTSIDE?
OR, ARE YOU SAYING THAT THERE ARE INSURGENTS ALREADY WITHIN?
THAT IS SYNONYMOUS WITH ADMITTING THAT YOUR EN IS NO BETTER THAN A SIEVE!
WELL?!
...
YOU ARE RIGHT, SIRE.
MY EN, IF ONLY ON THE OUTSIDE, WOULD NOT BE ABLE TO SENSE INTRUDERS COMING FROM UNDERGROUND, FOR EXAMPLE.
AND IF THERE WERE INSURGENTS AMONG THOSE PERMITTED ENTRY, I DO NOT HAVE THE ABILITY TO DETECT THEM.

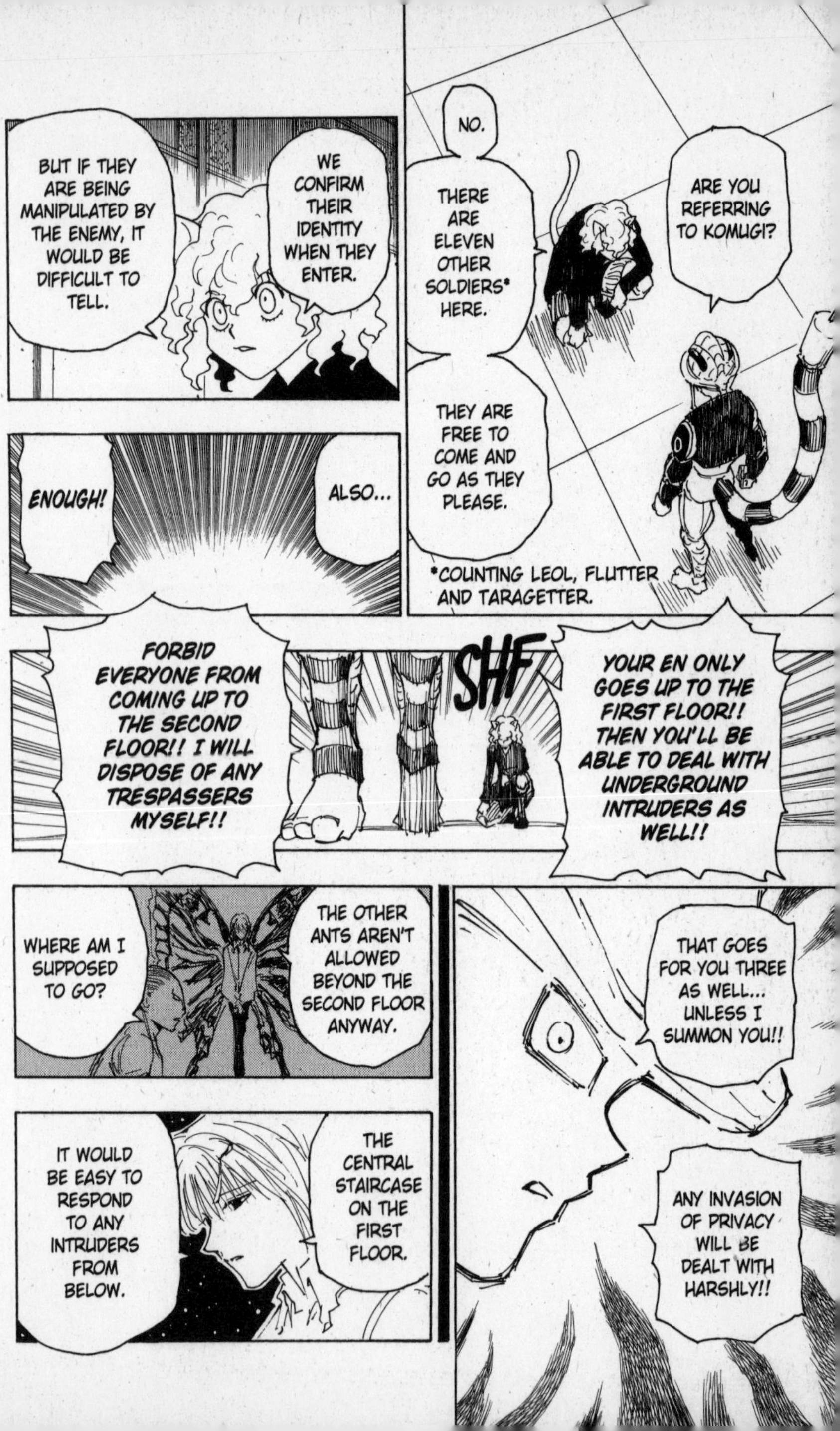

ARE YOU REFERRING TO KOMUGI?
NO.
THERE ARE ELEVEN OTHER SOLDIERS* HERE.
THEY ARE FREE TO COME AND GO AS THEY PLEASE.
*COUNTING LEOL, FLUTTER AND TARAGETTER.
WE CONFIRM THEIR IDENTITY WHEN THEY ENTER.
BUT IF THEY ARE BEING MANIPULATED BY THE ENEMY, IT WOULD BE DIFFICULT TO TELL.
ALSO...
ENOUGH!
YOUR EN ONLY GOES UP TO THE FIRST FLOOR!! THEN YOU'LL BE ABLE TO DEAL WITH UNDERGROUND INTRUDERS AS WELL!!
SHF
FORBID EVERYONE FROM COMING UP TO THE SECOND FLOOR!! I WILL DISPOSE OF ANY TRESPASSERS MYSELF!!
THAT GOES FOR YOU THREE AS WELL... UNLESS I SUMMON YOU!!
ANY INVASION OF PRIVACY WILL BE DEALT WITH HARSHLY!!
THE OTHER ANTS AREN'T ALLOWED BEYOND THE SECOND FLOOR ANYWAY.
WHERE AM I SUPPOSED TO GO?
THE CENTRAL STAIRCASE ON THE FIRST FLOOR.
IT WOULD BE EASY TO RESPOND TO ANY INTRUDERS FROM BELOW.

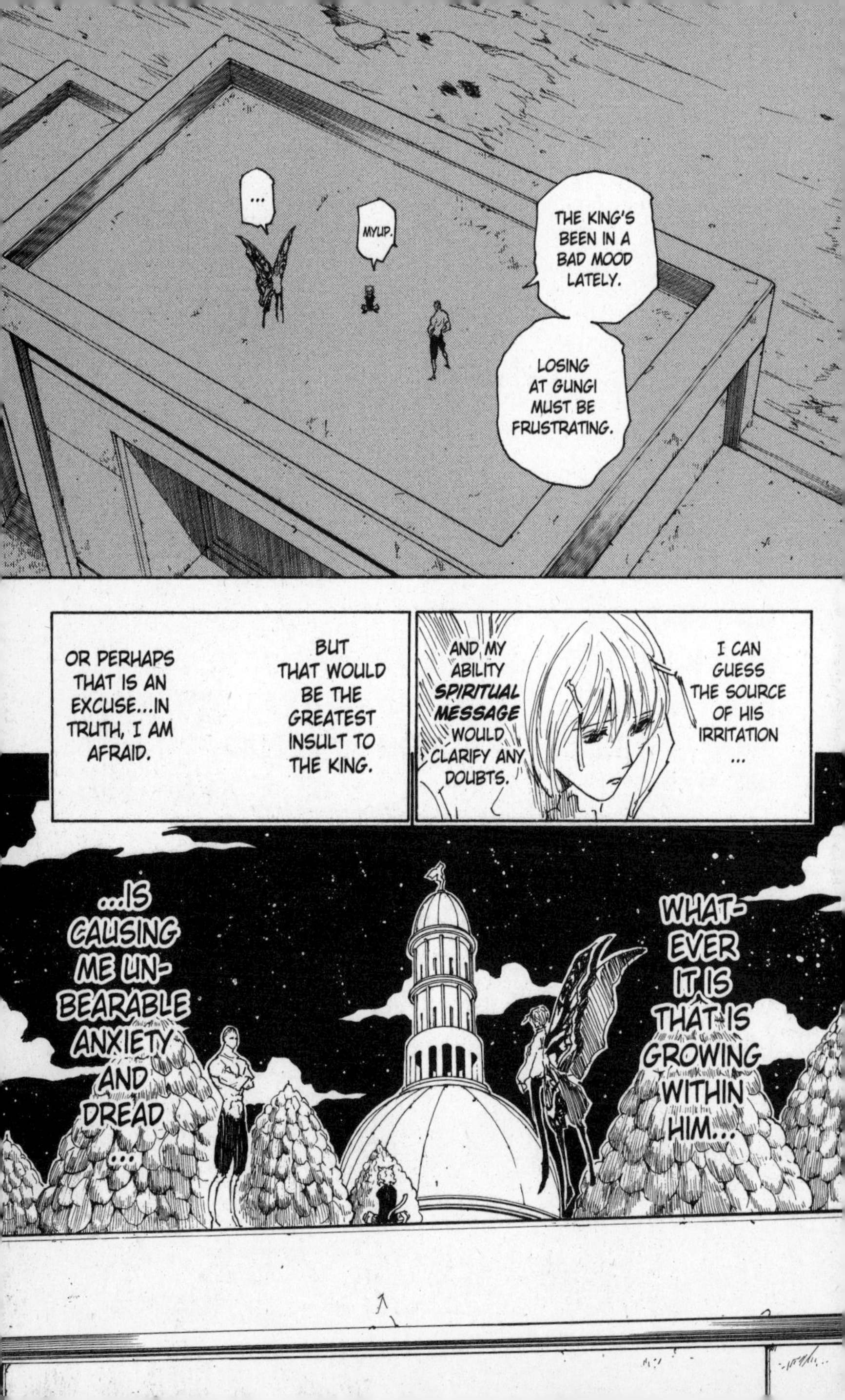
THE KING'S BEEN IN A BAD MOOD LATELY.
LOSING AT GUNGI MUST BE FRUSTRATING.
MYUP.
...
I CAN GUESS THE SOURCE OF HIS IRRITATION...
AND MY ABILITY **SPIRITUAL MESSAGE** WOULD CLARIFY ANY DOUBTS.
BUT THAT WOULD BE THE GREATEST INSULT TO THE KING.
OR PERHAPS THAT IS AN EXCUSE...IN TRUTH, I AM AFRAID.
WHAT-EVER IT IS THAT IS GROWING WITHIN HIM...
...IS CAUSING ME UN-BEARABLE ANXIETY AND DREAD...

AN APOLOGY AND AN EXPLANATION.

I AM SINCERELY SORRY THAT THE RESULTS OF THE THIRD HUNTER EXAM HAVE BEEN UNBELIEVABLY DELAYED. I REALLY WANTED TO GO THROUGH EACH AND EVERY APPLICATION AND ROLL THE DICE MYSELF. AND NOW, HERE ARE THE RESULTS!! WE HAD A GRAND TOTAL OF 4,336 ENTRIES!! THANK YOU FOR YOUR PARTICIPATION!! I WOULD LIKE TO DESCRIBE THE EXAM PROCESS AND POST THE RESULTS AND COMMENTS IN THIS VOLUME!! IT'S BEEN SO LONG THAT I WOULDN'T BE SURPRISED IF MANY OF YOU HAVE FORGOTTEN WHAT NAME YOU USED...PLEASE PUT UP WITH MY SELFISH WAYS!! LET'S GET STARTED!!!!

I'm sorry.

Chapter 262: Charge: Part 2

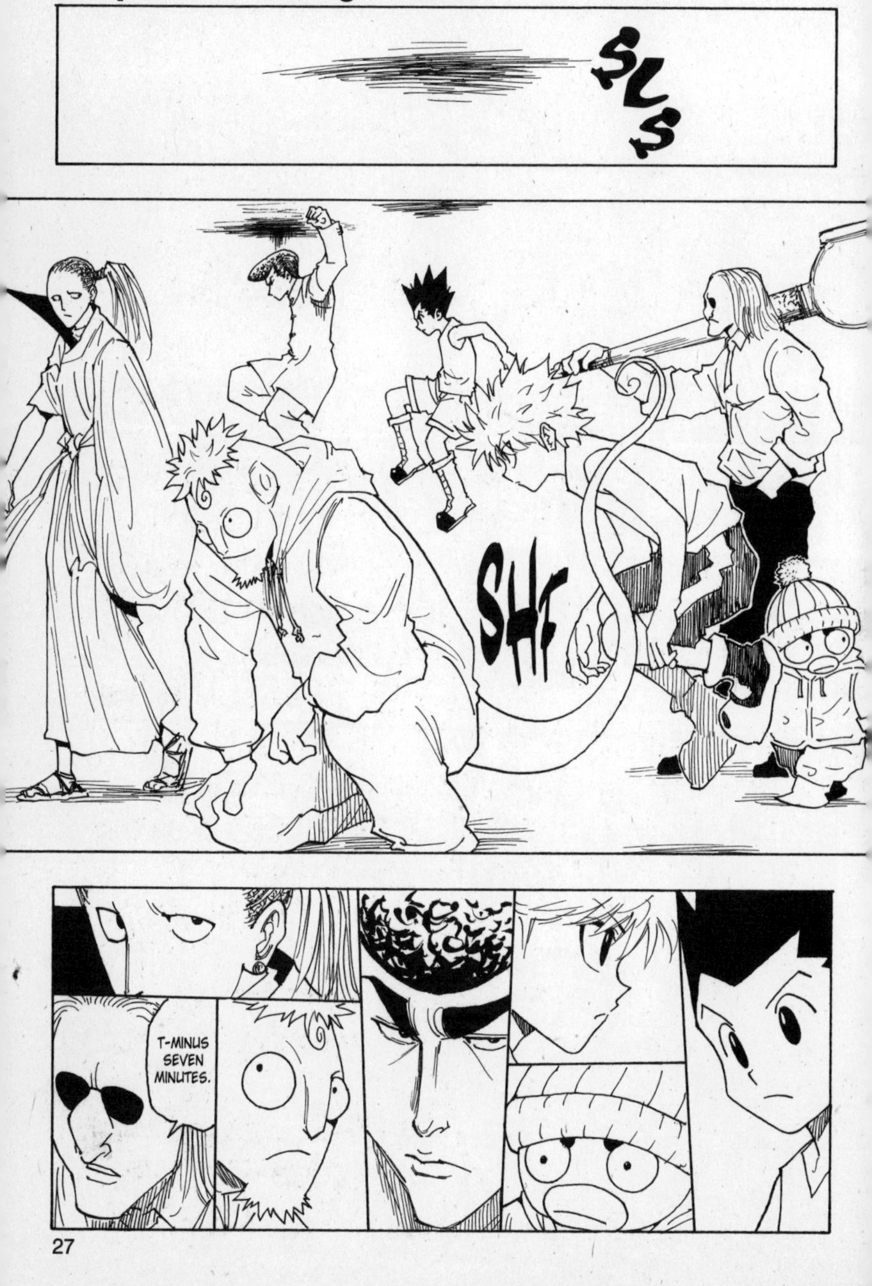
SLS
SHF
T-MINUS SEVEN MINUTES.

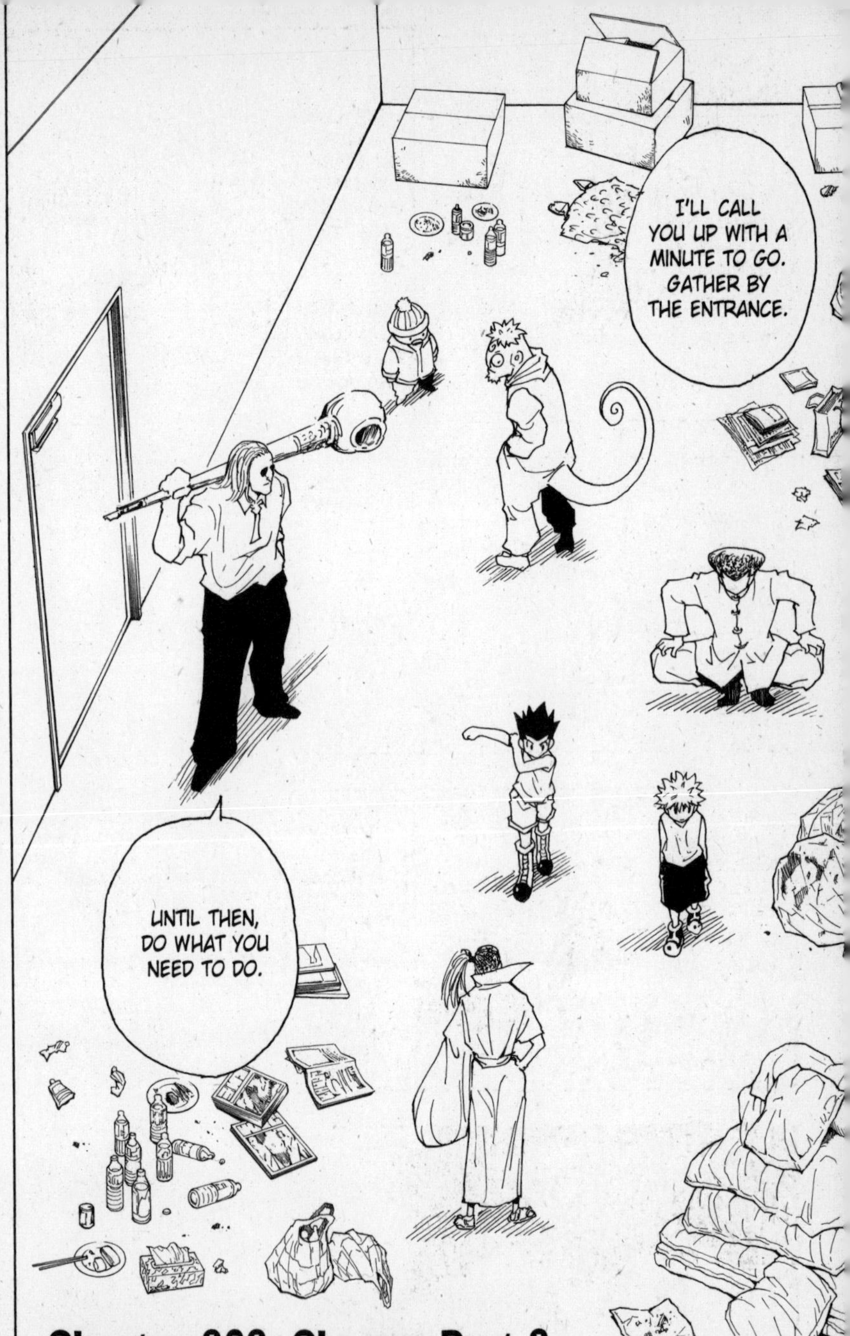
I'LL CALL YOU UP WITH A MINUTE TO GO. GATHER BY THE ENTRANCE.
UNTIL THEN, DO WHAT YOU NEED TO DO.

Chapter 262: Charge: Part 2

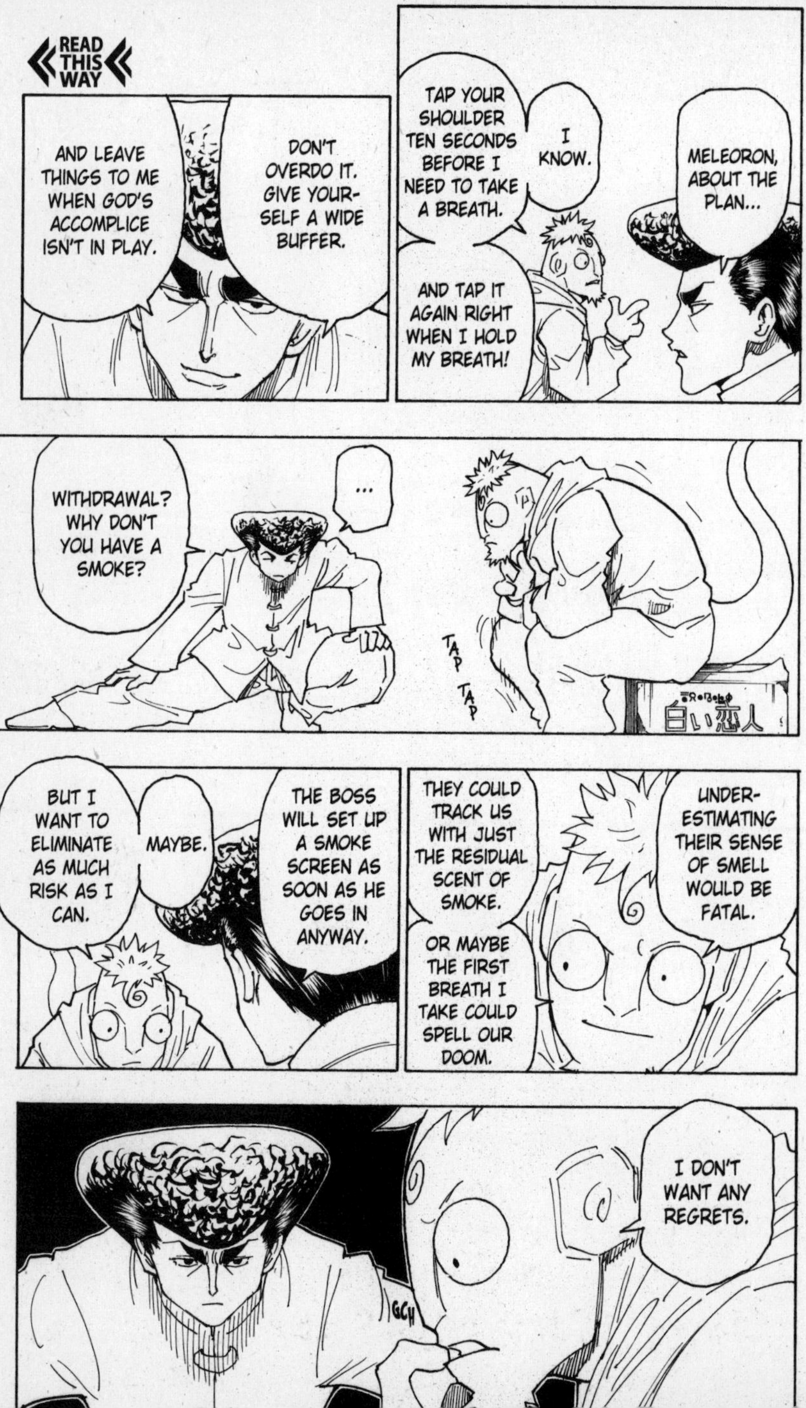
READ THIS WAY
MELEORON, ABOUT THE PLAN...
I KNOW.
TAP YOUR SHOULDER TEN SECONDS BEFORE I NEED TO TAKE A BREATH.
AND TAP IT AGAIN RIGHT WHEN I HOLD MY BREATH!
DON'T OVERDO IT. GIVE YOURSELF A WIDE BUFFER.
AND LEAVE THINGS TO ME WHEN GOD'S ACCOMPLICE ISN'T IN PLAY.
...
WITHDRAWAL? WHY DON'T YOU HAVE A SMOKE?
白い恋人
TAP TAP
UNDER-ESTIMATING THEIR SENSE OF SMELL WOULD BE FATAL.
THEY COULD TRACK US WITH JUST THE RESIDUAL SCENT OF SMOKE.
OR MAYBE THE FIRST BREATH I TAKE COULD SPELL OUR DOOM.
THE BOSS WILL SET UP A SMOKE SCREEN AS SOON AS HE GOES IN ANYWAY.
MAYBE.
BUT I WANT TO ELIMINATE AS MUCH RISK AS I CAN.
I DON'T WANT ANY REGRETS.
GCH

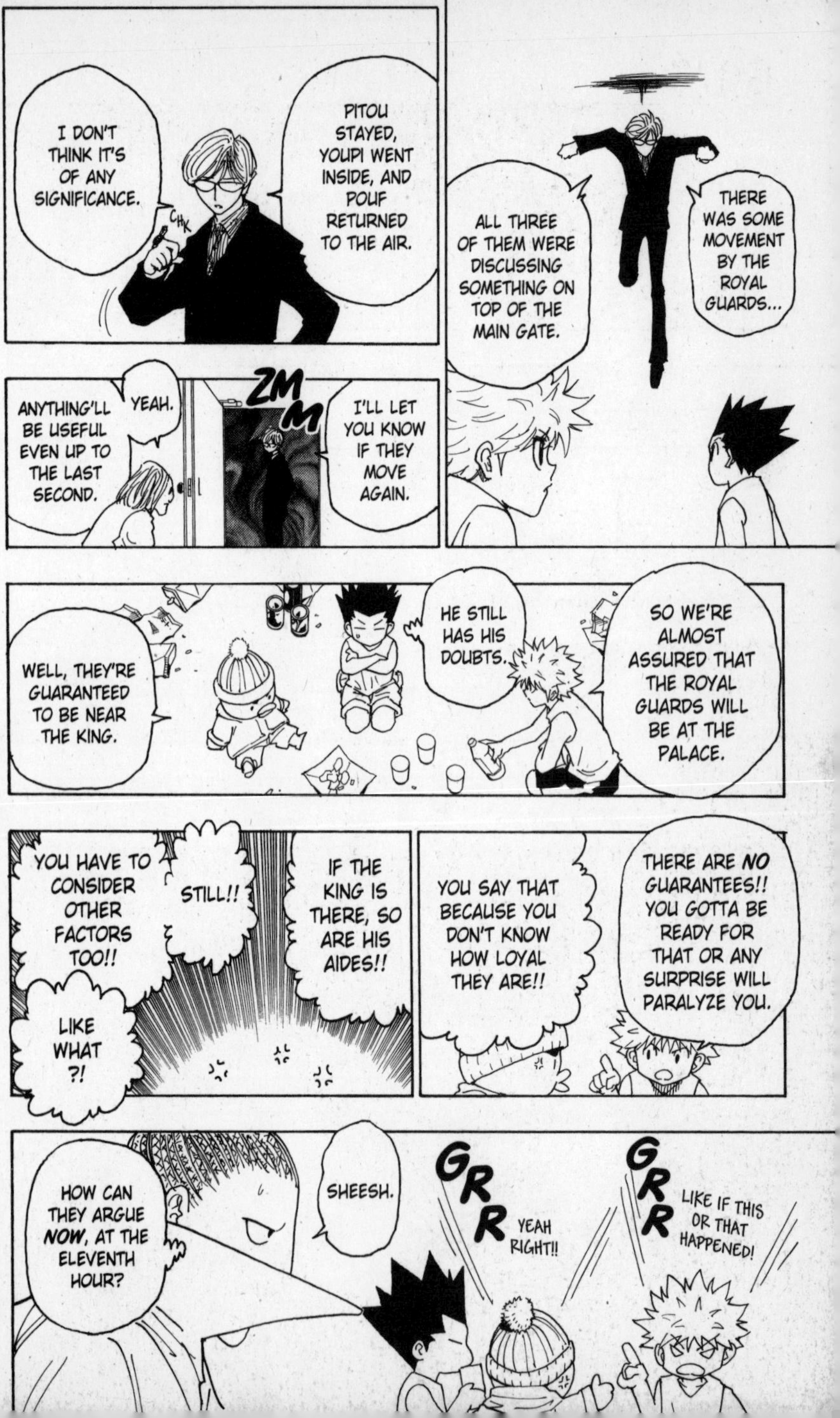
THERE WAS SOME MOVEMENT BY THE ROYAL GUARDS...
ALL THREE OF THEM WERE DISCUSSING SOMETHING ON TOP OF THE MAIN GATE.
PITOU STAYED, YOUPI WENT INSIDE, AND POUF RETURNED TO THE AIR.
I DON'T THINK IT'S OF ANY SIGNIFICANCE.
CHK
I'LL LET YOU KNOW IF THEY MOVE AGAIN.
ZMM
YEAH.
ANYTHING'LL BE USEFUL EVEN UP TO THE LAST SECOND.
SO WE'RE ALMOST ASSURED THAT THE ROYAL GUARDS WILL BE AT THE PALACE.
HE STILL HAS HIS DOUBTS.
WELL, THEY'RE GUARANTEED TO BE NEAR THE KING.
THERE ARE NO GUARANTEES!! YOU GOTTA BE READY FOR THAT OR ANY SURPRISE WILL PARALYZE YOU.
YOU SAY THAT BECAUSE YOU DON'T KNOW HOW LOYAL THEY ARE!!
IF THE KING IS THERE, SO ARE HIS AIDES!!
STILL!!
YOU HAVE TO CONSIDER OTHER FACTORS TOO!!
LIKE WHAT ?!
GRR
LIKE IF THIS OR THAT HAPPENED!
GRR
YEAH RIGHT!!
SHEESH.
HOW CAN THEY ARGUE NOW, AT THE ELEVENTH HOUR?

READ THIS WAY

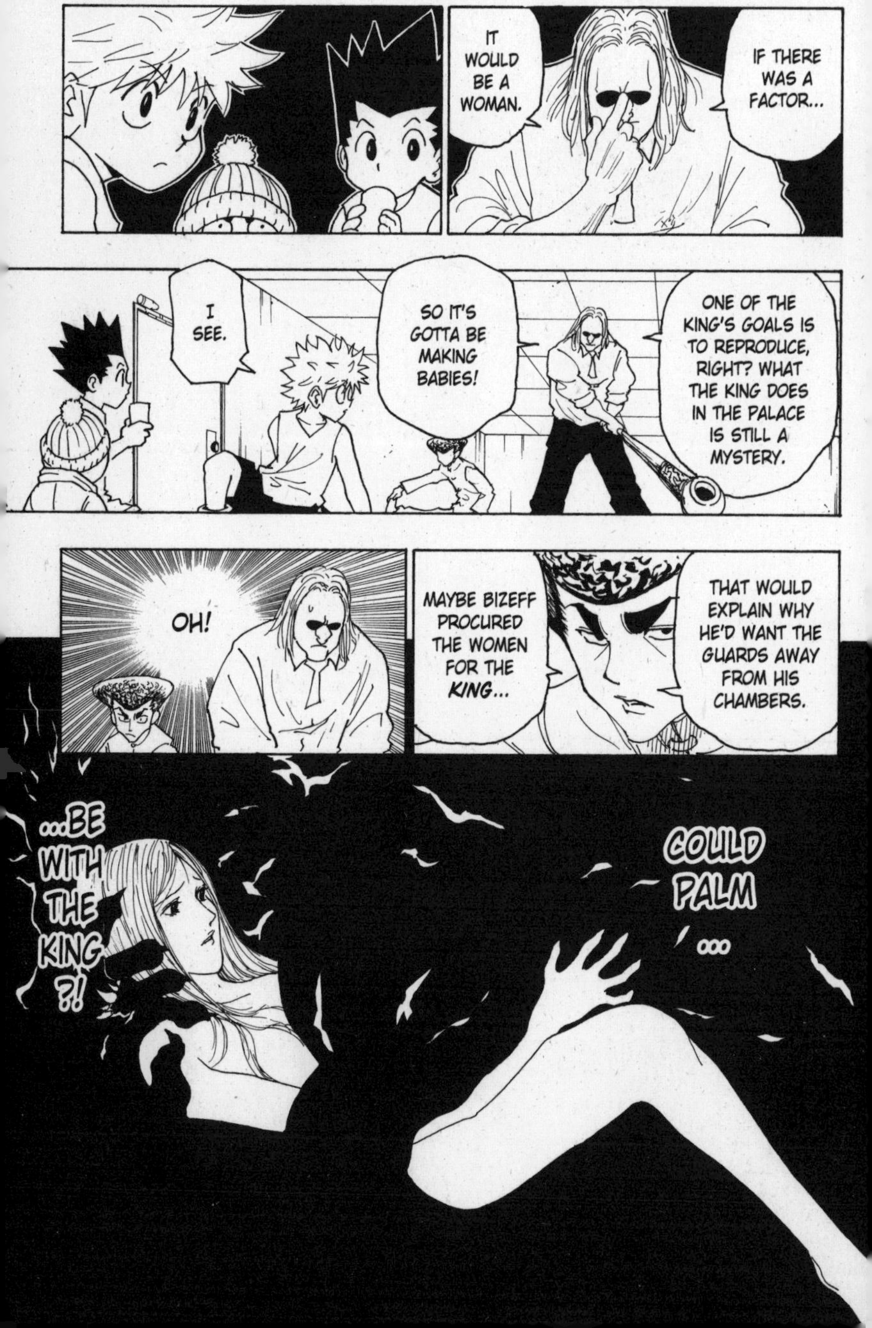
IF THERE WAS A FACTOR...
IT WOULD BE A WOMAN.
ONE OF THE KING'S GOALS IS TO REPRODUCE, RIGHT? WHAT THE KING DOES IN THE PALACE IS STILL A MYSTERY.
SO IT'S GOTTA BE MAKING BABIES!
I SEE.
THAT WOULD EXPLAIN WHY HE'D WANT THE GUARDS AWAY FROM HIS CHAMBERS.
MAYBE BIZEFF PROCURED THE WOMEN FOR THE *KING*...
OH!
COULD PALM...
...BE WITH THE KING?!

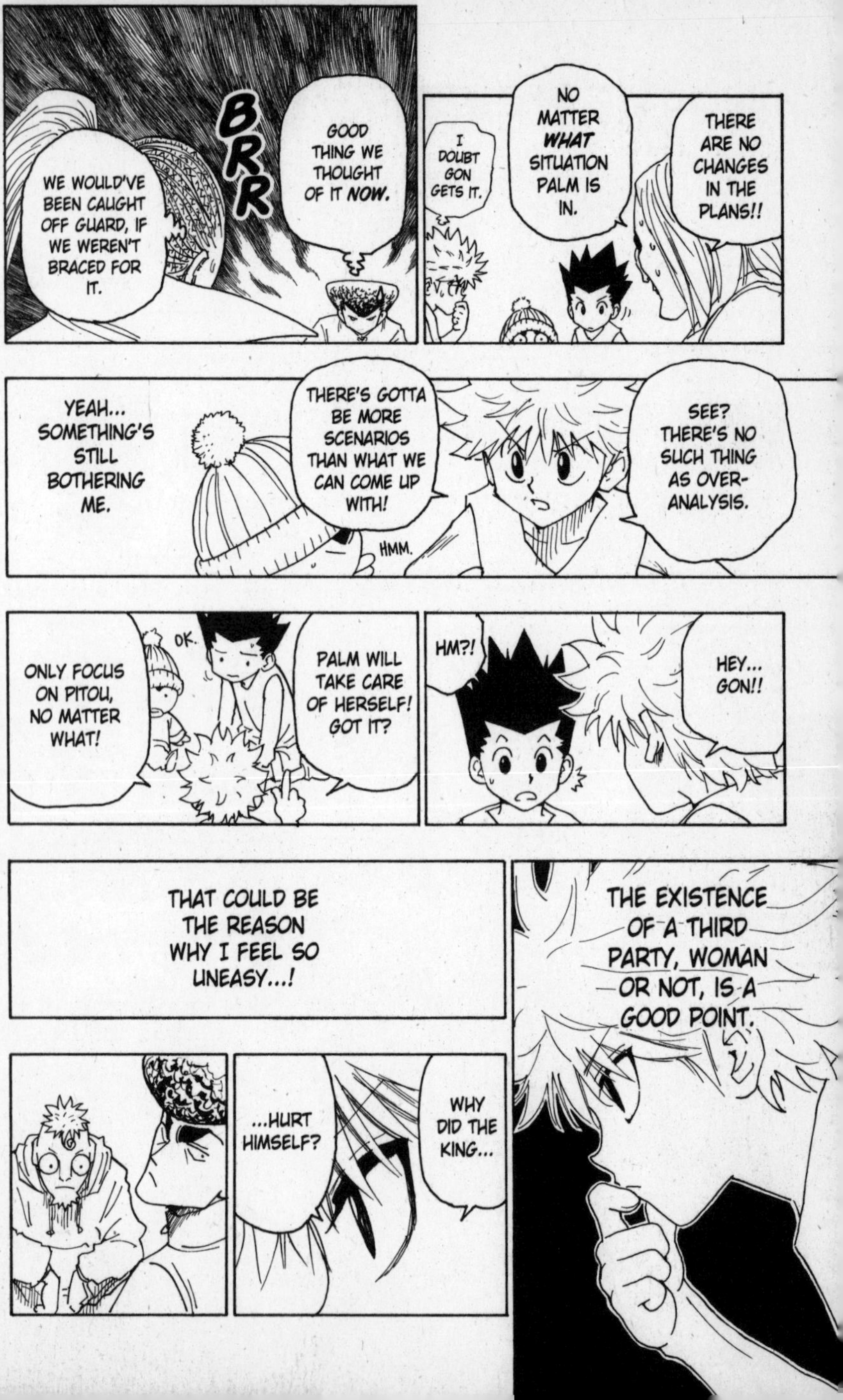
THERE ARE NO CHANGES IN THE PLANS!!
NO MATTER *WHAT* SITUATION PALM IS IN.
I DOUBT GON GETS IT.
GOOD THING WE THOUGHT OF IT *NOW*.
BRR
WE WOULD'VE BEEN CAUGHT OFF GUARD, IF WE WEREN'T BRACED FOR IT.
SEE? THERE'S NO SUCH THING AS OVER-ANALYSIS.
THERE'S GOTTA BE MORE SCENARIOS THAN WHAT WE CAN COME UP WITH!
HMM.
YEAH... SOMETHING'S STILL BOTHERING ME.
HEY... GON!!
HM?!
PALM WILL TAKE CARE OF HERSELF! GOT IT?
OK.
ONLY FOCUS ON PITOU, NO MATTER WHAT!
THE EXISTENCE OF A THIRD PARTY, WOMAN OR NOT, IS A GOOD POINT.
THAT COULD BE THE REASON WHY I FEEL SO UNEASY...!
WHY DID THE KING...
...HURT HIMSELF?

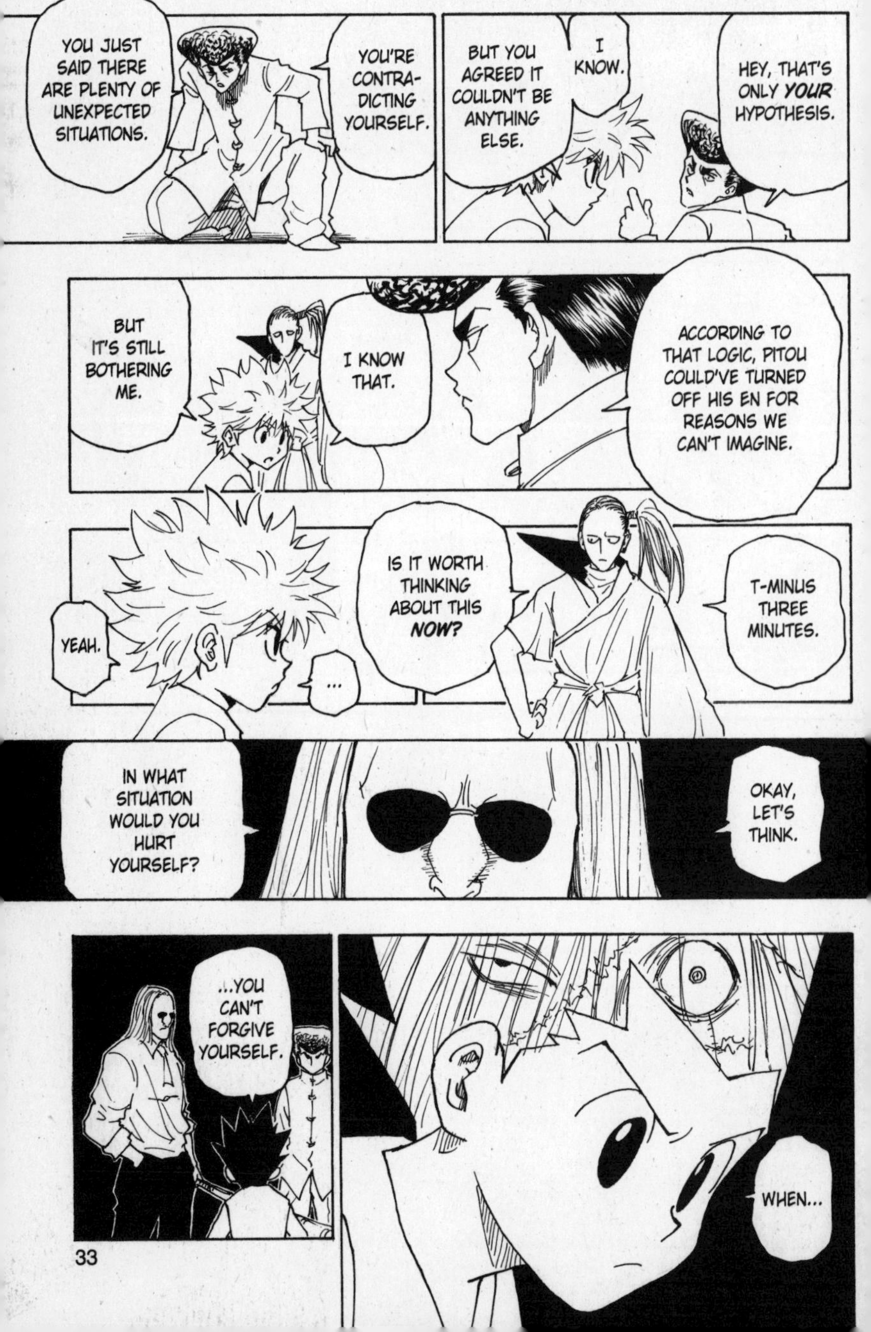
HEY, THAT'S ONLY *YOUR* HYPOTHESIS.
I KNOW.
BUT YOU AGREED IT COULDN'T BE ANYTHING ELSE.
YOU'RE CONTRA-DICTING YOURSELF.
YOU JUST SAID THERE ARE PLENTY OF UNEXPECTED SITUATIONS.
ACCORDING TO THAT LOGIC, PITOU COULD'VE TURNED OFF HIS EN FOR REASONS WE CAN'T IMAGINE.
I KNOW THAT.
BUT IT'S STILL BOTHERING ME.
T-MINUS THREE MINUTES.
IS IT WORTH THINKING ABOUT THIS *NOW?*
...
YEAH.
OKAY, LET'S THINK.
IN WHAT SITUATION WOULD YOU HURT YOURSELF?
WHEN...
...YOU CAN'T FORGIVE YOURSELF.

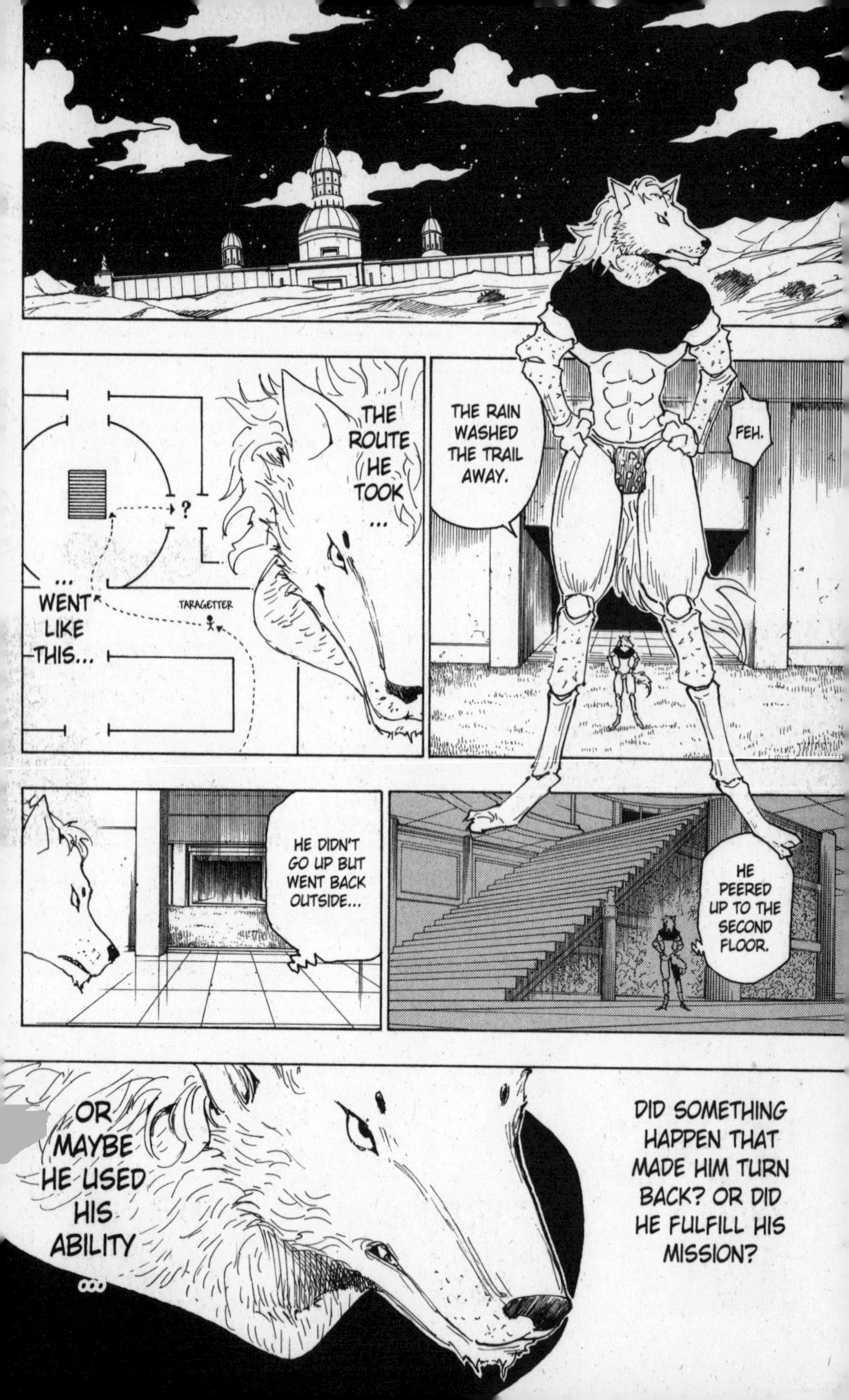
FEH.
THE RAIN WASHED THE TRAIL AWAY.
THE ROUTE HE TOOK ...
?
TARAGETTER
... WENT LIKE THIS...
HE PEERED UP TO THE SECOND FLOOR.
HE DIDN'T GO UP BUT WENT BACK OUTSIDE...
DID SOMETHING HAPPEN THAT MADE HIM TURN BACK? OR DID HE FULFILL HIS MISSION?
OR MAYBE HE USED HIS ABILITY ...

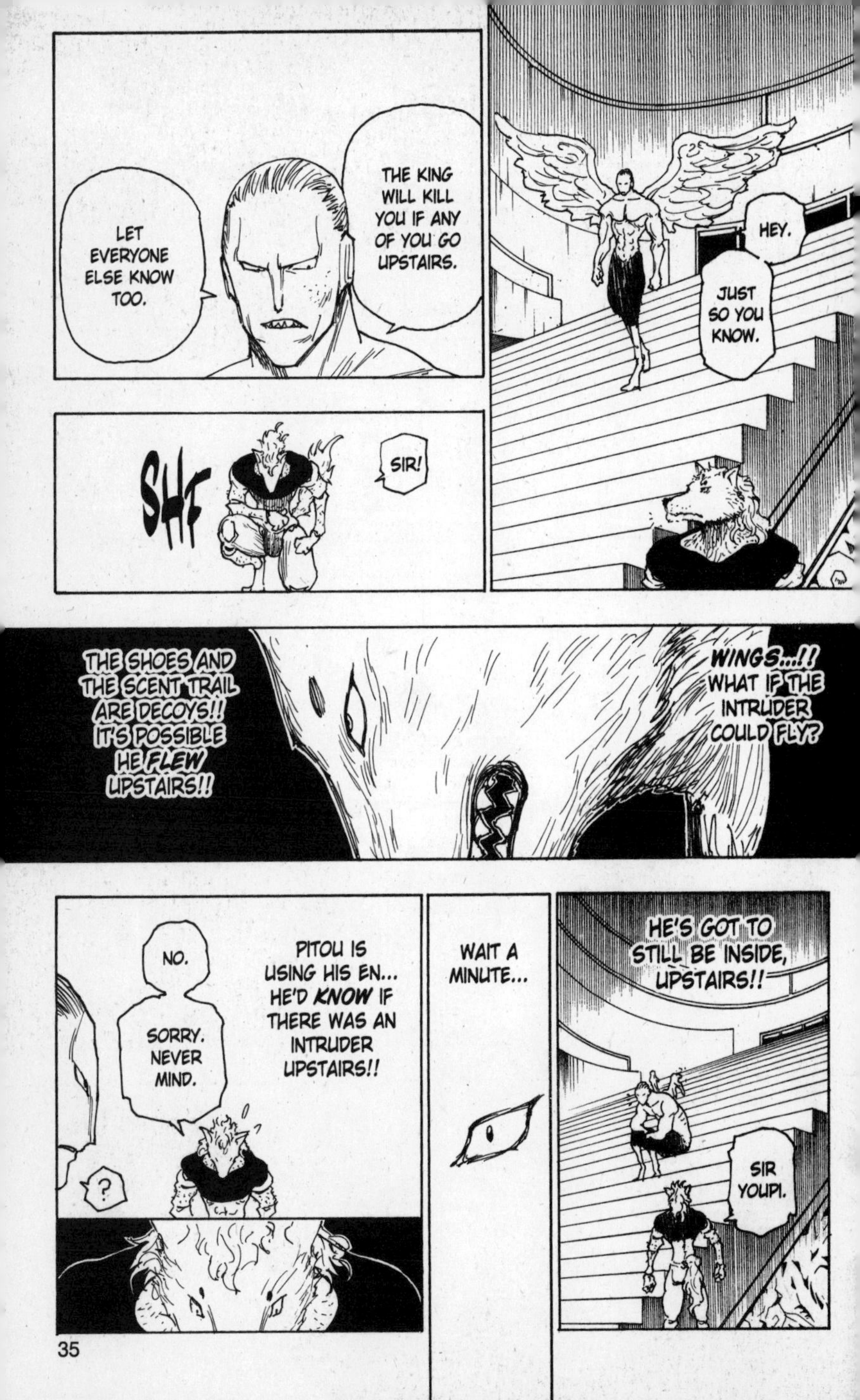
HEY.
JUST SO YOU KNOW.
THE KING WILL KILL YOU IF ANY OF YOU GO UPSTAIRS.
LET EVERYONE ELSE KNOW TOO.
SIR!
SHF
WINGS...!! WHAT IF THE INTRUDER COULD FLY?
THE SHOES AND THE SCENT TRAIL ARE DECOYS!! IT'S POSSIBLE HE FLEW UPSTAIRS!!
HE'S GOT TO STILL BE INSIDE, UPSTAIRS!!
SIR YOUPI.
WAIT A MINUTE...
PITOU IS USING HIS EN... HE'D KNOW IF THERE WAS AN INTRUDER UPSTAIRS!!
NO.
SORRY. NEVER MIND.
?

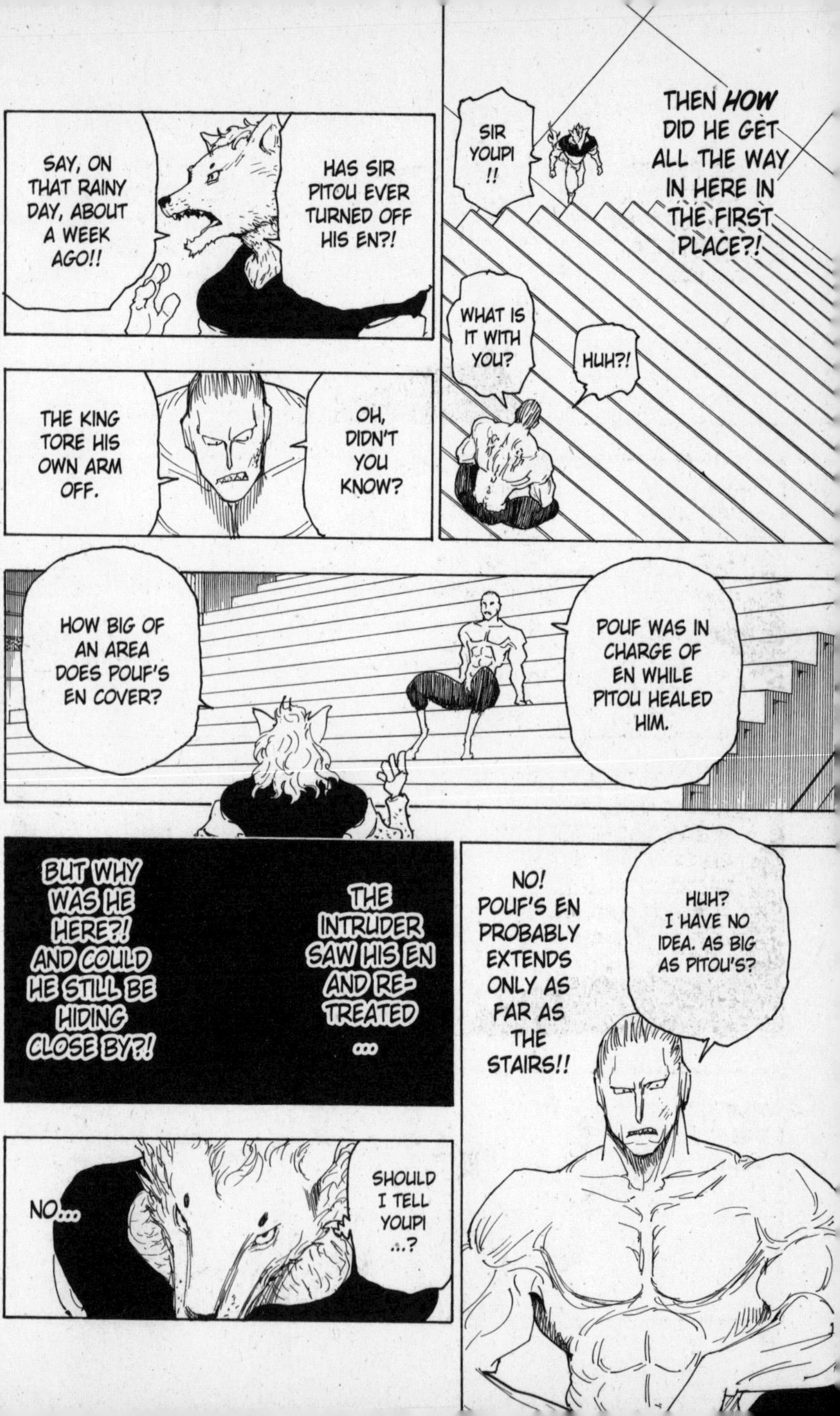

THEN HOW DID HE GET ALL THE WAY IN HERE IN THE FIRST PLACE?!
SIR YOUPI !!
HUH?!
WHAT IS IT WITH YOU?
HAS SIR PITOU EVER TURNED OFF HIS EN?!
SAY, ON THAT RAINY DAY, ABOUT A WEEK AGO!!
OH, DIDN'T YOU KNOW?
THE KING TORE HIS OWN ARM OFF.
POUF WAS IN CHARGE OF EN WHILE PITOU HEALED HIM.
HOW BIG OF AN AREA DOES POUF'S EN COVER?
HUH? I HAVE NO IDEA. AS BIG AS PITOU'S?
NO! POUF'S EN PROBABLY EXTENDS ONLY AS FAR AS THE STAIRS!!
THE INTRUDER SAW HIS EN AND RE-TREATED ...
BUT WHY WAS HE HERE?! AND COULD HE STILL BE HIDING CLOSE BY?!
SHOULD I TELL YOUPI ...?
NO...

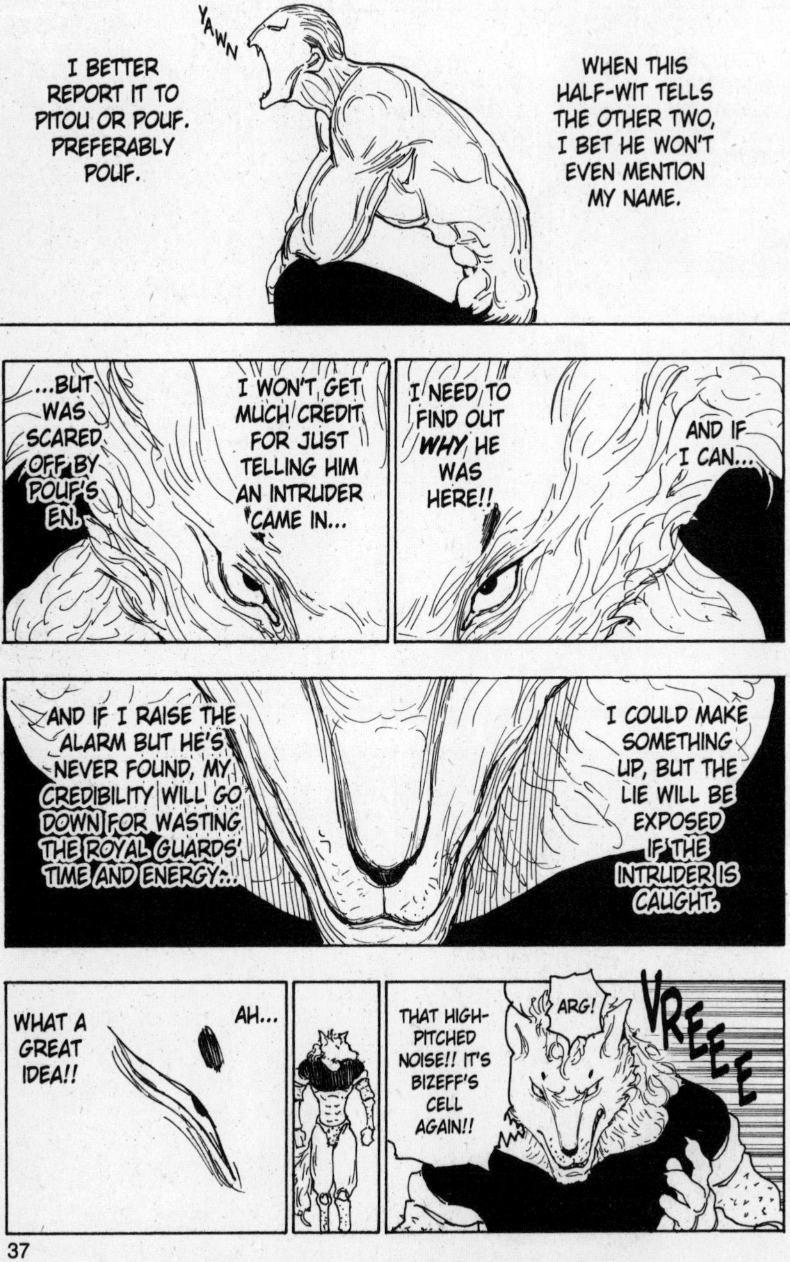
WHEN THIS HALF-WIT TELLS THE OTHER TWO, I BET HE WON'T EVEN MENTION MY NAME.
YAWN
I BETTER REPORT IT TO PITOU OR POUF. PREFERABLY POUF.
I NEED TO FIND OUT WHY HE WAS HERE!!
AND IF I CAN...
I WON'T GET MUCH CREDIT FOR JUST TELLING HIM AN INTRUDER CAME IN...
...BUT WAS SCARED OFF BY POUF'S EN.
I COULD MAKE SOMETHING UP, BUT THE LIE WILL BE EXPOSED IF THE INTRUDER IS CAUGHT.
AND IF I RAISE THE ALARM BUT HE'S NEVER FOUND, MY CREDIBILITY WILL GO DOWN FOR WASTING THE ROYAL GUARDS' TIME AND ENERGY...
VREEE
ARG!
THAT HIGH-PITCHED NOISE!! IT'S BIZEFF'S CELL AGAIN!!
AH...
WHAT A GREAT IDEA!!

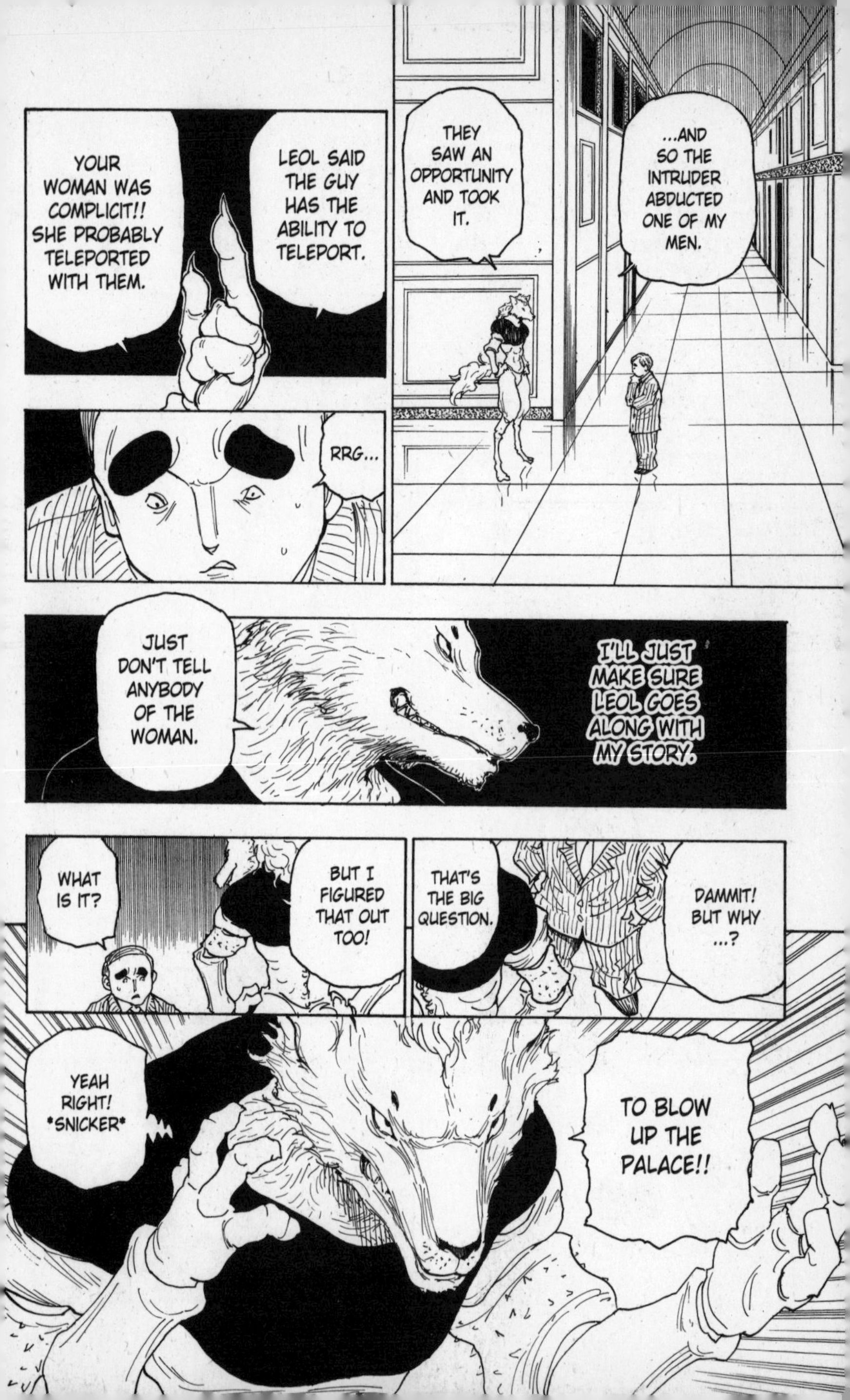
...AND SO THE INTRUDER ABDUCTED ONE OF MY MEN.
THEY SAW AN OPPORTUNITY AND TOOK IT.
LEOL SAID THE GUY HAS THE ABILITY TO TELEPORT.
YOUR WOMAN WAS COMPLICIT!! SHE PROBABLY TELEPORTED WITH THEM.
RRG...
I'LL JUST MAKE SURE LEOL GOES ALONG WITH MY STORY.
JUST DON'T TELL ANYBODY OF THE WOMAN.
DAMMIT! BUT WHY ...?
THAT'S THE BIG QUESTION.
BUT I FIGURED THAT OUT TOO!
WHAT IS IT?
TO BLOW UP THE PALACE!!
YEAH RIGHT! *SNICKER*

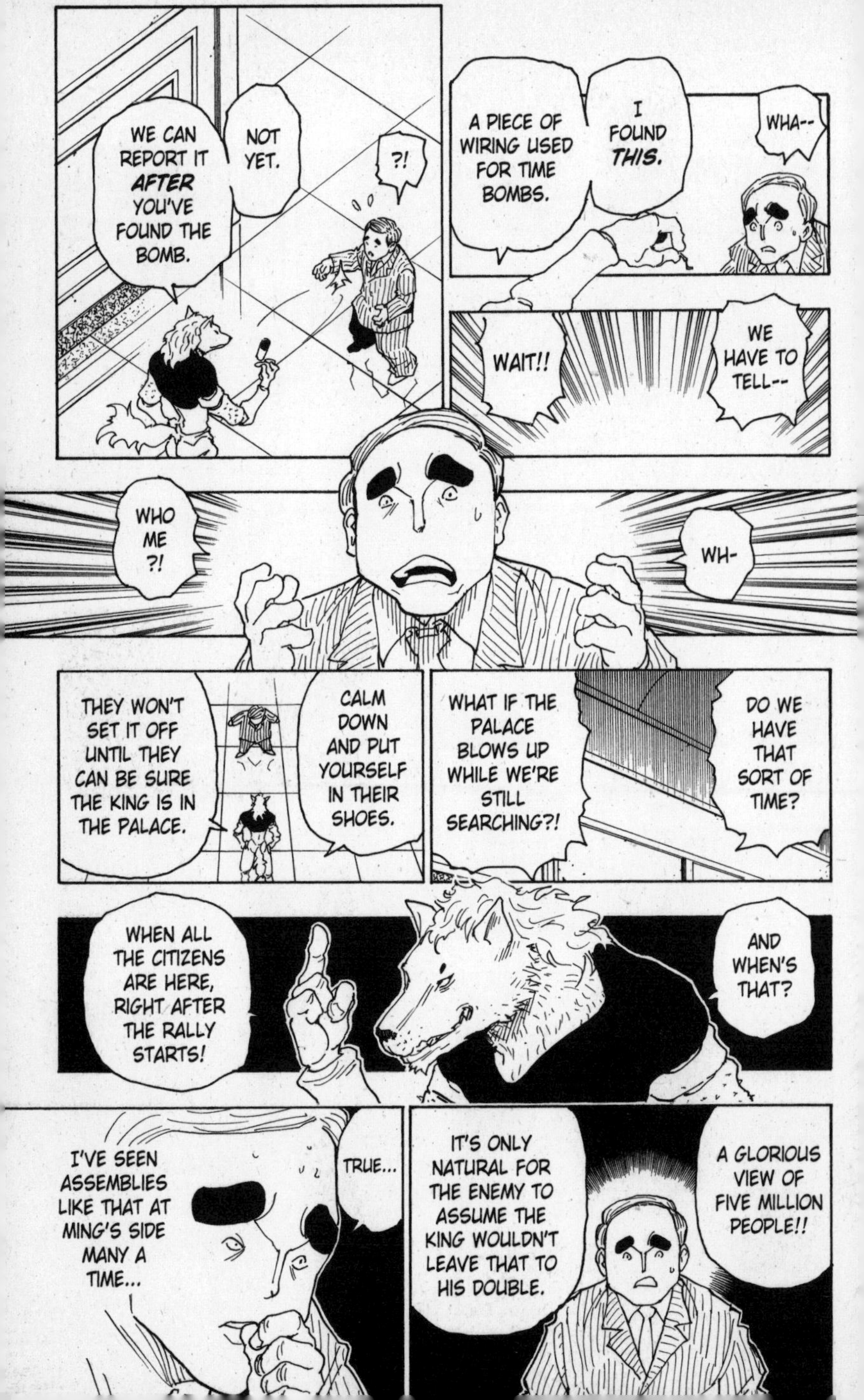
WHA--
I FOUND THIS.
A PIECE OF WIRING USED FOR TIME BOMBS.
WE HAVE TO TELL--
WAIT!!
?!
NOT YET.
WE CAN REPORT IT AFTER YOU'VE FOUND THE BOMB.
WH-
WHO ME ?!
DO WE HAVE THAT SORT OF TIME?
WHAT IF THE PALACE BLOWS UP WHILE WE'RE STILL SEARCHING?!
CALM DOWN AND PUT YOURSELF IN THEIR SHOES.
THEY WON'T SET IT OFF UNTIL THEY CAN BE SURE THE KING IS IN THE PALACE.
AND WHEN'S THAT?
WHEN ALL THE CITIZENS ARE HERE, RIGHT AFTER THE RALLY STARTS!
A GLORIOUS VIEW OF FIVE MILLION PEOPLE!!
IT'S ONLY NATURAL FOR THE ENEMY TO ASSUME THE KING WOULDN'T LEAVE THAT TO HIS DOUBLE.
TRUE...
I'VE SEEN ASSEMBLIES LIKE THAT AT MING'S SIDE MANY A TIME...

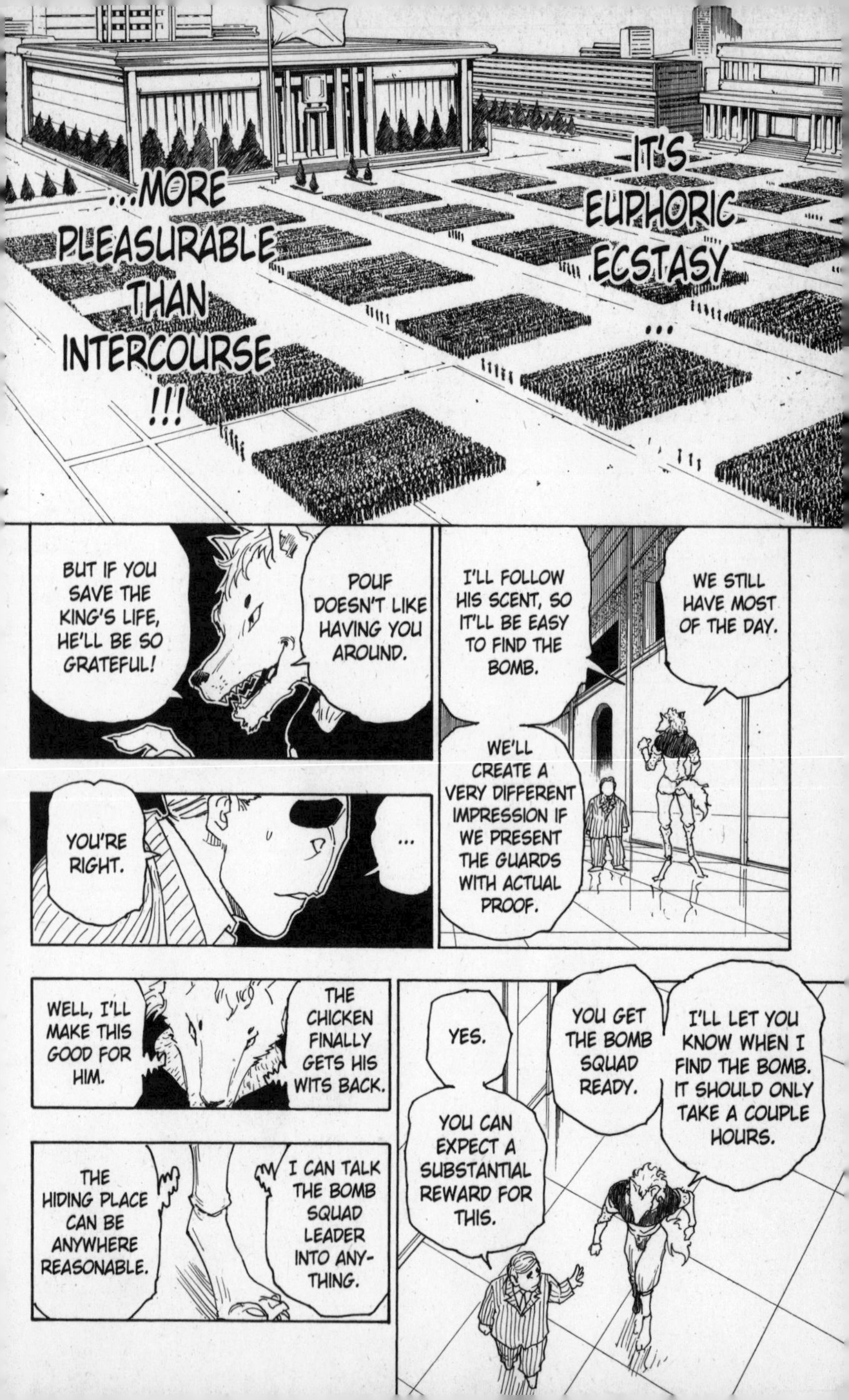
IT'S EUPHORIC ECSTASY...
...MORE PLEASURABLE THAN INTERCOURSE!!!
WE STILL HAVE MOST OF THE DAY.
I'LL FOLLOW HIS SCENT, SO IT'LL BE EASY TO FIND THE BOMB.
WE'LL CREATE A VERY DIFFERENT IMPRESSION IF WE PRESENT THE GUARDS WITH ACTUAL PROOF.
POUF DOESN'T LIKE HAVING YOU AROUND.
BUT IF YOU SAVE THE KING'S LIFE, HE'LL BE SO GRATEFUL!
...
YOU'RE RIGHT.
I'LL LET YOU KNOW WHEN I FIND THE BOMB. IT SHOULD ONLY TAKE A COUPLE HOURS.
YOU GET THE BOMB SQUAD READY.
YES.
YOU CAN EXPECT A SUBSTANTIAL REWARD FOR THIS.
THE CHICKEN FINALLY GETS HIS WITS BACK.
WELL, I'LL MAKE THIS GOOD FOR HIM.
I CAN TALK THE BOMB SQUAD LEADER INTO ANYTHING.
THE HIDING PLACE CAN BE ANYWHERE REASONABLE.

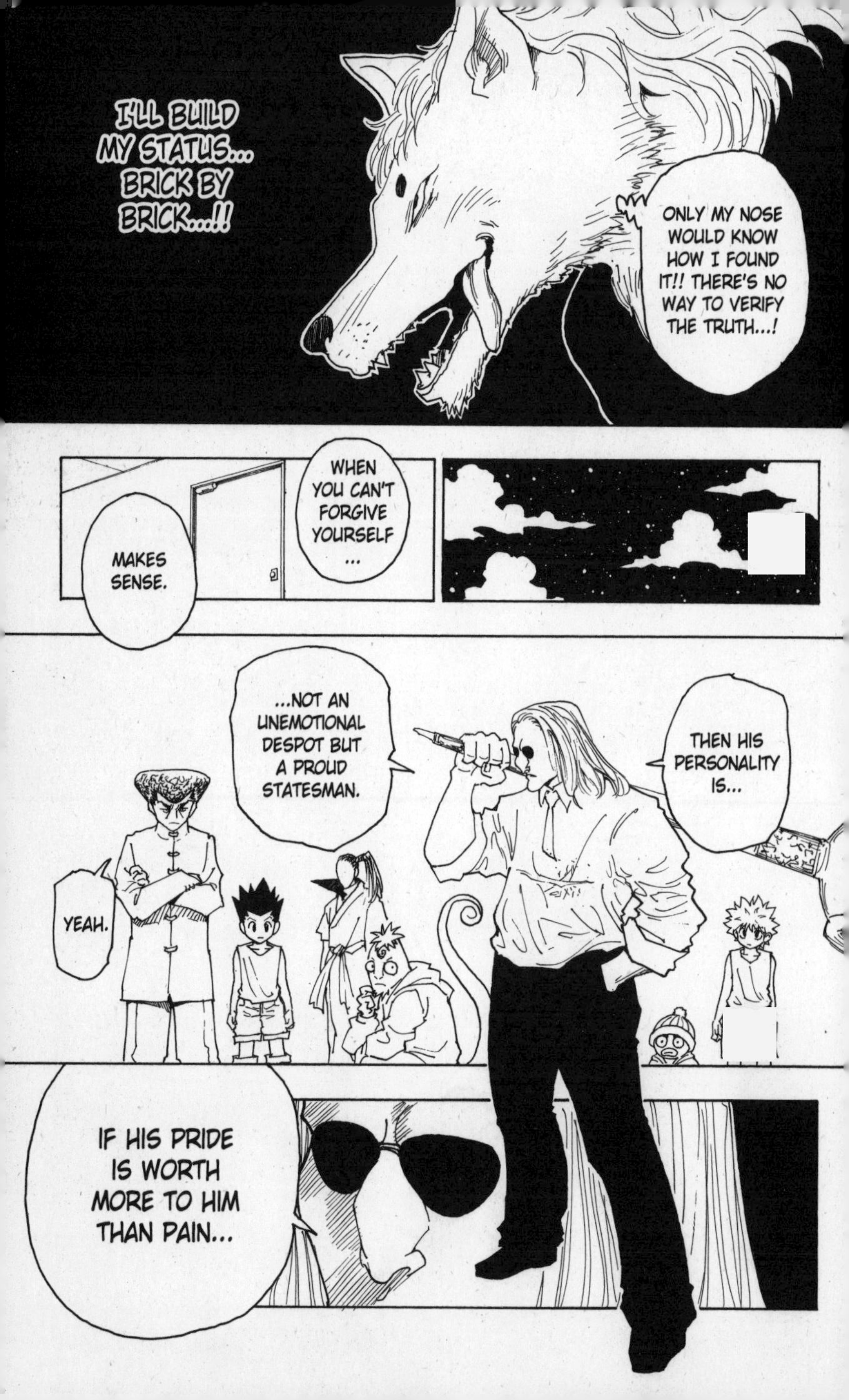
ONLY MY NOSE WOULD KNOW HOW I FOUND IT!! THERE'S NO WAY TO VERIFY THE TRUTH...!
I'LL BUILD MY STATUS... BRICK BY BRICK...!!
WHEN YOU CAN'T FORGIVE YOURSELF...
MAKES SENSE.
THEN HIS PERSONALITY IS...
...NOT AN UNEMOTIONAL DESPOT BUT A PROUD STATESMAN.
YEAH.
IF HIS PRIDE IS WORTH MORE TO HIM THAN PAIN...

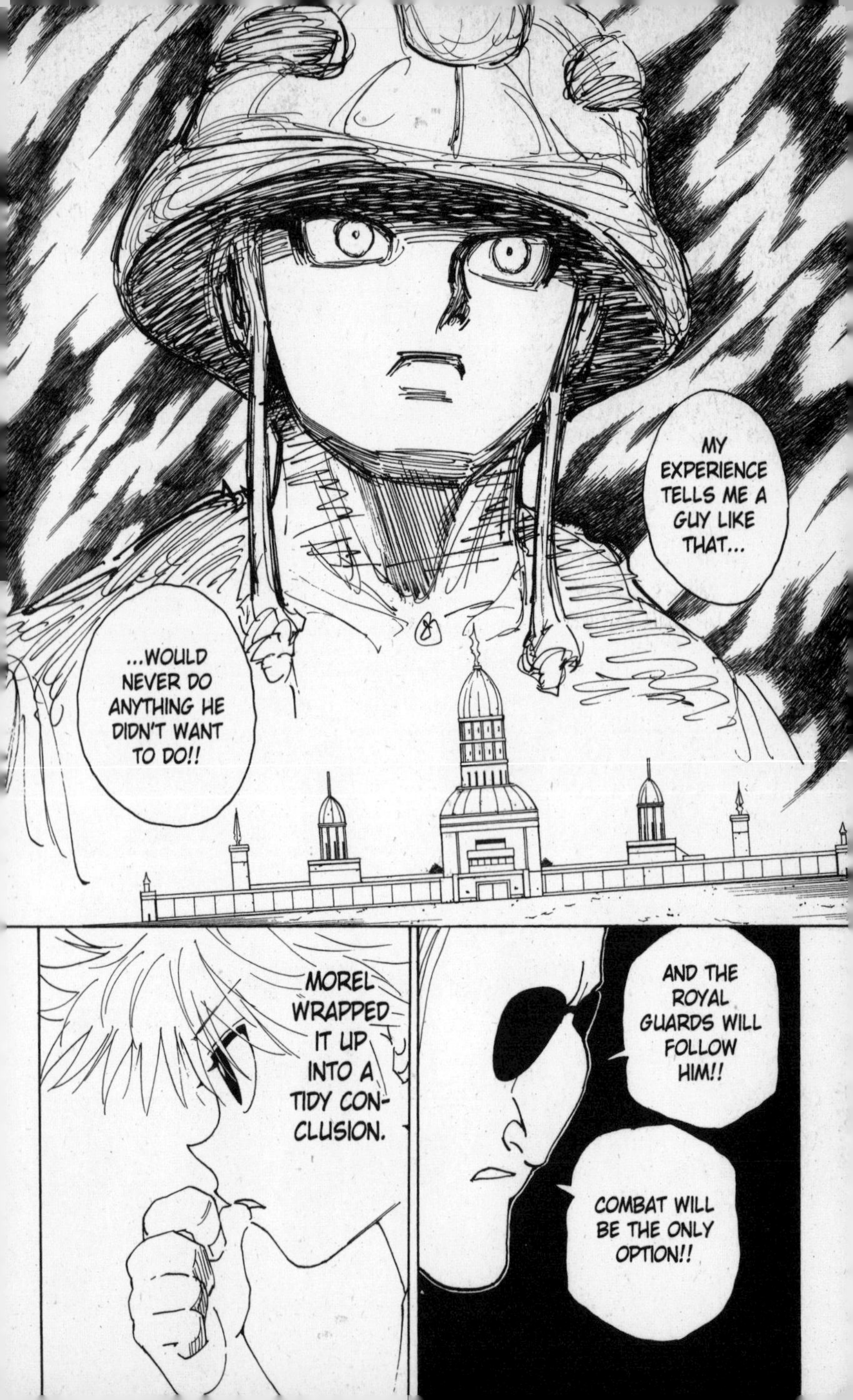
MY EXPERIENCE TELLS ME A GUY LIKE THAT...
...WOULD NEVER DO ANYTHING HE DIDN'T WANT TO DO!!
AND THE ROYAL GUARDS WILL FOLLOW HIM!!
COMBAT WILL BE THE ONLY OPTION!!
MOREL WRAPPED IT UP INTO A TIDY CON-CLUSION.

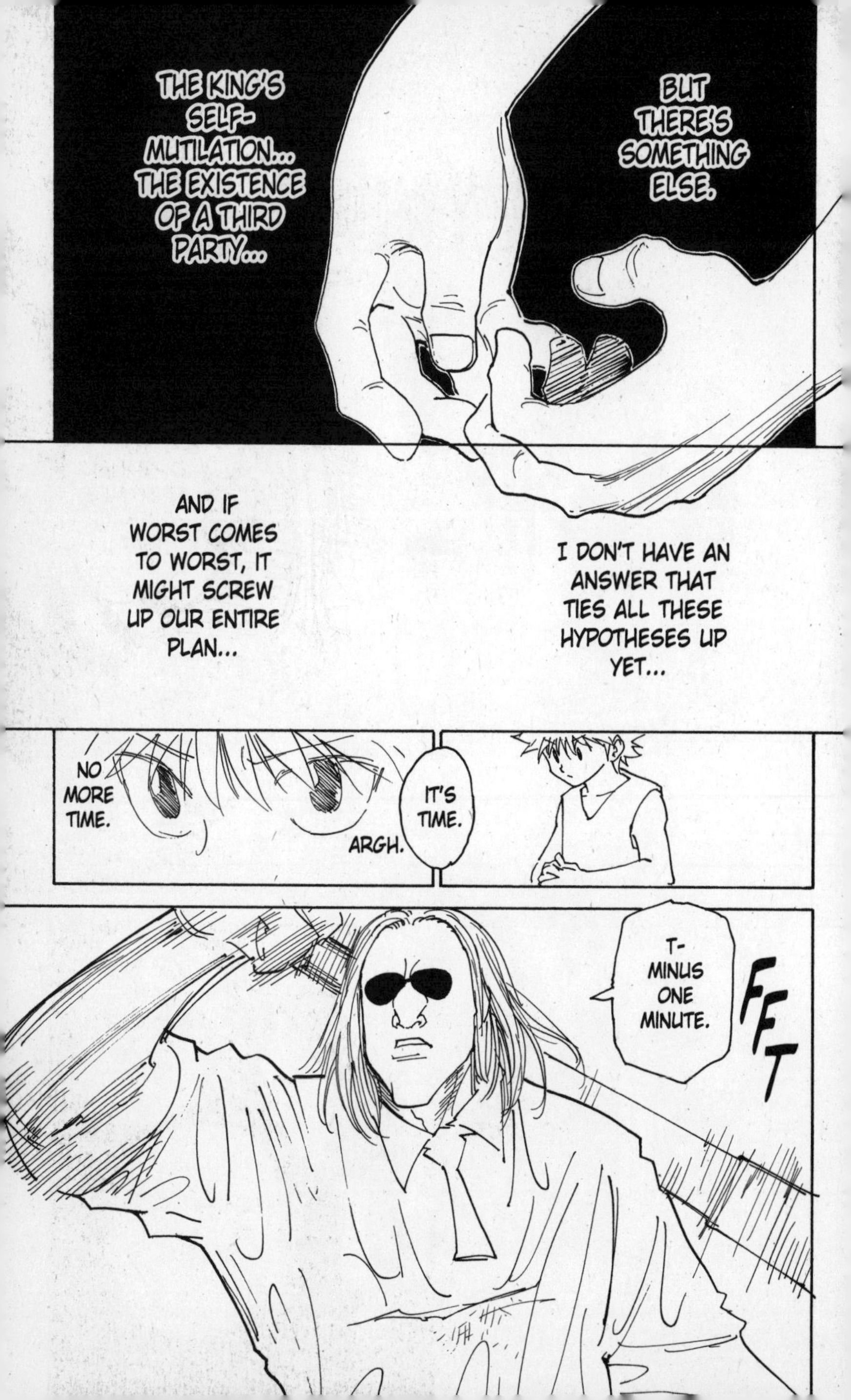
BUT THERE'S SOMETHING ELSE.
THE KING'S SELF-MUTILATION... THE EXISTENCE OF A THIRD PARTY...
I DON'T HAVE AN ANSWER THAT TIES ALL THESE HYPOTHESES UP YET...
AND IF WORST COMES TO WORST, IT MIGHT SCREW UP OUR ENTIRE PLAN...
IT'S TIME.
ARGH.
NO MORE TIME.
FFT
T-MINUS ONE MINUTE.

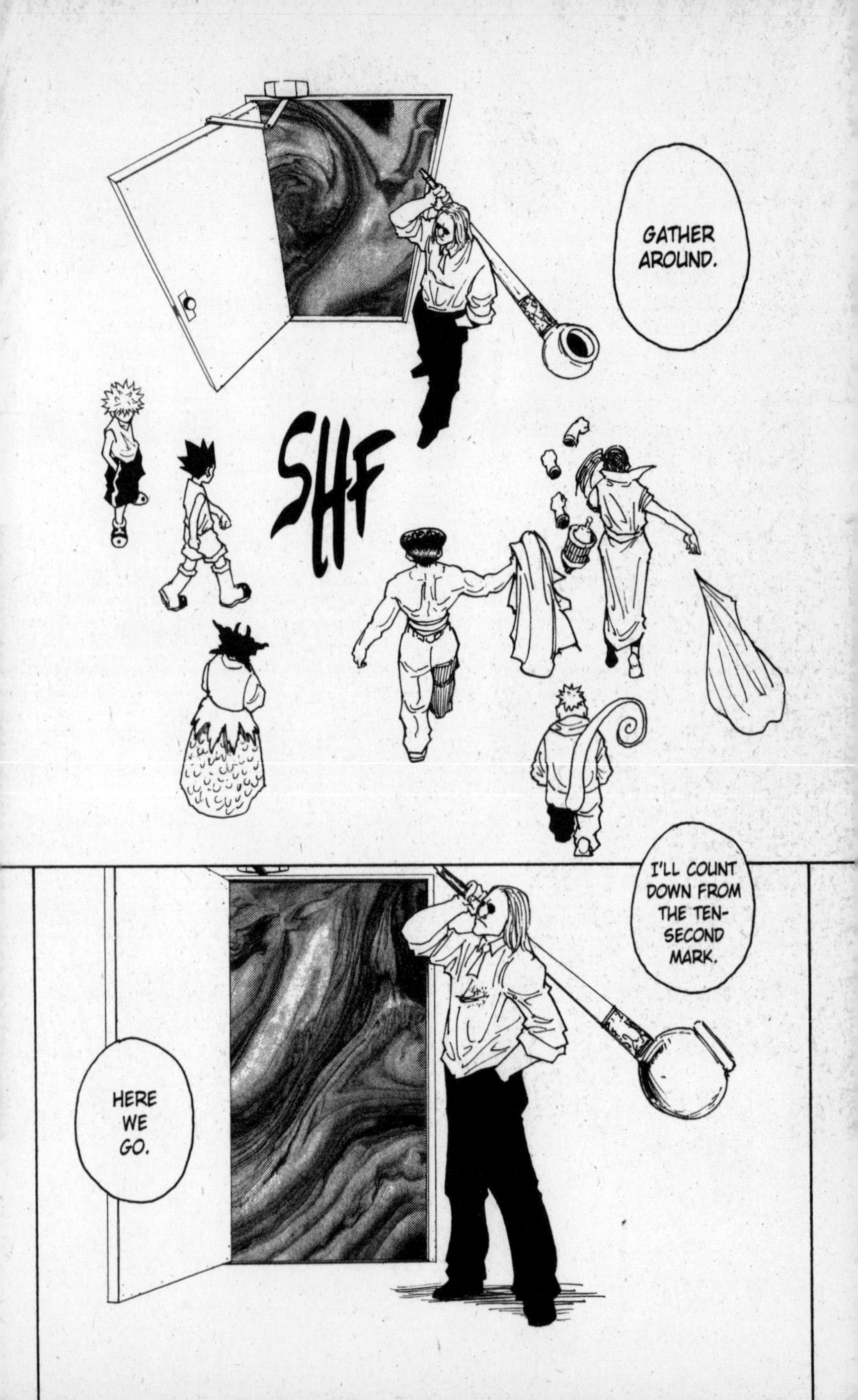
GATHER AROUND.
SHF
I'LL COUNT DOWN FROM THE TEN-SECOND MARK.
HERE WE GO.

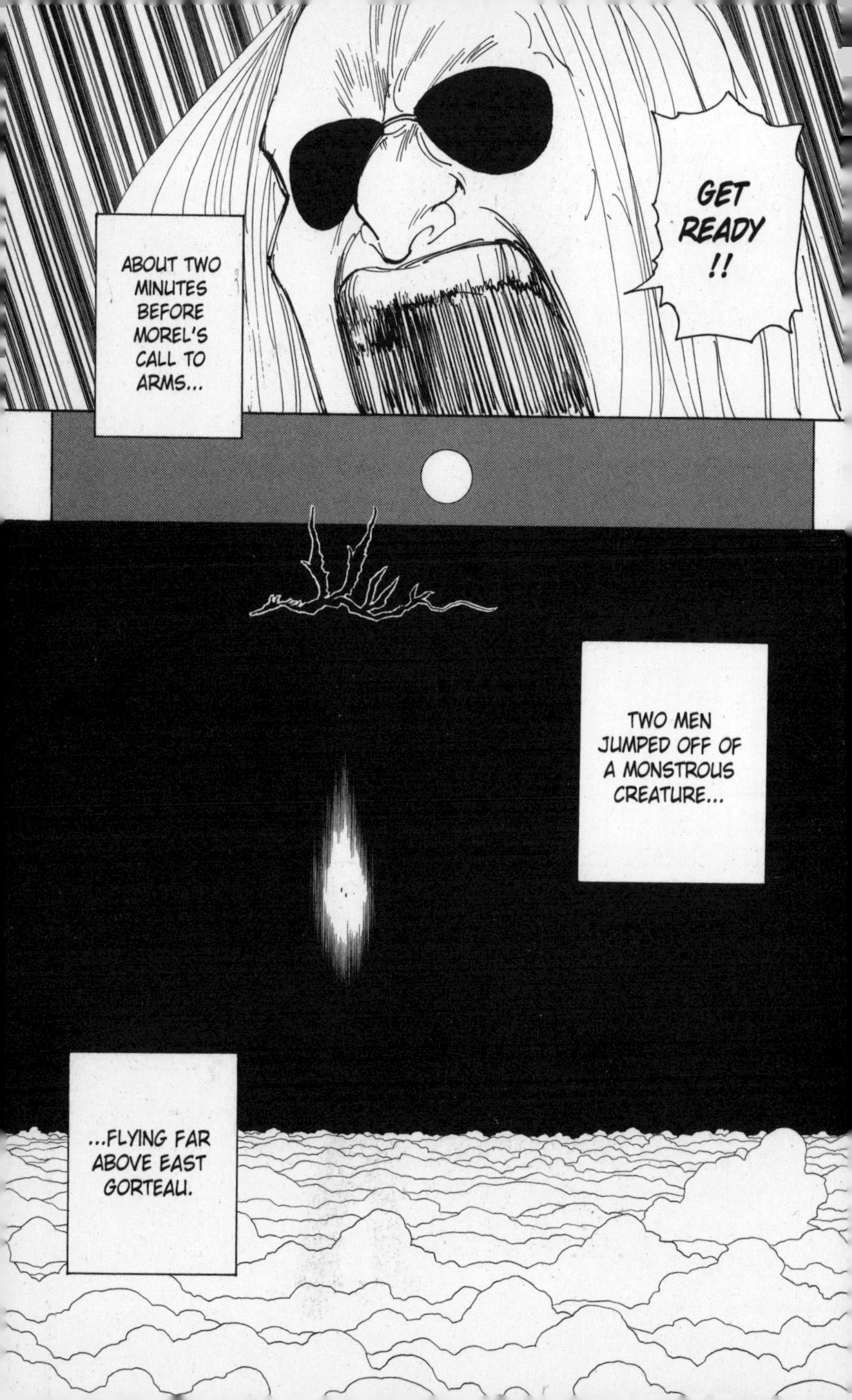
GET READY !!
ABOUT TWO MINUTES BEFORE MOREL'S CALL TO ARMS...
TWO MEN JUMPED OFF OF A MONSTROUS CREATURE...
...FLYING FAR ABOVE EAST GORTEAU.

ROUND ONE: BEACH FLAGS

◎ FOUR PEOPLE PER MATCH, WITH ONE PERSON
ADVANCING TO THE NEXT ROUND.

THE SCORES WERE TALLIED BY AGILITY + DIE
ROLL (REGULAR D6).
IF THERE'S A TIE, IT'S BROKEN BY THEIR TIMING STATS.
IF THERE'S ANOTHER TIE, I KEEP ROLLING UNTIL THERE'S
A WINNER.

Thanks for all the messages!!

THE POOL OF APPLICANTS
WAS REDUCED TO 1084. IT
TOOK ABOUT 15 HOURS TO
ROLL THE DICE.

THE HIGHEST SCORE WAS LIME WITH 16 POINTS!!
THERE WERE FIVE PEOPLE TIED FOR SECOND PLACE
WITH 15 POINTS: PINO, KAMAKURA, CAPTAIN FUJITA,
HANTASAN AND DORADORA PONPON.

○ PEOPLE WITH AGILITY OF 1 OR 0 ALL FAILED. ACCORDING
TO THE LUCK OF THE DRAW ON THEIR OPPONENTS,
THERE WERE CASES OF PEOPLE LOSING EVEN WITH A
SCORE OF 15, OR WINNING WITH A SCORE OF 5.
MY ROLLING WAS PUNCTUATED WITH OCCASIONAL
OUTBURSTS OF "WHOA, WHAT ARE THE CHANCES?!"
THERE WAS A SUPER INTENSE BATTLE WHERE I HAD
TO ROLL THE DICE FOUR TIMES TO FINALLY SETTLE
THE MATCH.

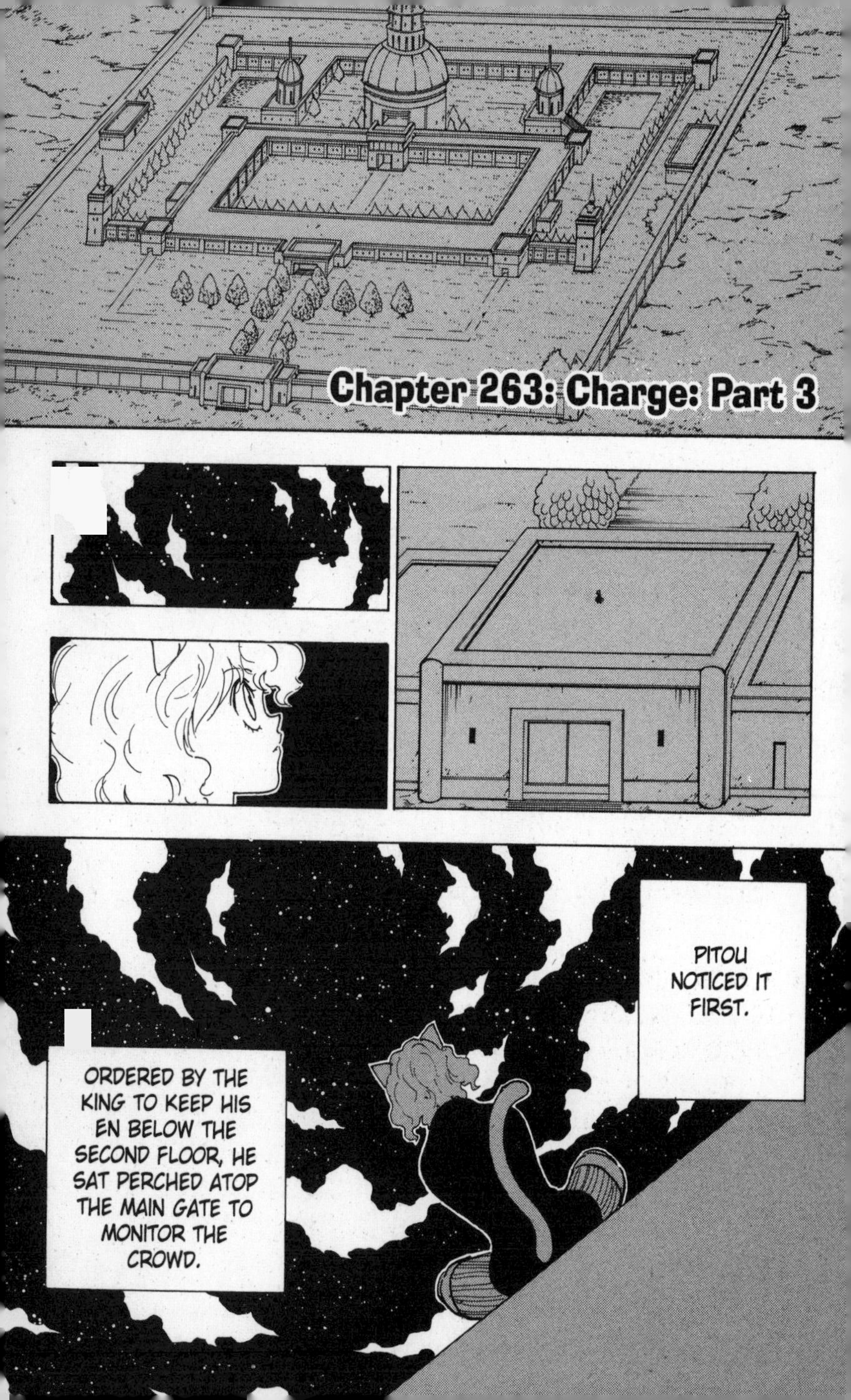
Chapter 263: Charge: Part 3
PITOU NOTICED IT FIRST.
ORDERED BY THE KING TO KEEP HIS EN BELOW THE SECOND FLOOR, HE SAT PERCHED ATOP THE MAIN GATE TO MONITOR THE CROWD.

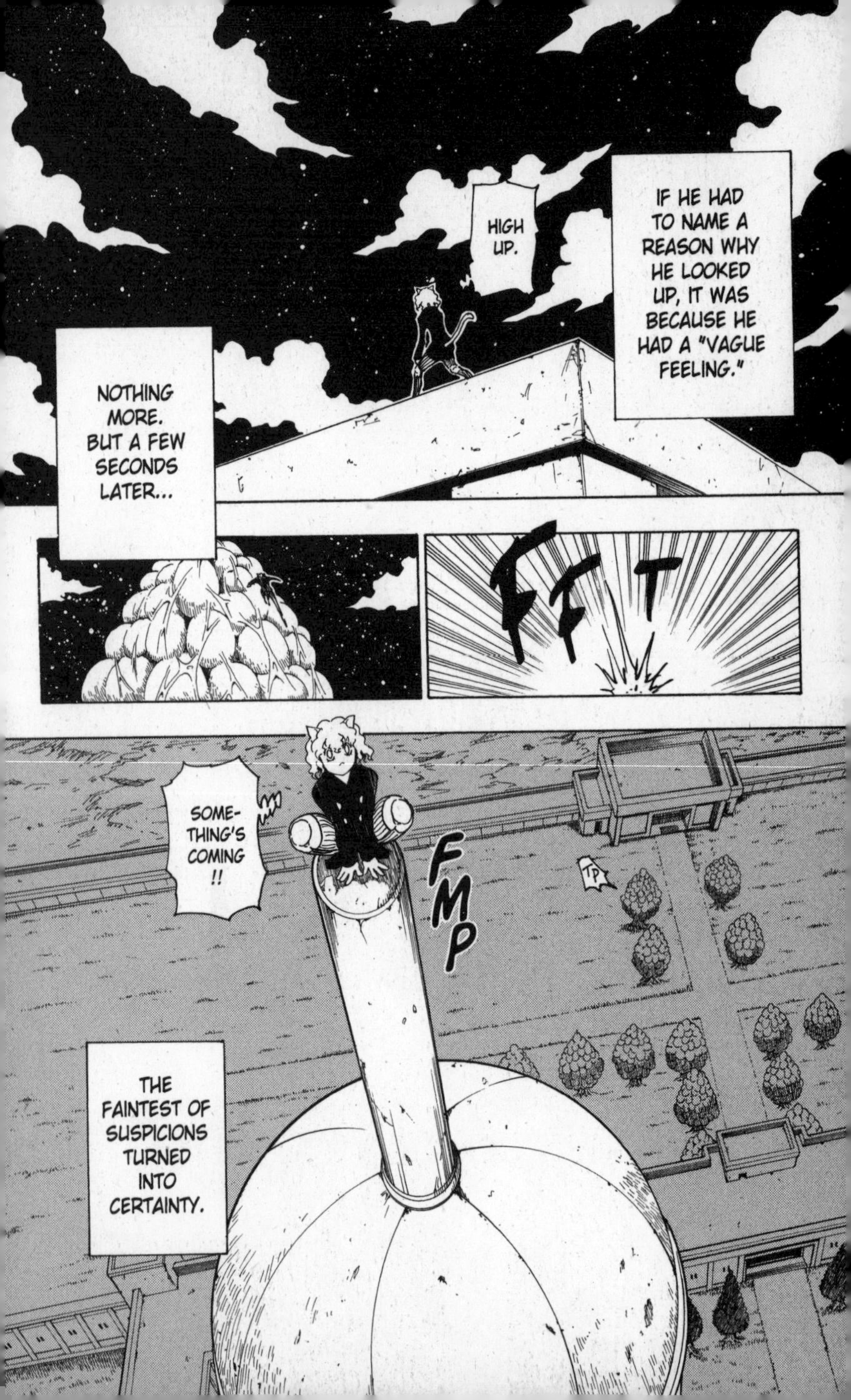
IF HE HAD TO NAME A REASON WHY HE LOOKED UP, IT WAS BECAUSE HE HAD A "VAGUE FEELING."
HIGH UP.
NOTHING MORE. BUT A FEW SECONDS LATER...
FFT
FMP
TP
SOME-THING'S COMING !!
THE FAINTEST OF SUSPICIONS TURNED INTO CERTAINTY.

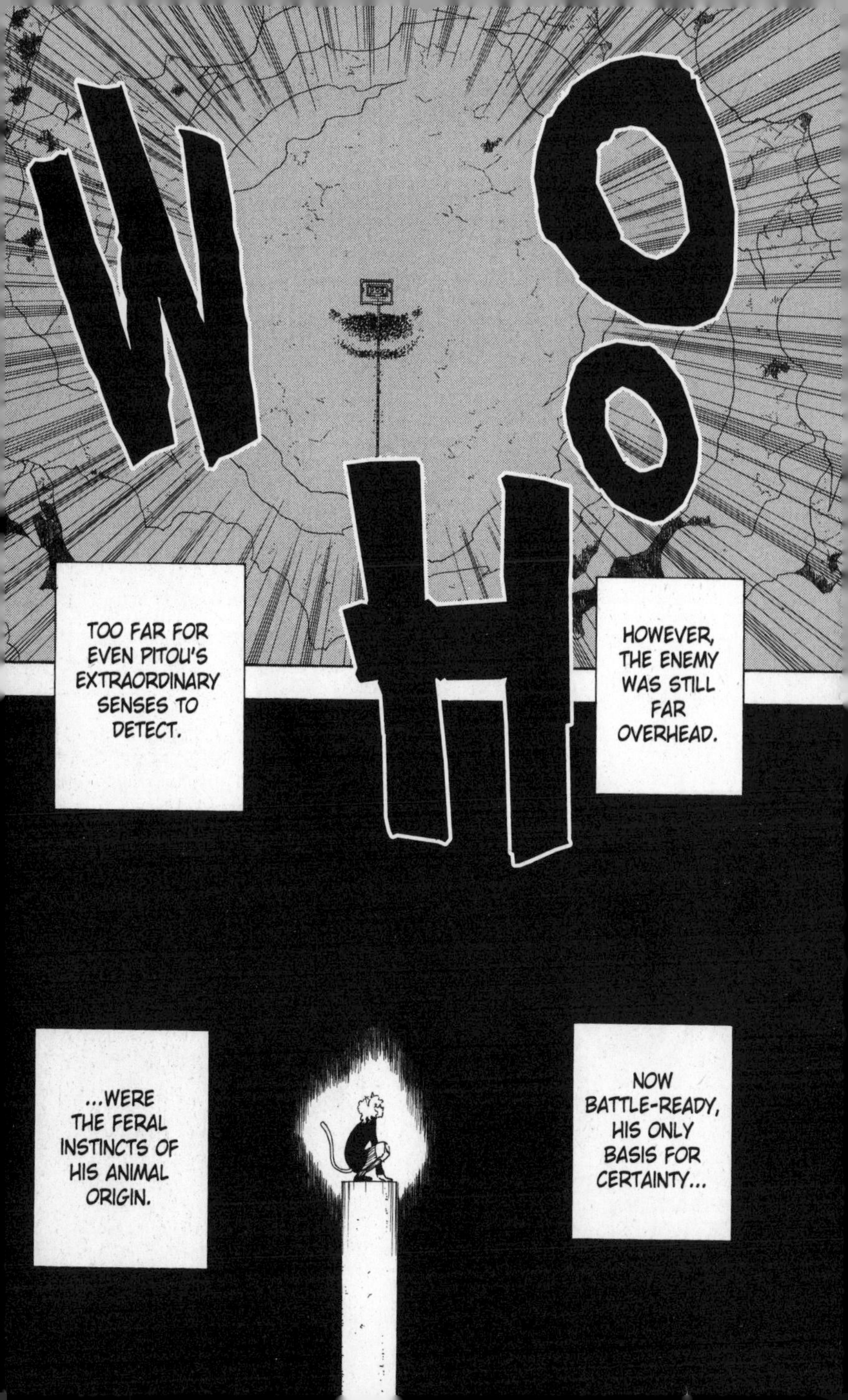
WHOO
HOWEVER, THE ENEMY WAS STILL FAR OVERHEAD.
TOO FAR FOR EVEN PITOU'S EXTRAORDINARY SENSES TO DETECT.
NOW BATTLE-READY, HIS ONLY BASIS FOR CERTAINTY...
...WERE THE FERAL INSTINCTS OF HIS ANIMAL ORIGIN.

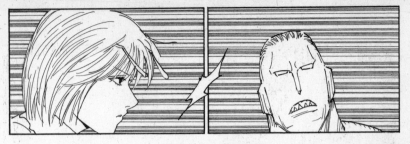

PITOU'S EN
IS GONE?

THIS
DESCENDING
AURA WAS SO
POWERFUL AND
THREATENING...

ROARR

...THAT IT
HEIGHTENED
PITOU'S INTUITION
MORE THAN
USUAL.

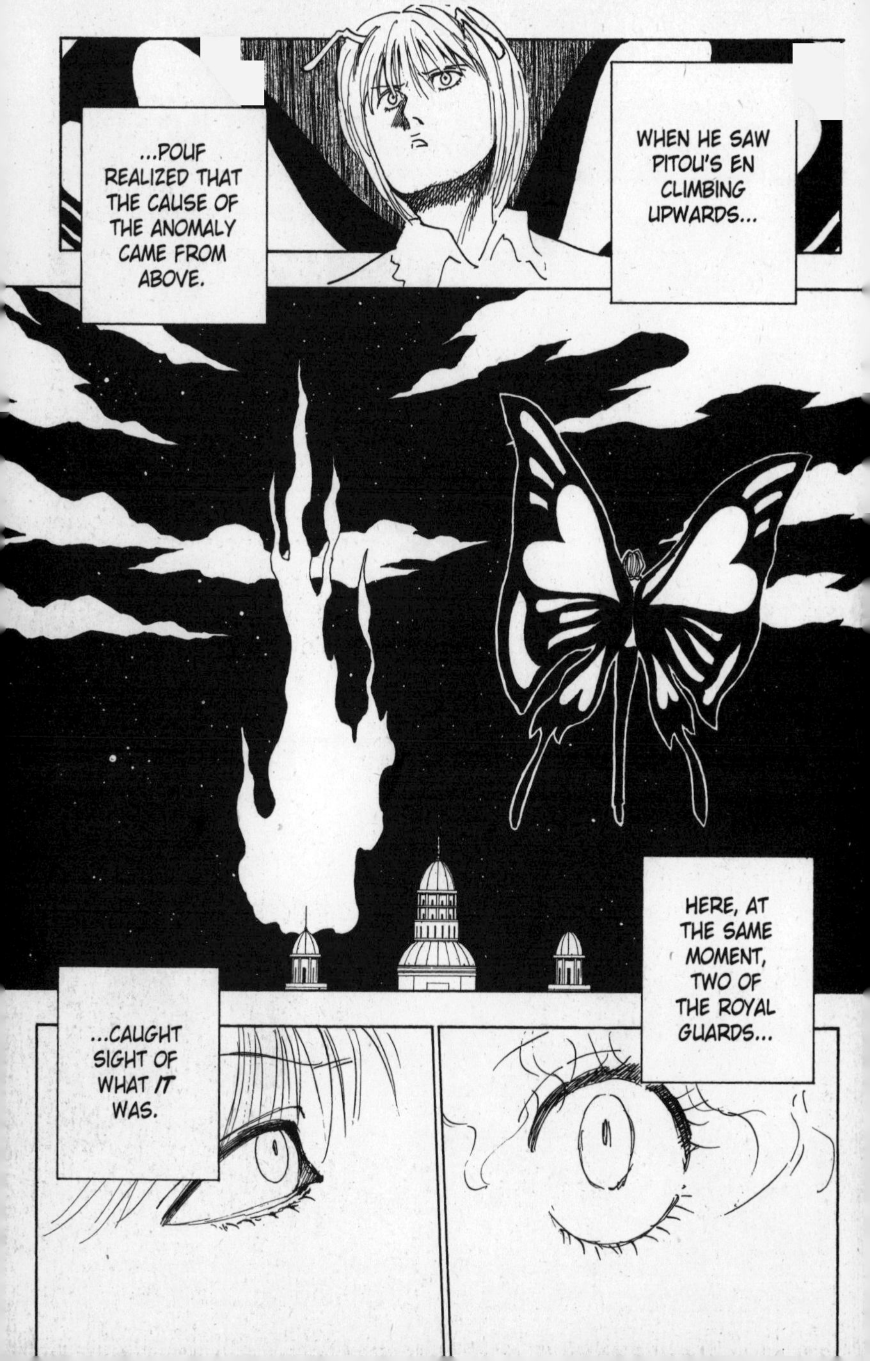
WHEN HE SAW PITOU'S EN CLIMBING UPWARDS...
...POUF REALIZED THAT THE CAUSE OF THE ANOMALY CAME FROM ABOVE.
HERE, AT THE SAME MOMENT, TWO OF THE ROYAL GUARDS...
...CAUGHT SIGHT OF WHAT *IT* WAS.

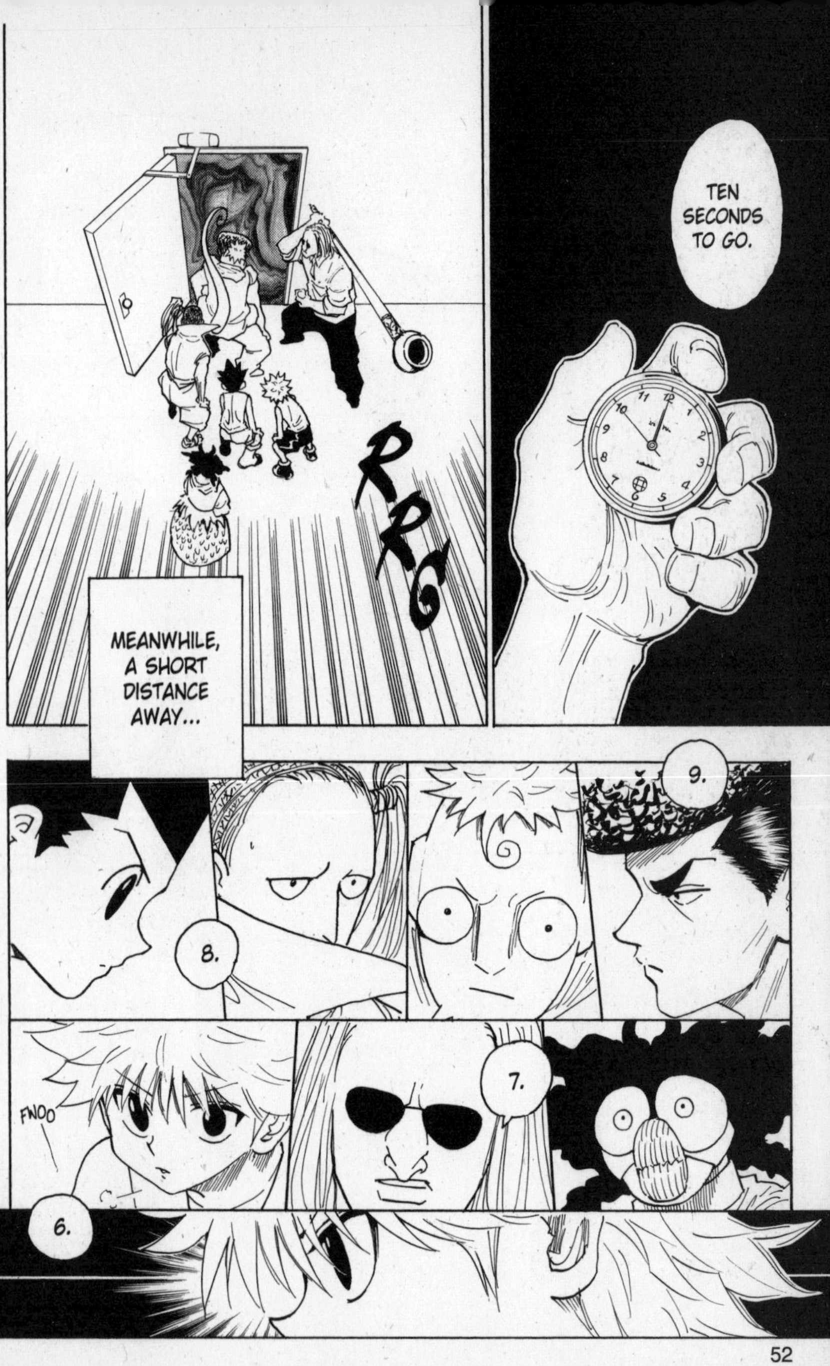
TEN SECONDS TO GO.
RRG
MEANWHILE, A SHORT DISTANCE AWAY...
9.
8.
7.
FWOO
6.

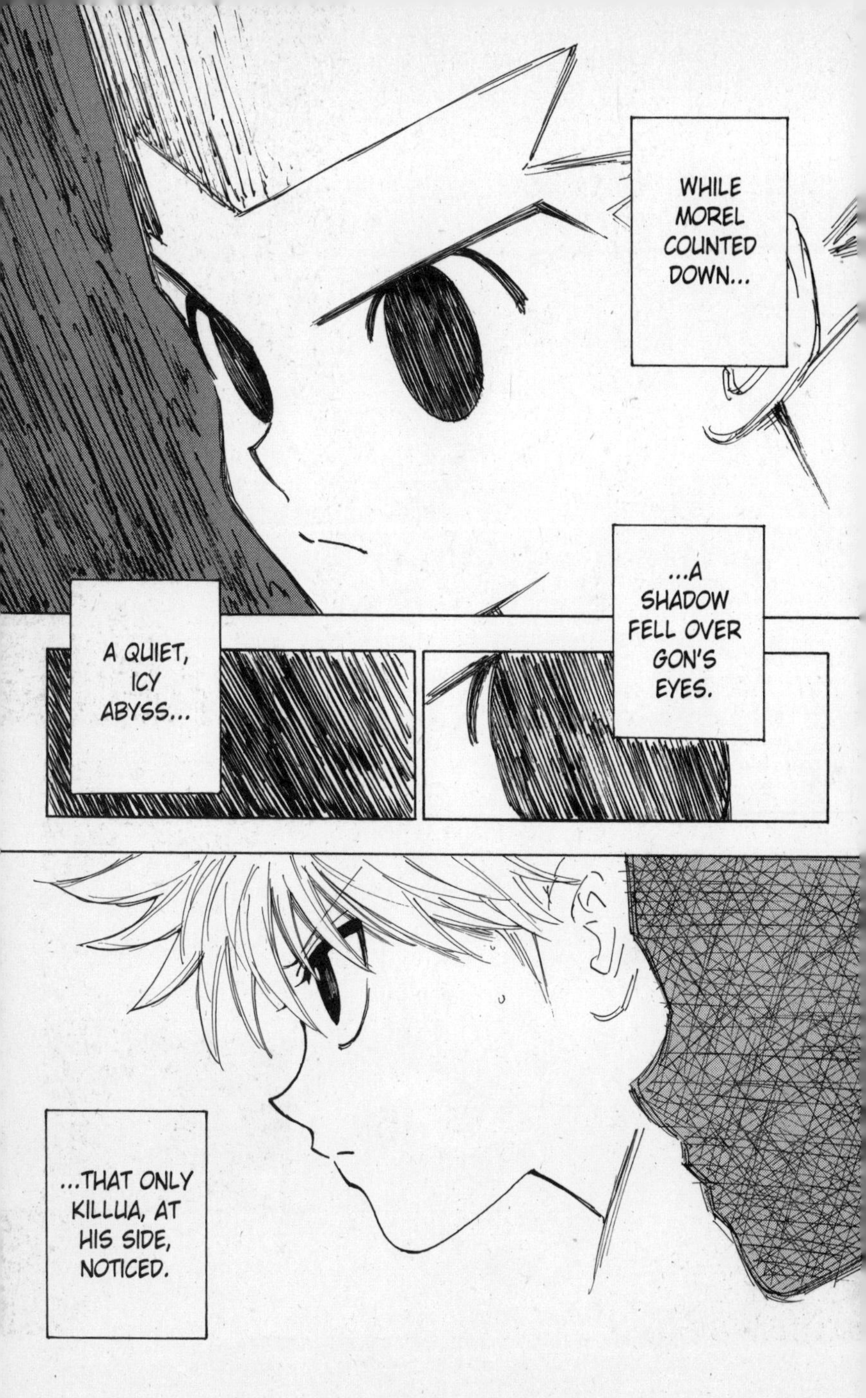
WHILE MOREL COUNTED DOWN...
...A SHADOW FELL OVER GON'S EYES.
A QUIET, ICY ABYSS...
...THAT ONLY KILLUA, AT HIS SIDE, NOTICED.

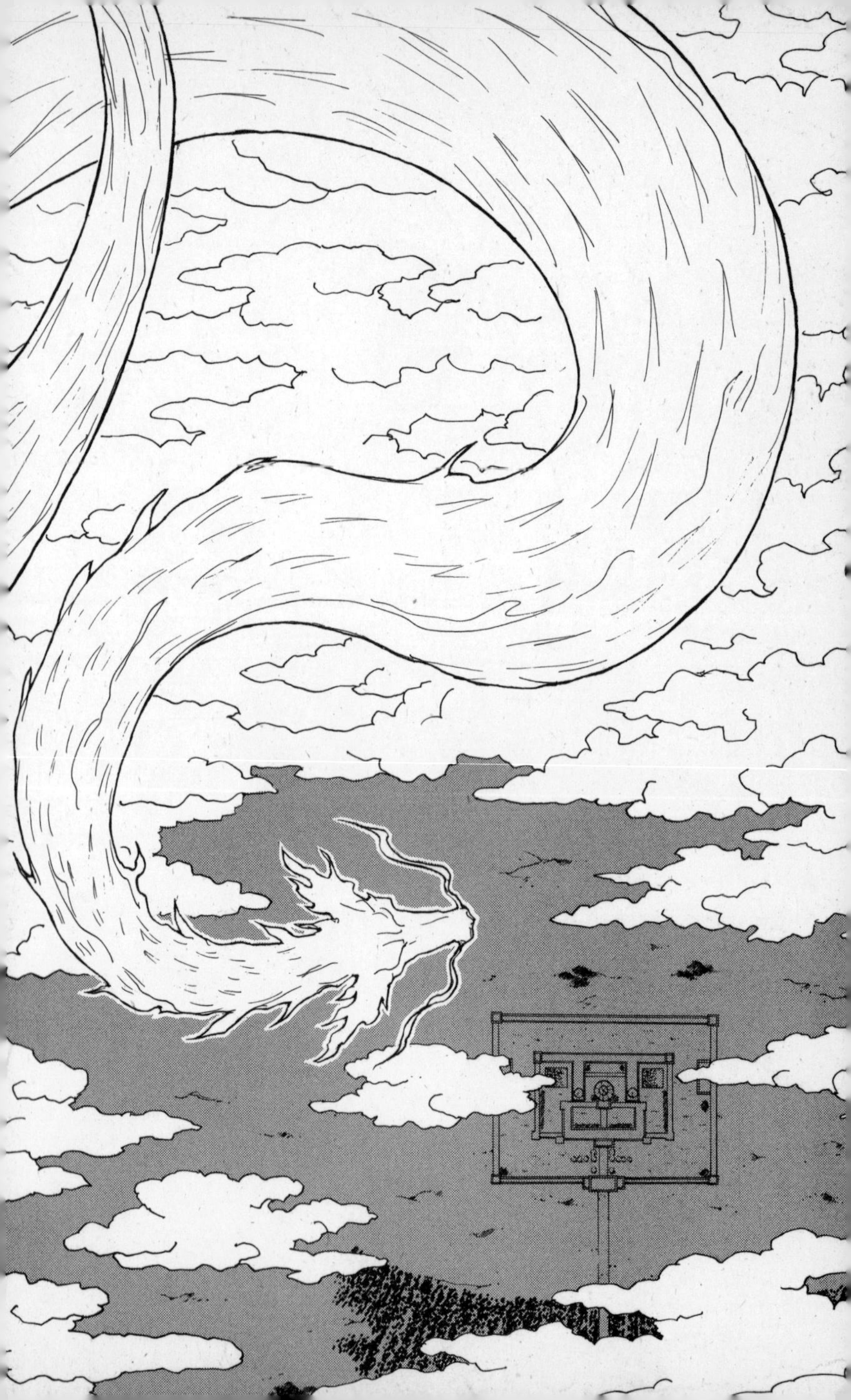

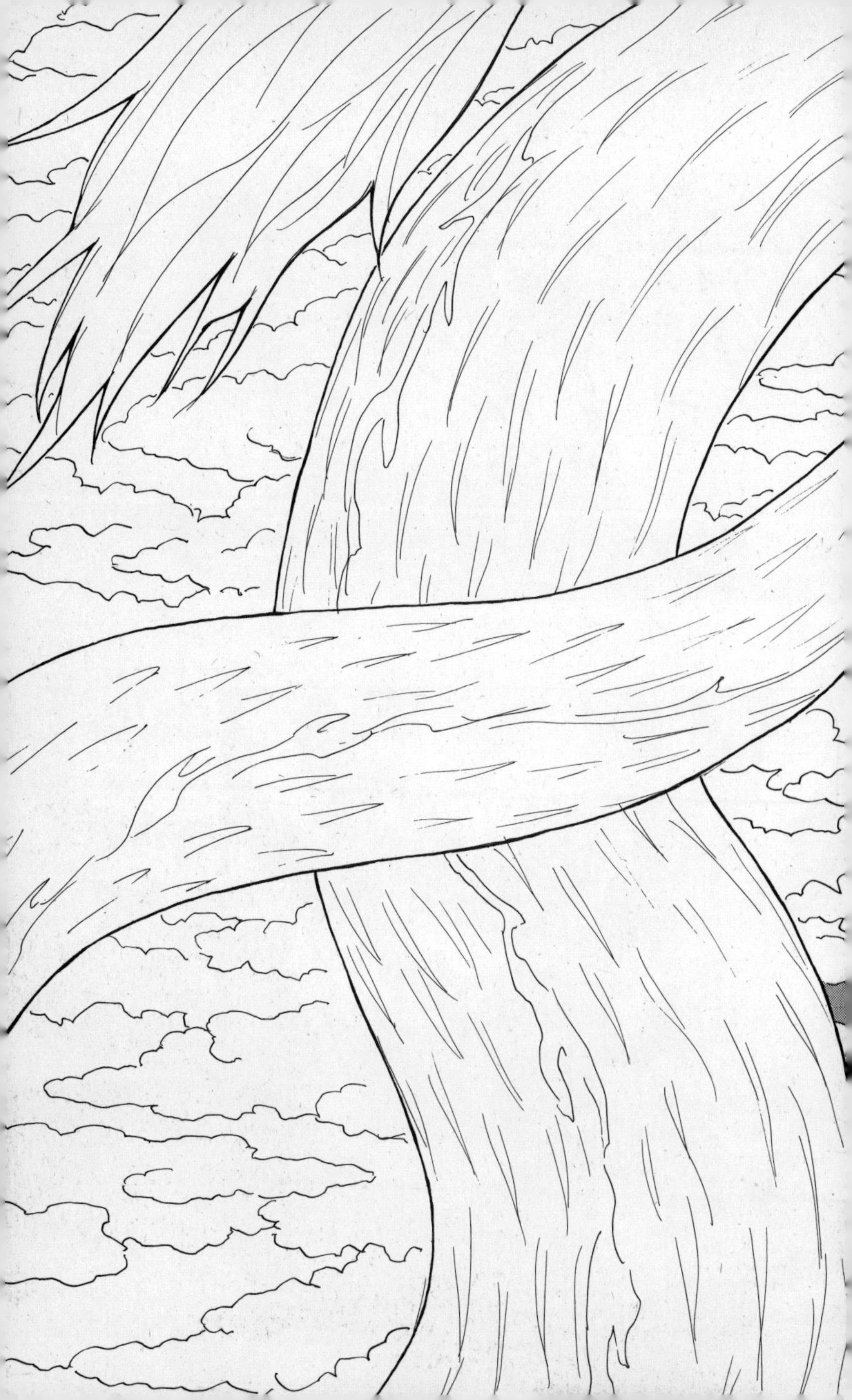

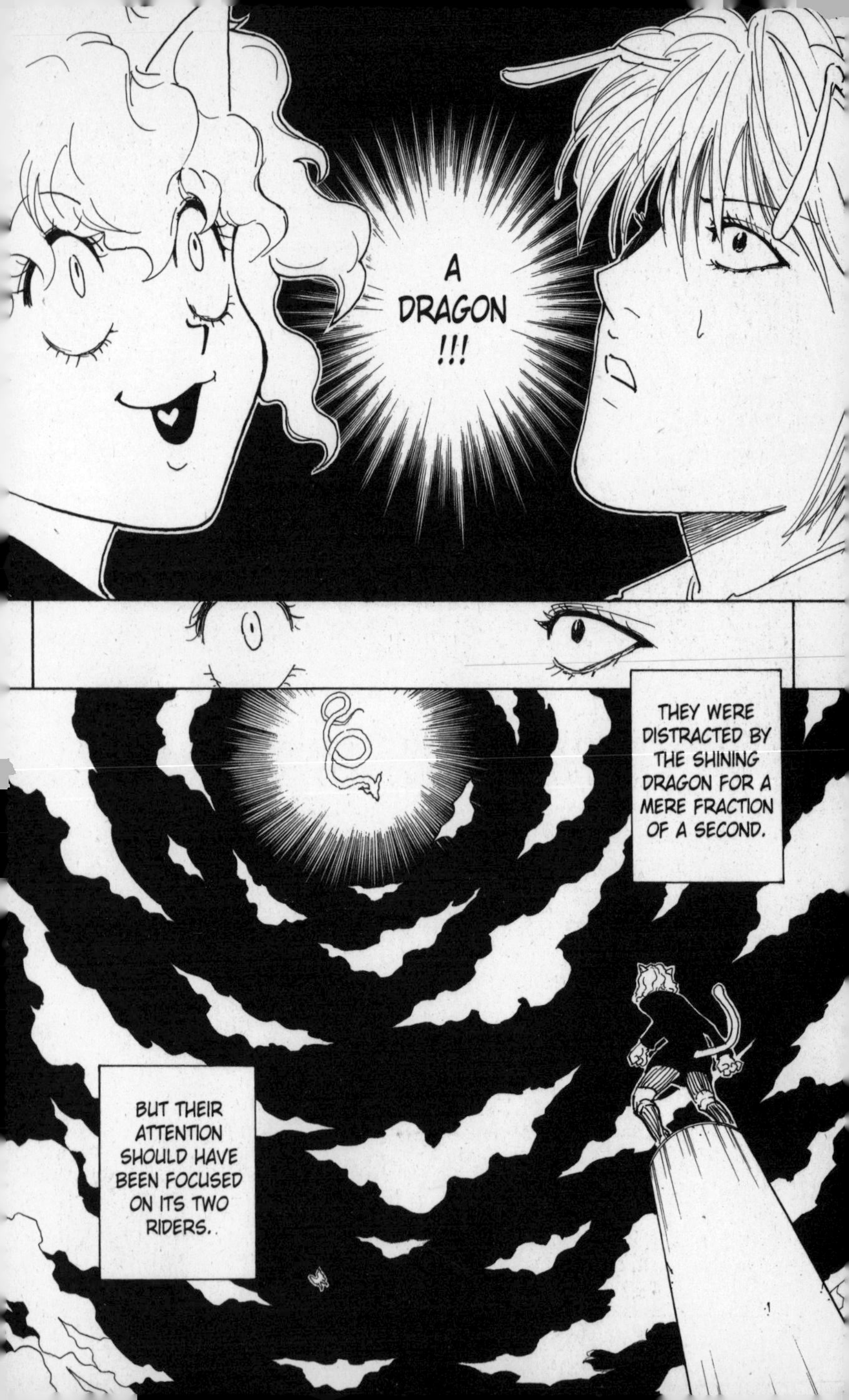
A DRAGON !!!
THEY WERE DISTRACTED BY THE SHINING DRAGON FOR A MERE FRACTION OF A SECOND.
BUT THEIR ATTENTION SHOULD HAVE BEEN FOCUSED ON ITS TWO RIDERS.

READ THIS WAY

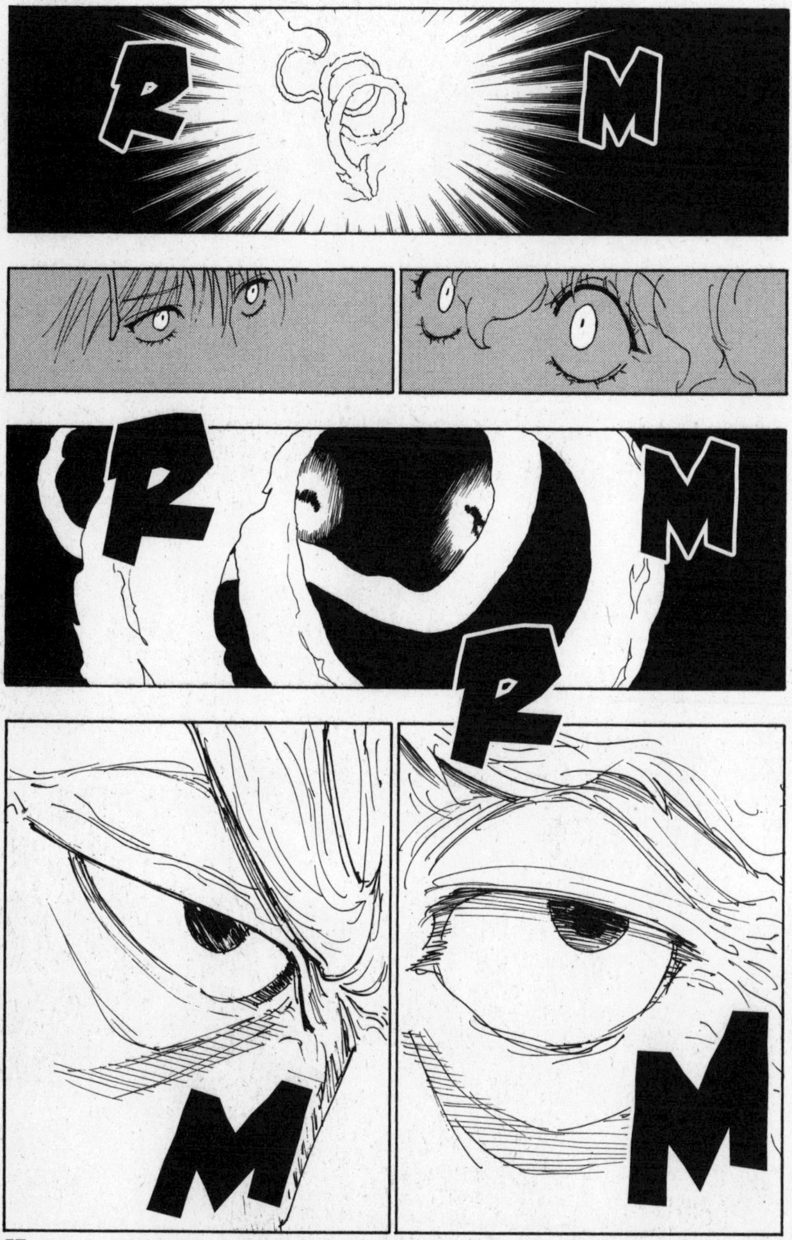

R
M
R
M
R
M
M

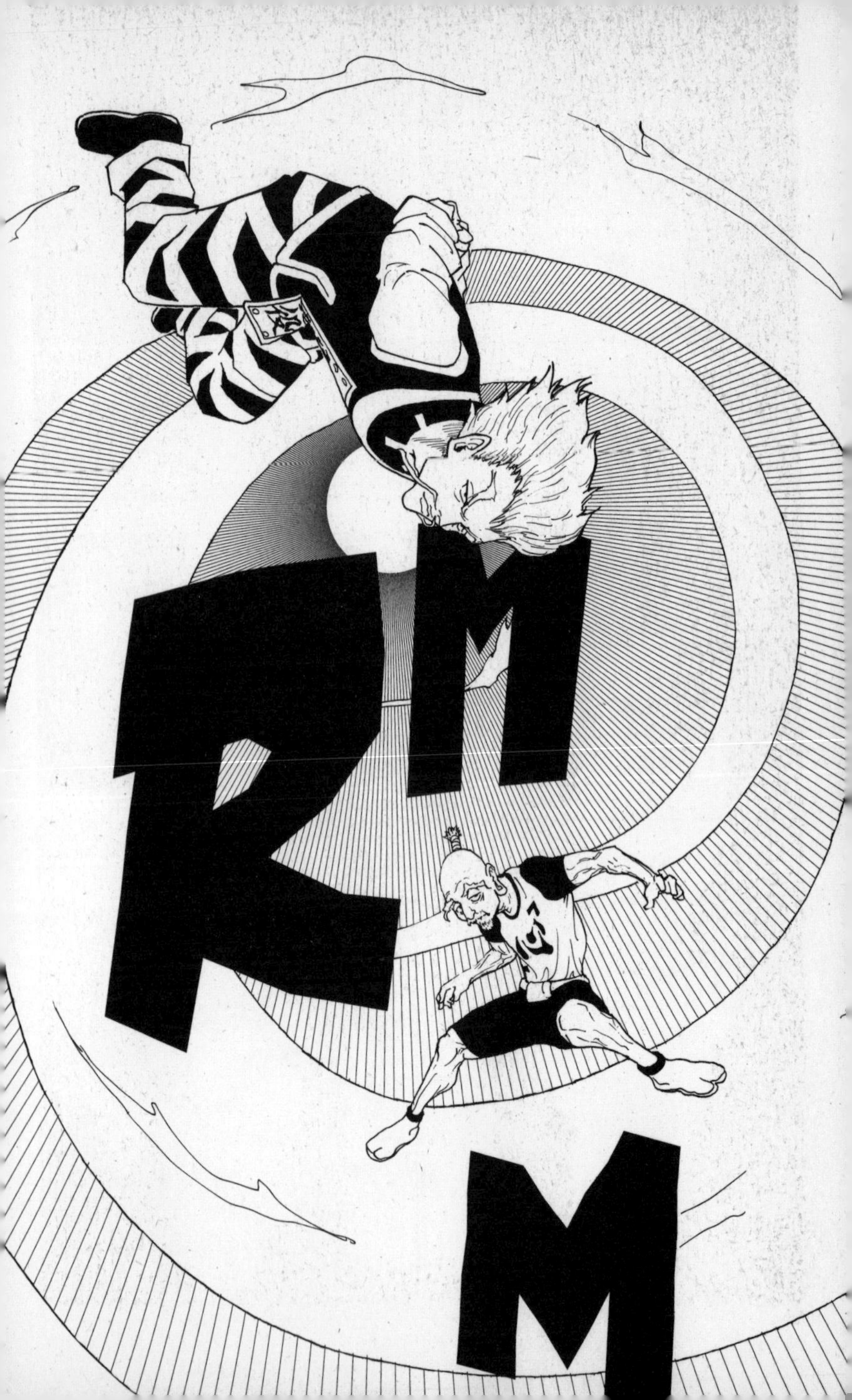
RMM

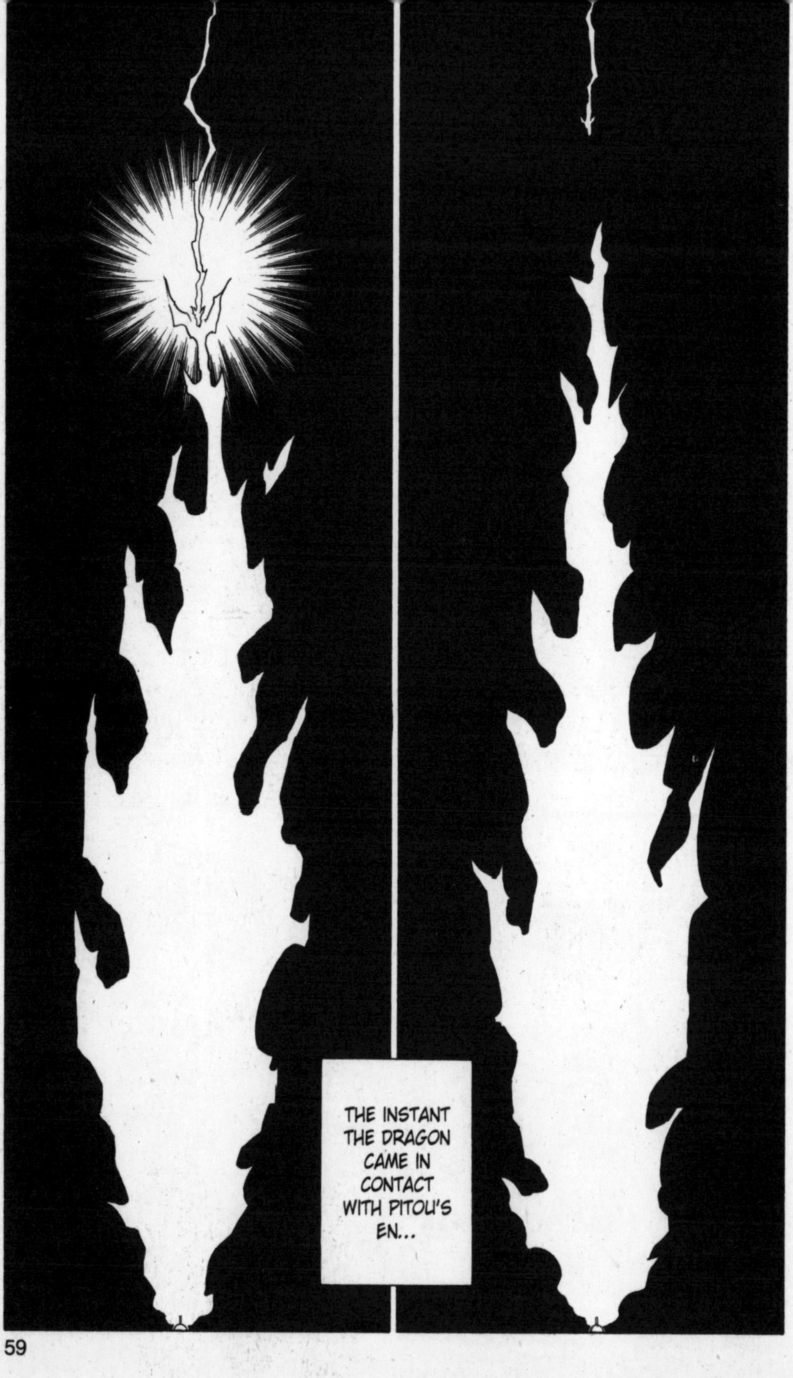
THE INSTANT THE DRAGON CAME IN CONTACT WITH PITOU'S EN...

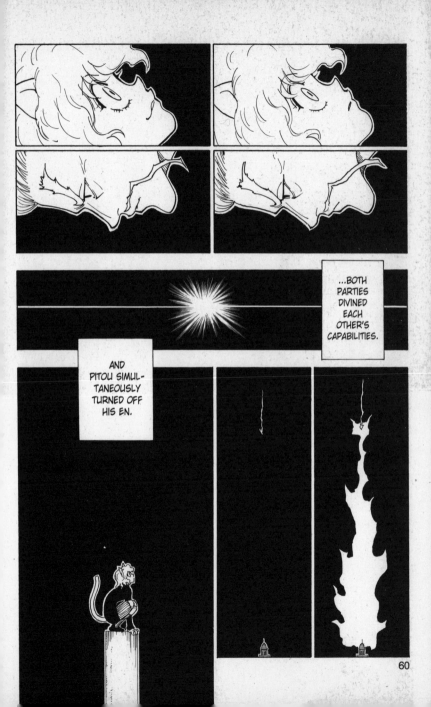

...BOTH PARTIES DIVINED EACH OTHER'S CAPABILITIES.

AND PITOU SIMULTANEOUSLY TURNED OFF HIS EN.

60

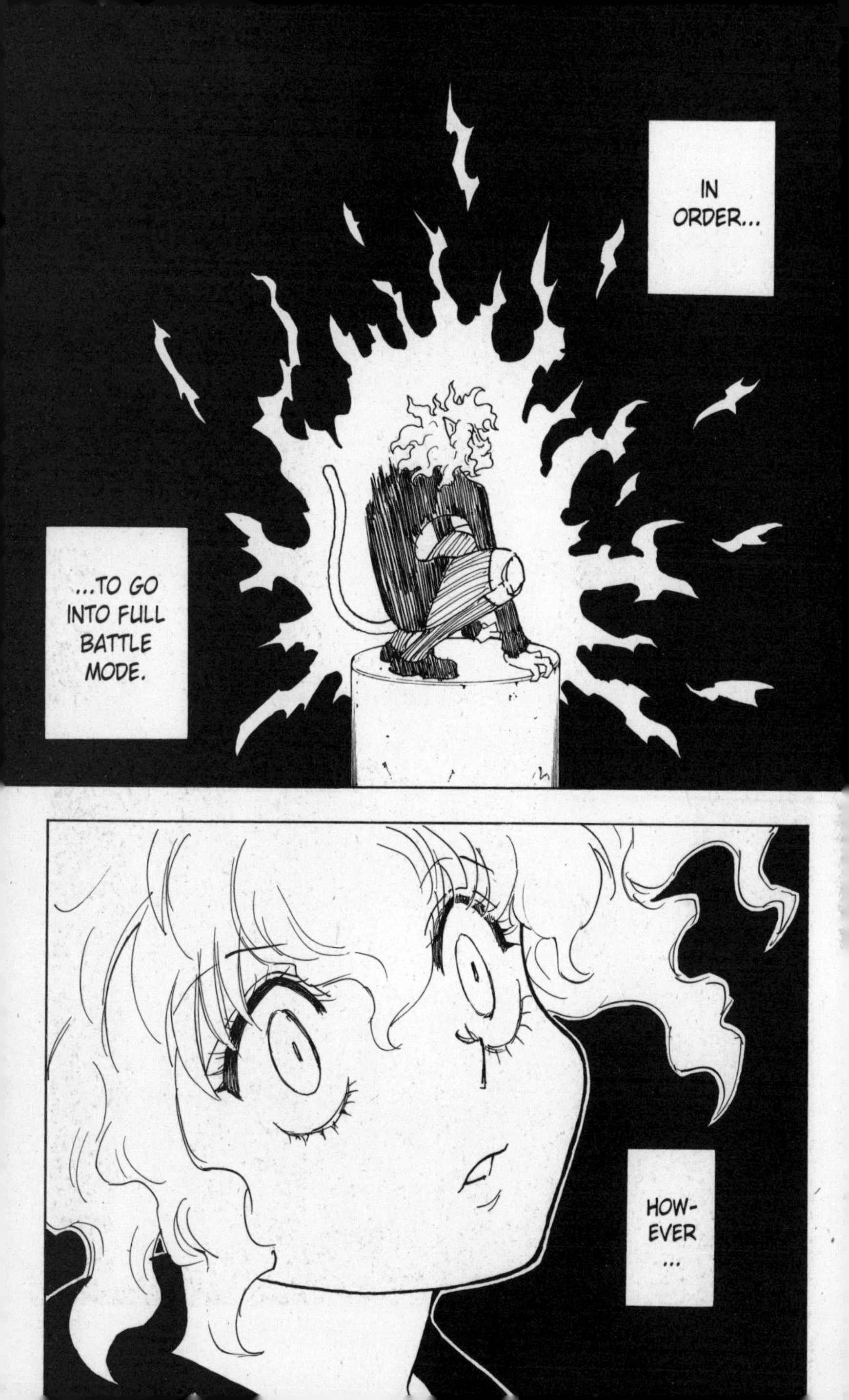
IN ORDER...
...TO GO INTO FULL BATTLE MODE.
HOW-EVER ...

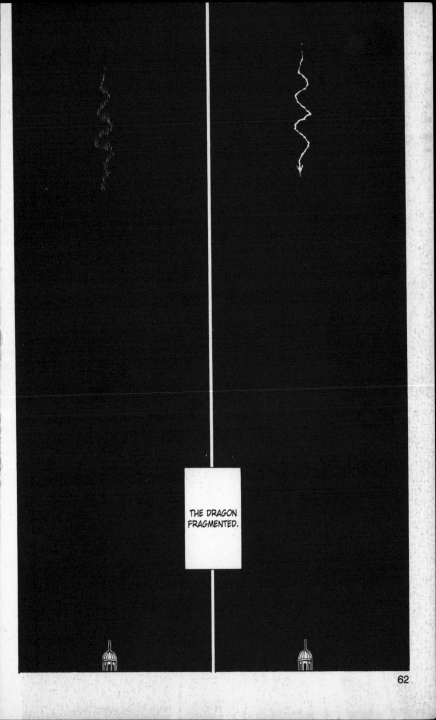

THE DRAGON
FRAGMENTED.

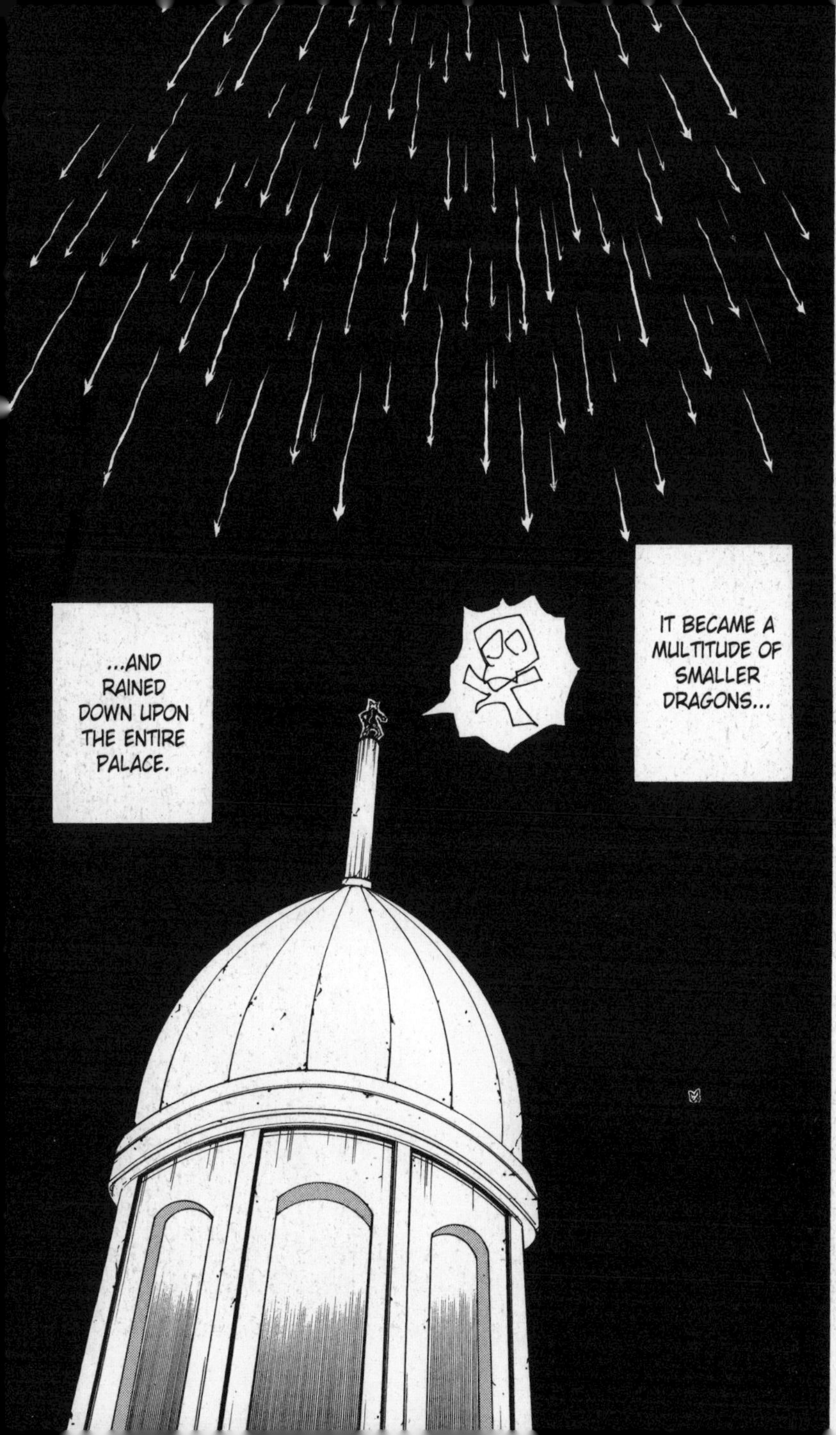
IT BECAME A MULTITUDE OF SMALLER DRAGONS...
...AND RAINED DOWN UPON THE ENTIRE PALACE.

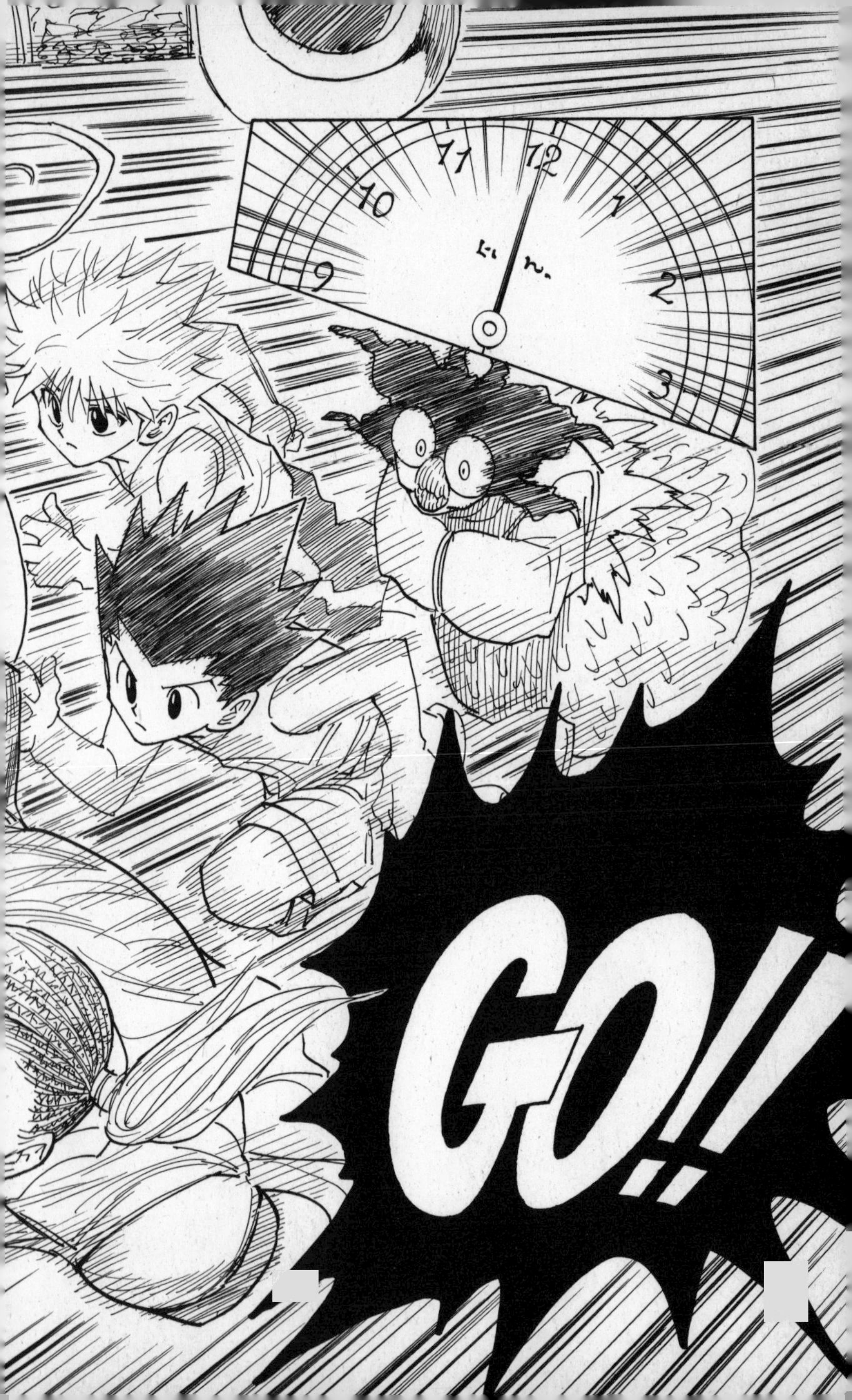
GO!!

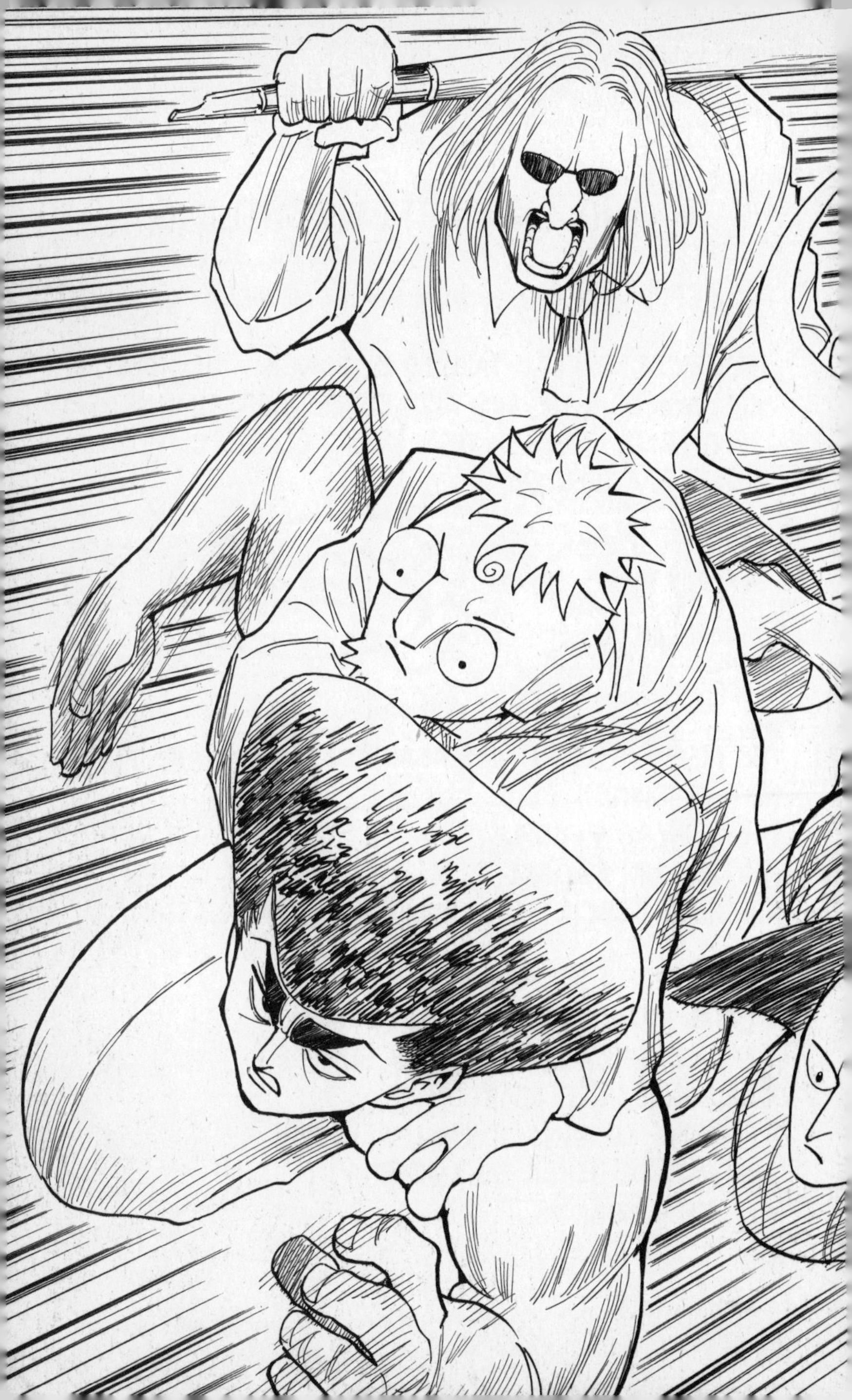

ROUND TWO: ARM WRESTLING

◎ TWO PEOPLE FACE OFF, WITH ONLY ONE ADVANCING.

THE SCORES WERE TALLIED BY POWER + DIE ROLL.
IN CASE OF A TIE, IT'S BROKEN BY THEIR TIMING STATS.
IF THERE'S ANOTHER TIE, I KEEP ROLLING UNTIL
THERE'S A WINNER.

NOW DOWN TO 542
HUNTERS. THE ROLLING
IS GOING WELL!!

THE HIGHEST SCORE WAS KEARI (OR IT COULD BE KIAI...)
WITH 13 POINTS!!
THERE WERE 9 PEOPLE TIED FOR SECOND PLACE WITH 12
POINTS: YUKI NAGARE, APOLLO, GING, BABY, BAYSTA,
KIRCHEIS, BLACK SPOT, CHUN X CHUN AND UKIDAMA.

○ THE LUCK OF THE DRAW WAS EVEN MORE
CRUCIAL THAN IN THE FIRST ROUND.
EVEN A HUNTER WITH A POWER STAT OF 1
COULD PASS DEPENDING ON HIS
OPPONENT, LOOKING TO FARE WELL IN
CONTESTS OF OTHER PARAMETERS IN
THE LATER ROUNDS.

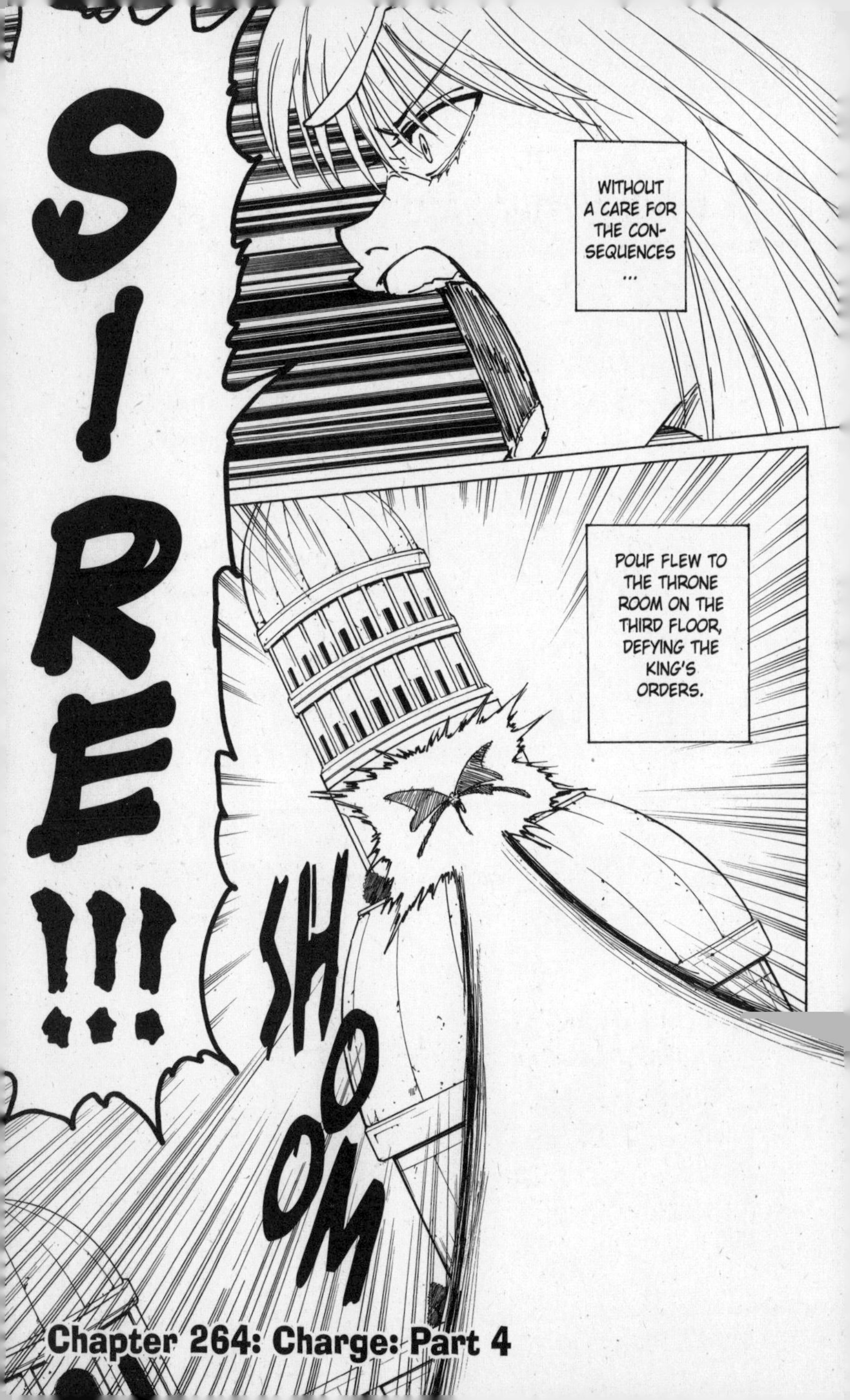
WITHOUT A CARE FOR THE CON-SEQUENCES ...
POUF FLEW TO THE THRONE ROOM ON THE THIRD FLOOR, DEFYING THE KING'S ORDERS.
SIRE!!!
SHOOOM

Chapter 264: Charge: Part 4

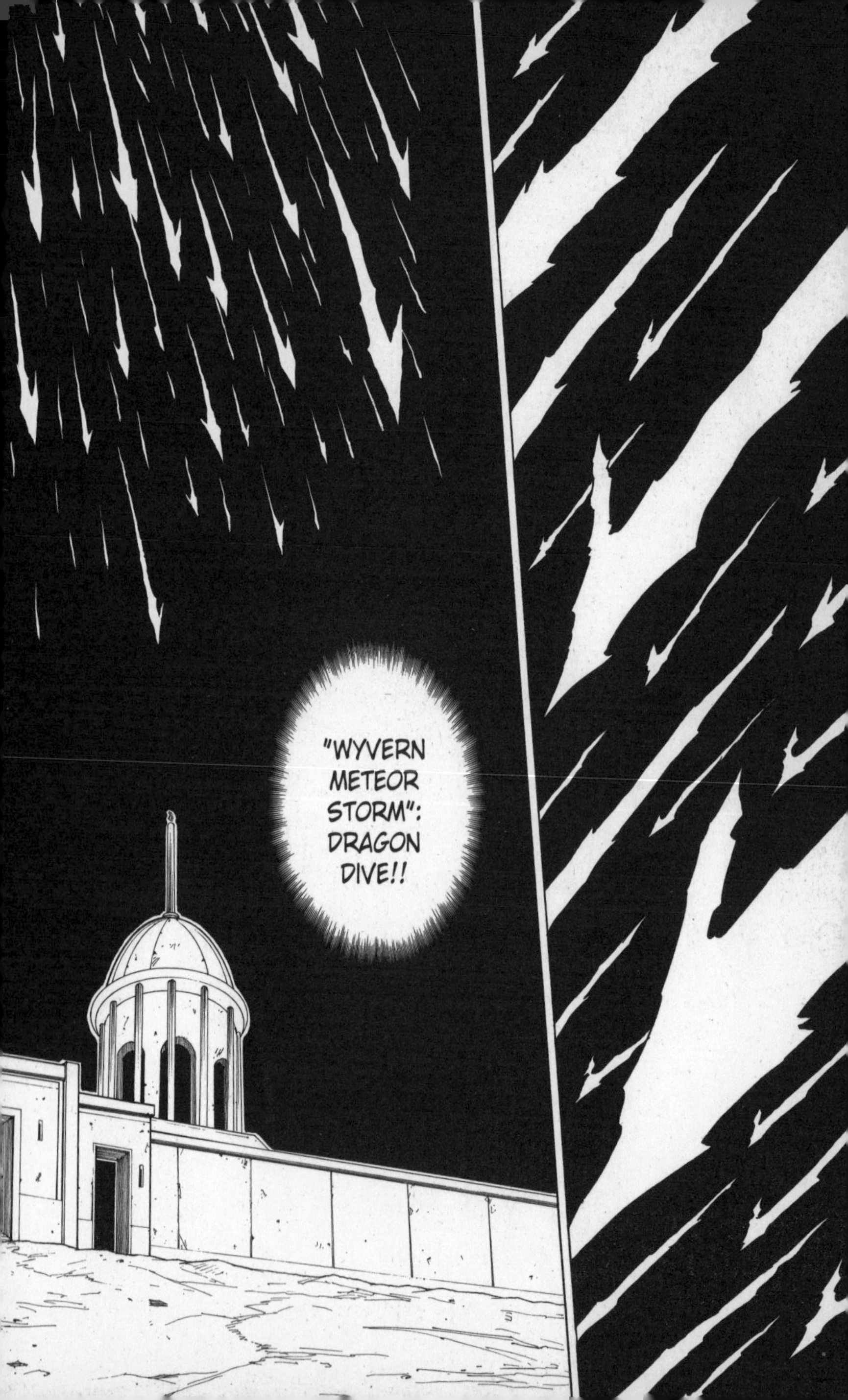
"WYVERN METEOR STORM": DRAGON DIVE!!

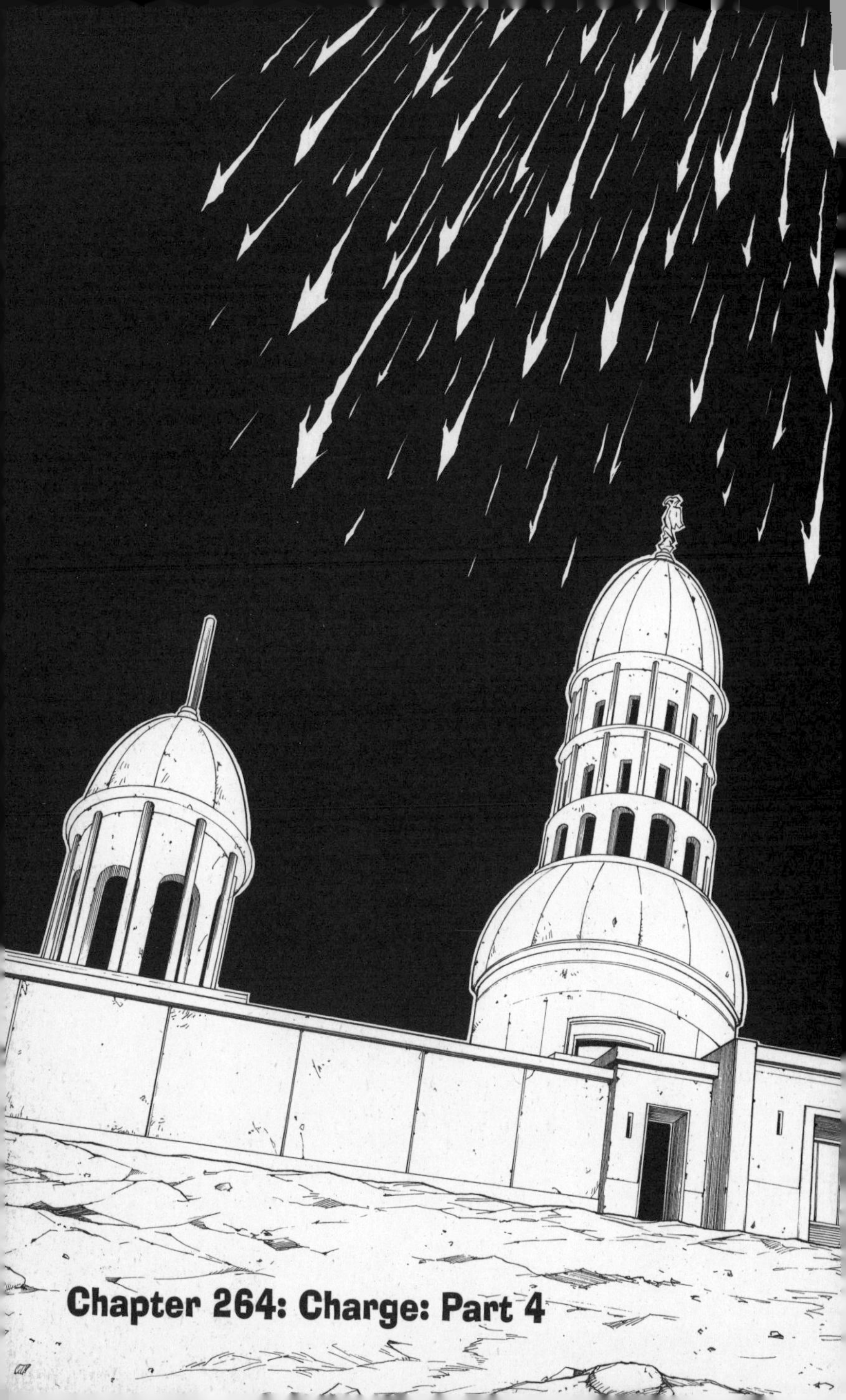

Chapter 264: Charge: Part 4

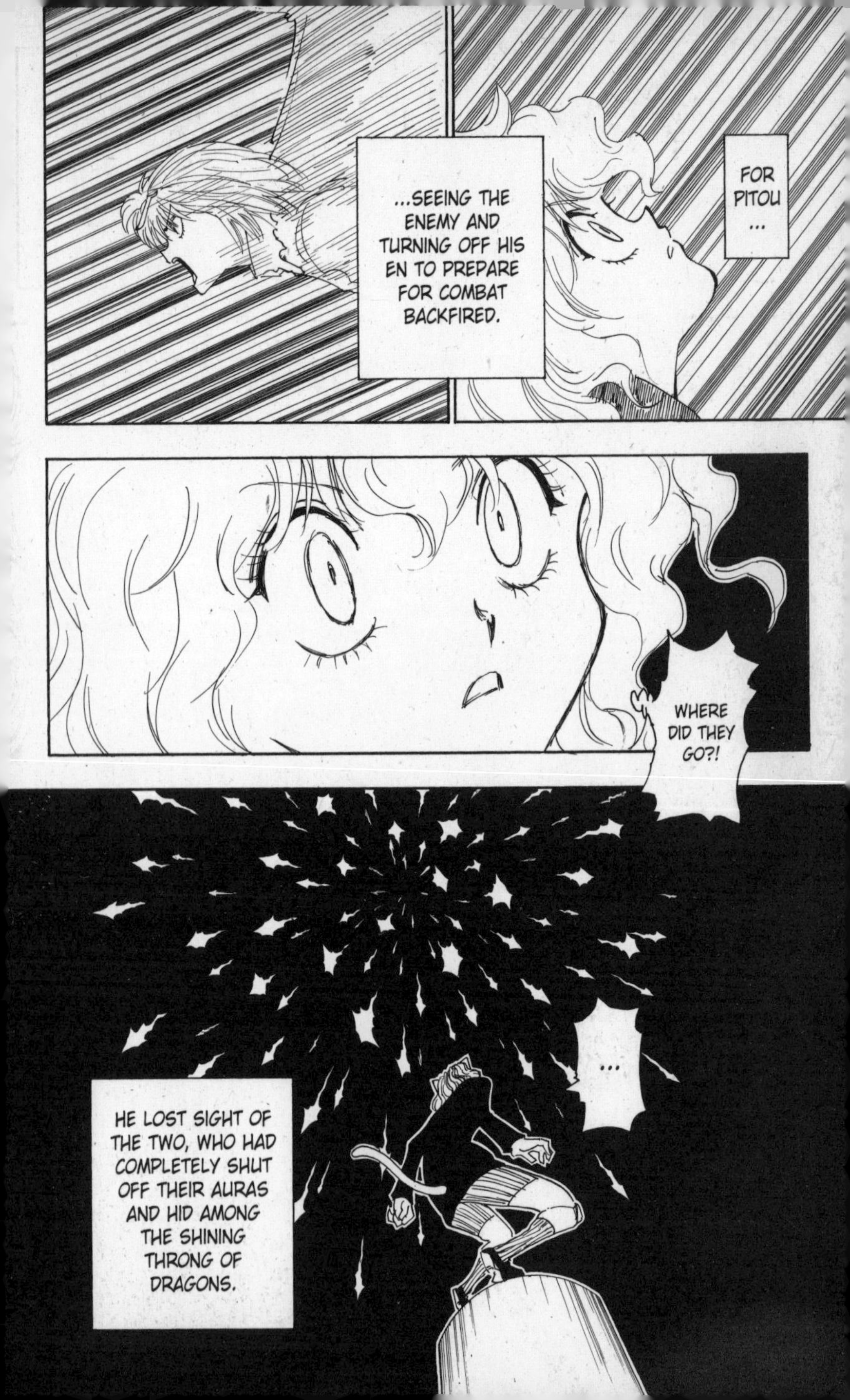
FOR PITOU ...
...SEEING THE ENEMY AND TURNING OFF HIS EN TO PREPARE FOR COMBAT BACKFIRED.
WHERE DID THEY GO?!
...
HE LOST SIGHT OF THE TWO, WHO HAD COMPLETELY SHUT OFF THEIR AURAS AND HID AMONG THE SHINING THRONG OF DRAGONS.

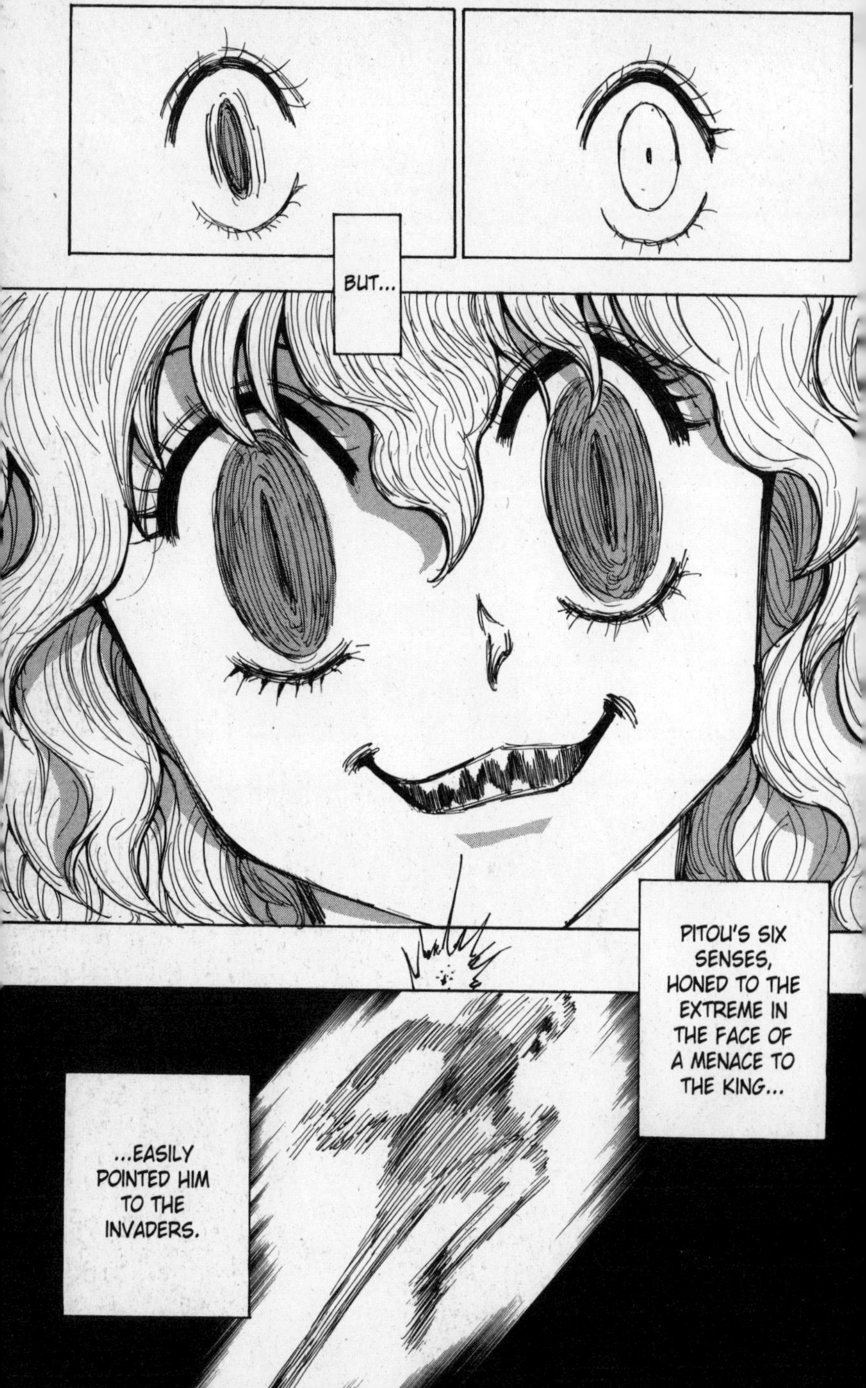
BUT...
PITOU'S SIX SENSES, HONED TO THE EXTREME IN THE FACE OF A MENACE TO THE KING...
...EASILY POINTED HIM TO THE INVADERS.

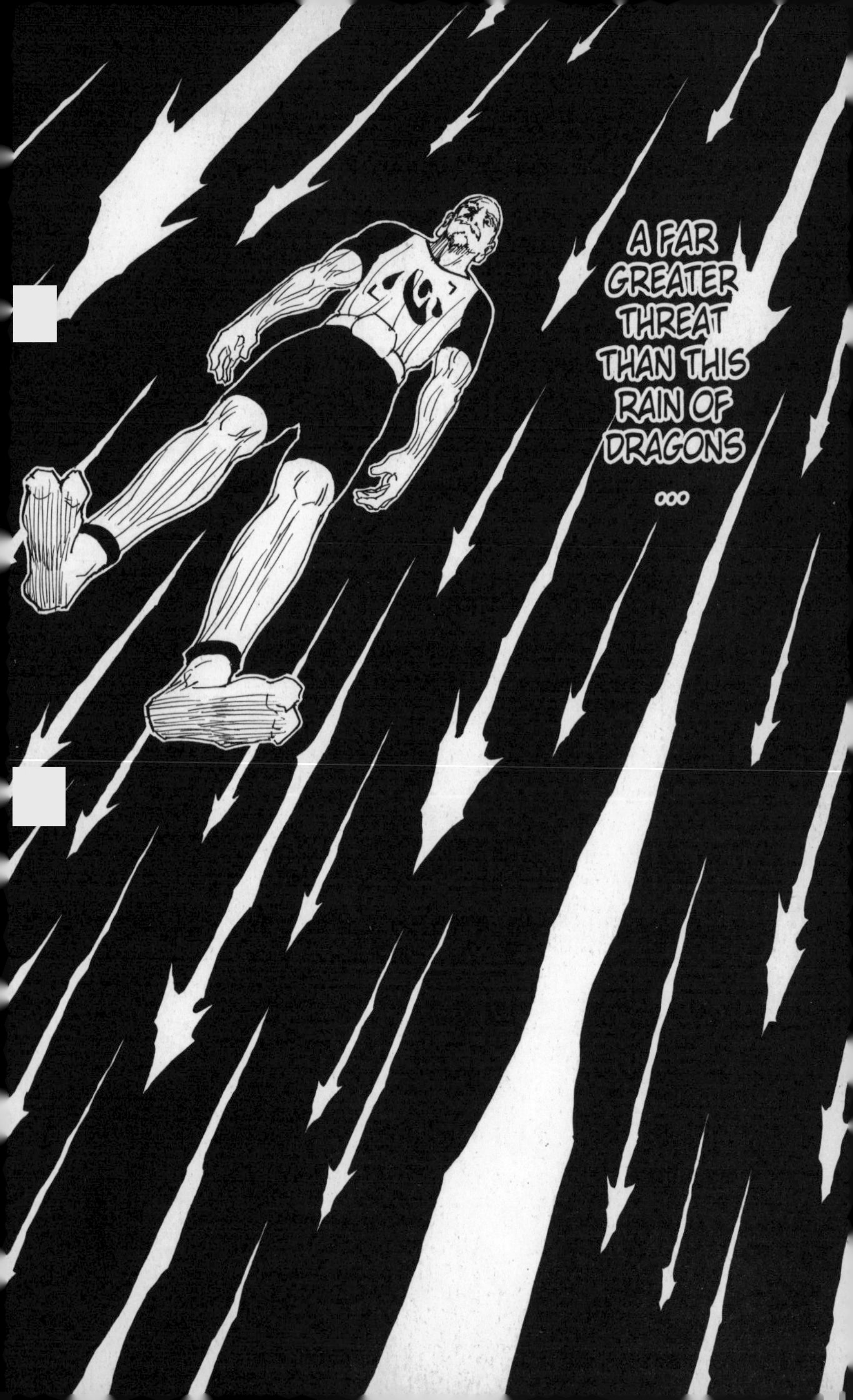
A FAR GREATER THREAT THAN THIS RAIN OF DRAGONS ...

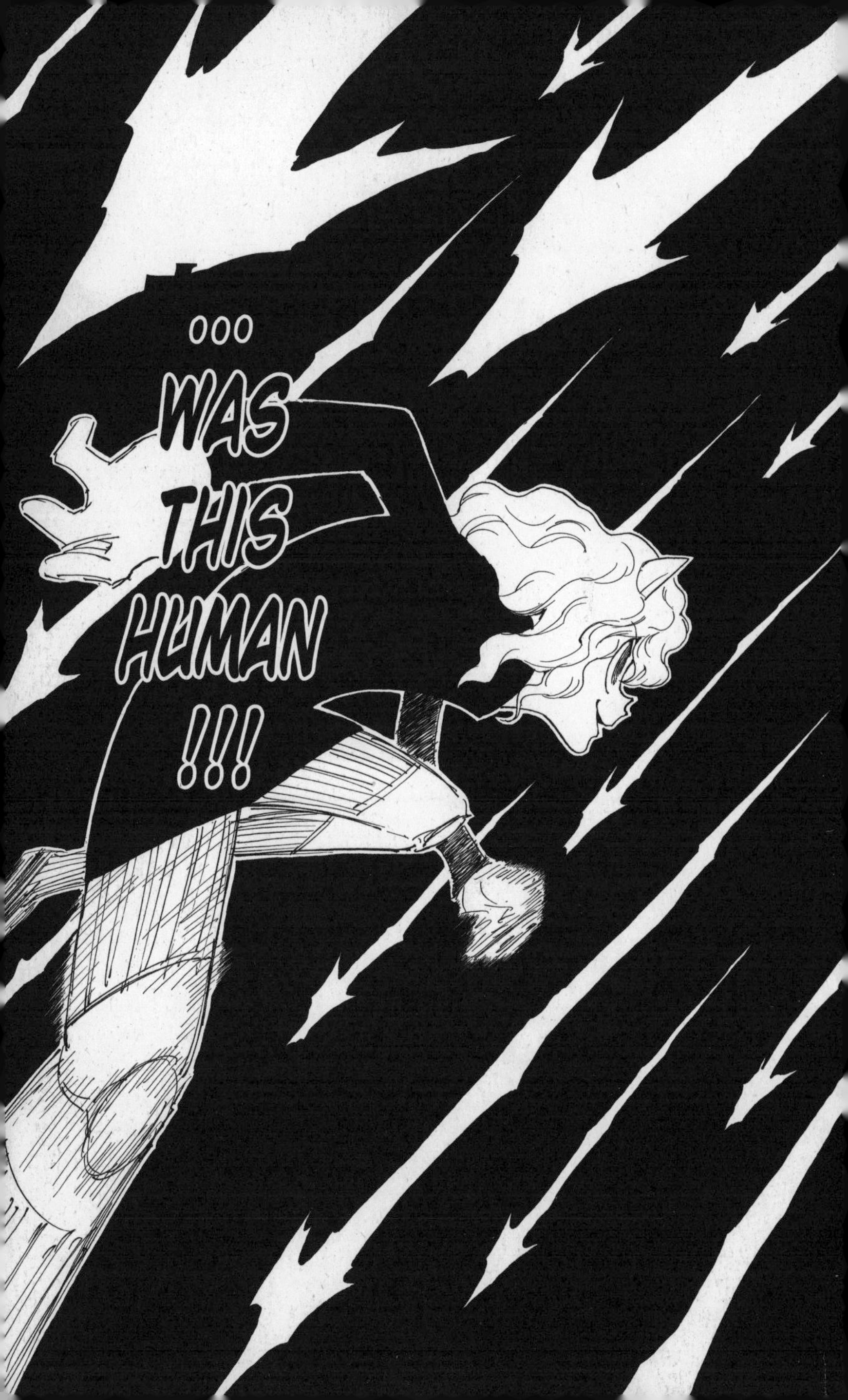
...WAS THIS HUMAN !!!

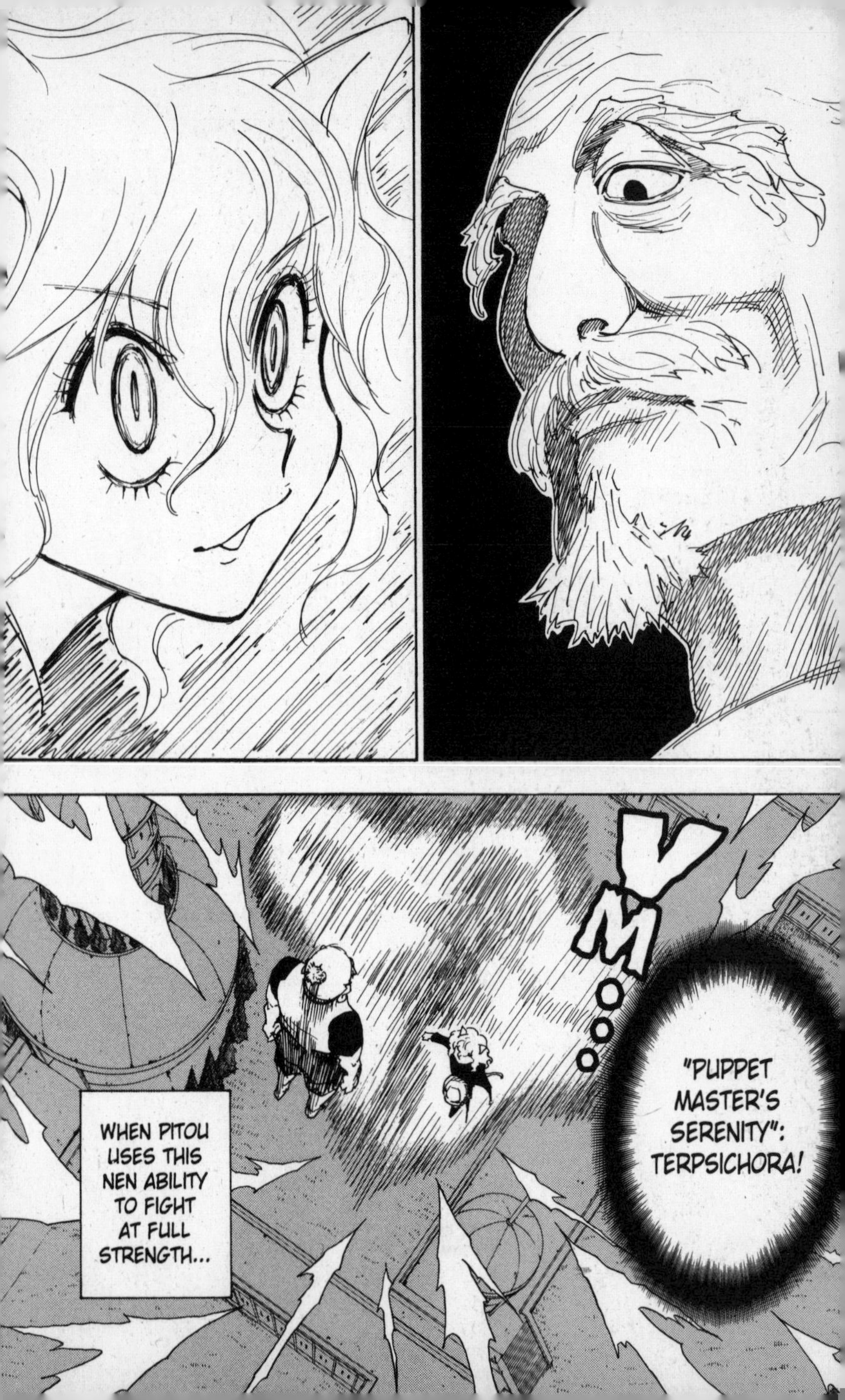
VMOOO
"PUPPET MASTER'S SERENITY": TERPSICHORA!
WHEN PITOU USES THIS NEN ABILITY TO FIGHT AT FULL STRENGTH...

READ THIS WAY

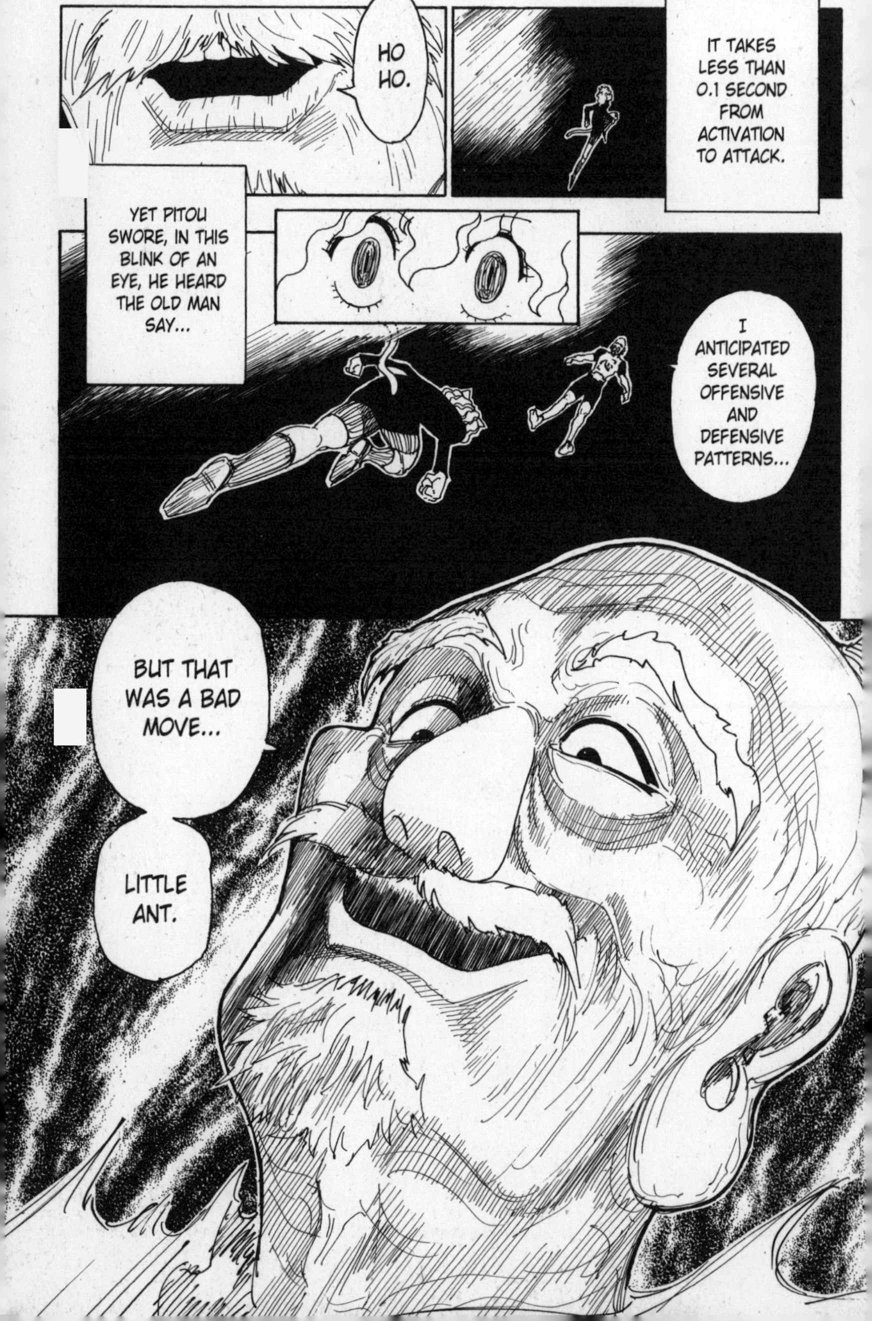

IT TAKES LESS THAN 0.1 SECOND FROM ACTIVATION TO ATTACK.
HO HO.
YET PITOU SWORE, IN THIS BLINK OF AN EYE, HE HEARD THE OLD MAN SAY...
I ANTICIPATED SEVERAL OFFENSIVE AND DEFENSIVE PATTERNS...
BUT THAT WAS A BAD MOVE...
LITTLE ANT.

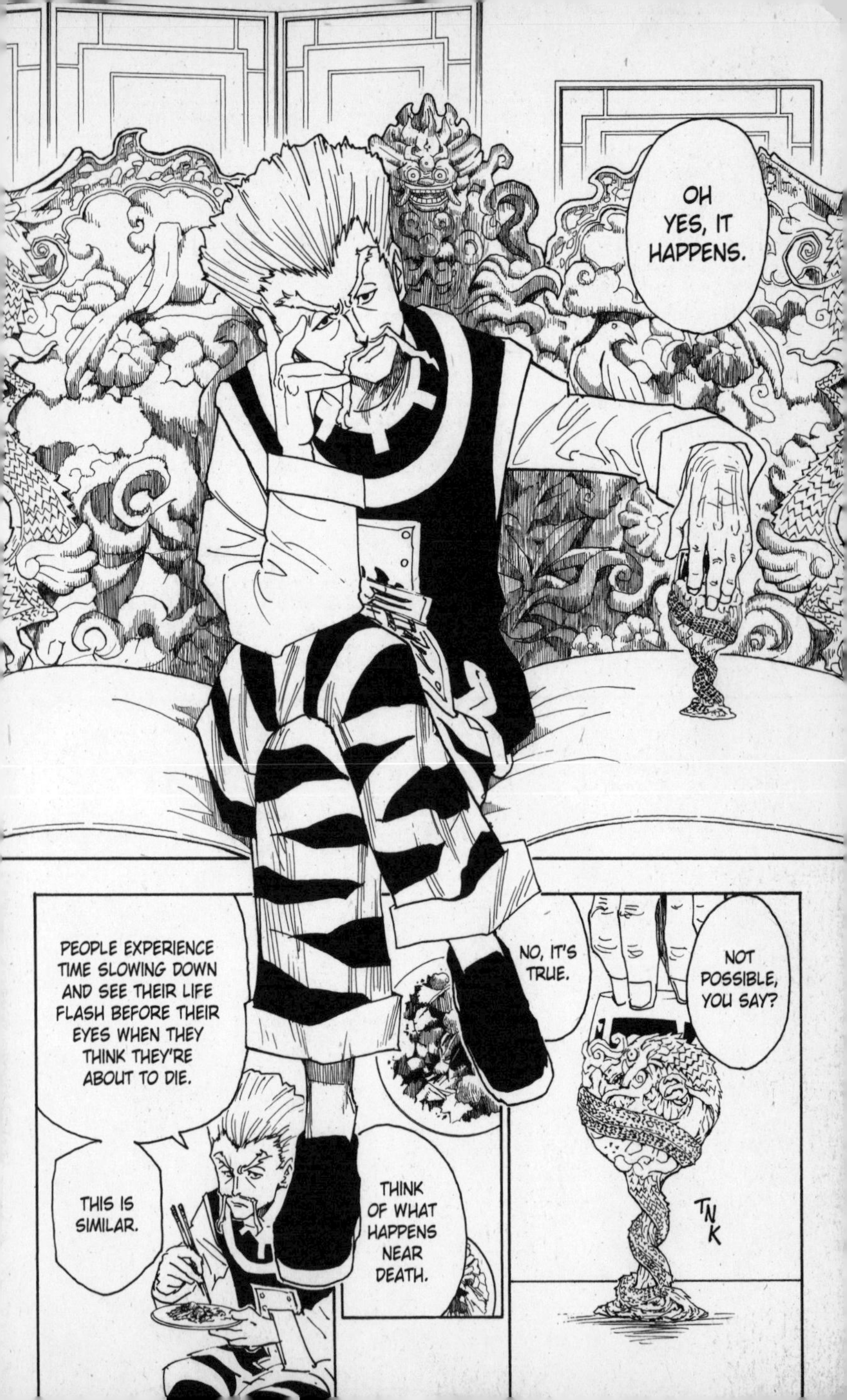
OH YES, IT HAPPENS.
NOT POSSIBLE, YOU SAY?
NO, IT'S TRUE.
TNK
THINK OF WHAT HAPPENS NEAR DEATH.
PEOPLE EXPERIENCE TIME SLOWING DOWN AND SEE THEIR LIFE FLASH BEFORE THEIR EYES WHEN THEY THINK THEY'RE ABOUT TO DIE.
THIS IS SIMILAR.

READ THIS WAY

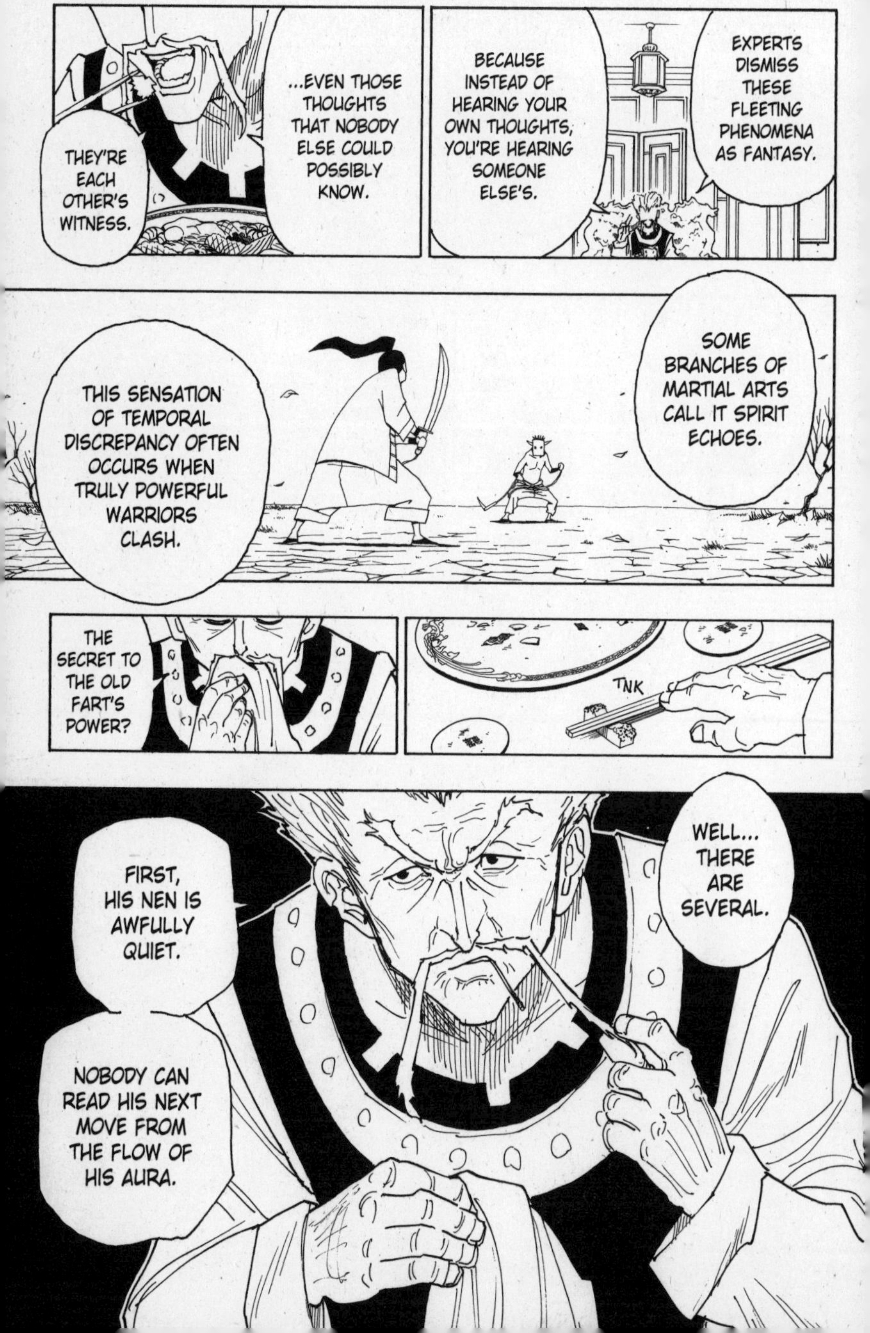
EXPERTS DISMISS THESE FLEETING PHENOMENA AS FANTASY.
BECAUSE INSTEAD OF HEARING YOUR OWN THOUGHTS, YOU'RE HEARING SOMEONE ELSE'S.
...EVEN THOSE THOUGHTS THAT NOBODY ELSE COULD POSSIBLY KNOW.
THEY'RE EACH OTHER'S WITNESS.
SOME BRANCHES OF MARTIAL ARTS CALL IT SPIRIT ECHOES.
THIS SENSATION OF TEMPORAL DISCREPANCY OFTEN OCCURS WHEN TRULY POWERFUL WARRIORS CLASH.
TNK
THE SECRET TO THE OLD FART'S POWER?
WELL... THERE ARE SEVERAL.
FIRST, HIS NEN IS AWFULLY QUIET.
NOBODY CAN READ HIS NEXT MOVE FROM THE FLOW OF HIS AURA.

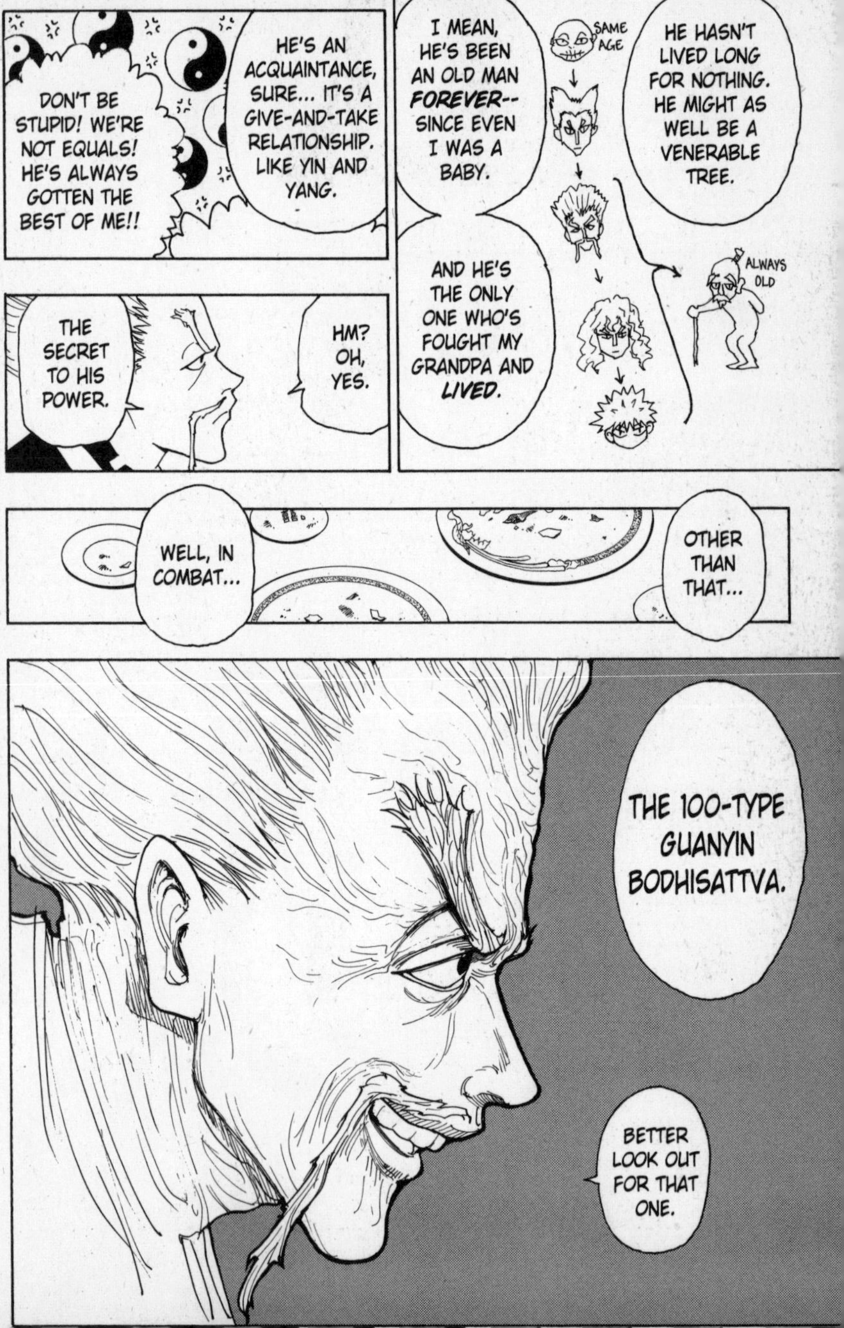
HE HASN'T LIVED LONG FOR NOTHING. HE MIGHT AS WELL BE A VENERABLE TREE.
SAME AGE
I MEAN, HE'S BEEN AN OLD MAN FOREVER-- SINCE EVEN I WAS A BABY.
ALWAYS OLD
AND HE'S THE ONLY ONE WHO'S FOUGHT MY GRANDPA AND LIVED.
HE'S AN ACQUAINTANCE, SURE... IT'S A GIVE-AND-TAKE RELATIONSHIP. LIKE YIN AND YANG.
DON'T BE STUPID! WE'RE NOT EQUALS! HE'S ALWAYS GOTTEN THE BEST OF ME!!
HM? OH, YES.
THE SECRET TO HIS POWER.
OTHER THAN THAT...
WELL, IN COMBAT...
THE 100-TYPE GUANYIN BODHISATTVA.
BETTER LOOK OUT FOR THAT ONE.

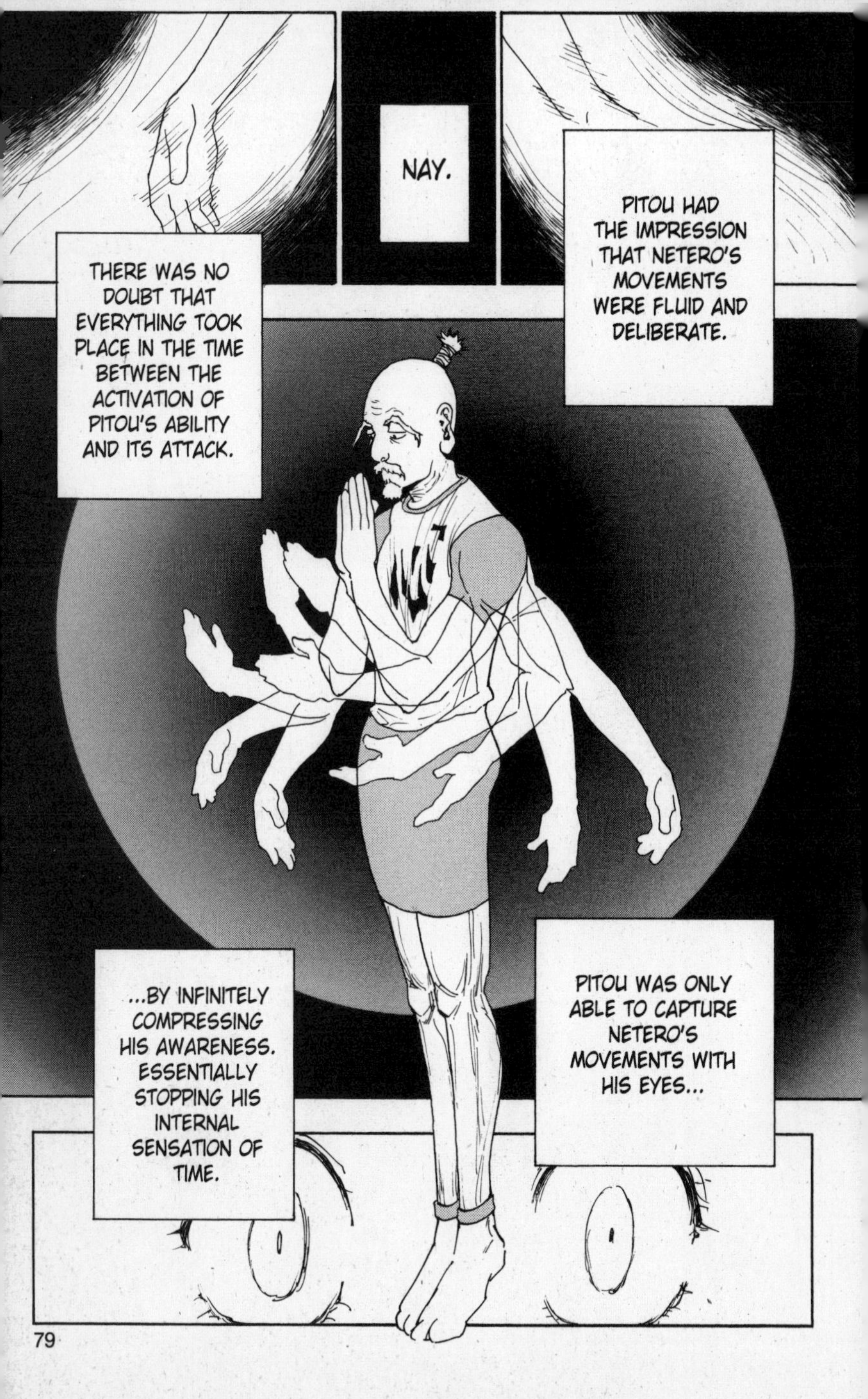

PITOU HAD THE IMPRESSION THAT NETERO'S MOVEMENTS WERE FLUID AND DELIBERATE.
NAY.
THERE WAS NO DOUBT THAT EVERYTHING TOOK PLACE IN THE TIME BETWEEN THE ACTIVATION OF PITOU'S ABILITY AND ITS ATTACK.
PITOU WAS ONLY ABLE TO CAPTURE NETERO'S MOVEMENTS WITH HIS EYES...
...BY INFINITELY COMPRESSING HIS AWARENESS. ESSENTIALLY STOPPING HIS INTERNAL SENSATION OF TIME.

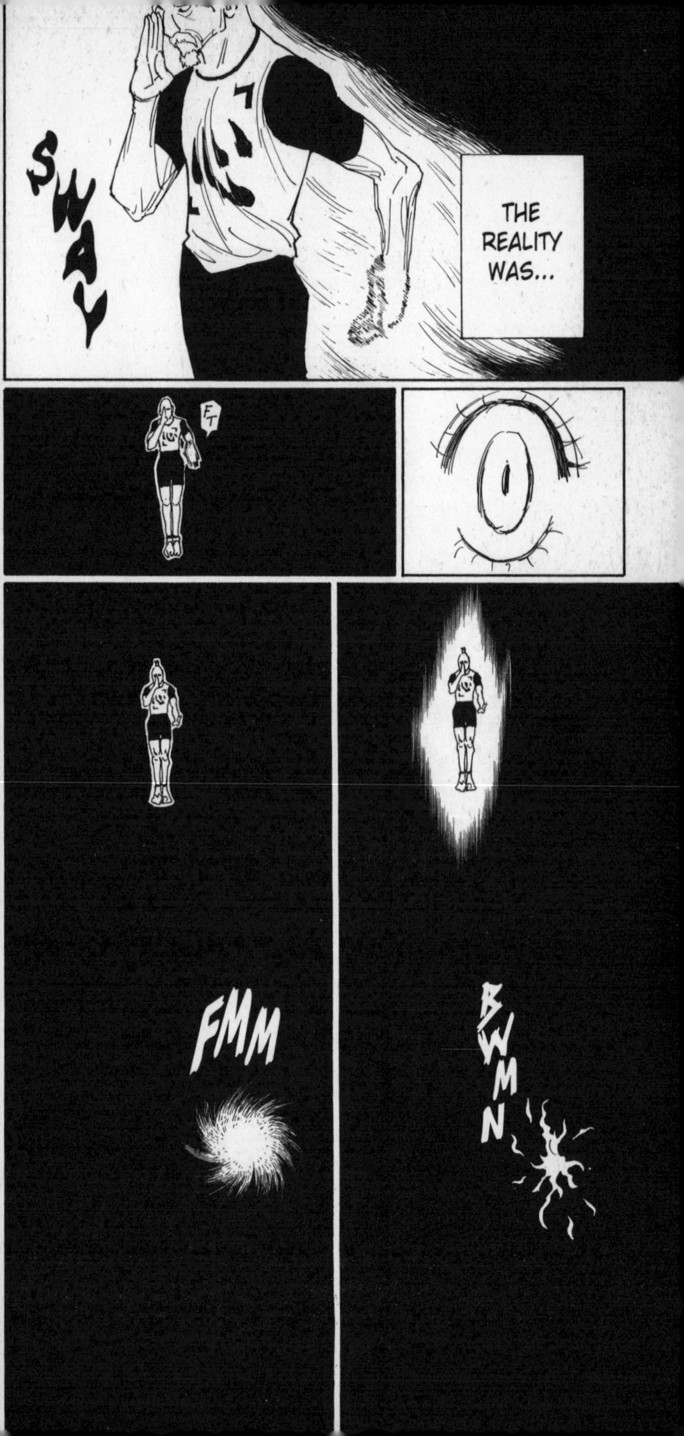
THE REALITY WAS...
SWAY
FT
BWMN
FMM

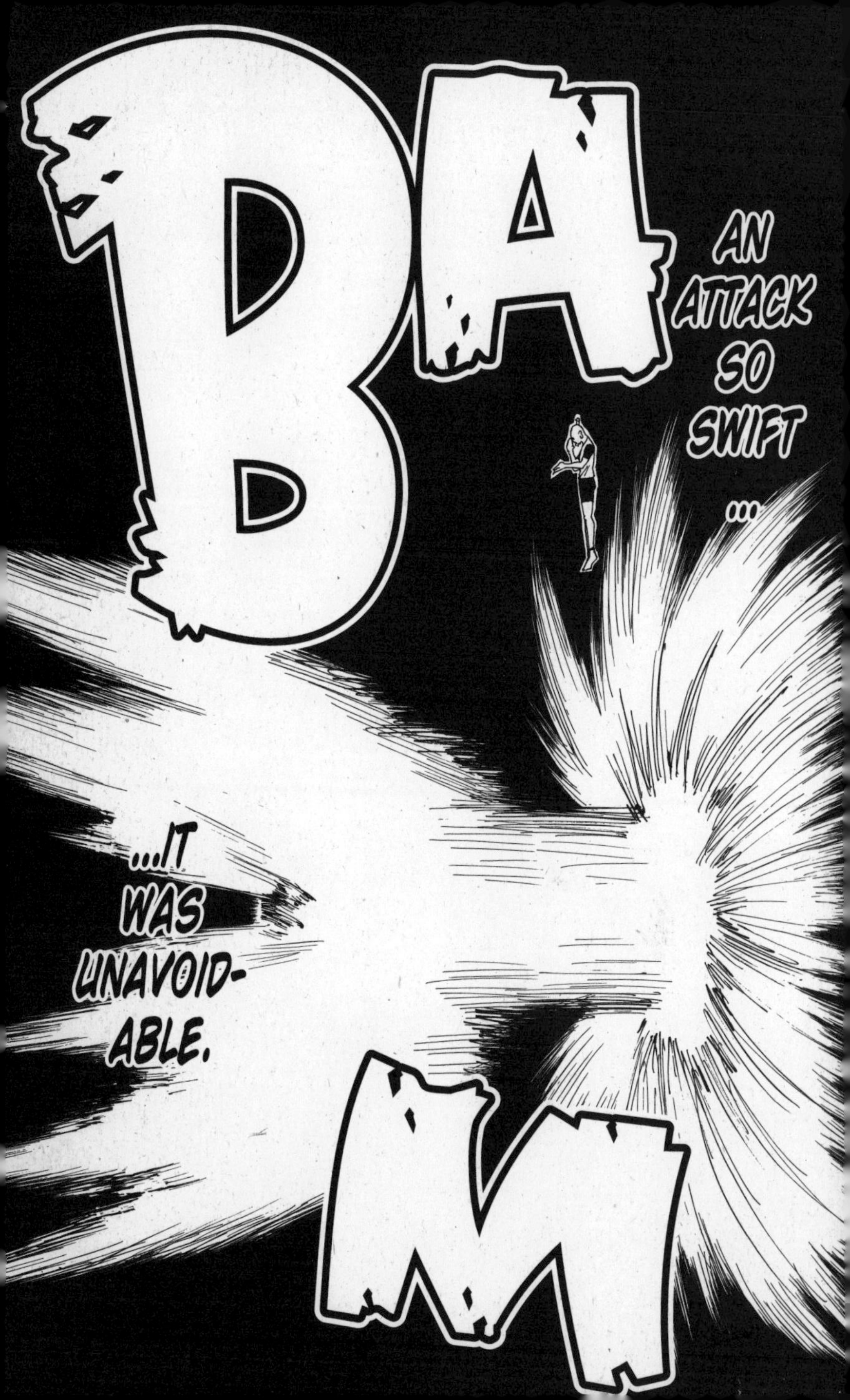
AN ATTACK SO SWIFT...
BAM
...IT WAS UNAVOID-ABLE.

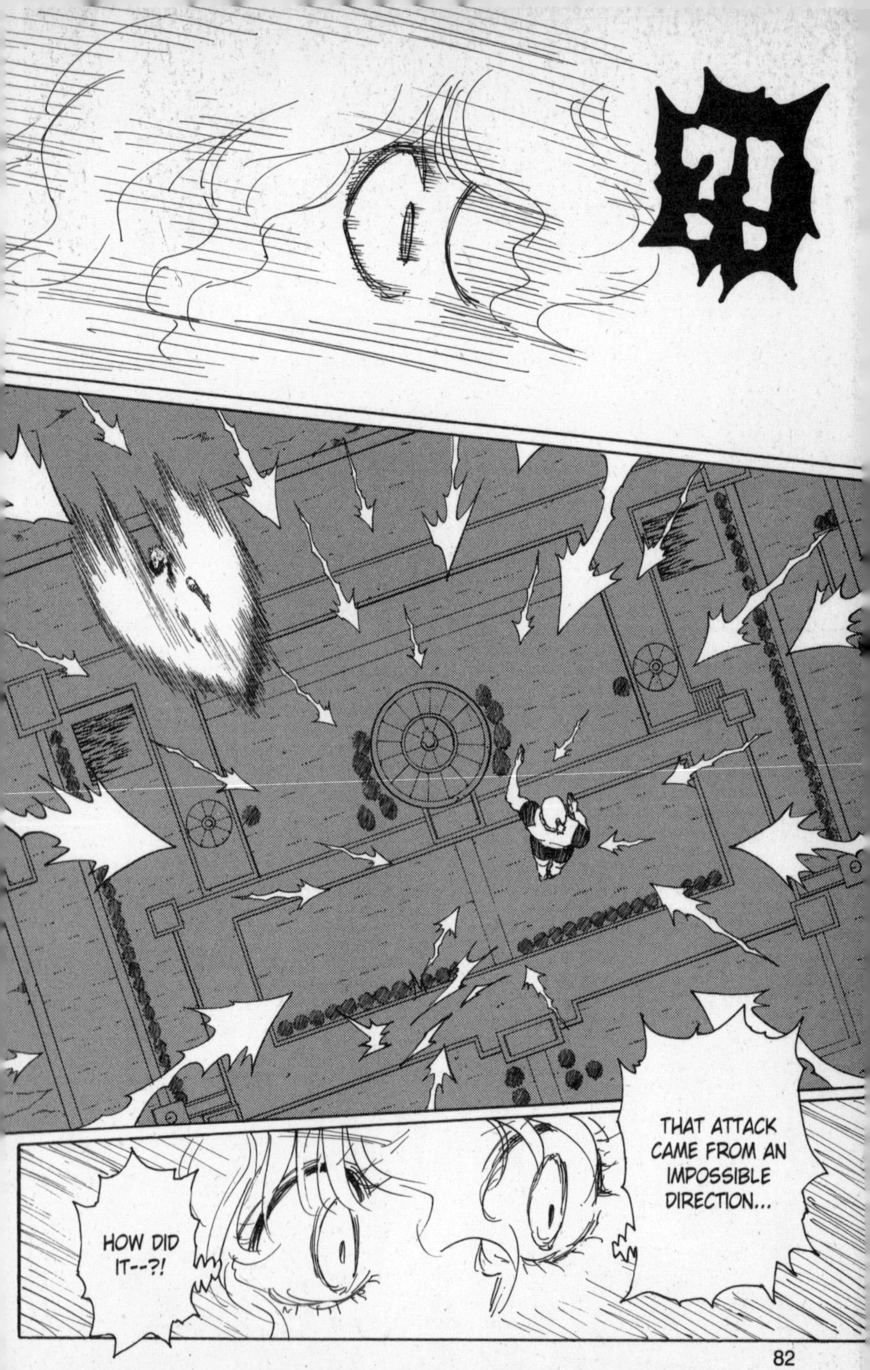
?!
THAT ATTACK CAME FROM AN IMPOSSIBLE DIRECTION...
HOW DID IT--?!

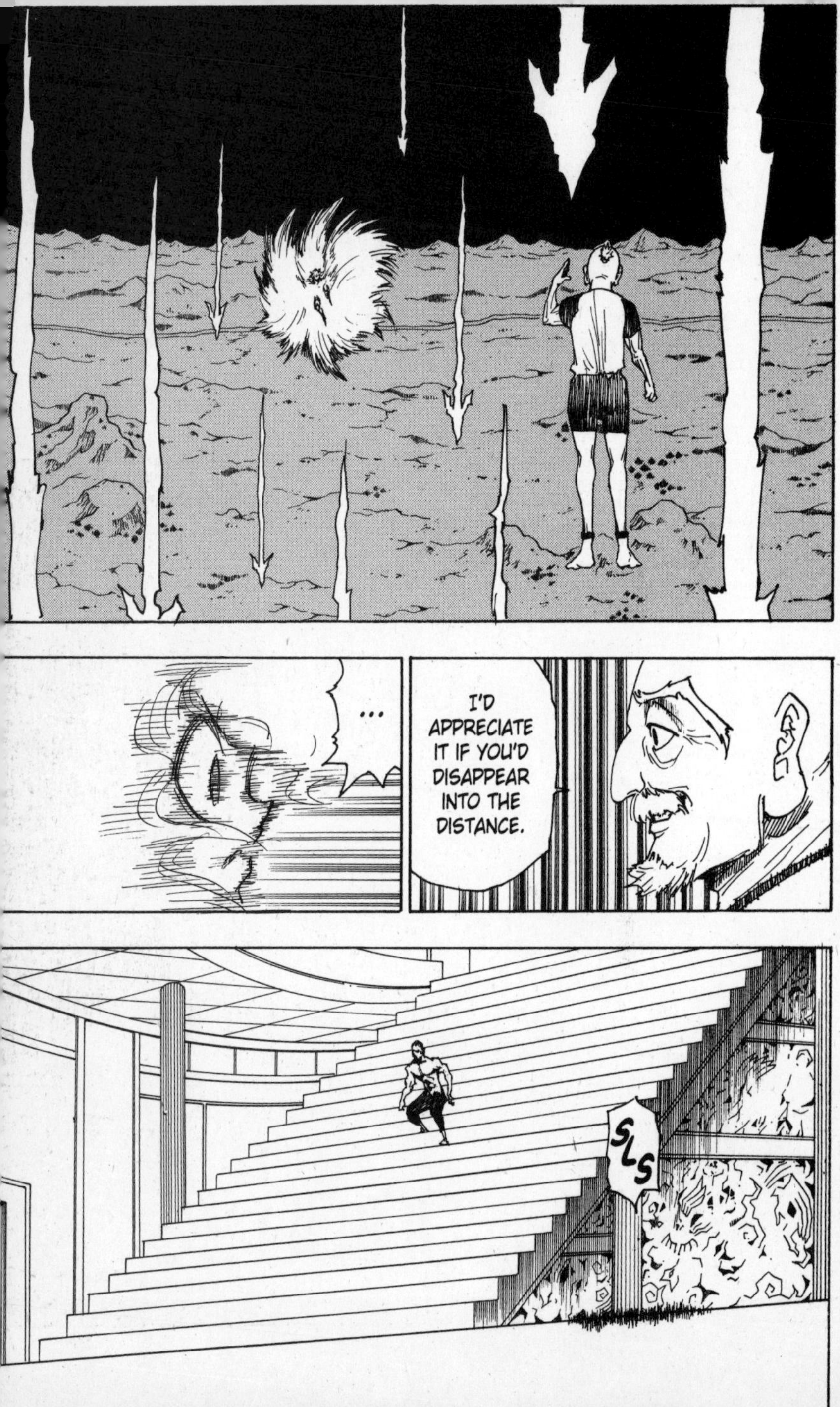
I'D APPRECIATE IT IF YOU'D DISAPPEAR INTO THE DISTANCE.
...
SLS

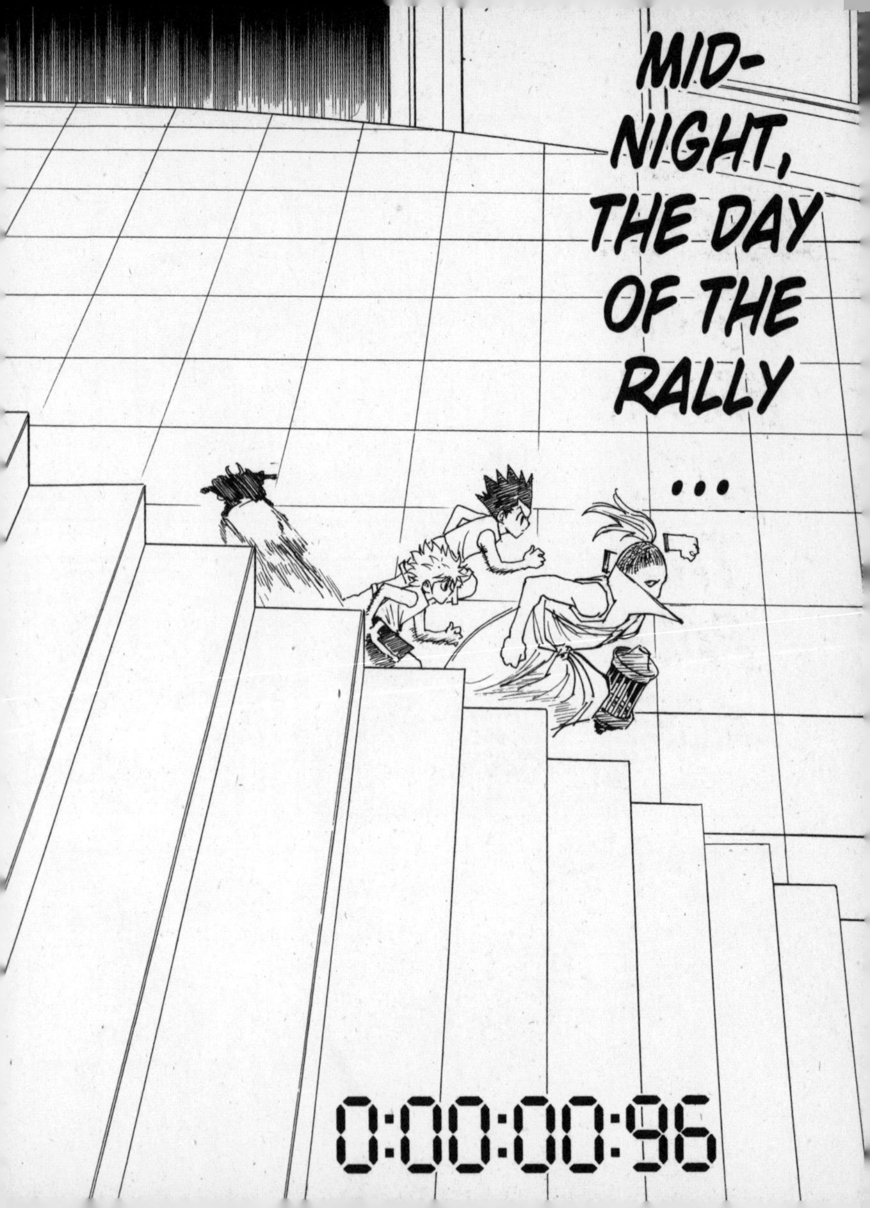
MID-NIGHT, THE DAY OF THE RALLY
...
0:00:00:96

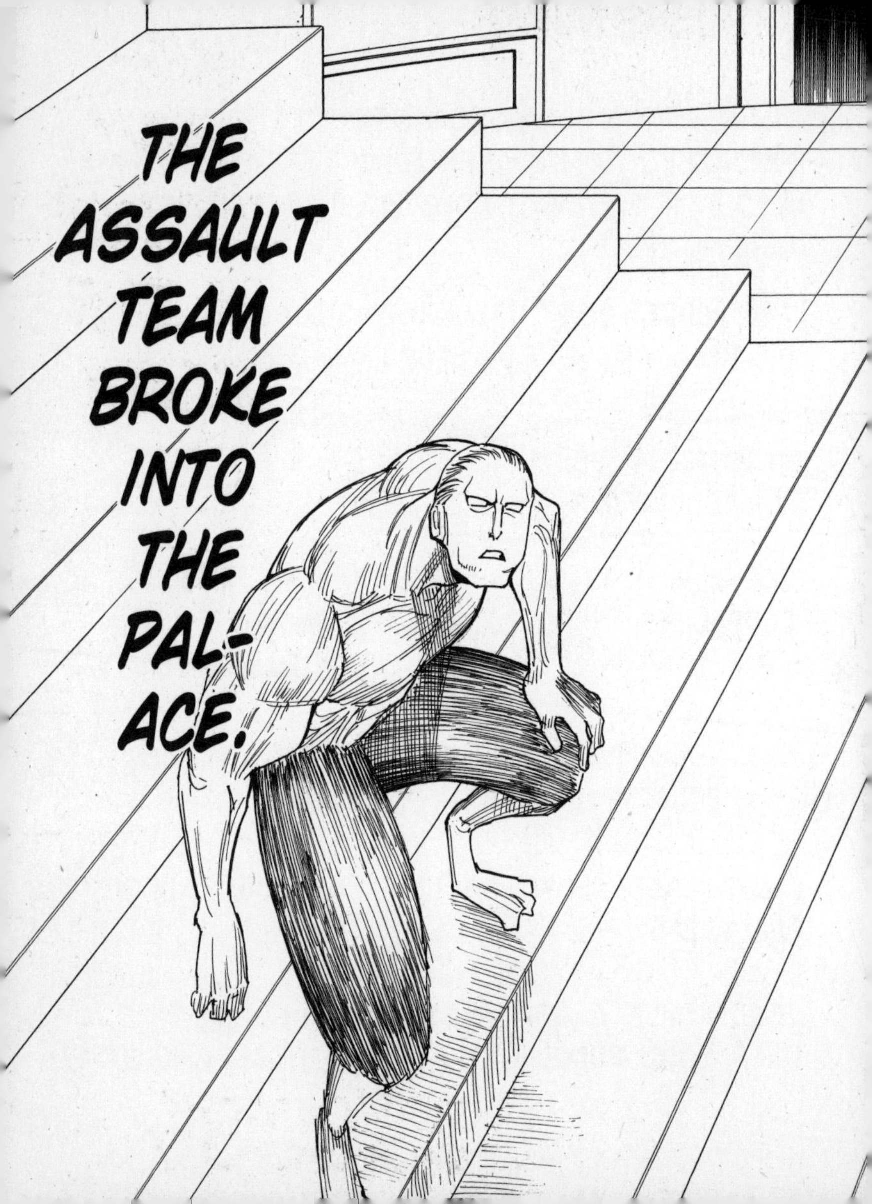
THE ASSAULT TEAM BROKE INTO THE PAL-ACE.

ROUND THREE: HIGH JUMP

1) TIMING STAT MINUS THE DIE ROLL MUST BE MORE THAN ZERO TO MAKE THE JUMP. ZERO OR LESS IS A FOUL. IF THE FIRST ROLL IS A FOUL, YOU GET A SECOND TRY.

2) THE SCORES WERE TALLIED BY JUMP STAT + DIE ROLL + RESULT OF STEP 1.

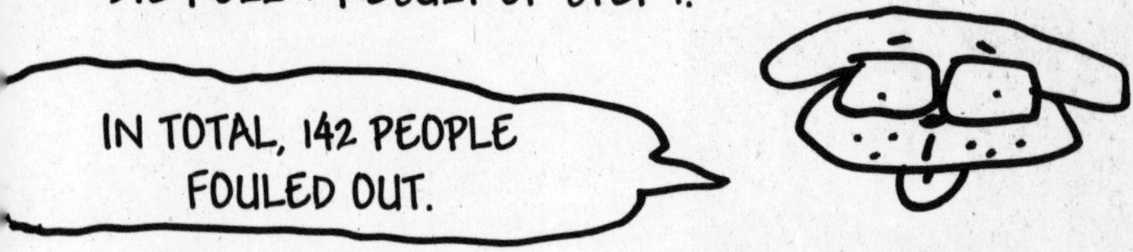
IN TOTAL, 142 PEOPLE FOULED OUT.

SCORE -	13	12	11	10	9	8	7	6	5	4	3	2
PEOPLE -	5	9	25	48	56	63	70	44	46	29	3	2

TOTAL: 400 PEOPLE

THERE WERE FIVE PEOPLE TIED FOR FIRST PLACE WITH 13 POINTS!! NINE TIED FOR SECOND.

FIRST PLACE: CLARE, CAGLIOSTRO, GODOR, BETTY AND PAZAS

SECOND PLACE: GONZALES, BERSERK, AYA, CALC, U-TA, SOUL, PUDDING, TAKECHIKA HYOZEI AND WASHU

○ UNFORTUNATELY, ALL HUNTERS WITH A TIMING STAT OF 0 WERE ELIMINATED.

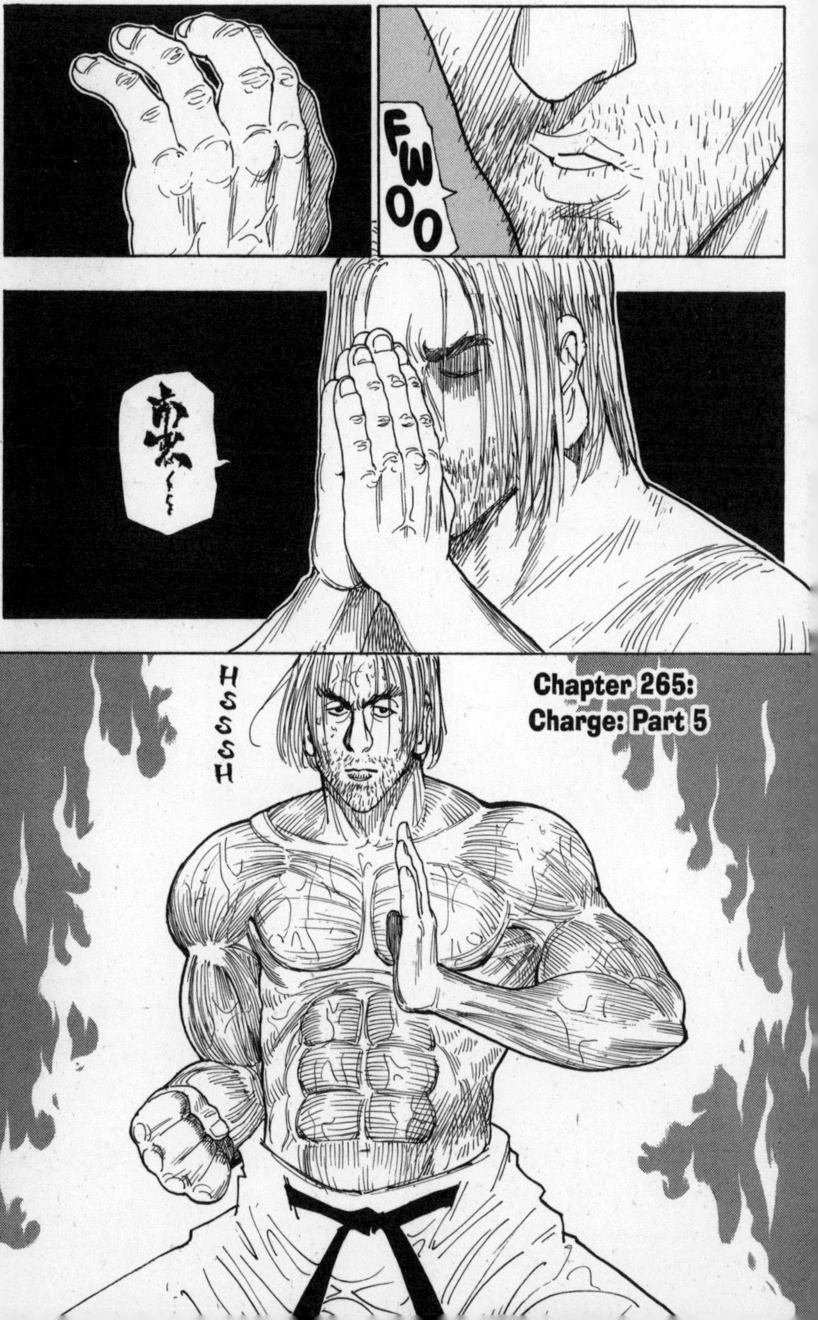
FWOO
南無
HSSSH
Chapter 265:
Charge: Part 5

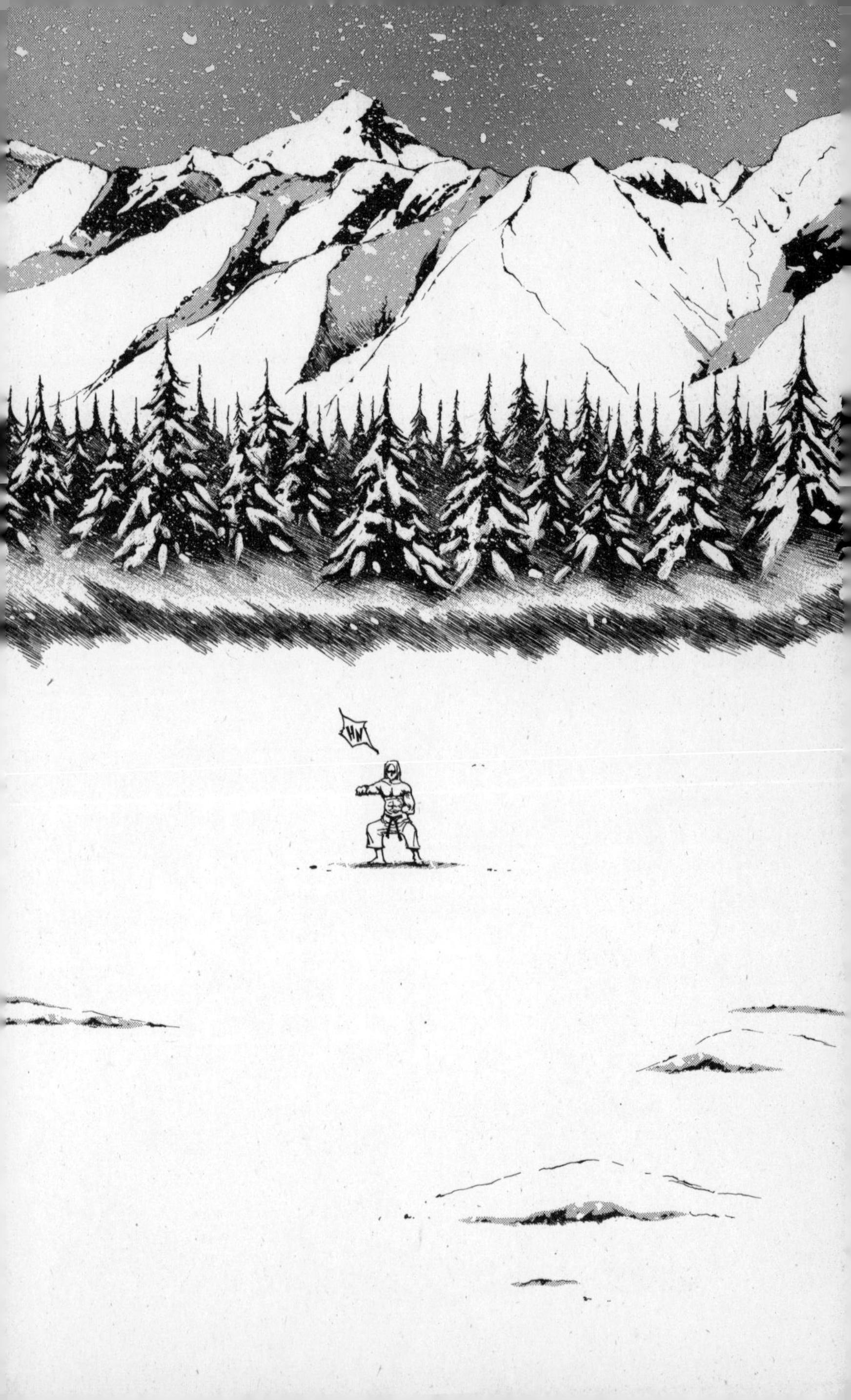
HN

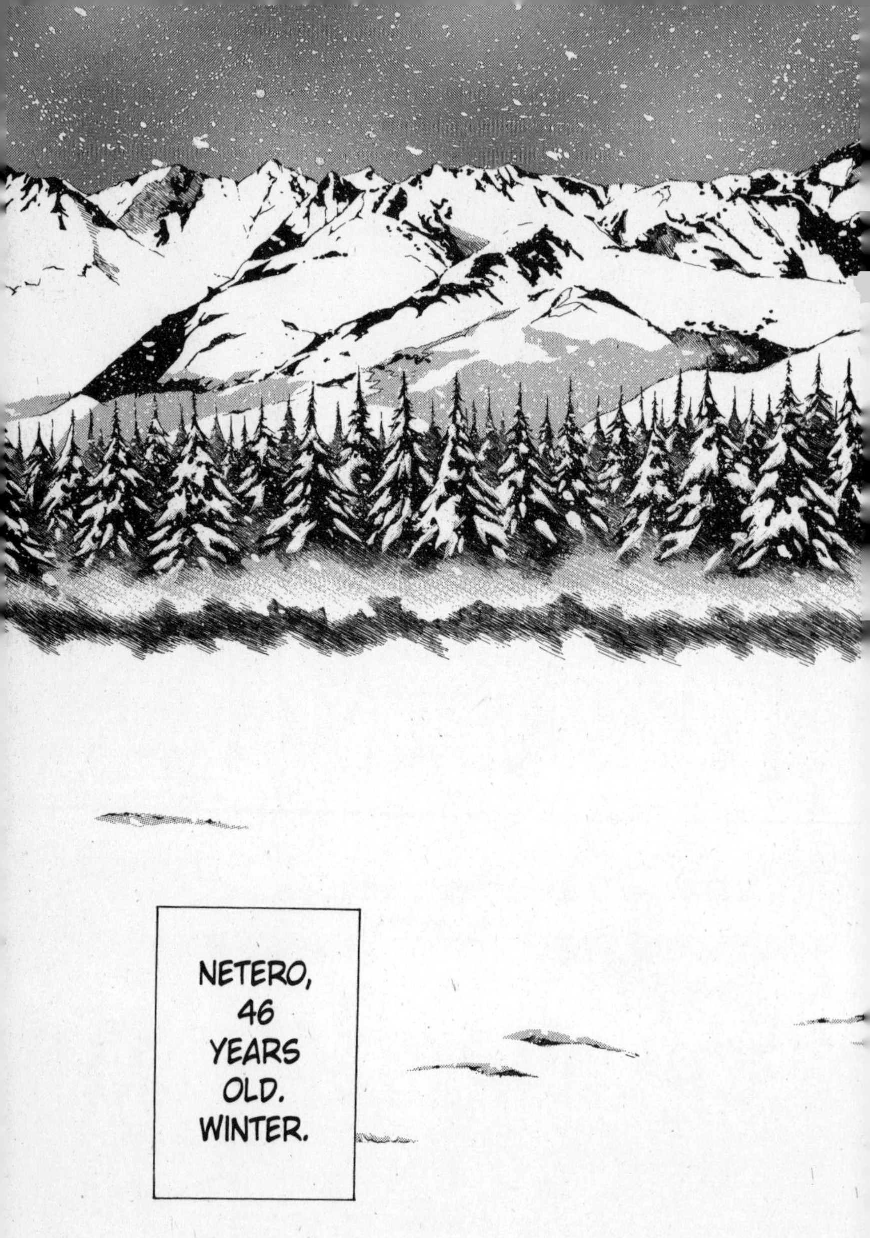
NETERO, 46 YEARS OLD. WINTER.

Chapter 265: Charge: Part 5

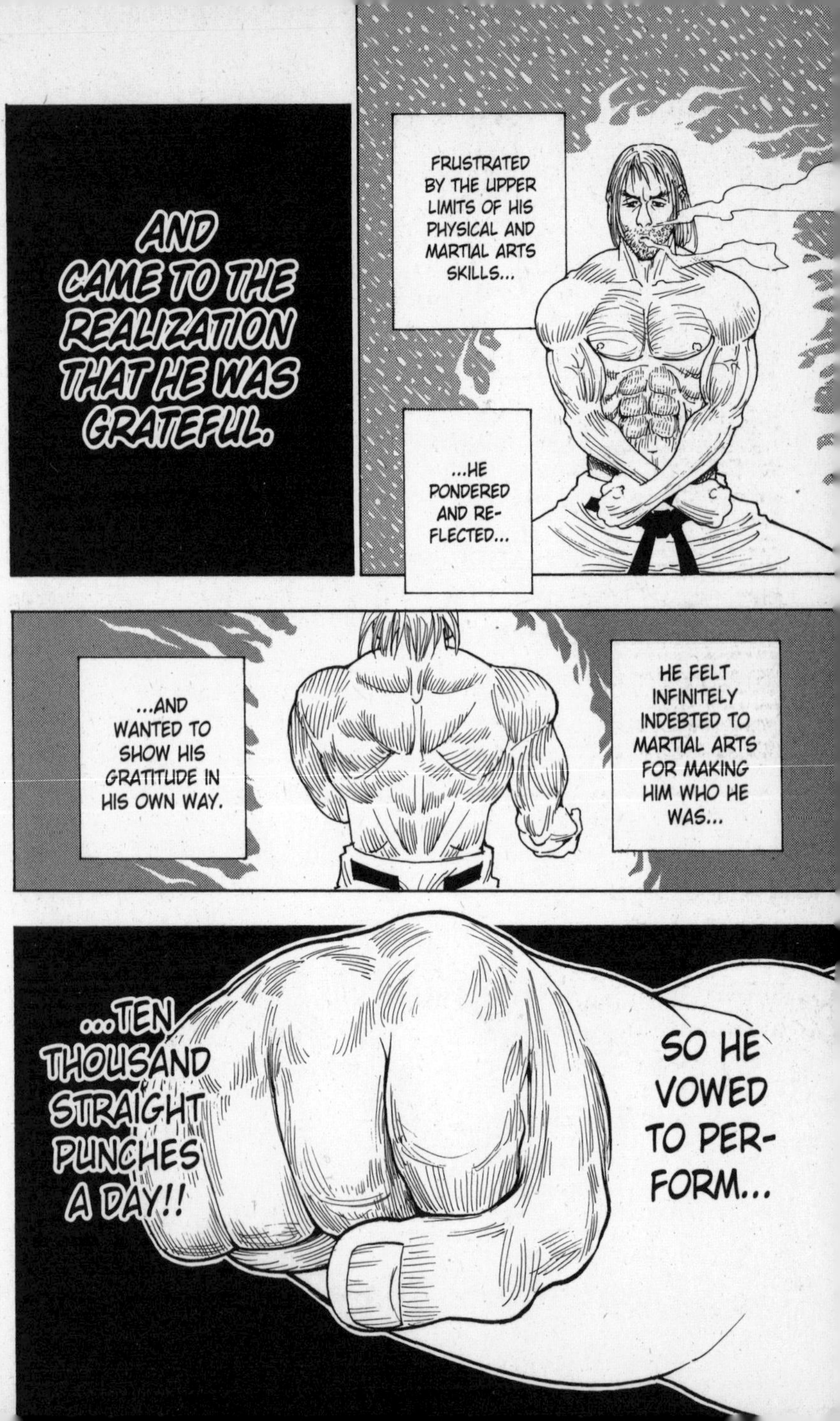
FRUSTRATED BY THE UPPER LIMITS OF HIS PHYSICAL AND MARTIAL ARTS SKILLS...
...HE PONDERED AND RE-FLECTED...
AND CAME TO THE REALIZATION THAT HE WAS GRATEFUL.
HE FELT INFINITELY INDEBTED TO MARTIAL ARTS FOR MAKING HIM WHO HE WAS...
...AND WANTED TO SHOW HIS GRATITUDE IN HIS OWN WAY.
SO HE VOWED TO PER-FORM...
...TEN THOUSAND STRAIGHT PUNCHES A DAY!!

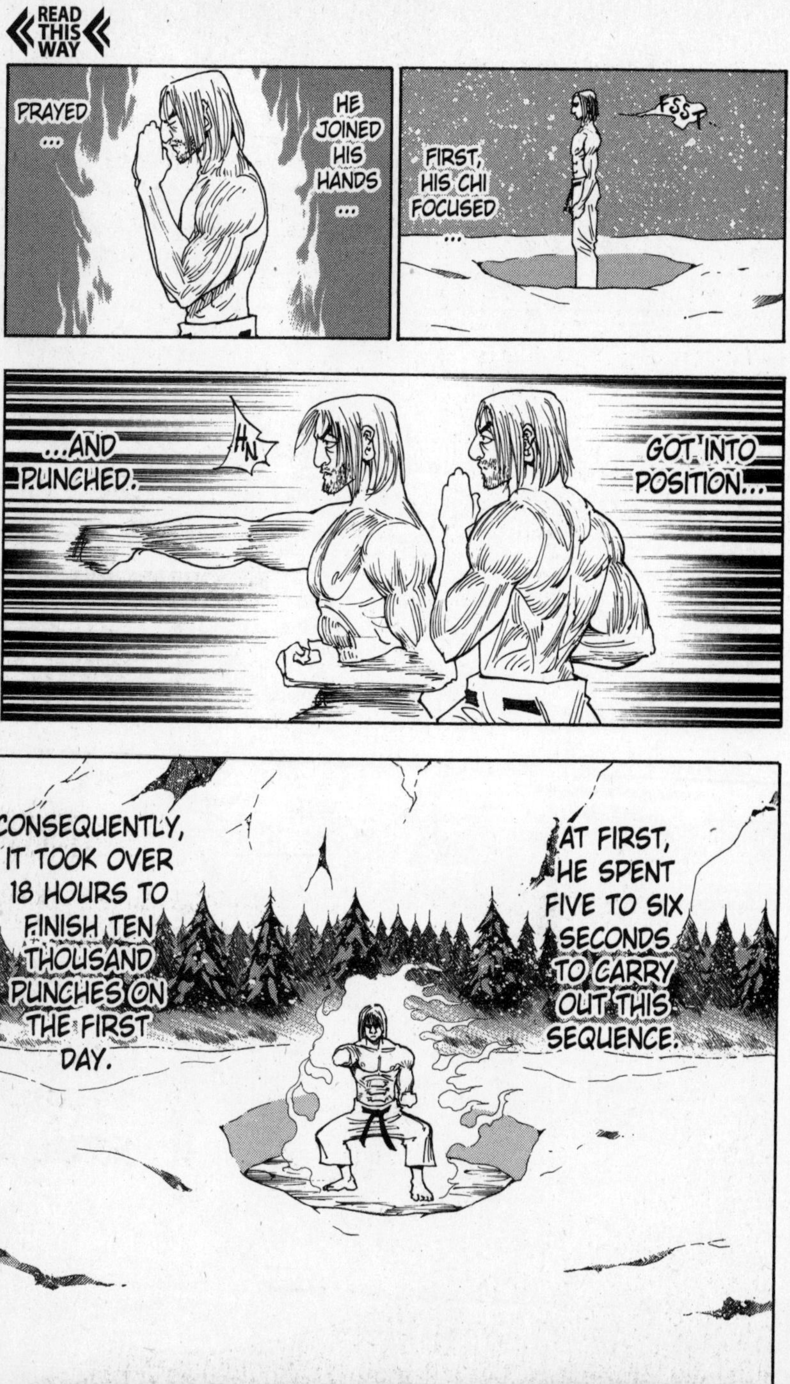
READ THIS WAY
FSST
FIRST, HIS CHI FOCUSED ...
HE JOINED HIS HANDS ...
PRAYED ...
GOT INTO POSITION...
HN
...AND PUNCHED.
AT FIRST, HE SPENT FIVE TO SIX SECONDS TO CARRY OUT THIS SEQUENCE.
CONSEQUENTLY, IT TOOK OVER 18 HOURS TO FINISH TEN THOUSAND PUNCHES ON THE FIRST DAY.

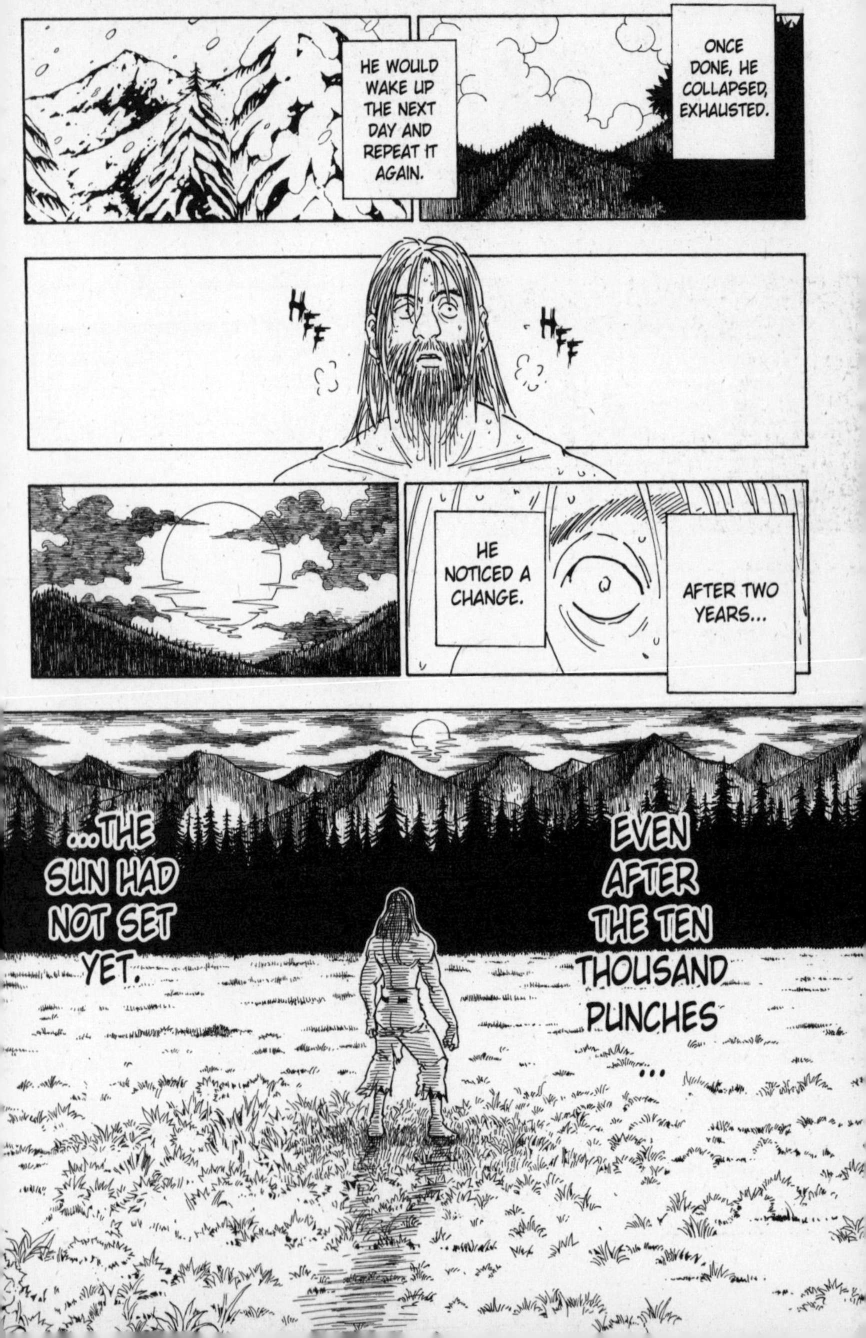
ONCE DONE, HE COLLAPSED, EXHAUSTED.
HE WOULD WAKE UP THE NEXT DAY AND REPEAT IT AGAIN.
HFF
HFF
AFTER TWO YEARS...
HE NOTICED A CHANGE.
EVEN AFTER THE TEN THOUSAND PUNCHES...
...THE SUN HAD NOT SET YET.

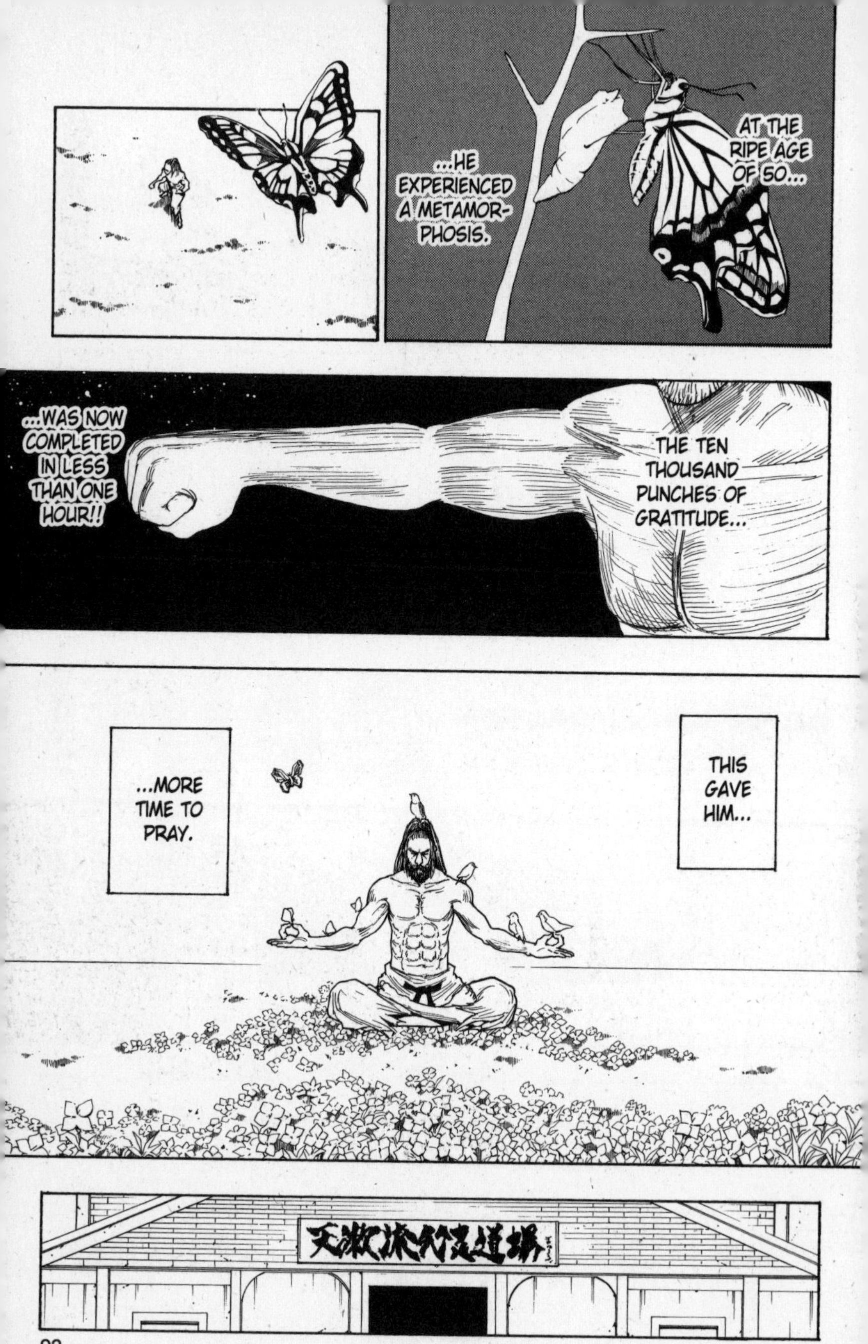
AT THE RIPE AGE OF 50...
...HE EXPERIENCED A METAMORPHOSIS.
THE TEN THOUSAND PUNCHES OF GRATITUDE...
...WAS NOW COMPLETED IN LESS THAN ONE HOUR!!
THIS GAVE HIM...
...MORE TIME TO PRAY.

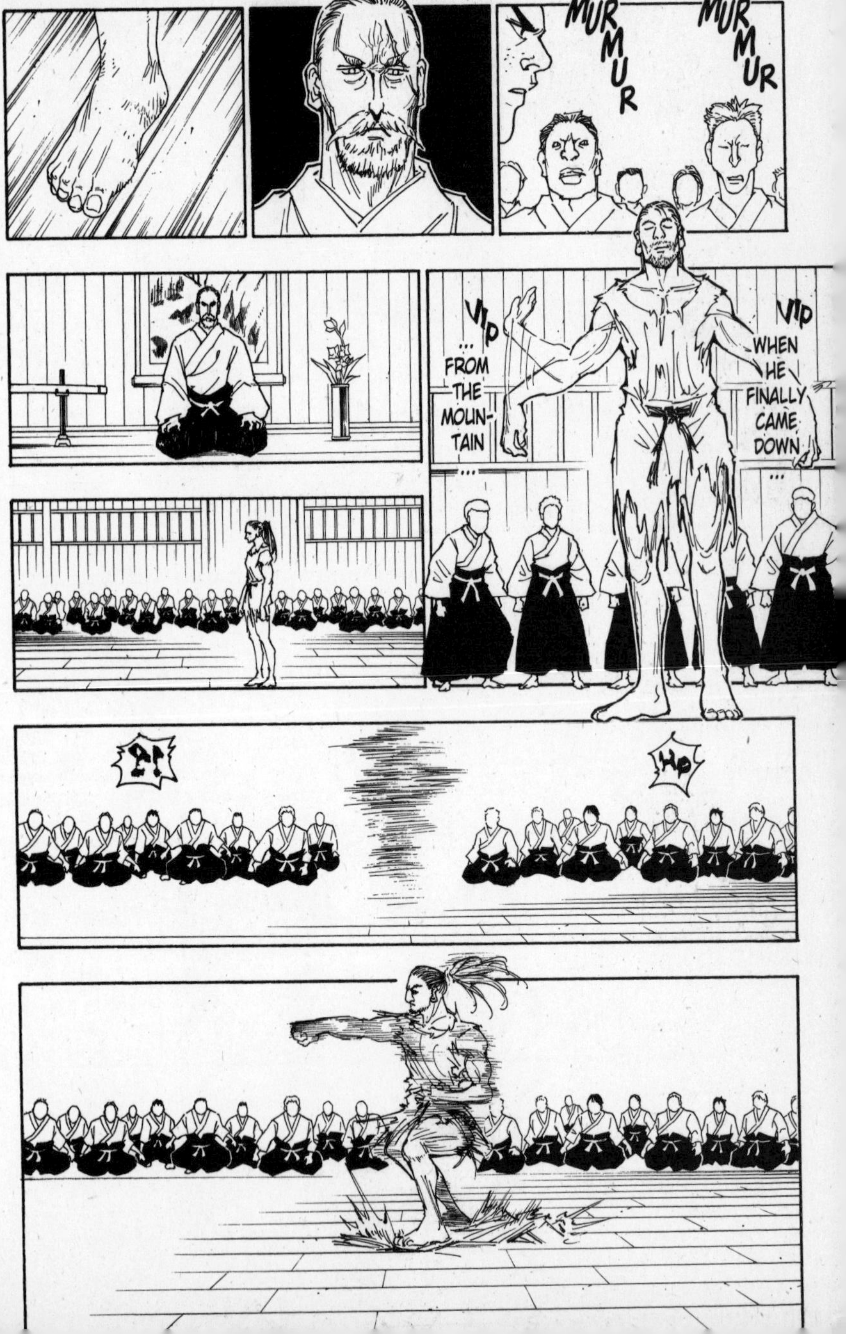
MURMUR
MURMUR
VIP
WHEN HE FINALLY CAME DOWN...
VIP
...FROM THE MOUNTAIN...
HP
?!

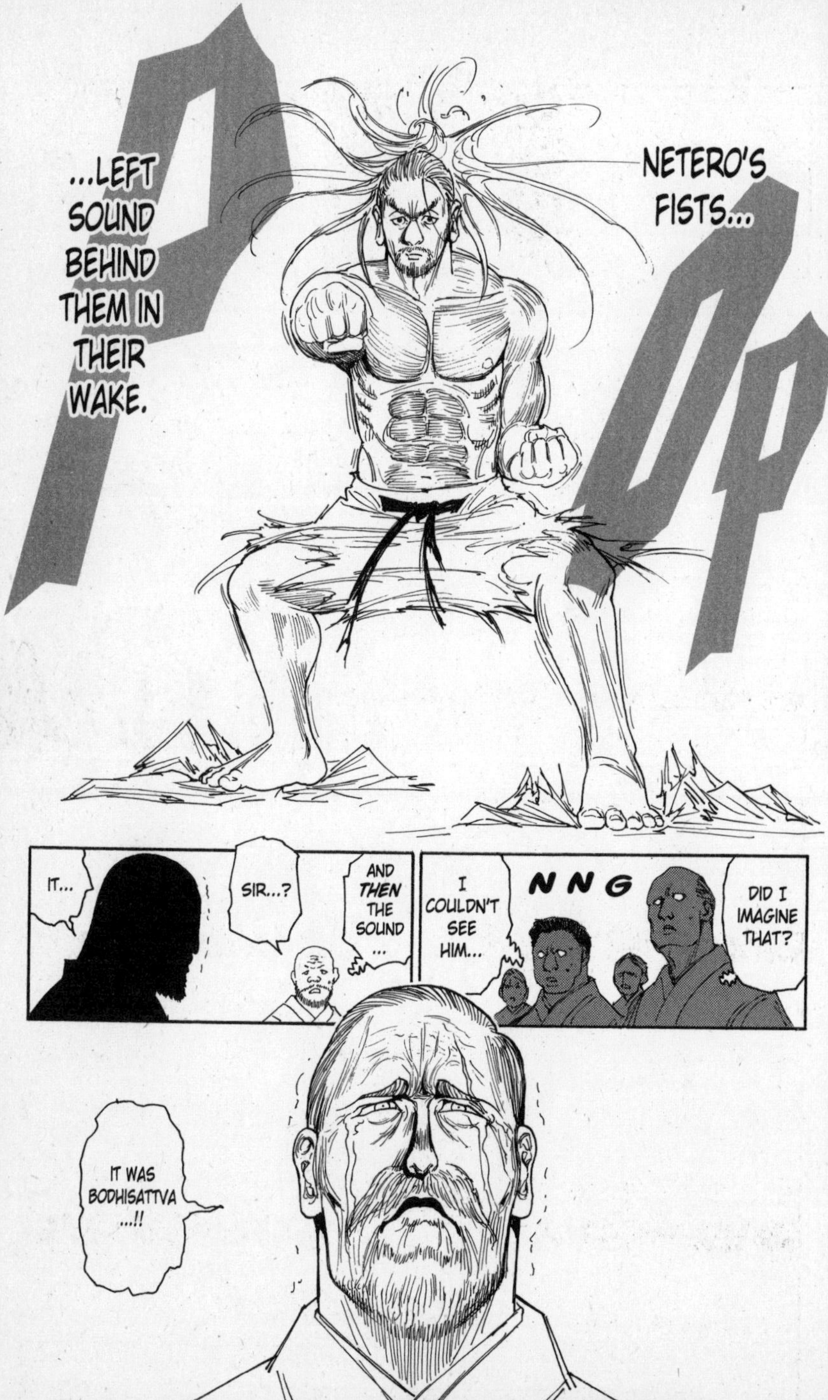
NETERO'S FISTS...
...LEFT SOUND BEHIND THEM IN THEIR WAKE.
POP
DID I IMAGINE THAT?
NNG
I COULDN'T SEE HIM...
AND *THEN* THE SOUND...
SIR...?
IT...
IT WAS BODHISATTVA...!!

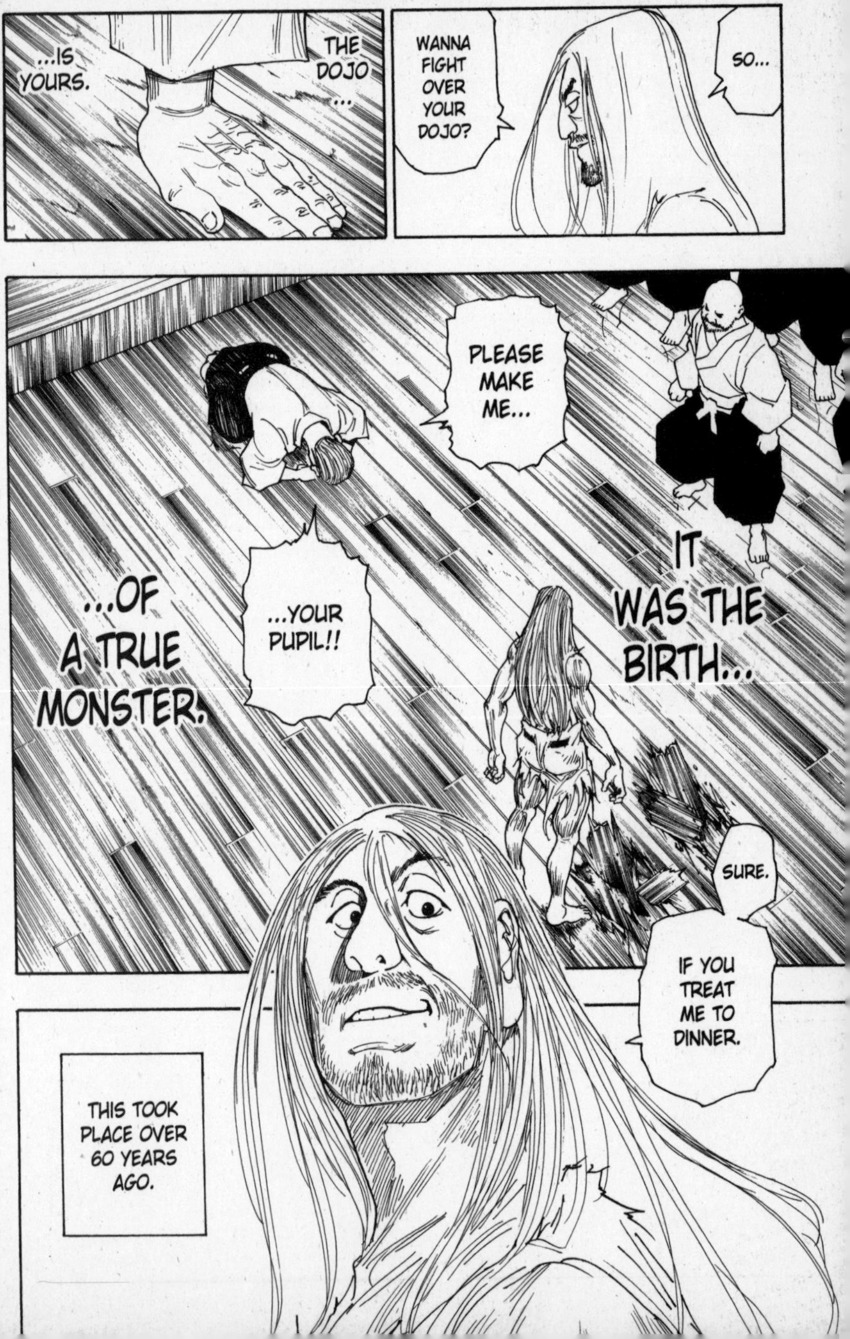
SO...
WANNA FIGHT OVER YOUR DOJO?
THE DOJO...
...IS YOURS.
PLEASE MAKE ME...
...YOUR PUPIL!!
IT WAS THE BIRTH...
...OF A TRUE MONSTER.
SURE.
IF YOU TREAT ME TO DINNER.
THIS TOOK PLACE OVER 60 YEARS AGO.

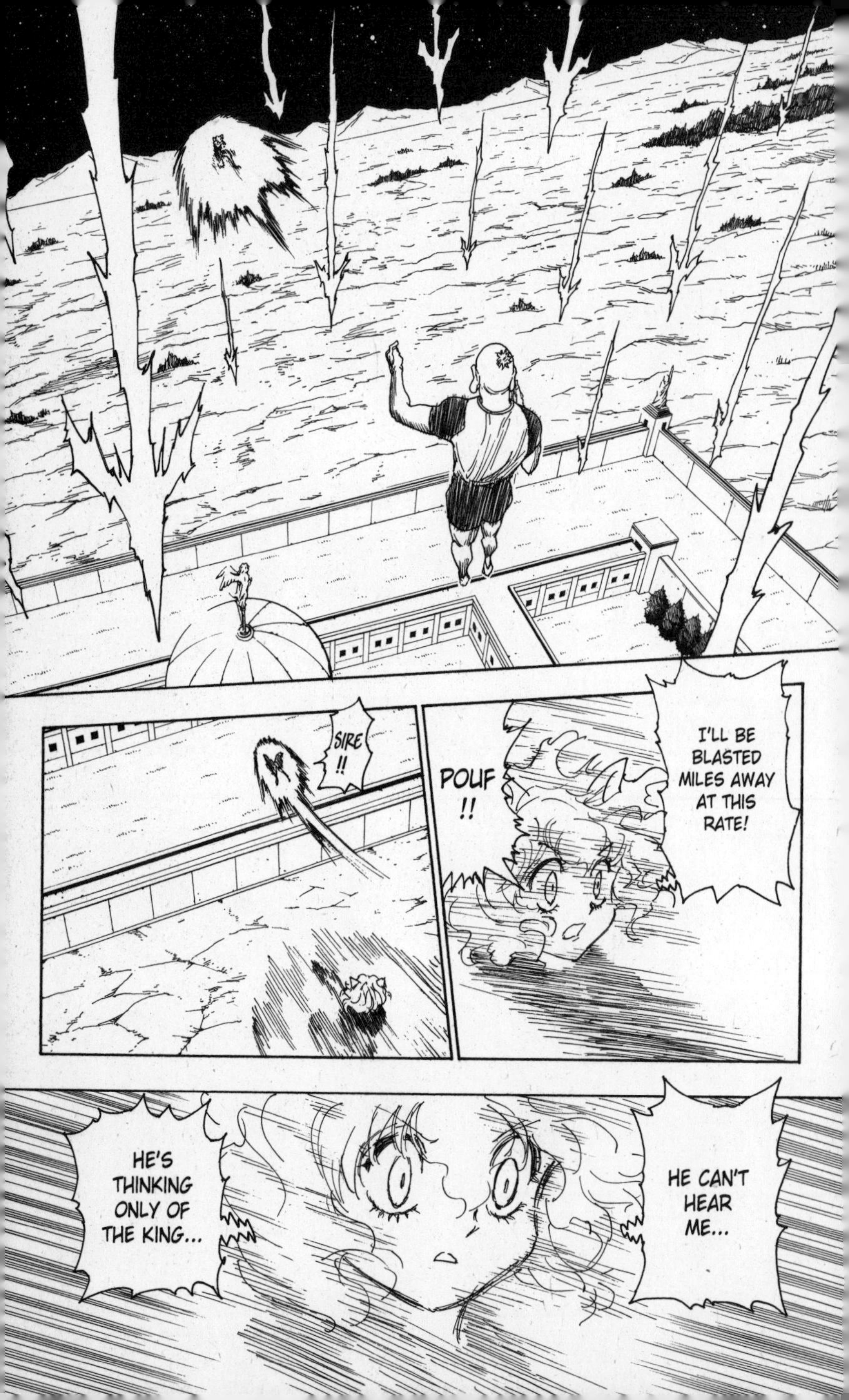
I'LL BE BLASTED MILES AWAY AT THIS RATE!
POUF !!
SIRE !!
HE CAN'T HEAR ME...
HE'S THINKING ONLY OF THE KING...

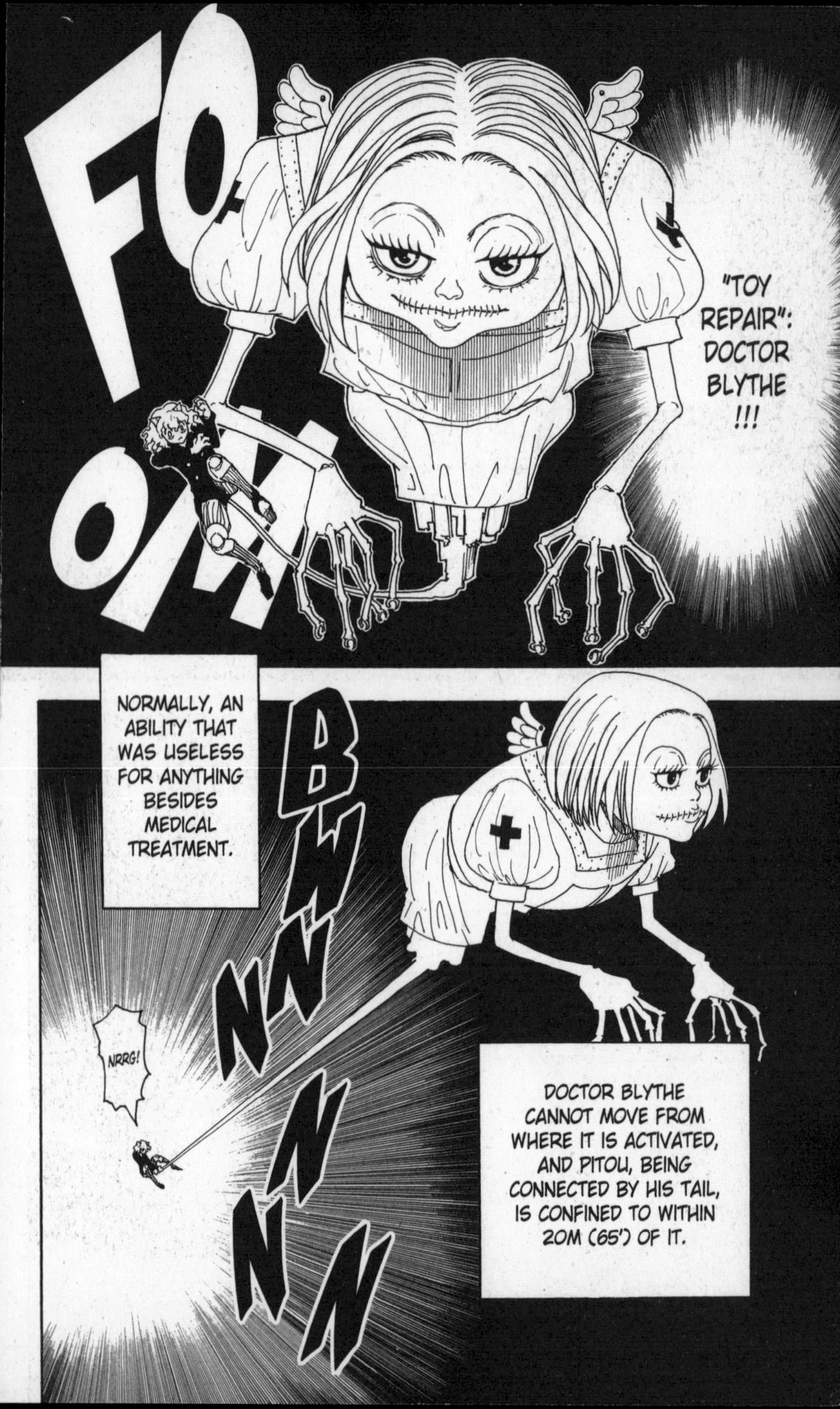
FOOOM
"TOY REPAIR": DOCTOR BLYTHE !!!
NORMALLY, AN ABILITY THAT WAS USELESS FOR ANYTHING BESIDES MEDICAL TREATMENT.
BWNNNNNNN
NRRG!
DOCTOR BLYTHE CANNOT MOVE FROM WHERE IT IS ACTIVATED, AND PITOU, BEING CONNECTED BY HIS TAIL, IS CONFINED TO WITHIN 20M (65') OF IT.

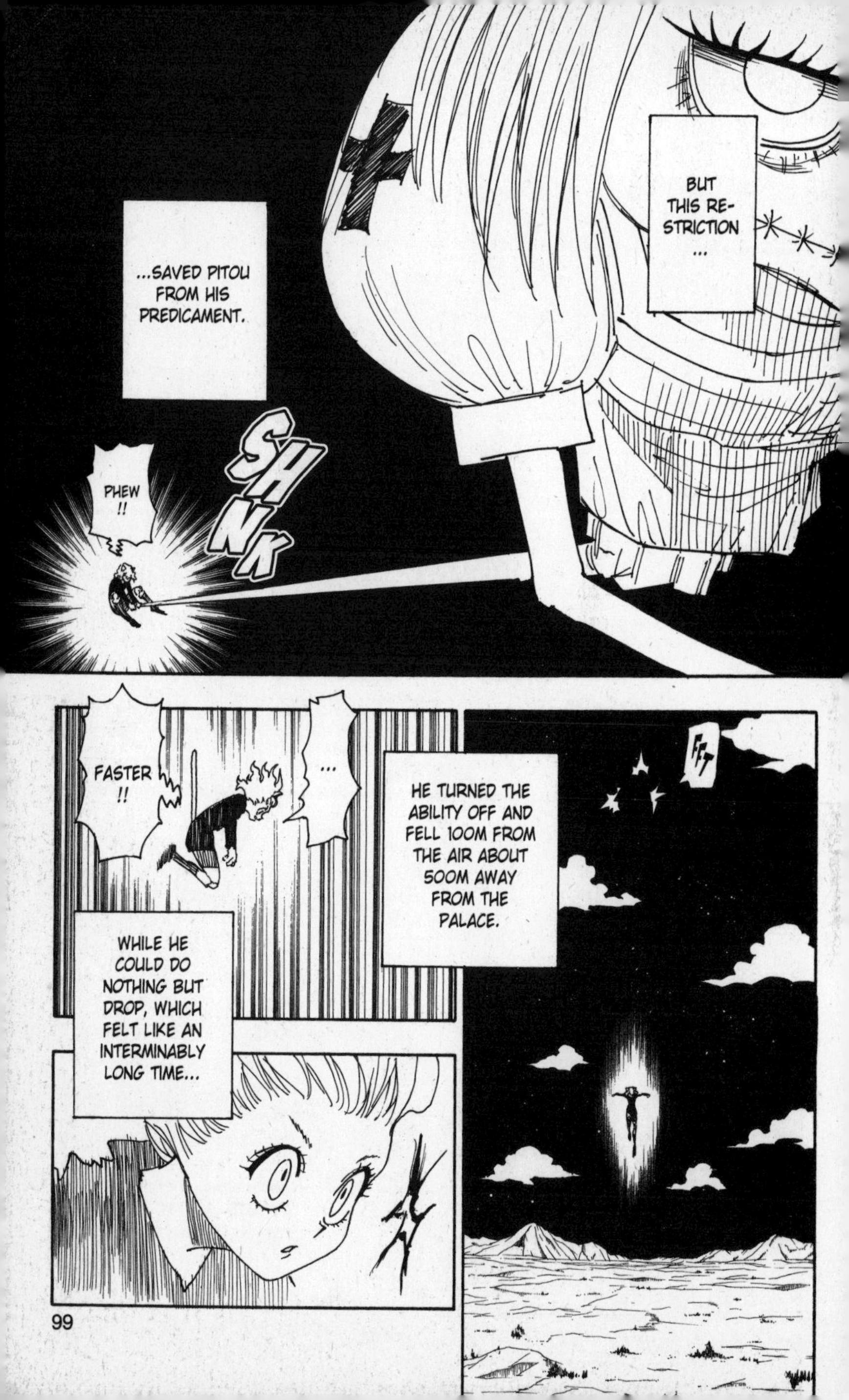
BUT THIS RE-STRICTION ...
...SAVED PITOU FROM HIS PREDICAMENT.
SHNK
PHEW !!
FFT
HE TURNED THE ABILITY OFF AND FELL 100M FROM THE AIR ABOUT 500M AWAY FROM THE PALACE.
...
FASTER !!
WHILE HE COULD DO NOTHING BUT DROP, WHICH FELT LIKE AN INTERMINABLY LONG TIME...

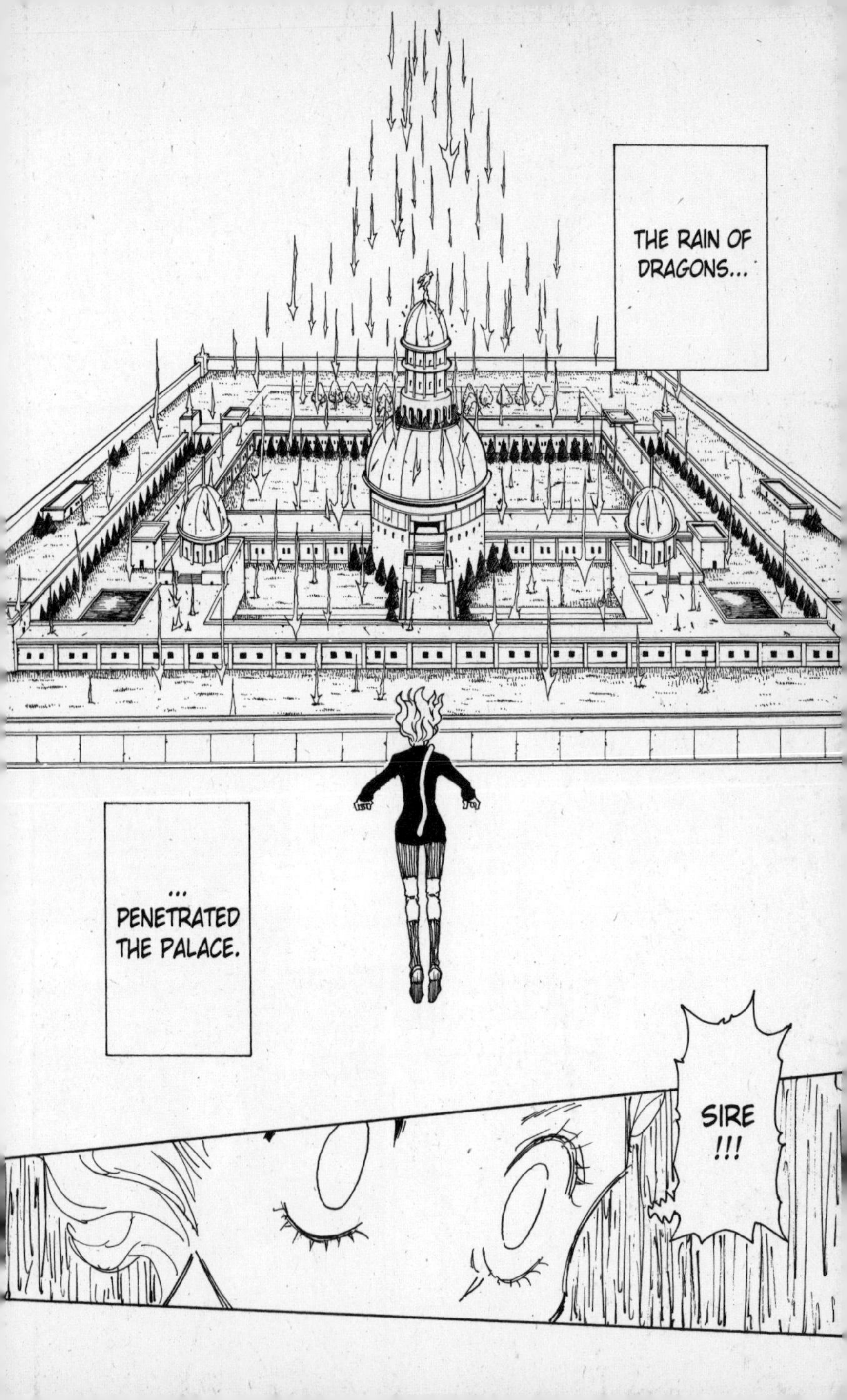
THE RAIN OF DRAGONS...
... PENETRATED THE PALACE.
SIRE !!!

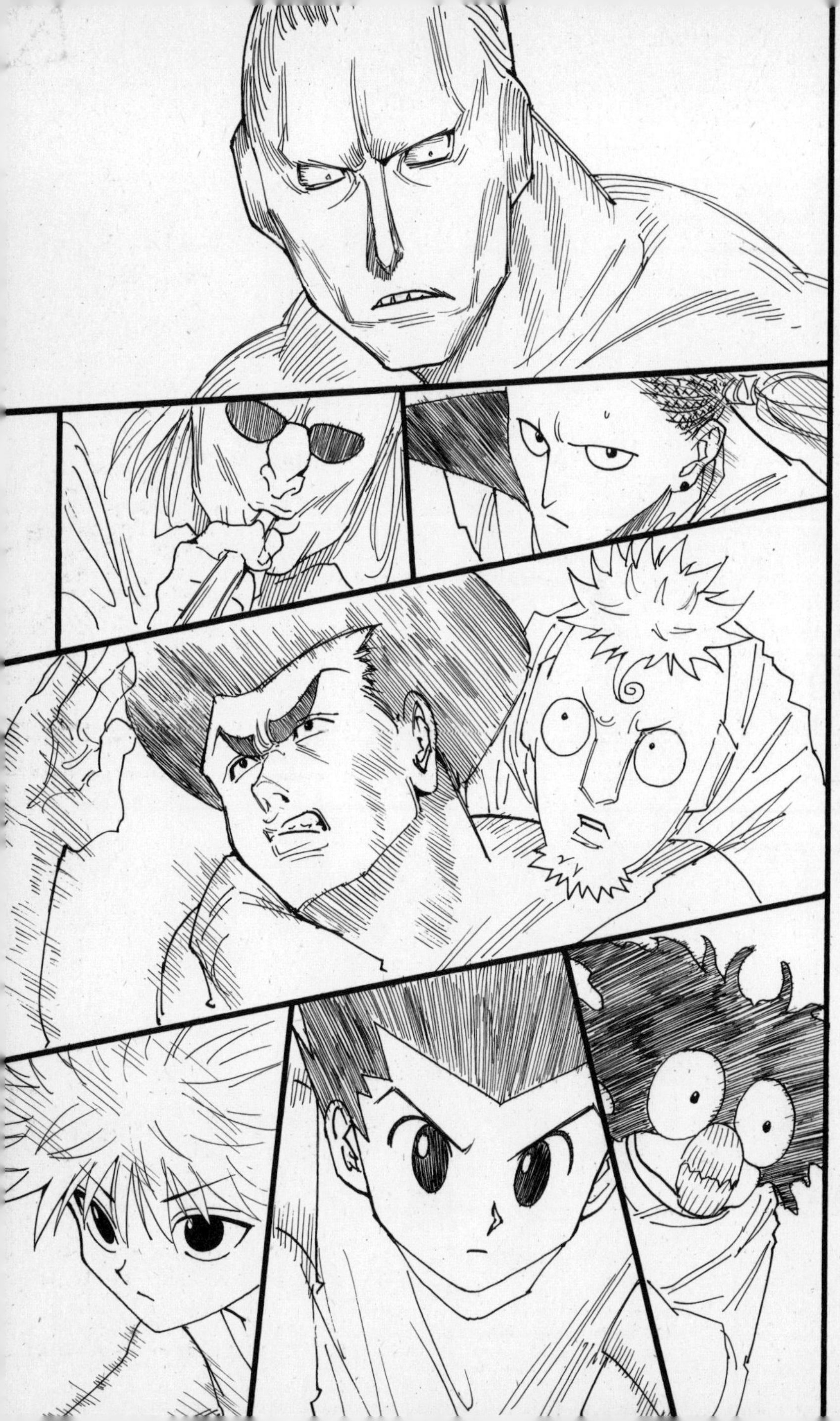

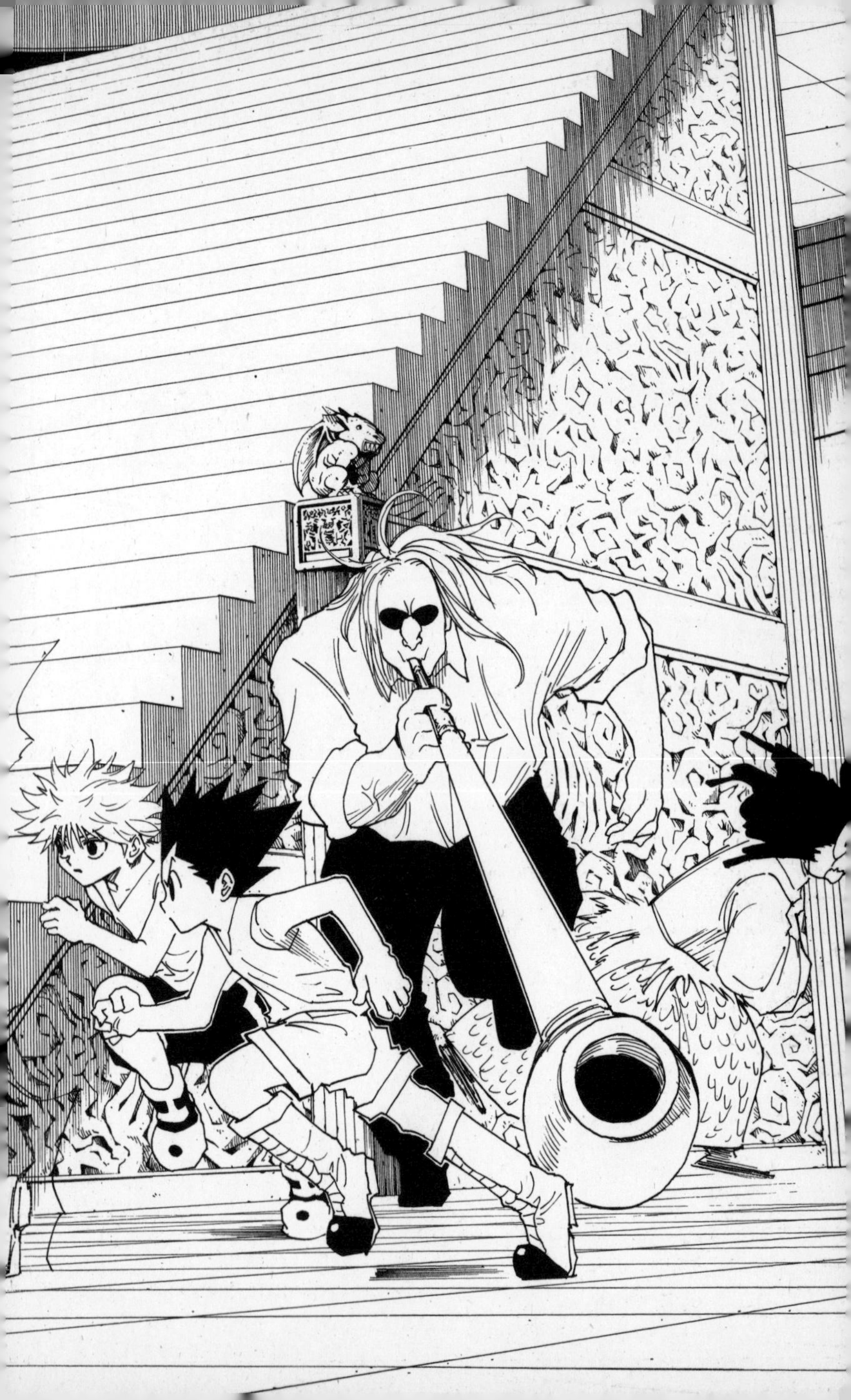

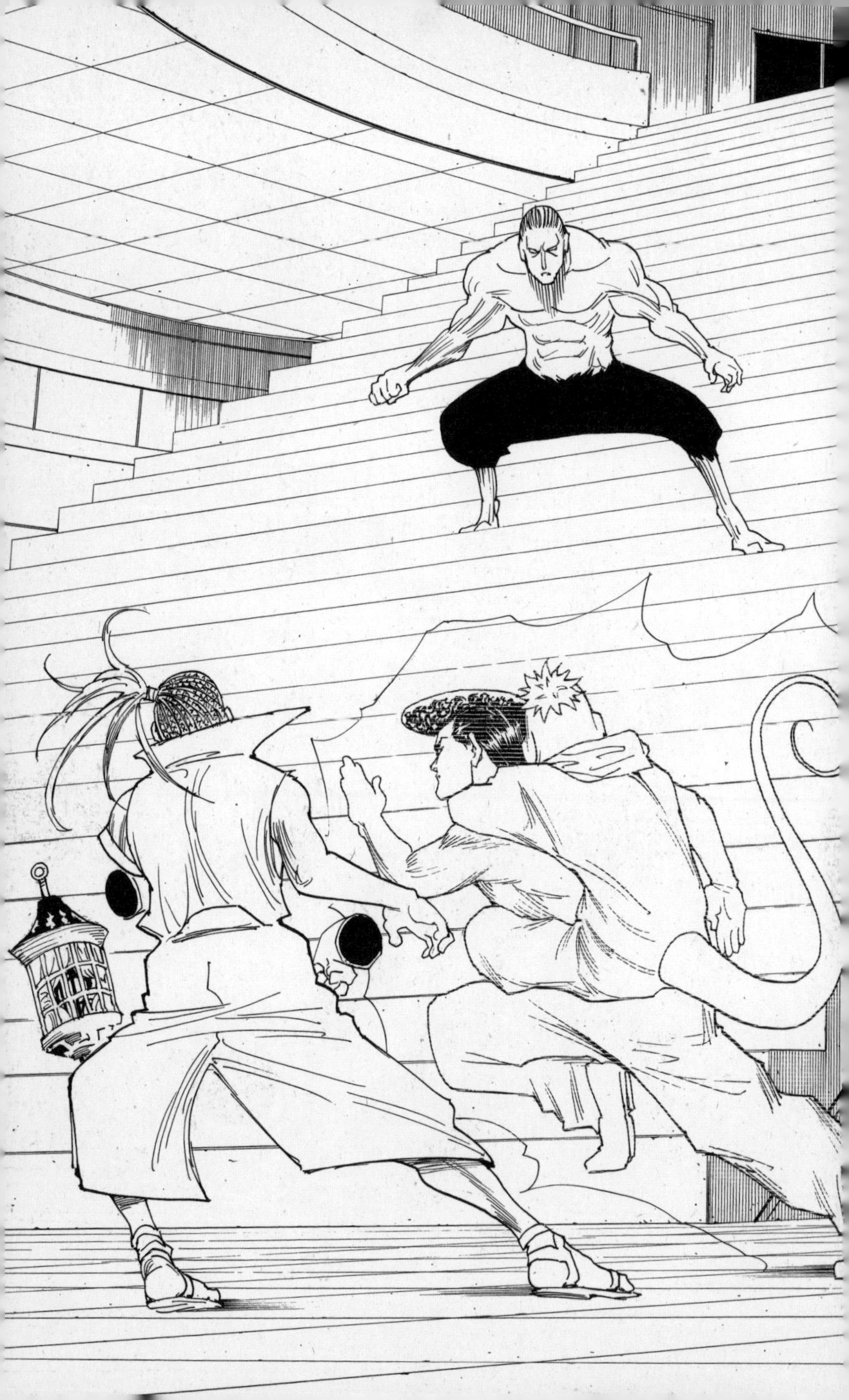

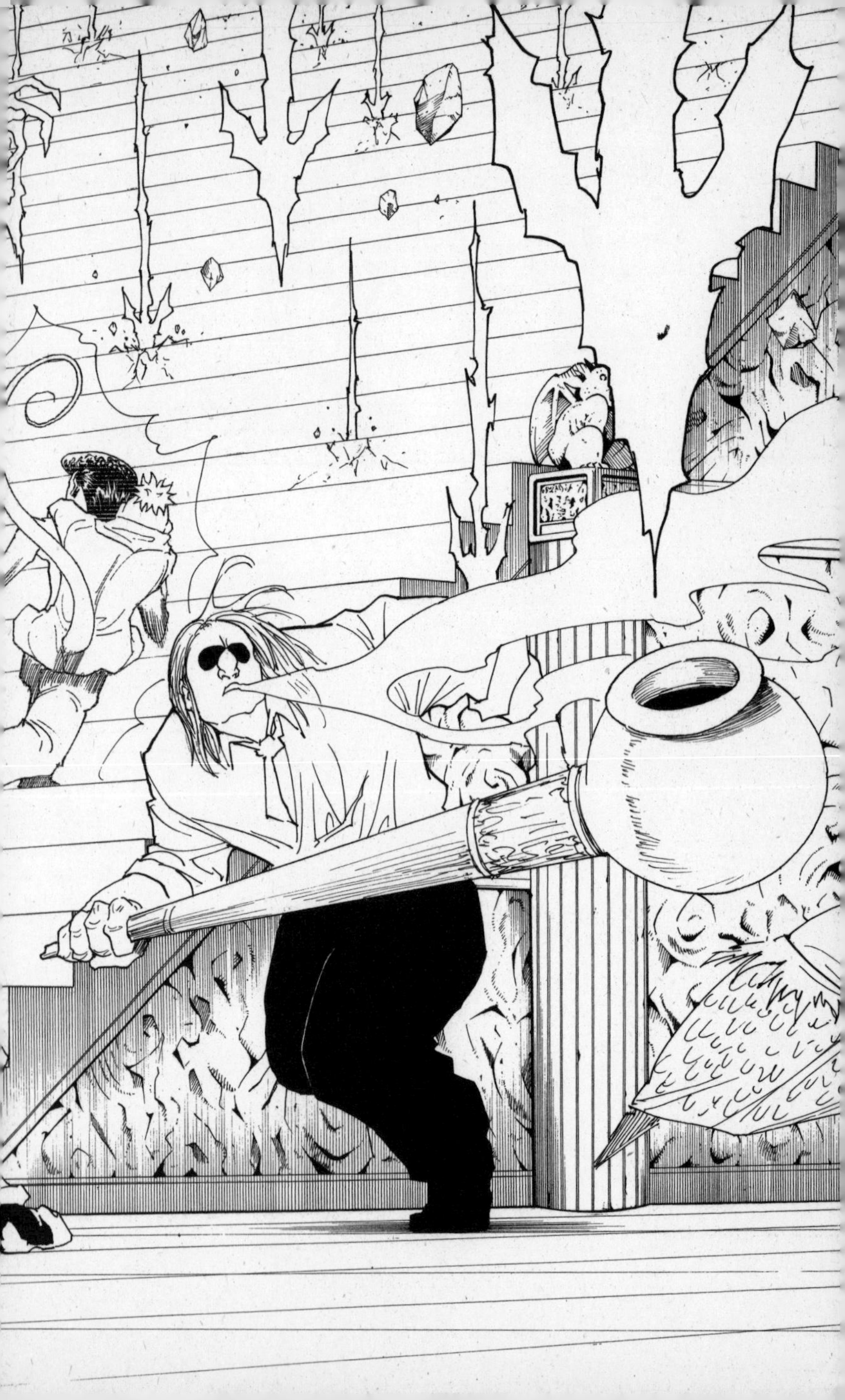

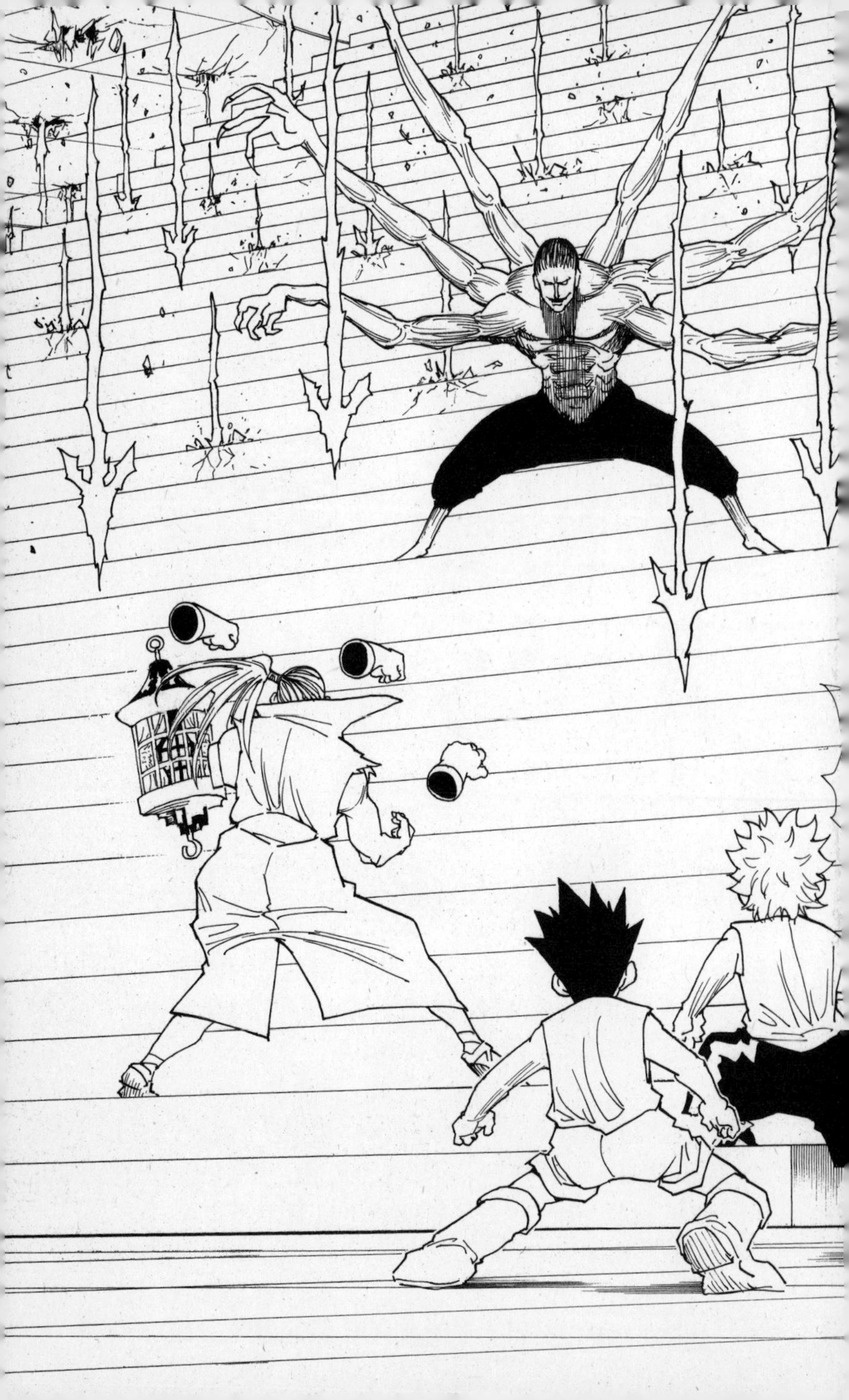

ROUND FOUR: JAVELIN

1) TIMING STAT MINUS THE DIE ROLL MUST BE MORE THAN ZERO TO MAKE THE THROW. ZERO OR LESS IS A FOUL. IF THE FIRST ROLL IS A FOUL, YOU GET A SECOND TRY.

2) THE SCORES WERE TALLIED BY POWER STAT + DIE ROLL + RESULT OF STEP 1.

THIS ROUND, 86 PEOPLE FOULED OUT.

SCORE -	14	13	12	11	10	9	8	7	6	5	4
PEOPLE -	2	10	23	33	44	59	64	31	29	13	6

TOTAL: 314 PEOPLE

THERE WERE TWO PEOPLE TIED FOR FIRST PLACE WITH 14 POINTS. TEN TIED FOR SECOND WITH 13 POINTS.

FIRST PLACE: EN AND CLARE

SECOND PLACE: RENGE, MICHAELUCY, ONIGIRI, SHINA-EMON, YOSHIKAWA CLASS 2-5, KANA, HIDE, SATOSHI, TODOROCKY AND IBIRO

○ ROUNDS THREE, FOUR AND FIVE WERE EVENTS WHERE TIMING STATS WERE CRUCIAL. IT WAS TOUGH FOR HUNTERS WITH LOW TIMING, BUT IF THEY SURVIVE, THE POINTS ALLOCATED TO OTHER STATS WILL COME IN USEFUL. CLARE GETS FIRST PLACE FOR TWO ROUNDS IN A ROW!! AWESOME!!

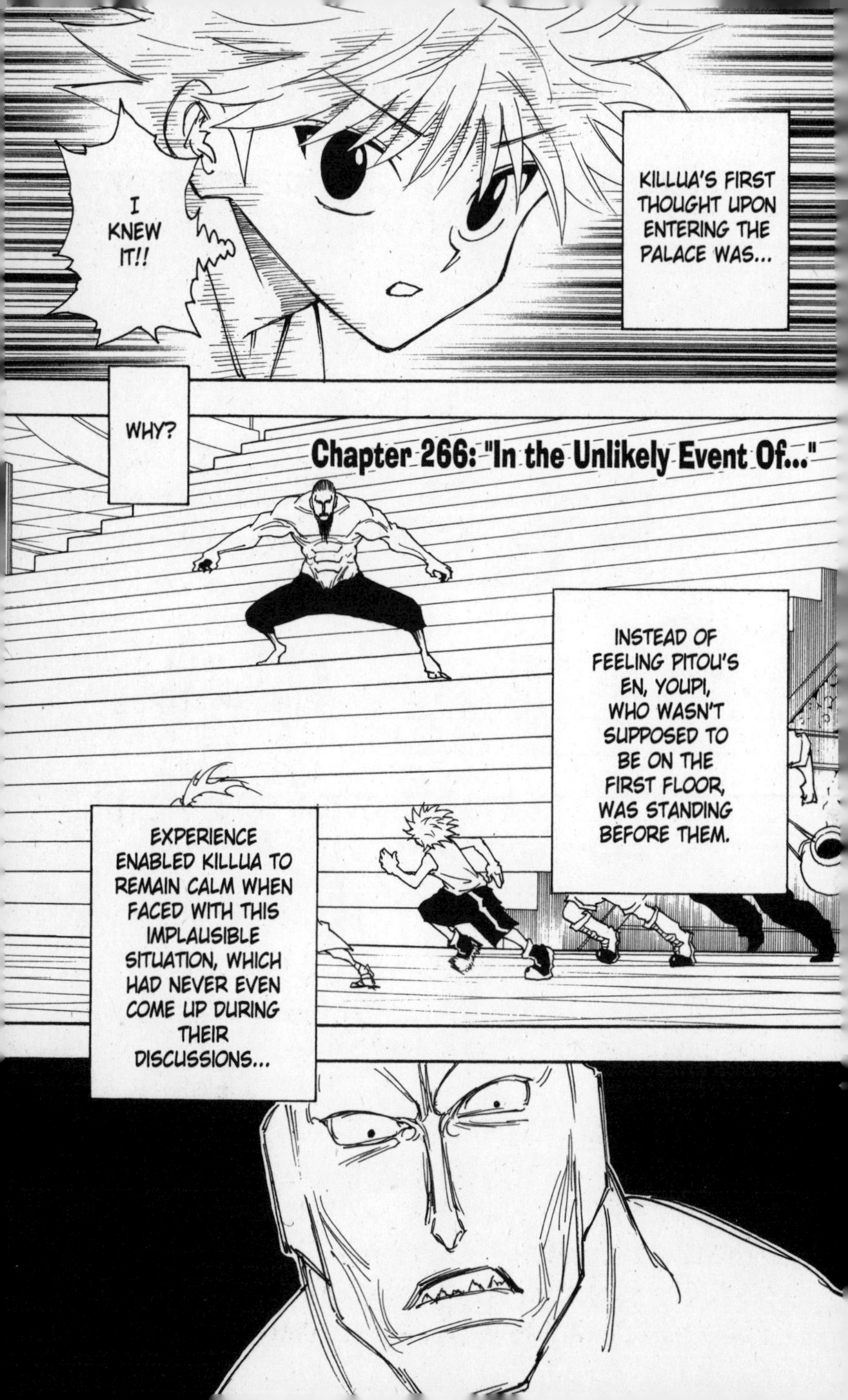
KILLUA'S FIRST THOUGHT UPON ENTERING THE PALACE WAS...
I KNEW IT!!
WHY?
Chapter 266: "In the Unlikely Event Of..."
INSTEAD OF FEELING PITOU'S EN, YOUPI, WHO WASN'T SUPPOSED TO BE ON THE FIRST FLOOR, WAS STANDING BEFORE THEM.
EXPERIENCE ENABLED KILLUA TO REMAIN CALM WHEN FACED WITH THIS IMPLAUSIBLE SITUATION, WHICH HAD NEVER EVEN COME UP DURING THEIR DISCUSSIONS...

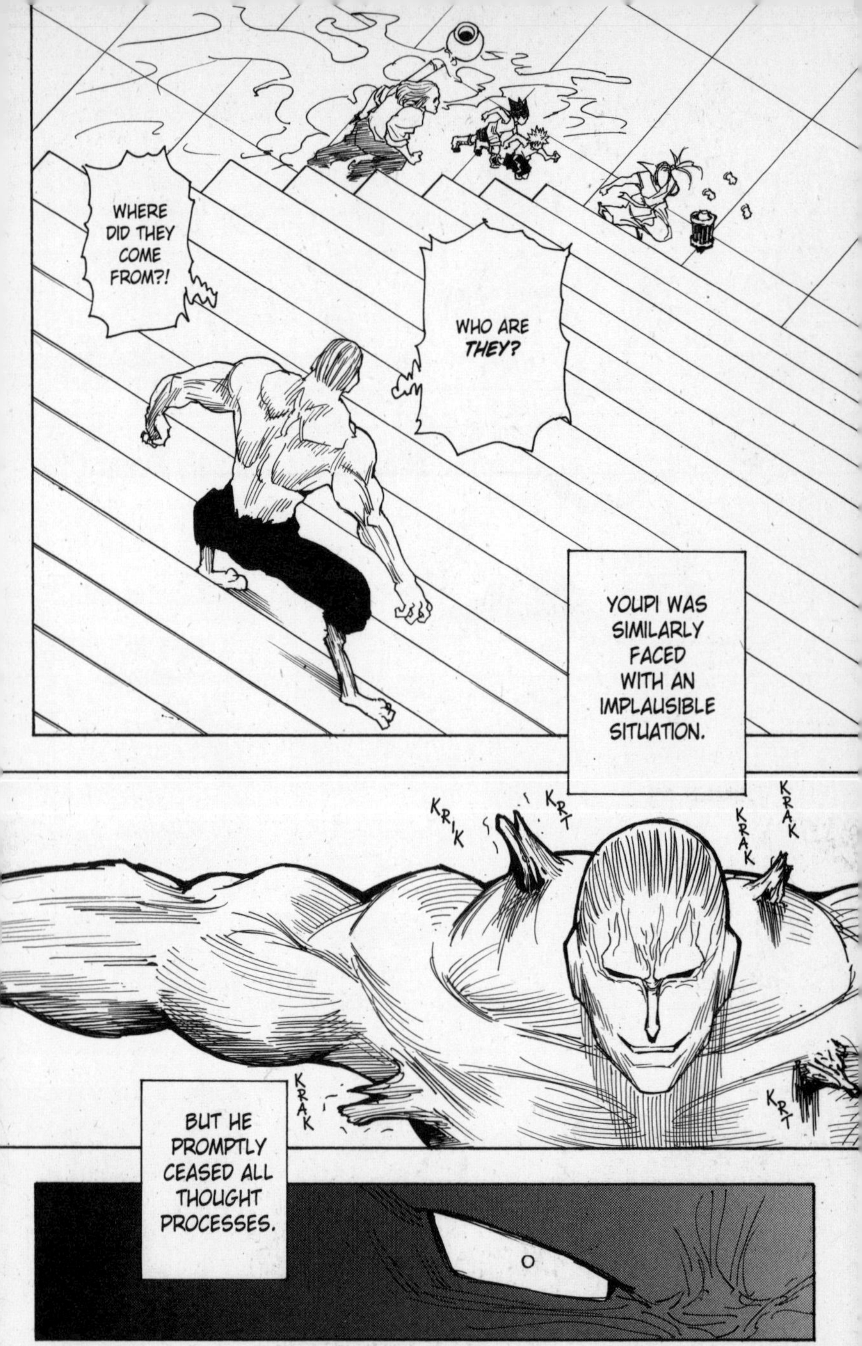
WHO ARE THEY?
WHERE DID THEY COME FROM?!
YOUPI WAS SIMILARLY FACED WITH AN IMPLAUSIBLE SITUATION.
KRAK
KRAK
KRT
KRIK
KRT
KRAK
BUT HE PROMPTLY CEASED ALL THOUGHT PROCESSES.

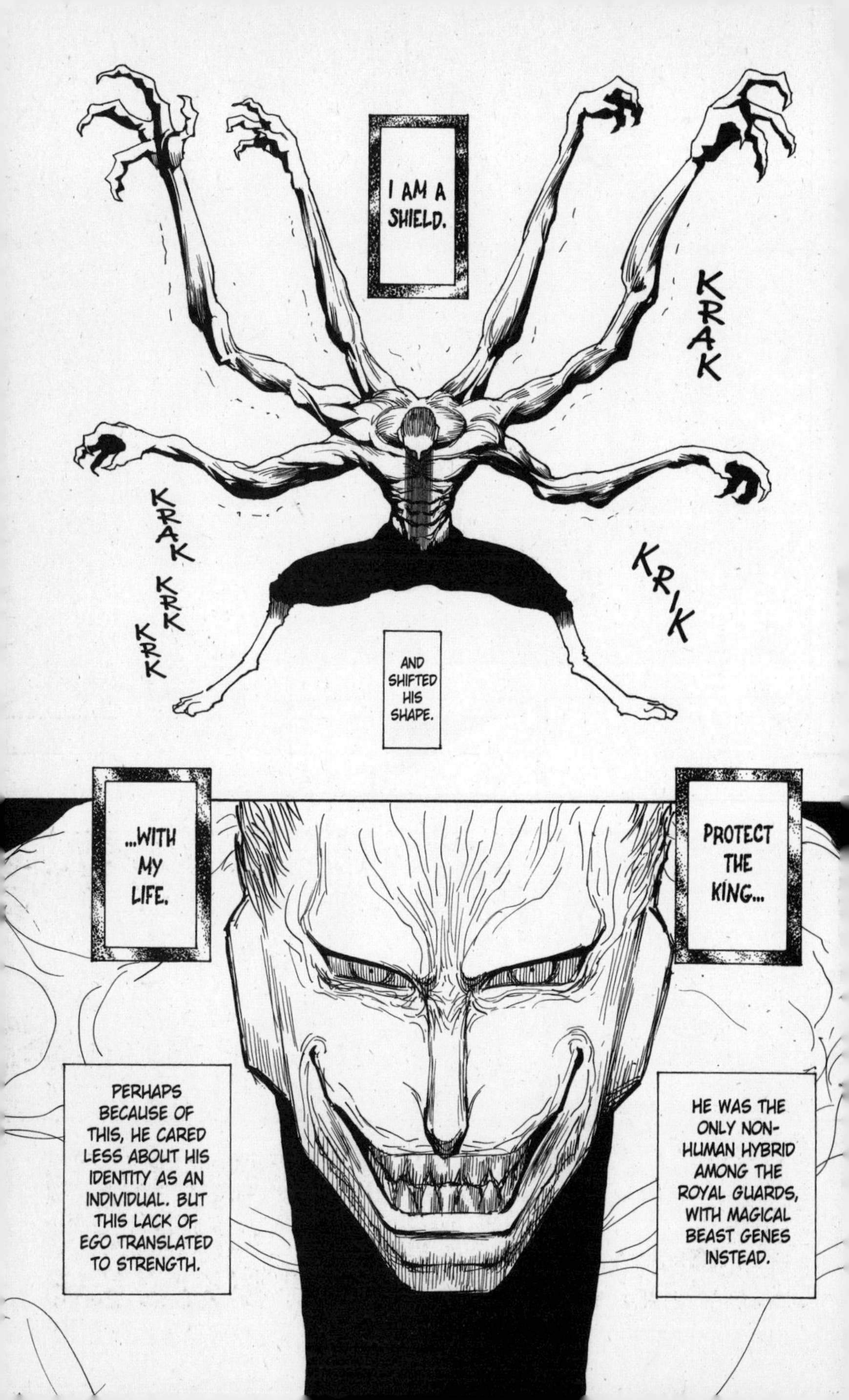
I AM A SHIELD.
KRAK
KRIK
KRAK KRK KRK
AND SHIFTED HIS SHAPE.
PROTECT THE KING...
...WITH MY LIFE.
HE WAS THE ONLY NON-HUMAN HYBRID AMONG THE ROYAL GUARDS, WITH MAGICAL BEAST GENES INSTEAD.
PERHAPS BECAUSE OF THIS, HE CARED LESS ABOUT HIS IDENTITY AS AN INDIVIDUAL. BUT THIS LACK OF EGO TRANSLATED TO STRENGTH.

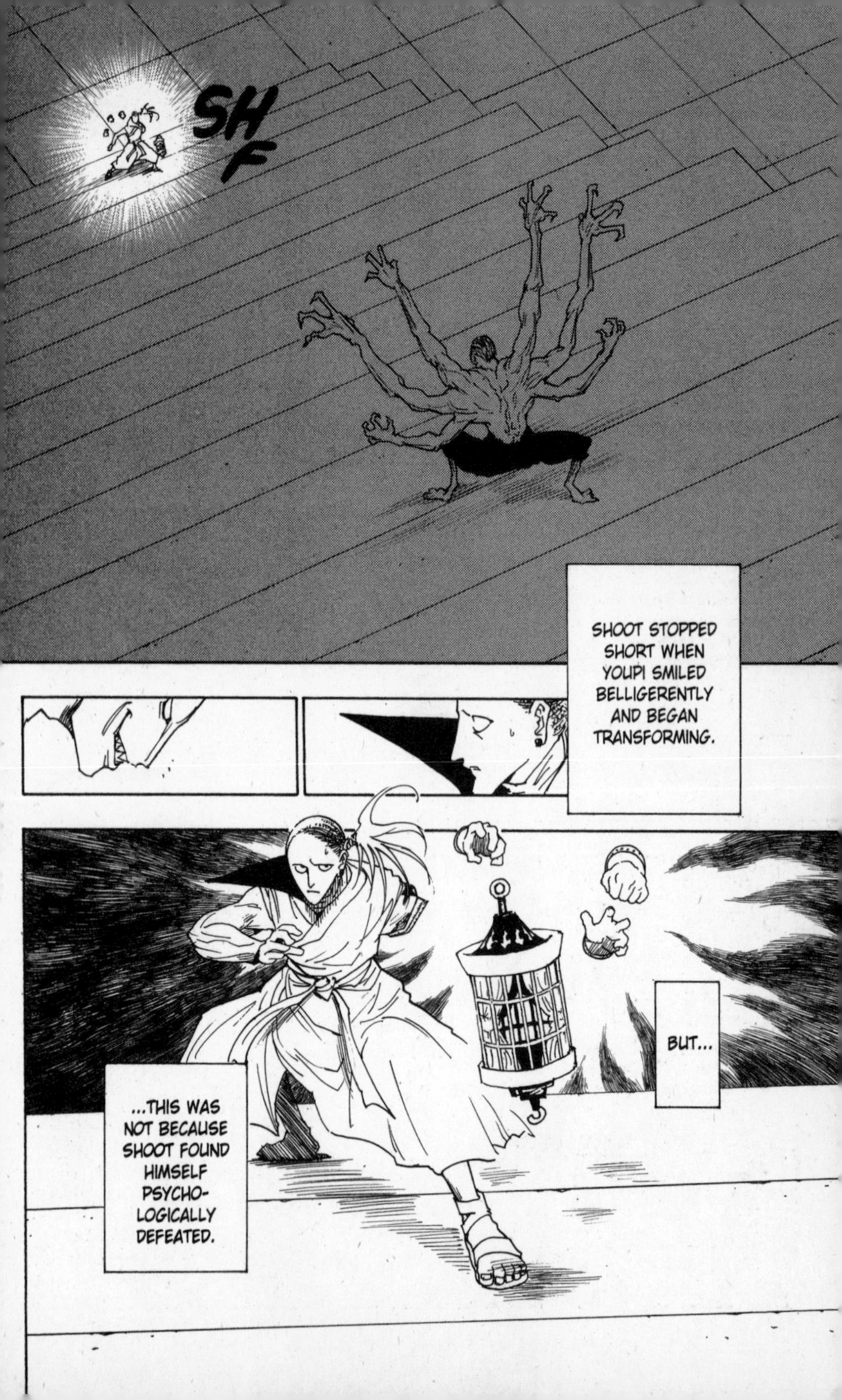
SHF
SHOOT STOPPED SHORT WHEN YOUPI SMILED BELLIGERENTLY AND BEGAN TRANSFORMING.
BUT...
...THIS WAS NOT BECAUSE SHOOT FOUND HIMSELF PSYCHO-LOGICALLY DEFEATED.

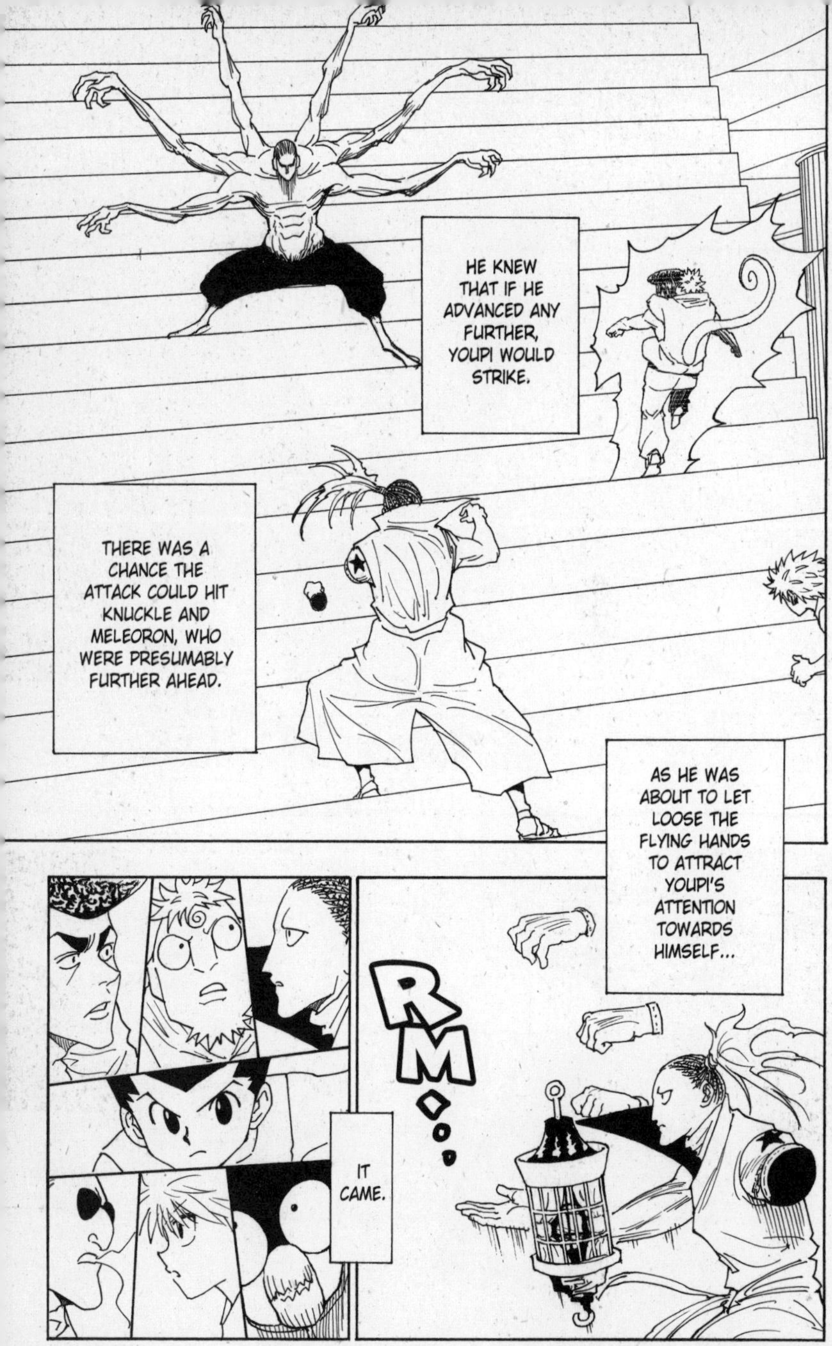
HE KNEW THAT IF HE ADVANCED ANY FURTHER, YOUPI WOULD STRIKE.
THERE WAS A CHANCE THE ATTACK COULD HIT KNUCKLE AND MELEORON, WHO WERE PRESUMABLY FURTHER AHEAD.
AS HE WAS ABOUT TO LET LOOSE THE FLYING HANDS TO ATTRACT YOUPI'S ATTENTION TOWARDS HIMSELF...
RMOO
IT CAME.

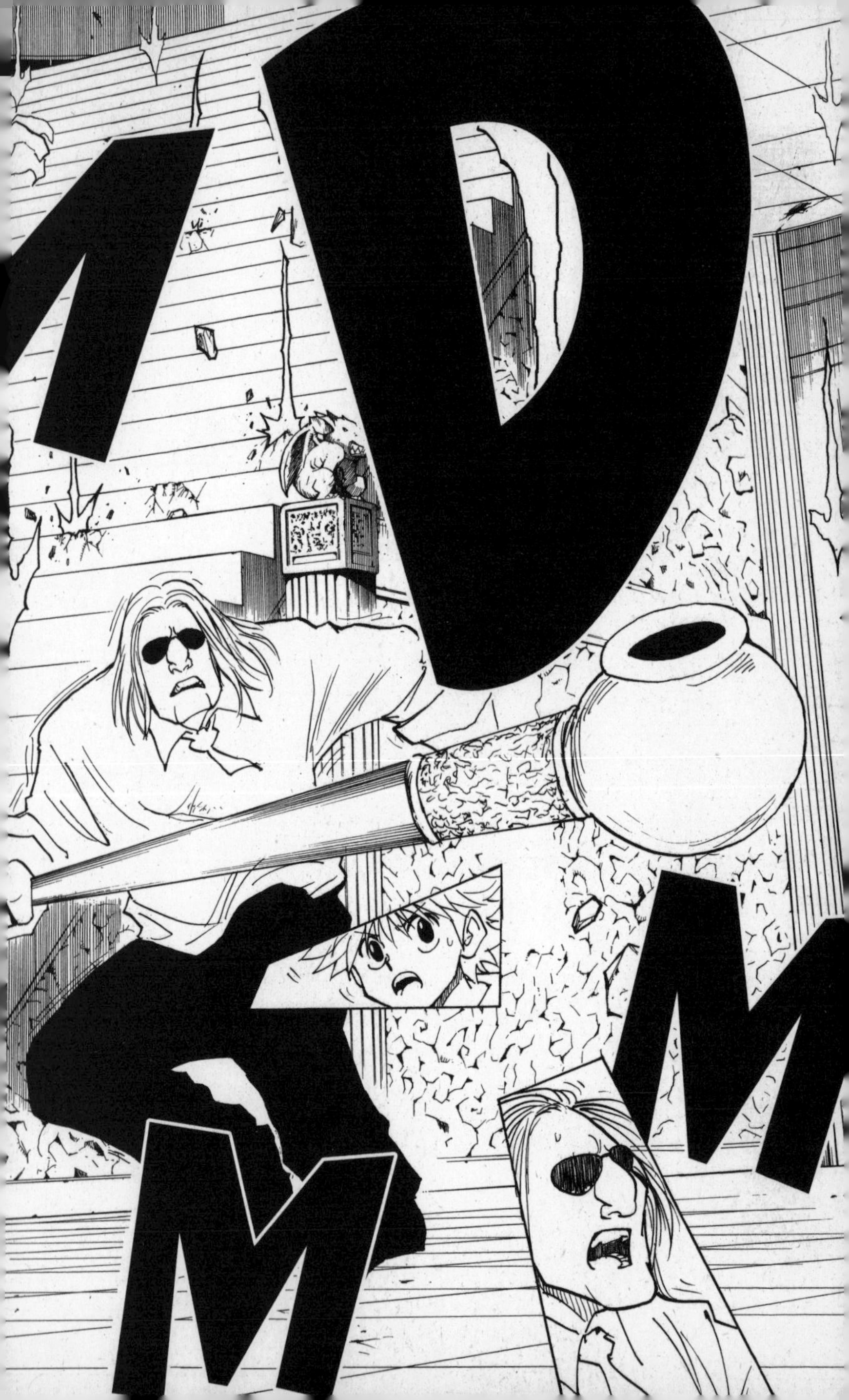

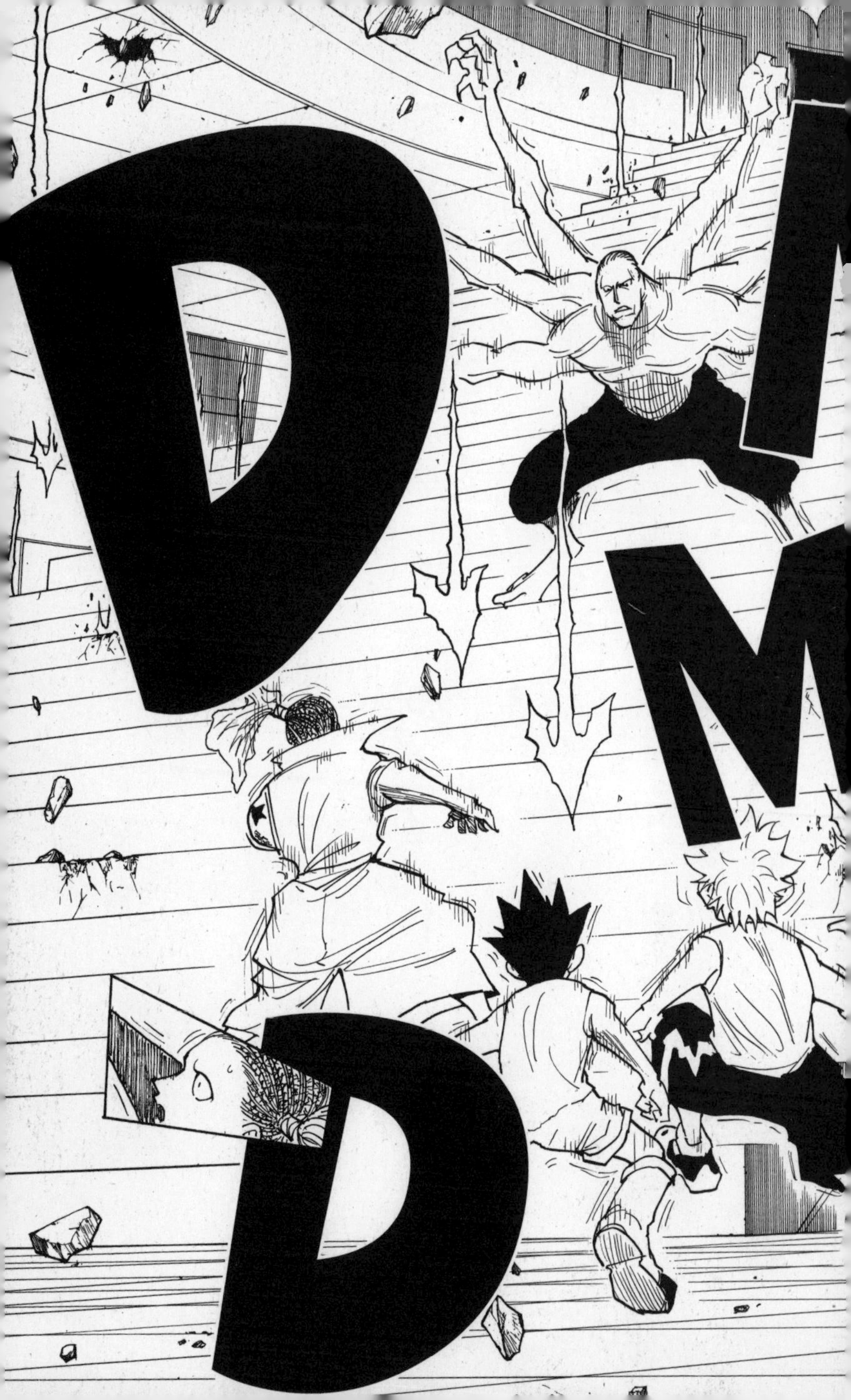

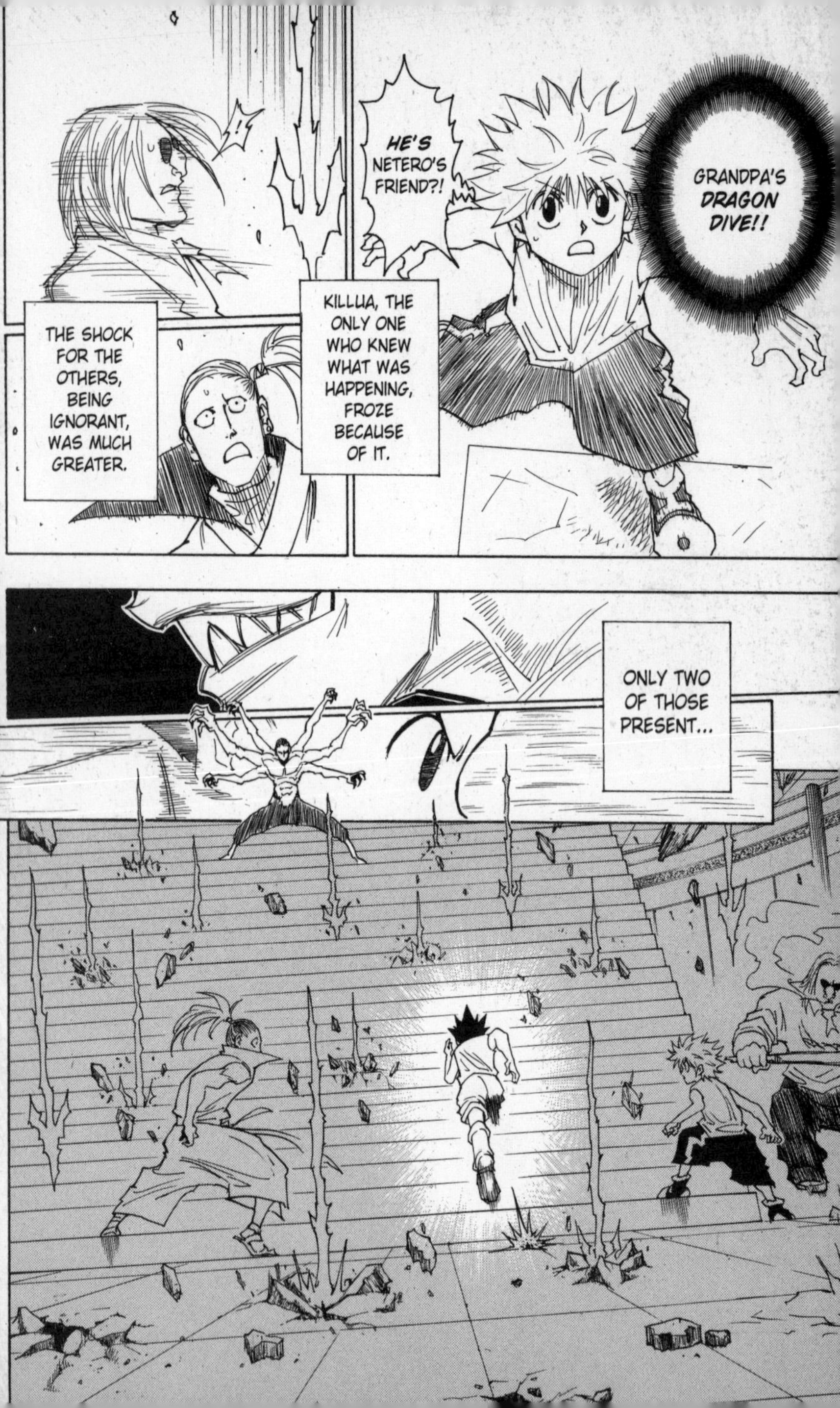
GRANDPA'S DRAGON DIVE!!
HE'S NETERO'S FRIEND?!
KILLUA, THE ONLY ONE WHO KNEW WHAT WAS HAPPENING, FROZE BECAUSE OF IT.
THE SHOCK FOR THE OTHERS, BEING IGNORANT, WAS MUCH GREATER.
ONLY TWO OF THOSE PRESENT...

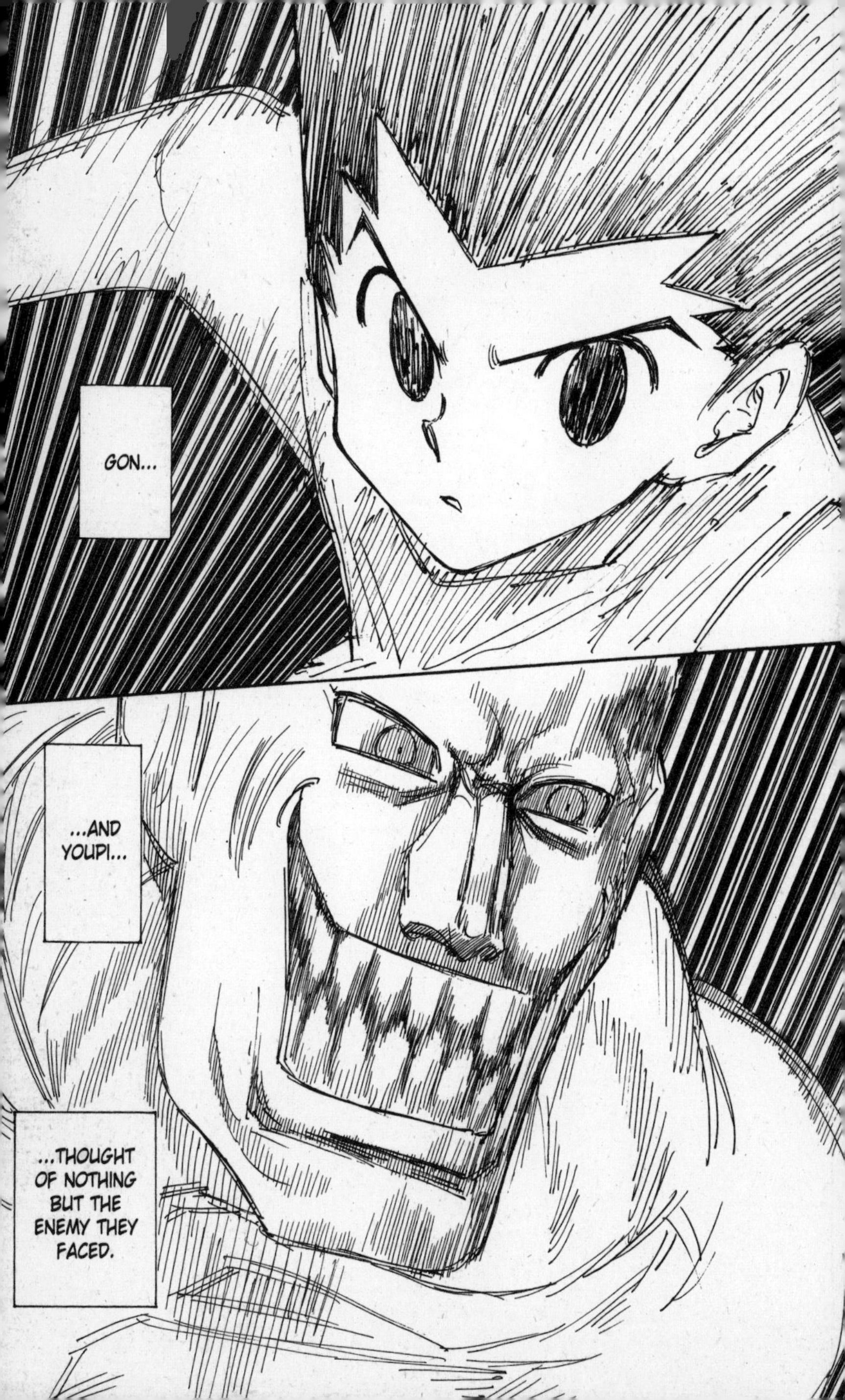
GON...
...AND YOUPI...
...THOUGHT OF NOTHING BUT THE ENEMY THEY FACED.

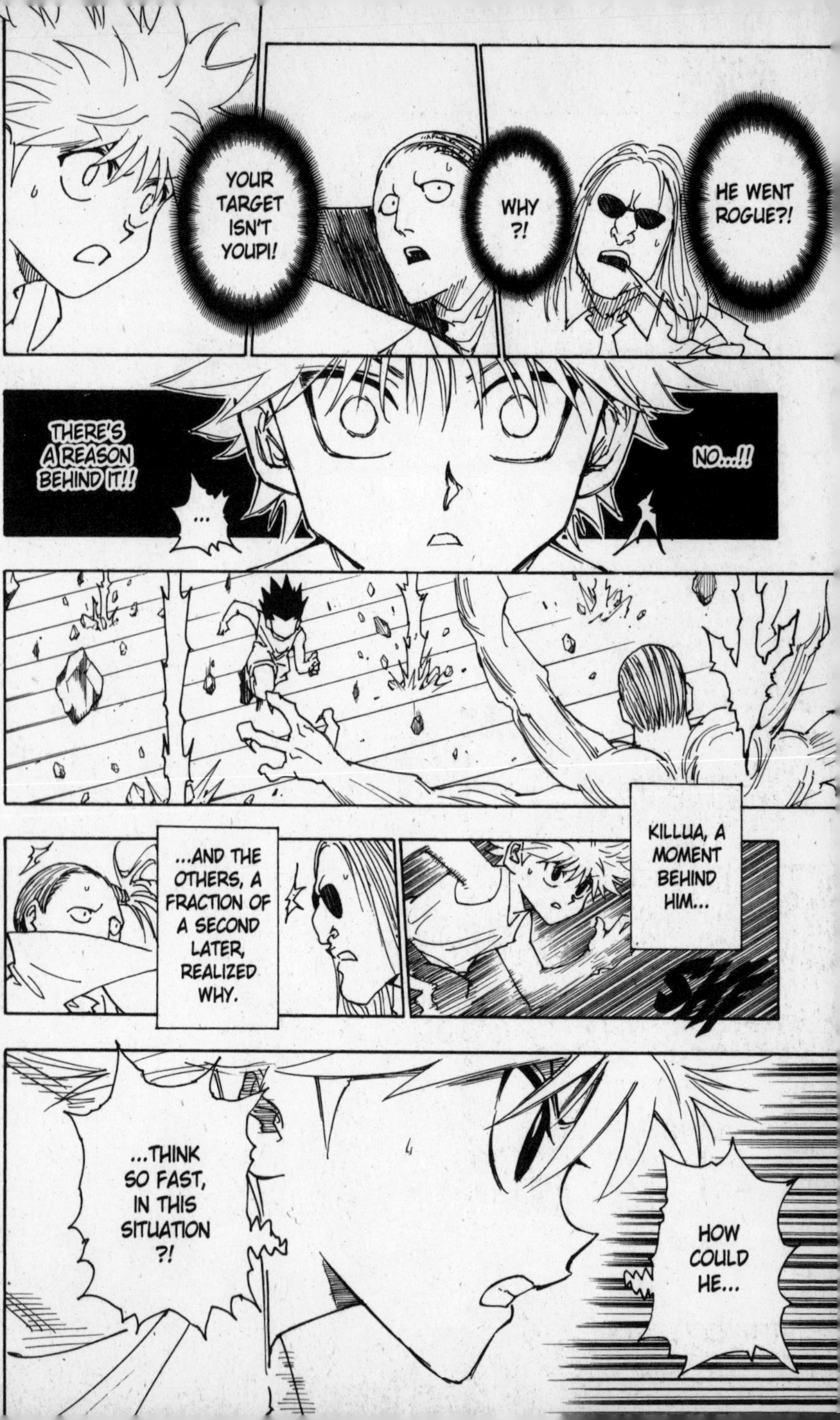
HE WENT ROGUE?!
WHY ?!
YOUR TARGET ISN'T YOUPI!
NO...!!
THERE'S A REASON BEHIND IT!!
...
KILLUA, A MOMENT BEHIND HIM...
SHF
...AND THE OTHERS, A FRACTION OF A SECOND LATER, REALIZED WHY.
HOW COULD HE...
...THINK SO FAST, IN THIS SITUATION ?!

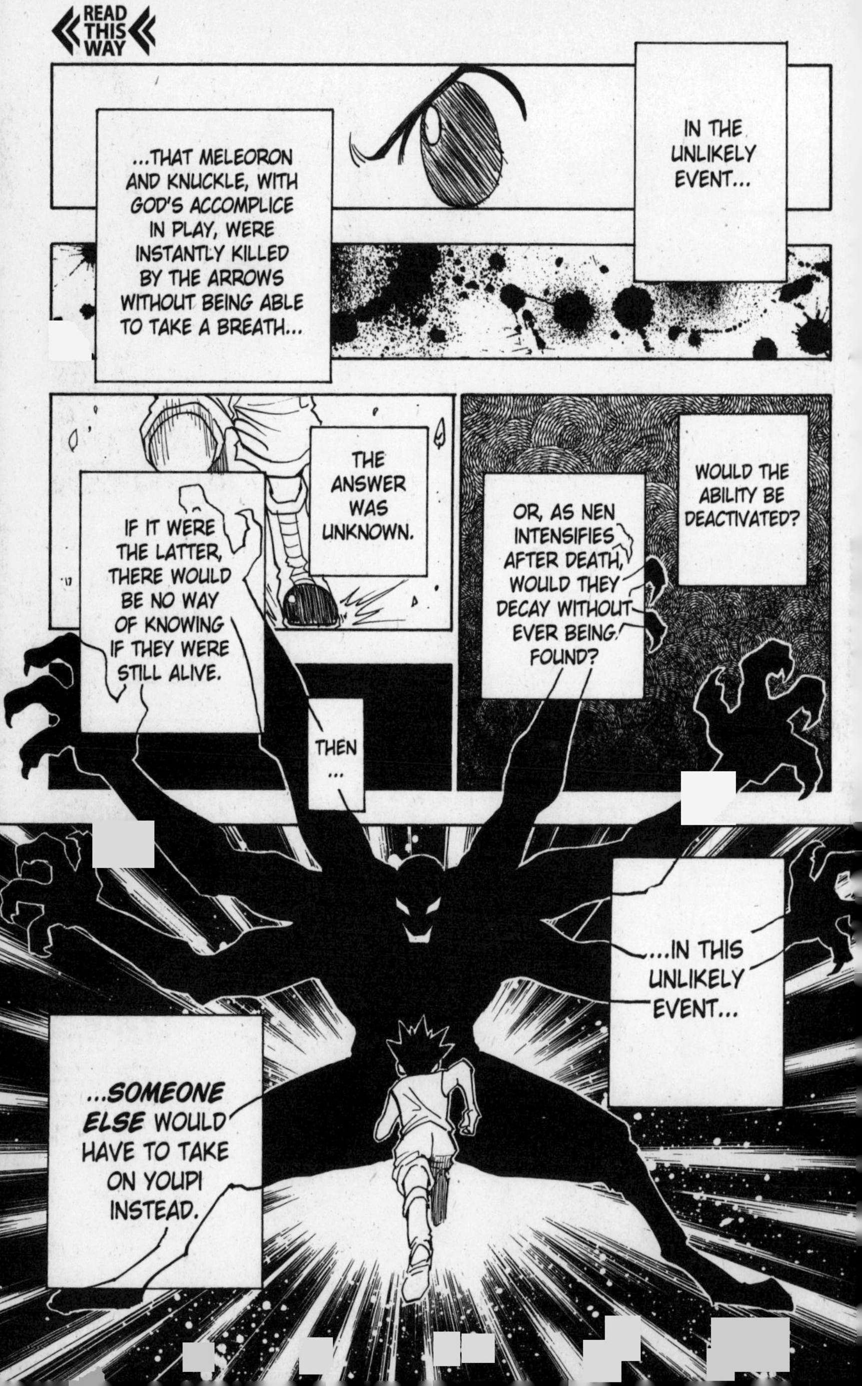
READ THIS WAY
IN THE UNLIKELY EVENT...
...THAT MELEORON AND KNUCKLE, WITH GOD'S ACCOMPLICE IN PLAY, WERE INSTANTLY KILLED BY THE ARROWS WITHOUT BEING ABLE TO TAKE A BREATH...
WOULD THE ABILITY BE DEACTIVATED?
OR, AS NEN INTENSIFIES AFTER DEATH, WOULD THEY DECAY WITHOUT EVER BEING FOUND?
THE ANSWER WAS UNKNOWN.
IF IT WERE THE LATTER, THERE WOULD BE NO WAY OF KNOWING IF THEY WERE STILL ALIVE.
THEN ...
...IN THIS UNLIKELY EVENT...
...SOMEONE ELSE WOULD HAVE TO TAKE ON YOUPI INSTEAD.

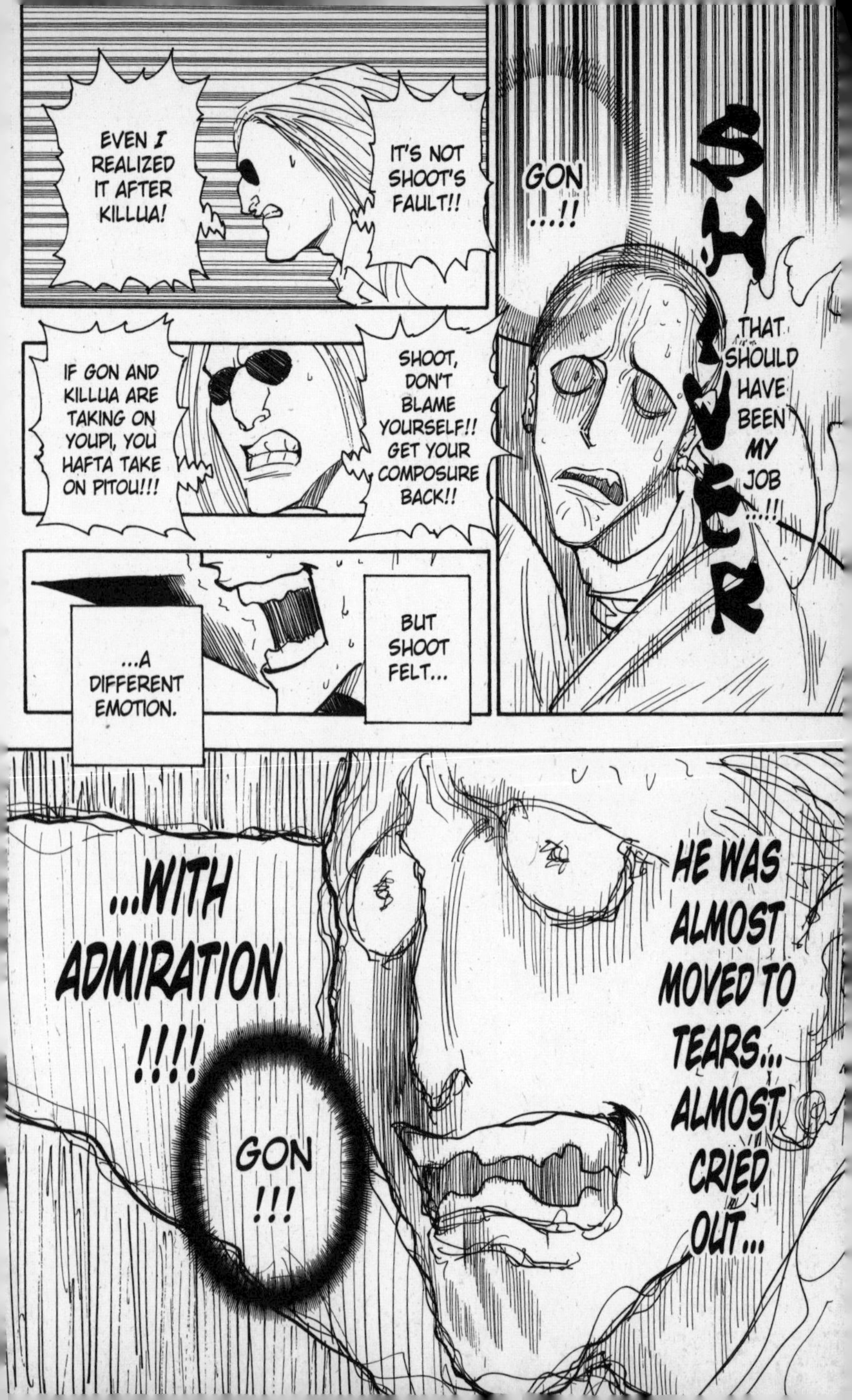
SHIVER
GON ...!!
THAT SHOULD HAVE BEEN MY JOB ...!!
IT'S NOT SHOOT'S FAULT!!
EVEN I REALIZED IT AFTER KILLUA!
SHOOT, DON'T BLAME YOURSELF!! GET YOUR COMPOSURE BACK!!
IF GON AND KILLUA ARE TAKING ON YOUPI, YOU HAFTA TAKE ON PITOU!!!
BUT SHOOT FELT...
...A DIFFERENT EMOTION.
HE WAS ALMOST MOVED TO TEARS... ALMOST CRIED OUT...
...WITH ADMIRATION !!!!
GON !!!

READ THIS WAY

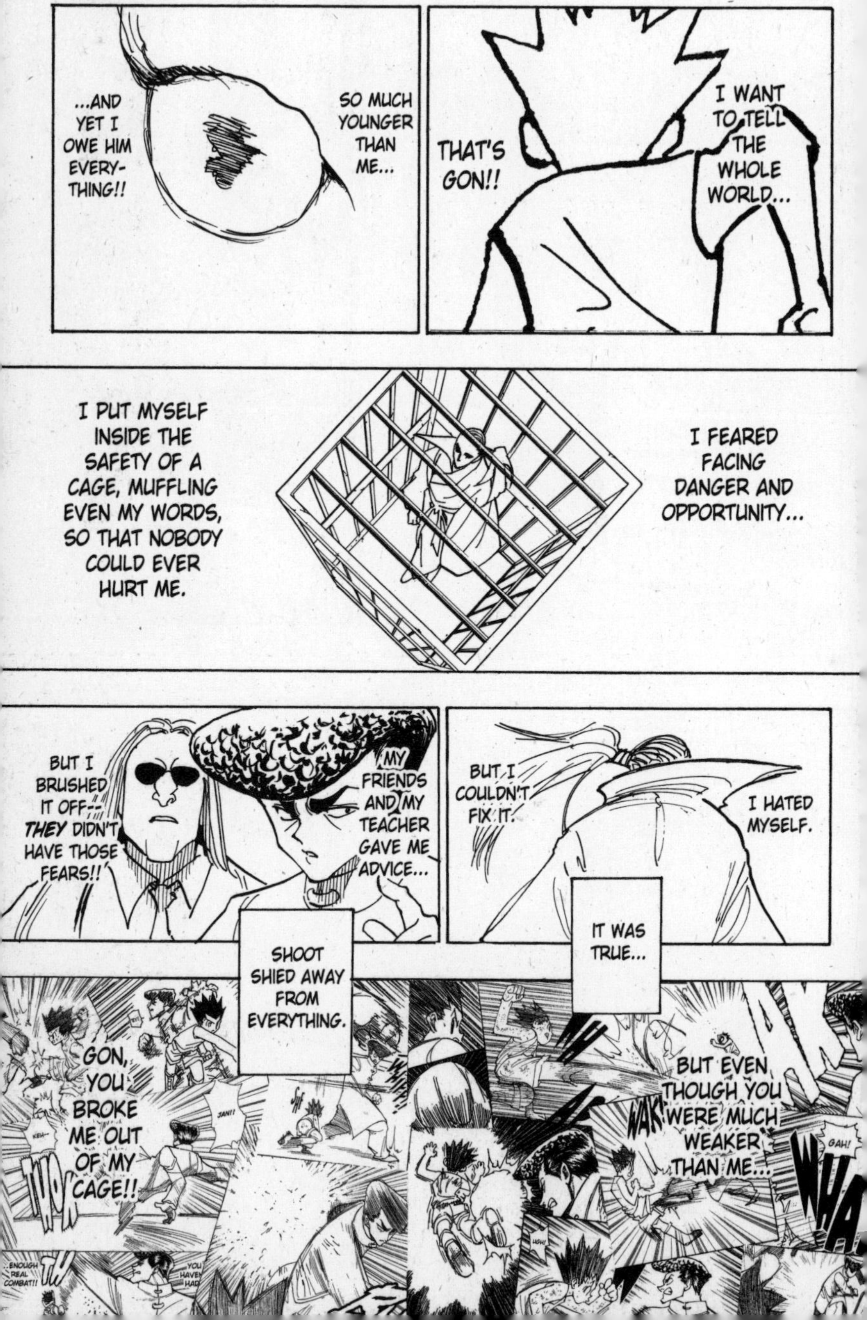
I WANT TO TELL THE WHOLE WORLD...
THAT'S GON!!
SO MUCH YOUNGER THAN ME...
...AND YET I OWE HIM EVERYTHING!!
I FEARED FACING DANGER AND OPPORTUNITY...
I PUT MYSELF INSIDE THE SAFETY OF A CAGE, MUFFLING EVEN MY WORDS, SO THAT NOBODY COULD EVER HURT ME.
I HATED MYSELF.
BUT I COULDN'T FIX IT.
IT WAS TRUE...
MY FRIENDS AND MY TEACHER GAVE ME ADVICE...
BUT I BRUSHED IT OFF-- *THEY* DIDN'T HAVE THOSE FEARS!!
SHOOT SHIED AWAY FROM EVERYTHING.
GAH!
WHA
BUT EVEN THOUGH YOU WERE MUCH WEAKER THAN ME...
WAK
JAN!!
GON, YOU BROKE ME OUT OF MY CAGE!!
THOK
ENOUGH REAL COMBAT!!

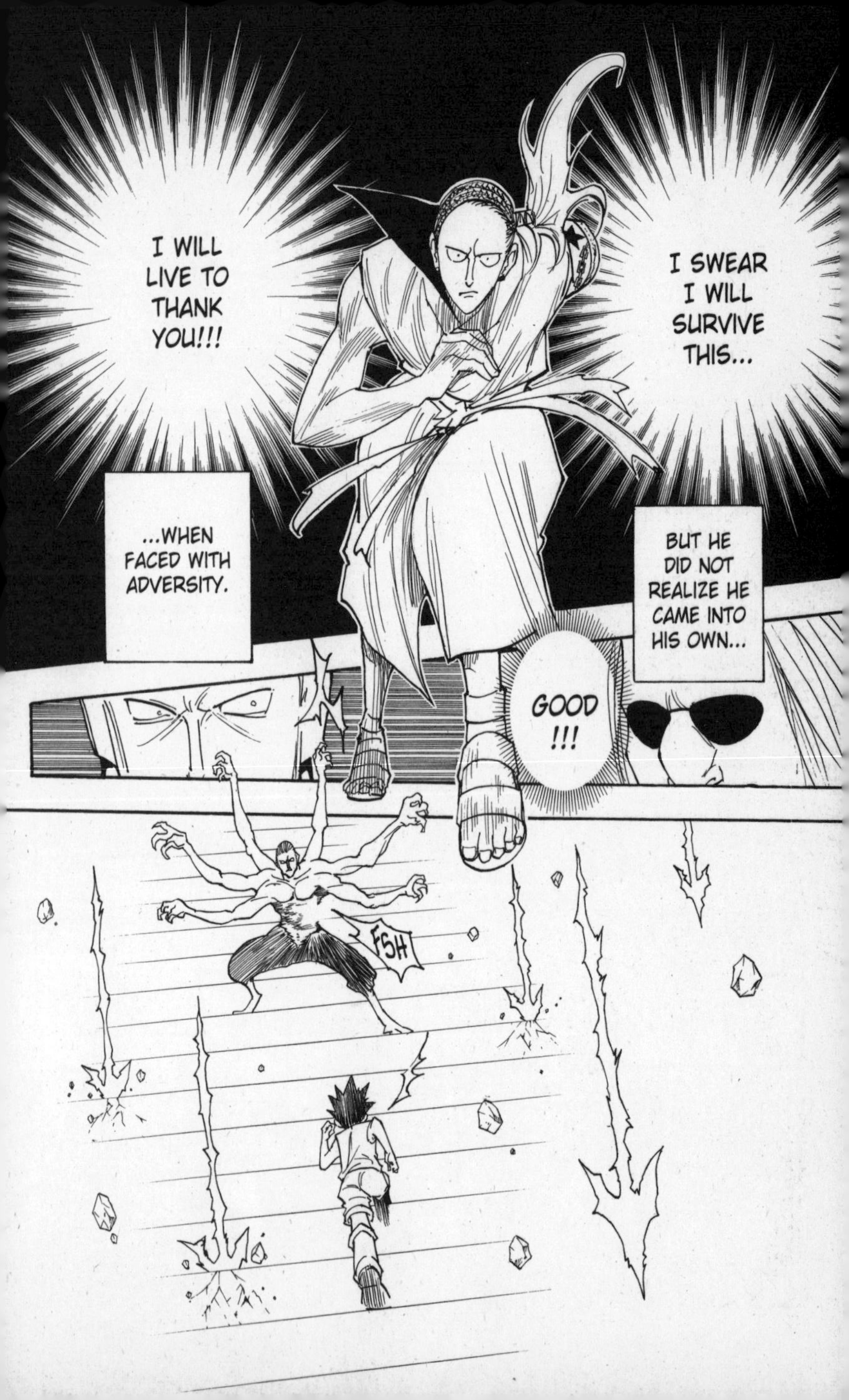
I SWEAR I WILL SURVIVE THIS...
I WILL LIVE TO THANK YOU!!!
BUT HE DID NOT REALIZE HE CAME INTO HIS OWN...
...WHEN FACED WITH ADVERSITY.
GOOD !!!
FSH

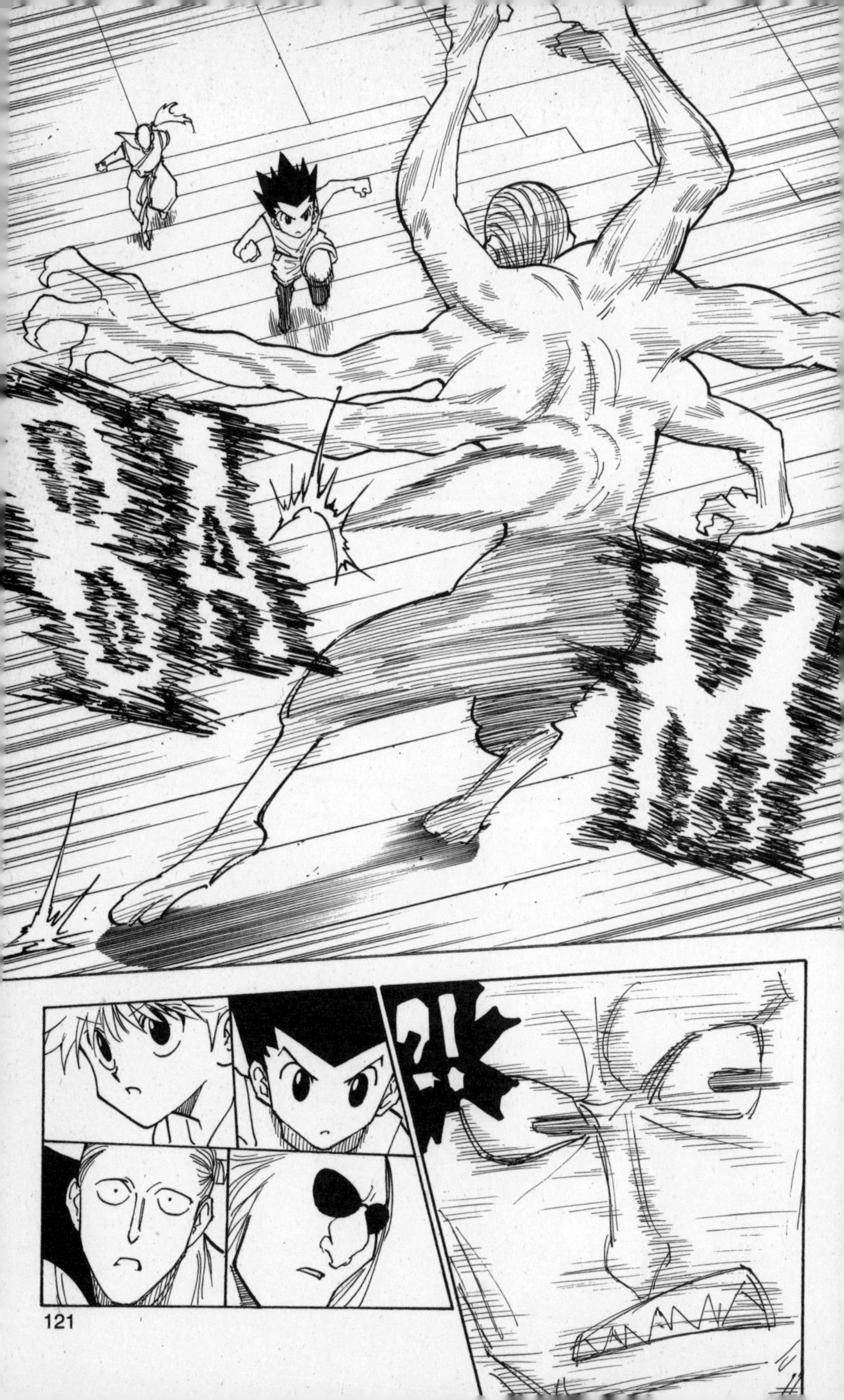
?!

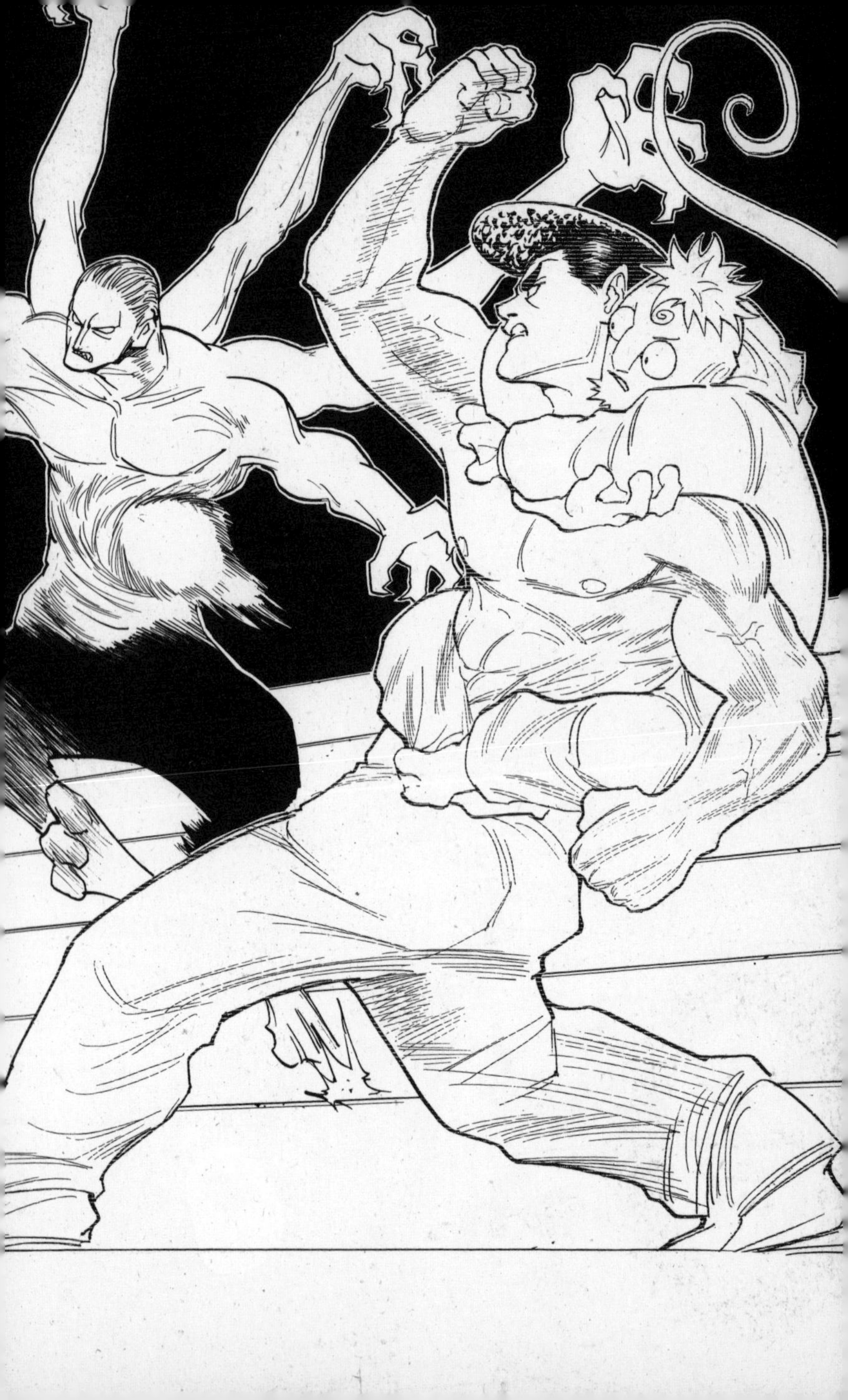

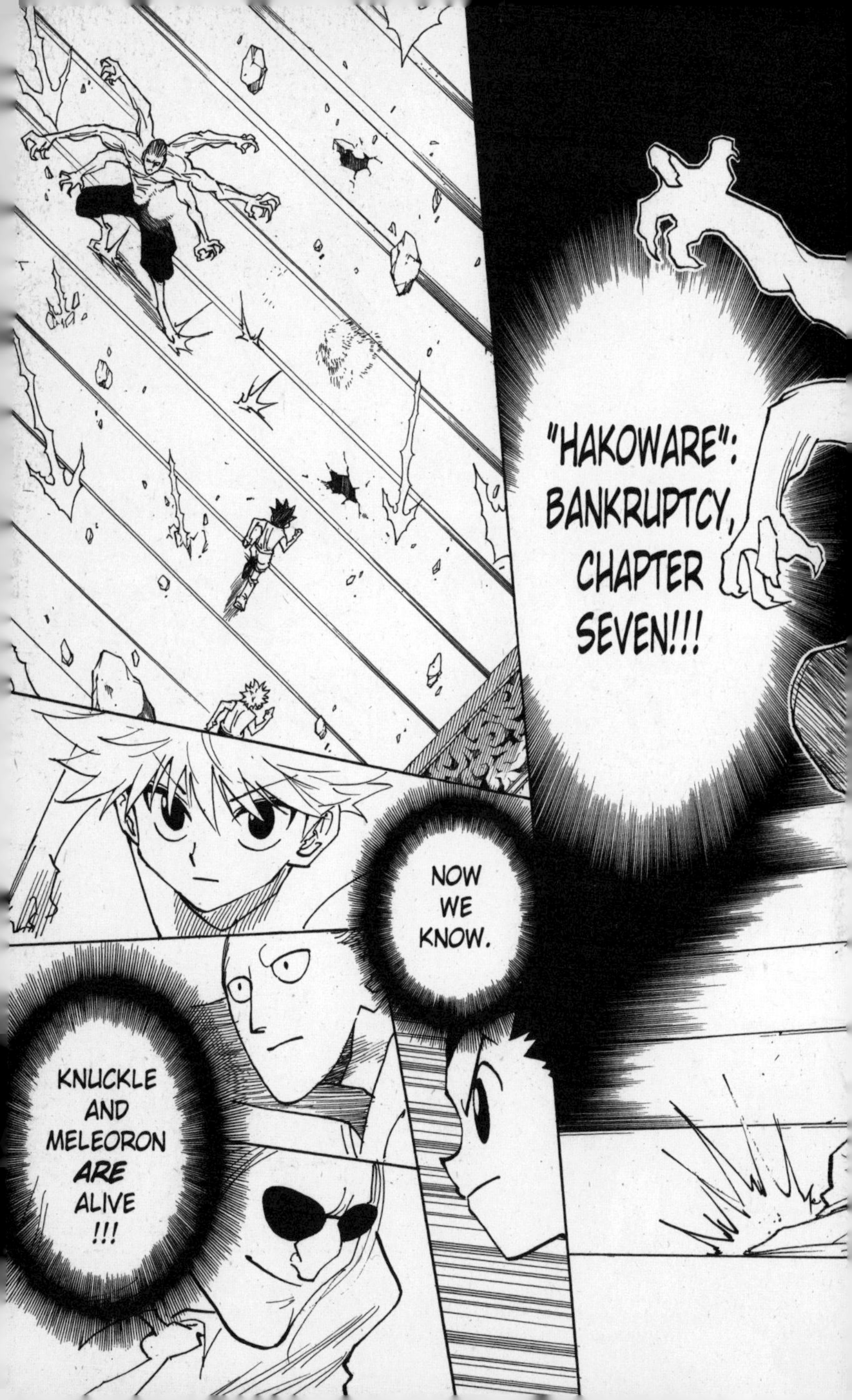
"HAKOWARE": BANKRUPTCY, CHAPTER SEVEN!!!
NOW WE KNOW.
KNUCKLE AND MELEORON ARE ALIVE!!!

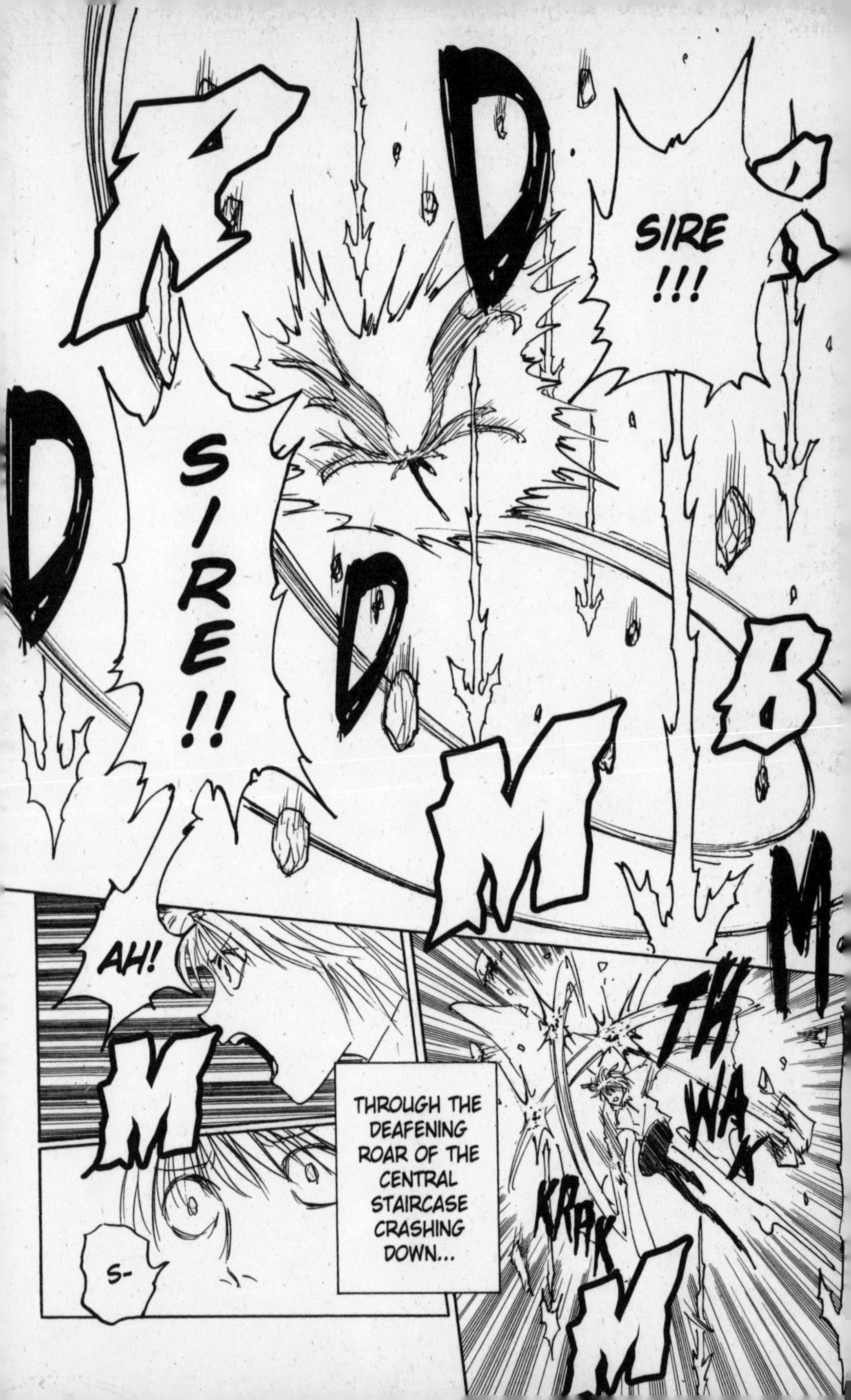
SIRE !!!
SIRE!!
THWAK
KRAK
THROUGH THE DEAFENING ROAR OF THE CENTRAL STAIRCASE CRASHING DOWN...
AH!
S-

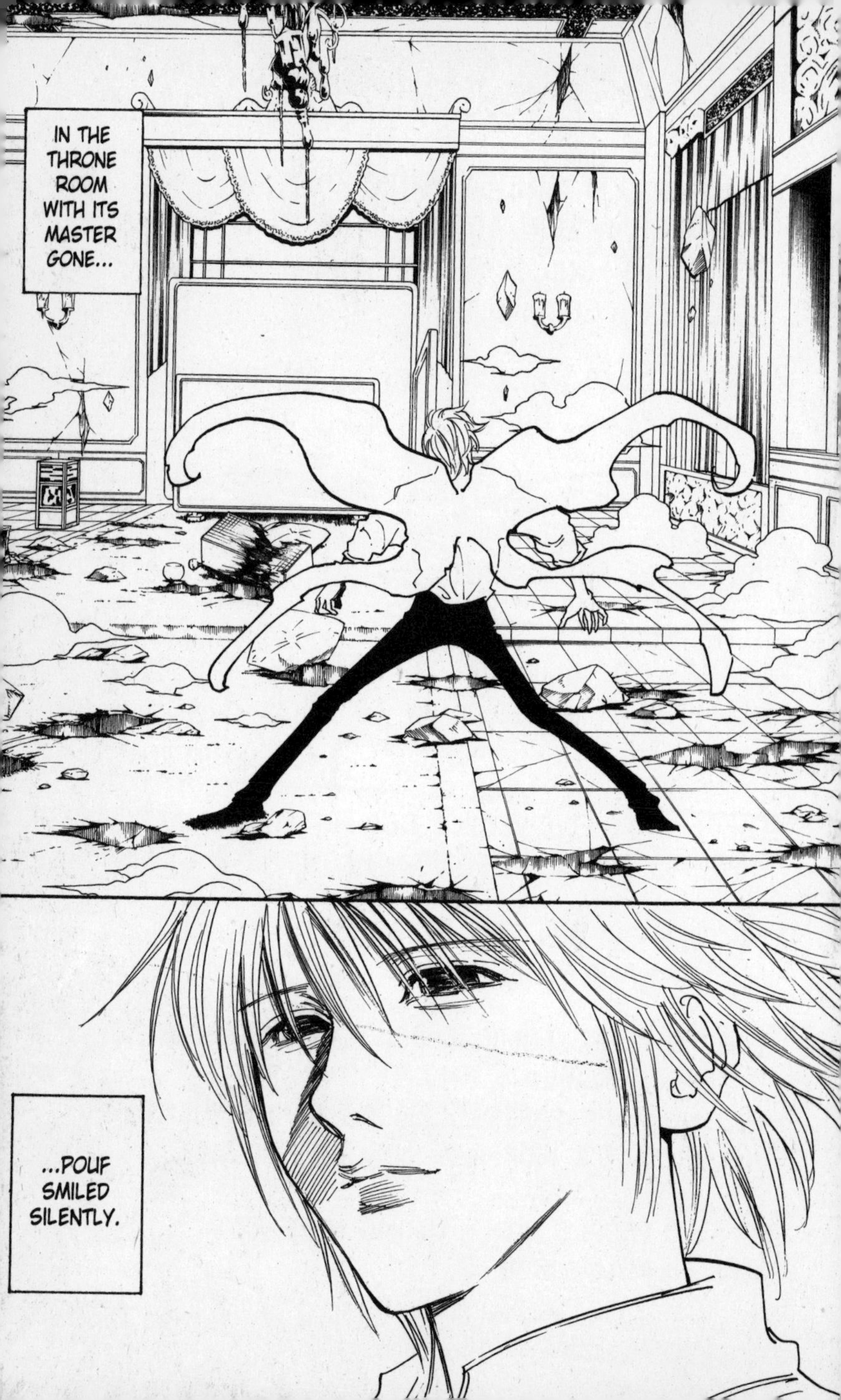
IN THE THRONE ROOM WITH ITS MASTER GONE...
...POUF SMILED SILENTLY.

ROUND FIVE: LONG JUMP

1) TIMING STAT MINUS THE DIE ROLL MUST BE MORE THAN ZERO TO MAKE THE JUMP. ZERO OR LESS IS A FOUL. IF THE FIRST ROLL IS A FOUL, YOU GET A SECOND TRY.

2) THE SCORES WERE TALLIED BY JUMP STAT + SPEED STAT + DIE ROLL + RESULT OF STEP 1.

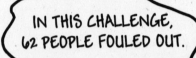

IN THIS CHALLENGE, 62 PEOPLE FOULED OUT.

SCORE -	17	16	15	14	13	12	11	10	9	8	7	6
PEOPLE -	5	16	26	33	38	44	29	32	17	9	2	1

TOTAL: 252 PEOPLE

THERE WERE FIVE PEOPLE TIED FOR FIRST PLACE WITH 17 POINTS. SIXTEEN TIED FOR SECOND WITH 16 POINTS.

FIRST PLACE: TEN-TEN, SETO BAKURA, ITO KING, GUSSURA AND TOSAKARION X

SECOND PLACE: FUMIO, ELDER MANDELA, BERSERK, R, KENJI, WACHHUND, FALCAO, K-WAFFLE, EM, KILLUA MIZUNO, ROCK-PAPER-SCISSORS, EVANS, YUKITO YŪRAKU, ACE 2, MORNING MUSUKO. AND CHIRO

○ ONLY 17 PEOPLE WITH A TIMING STAT LESS THAN 2 REMAINED!!

Chapter 267: Activation

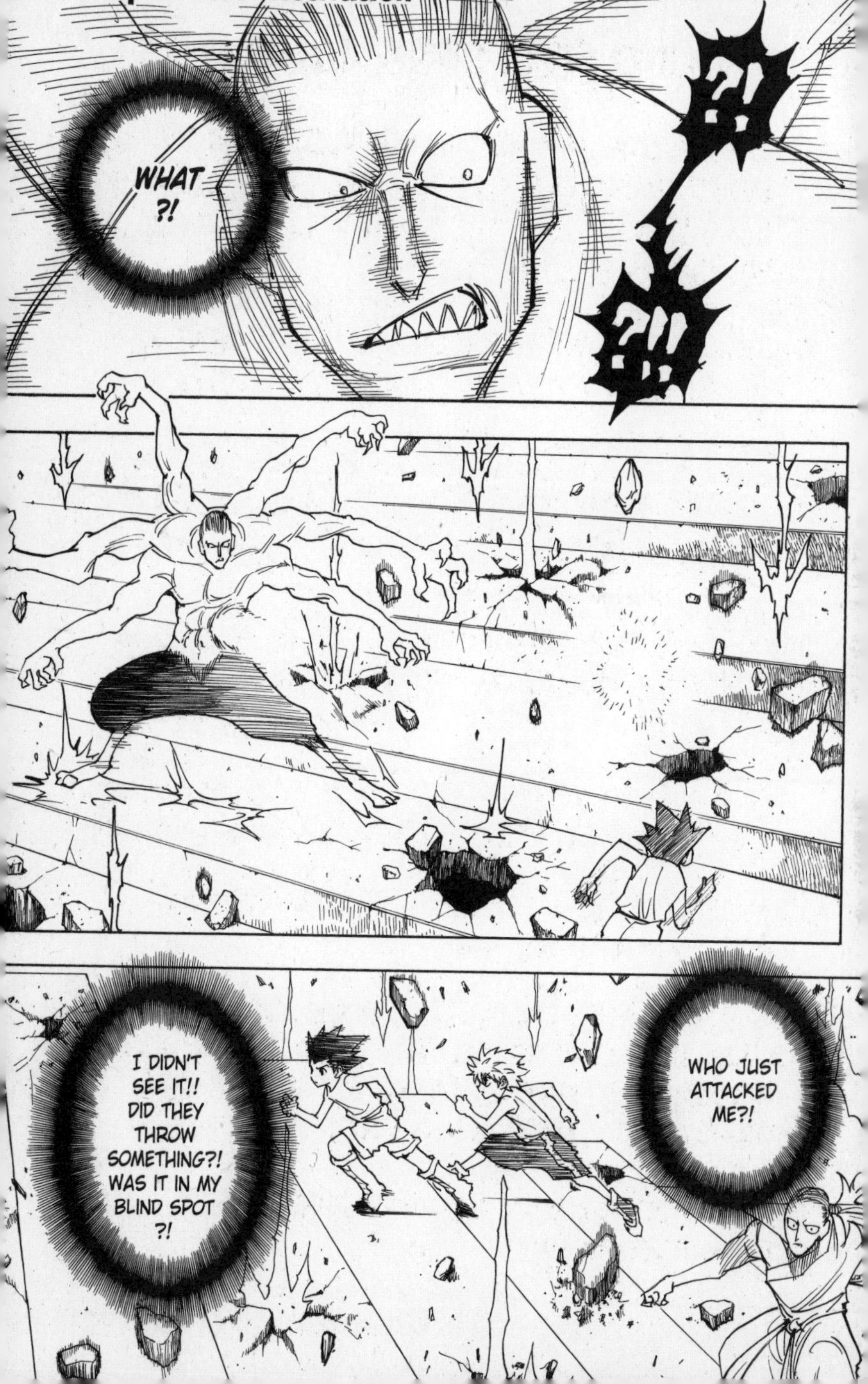
?!
?!!
WHAT ?!
WHO JUST ATTACKED ME?!
I DIDN'T SEE IT!! DID THEY THROW SOMETHING?! WAS IT IN MY BLIND SPOT ?!

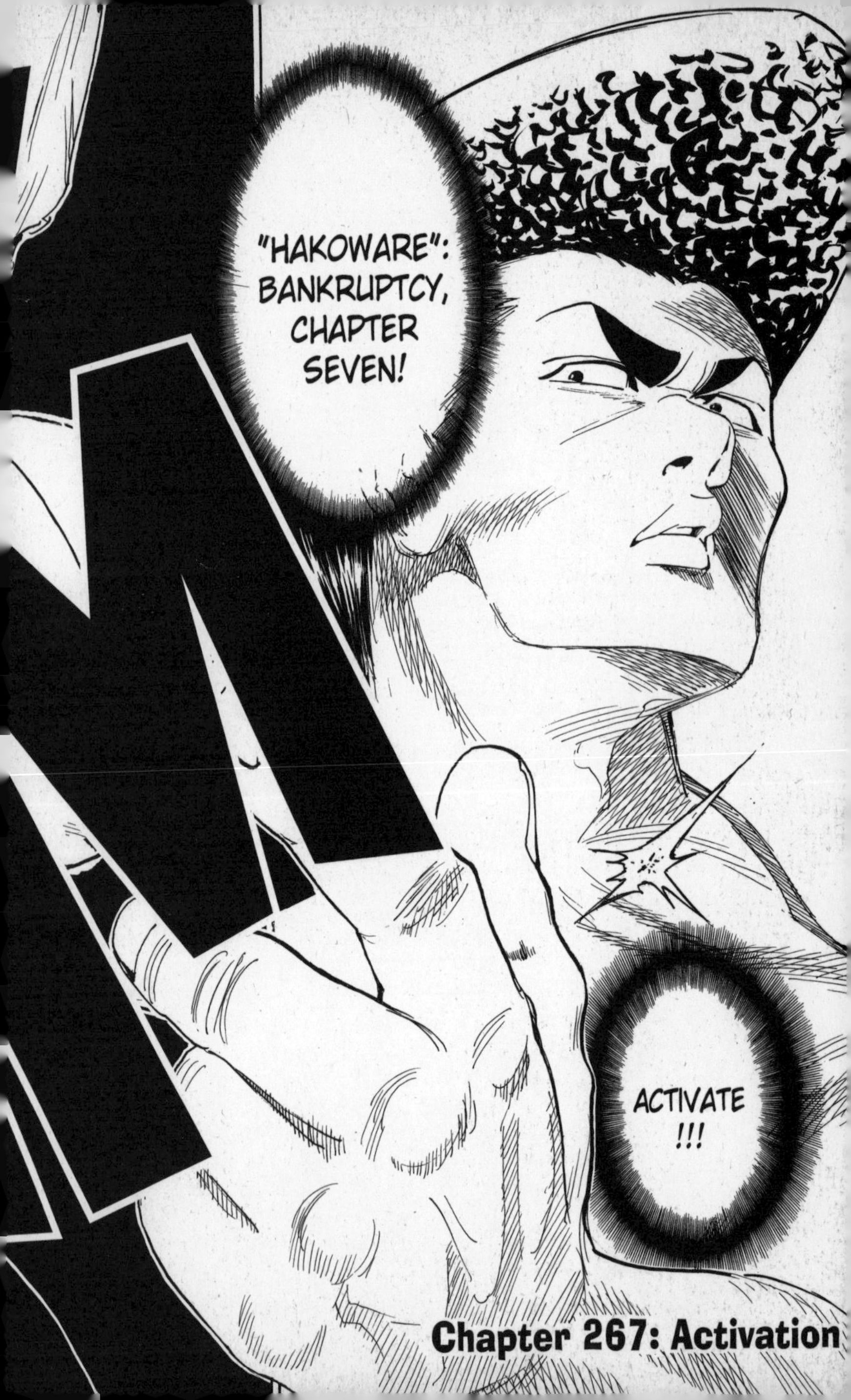
"HAKOWARE": BANKRUPTCY, CHAPTER SEVEN!
ACTIVATE !!!

Chapter 267: Activation

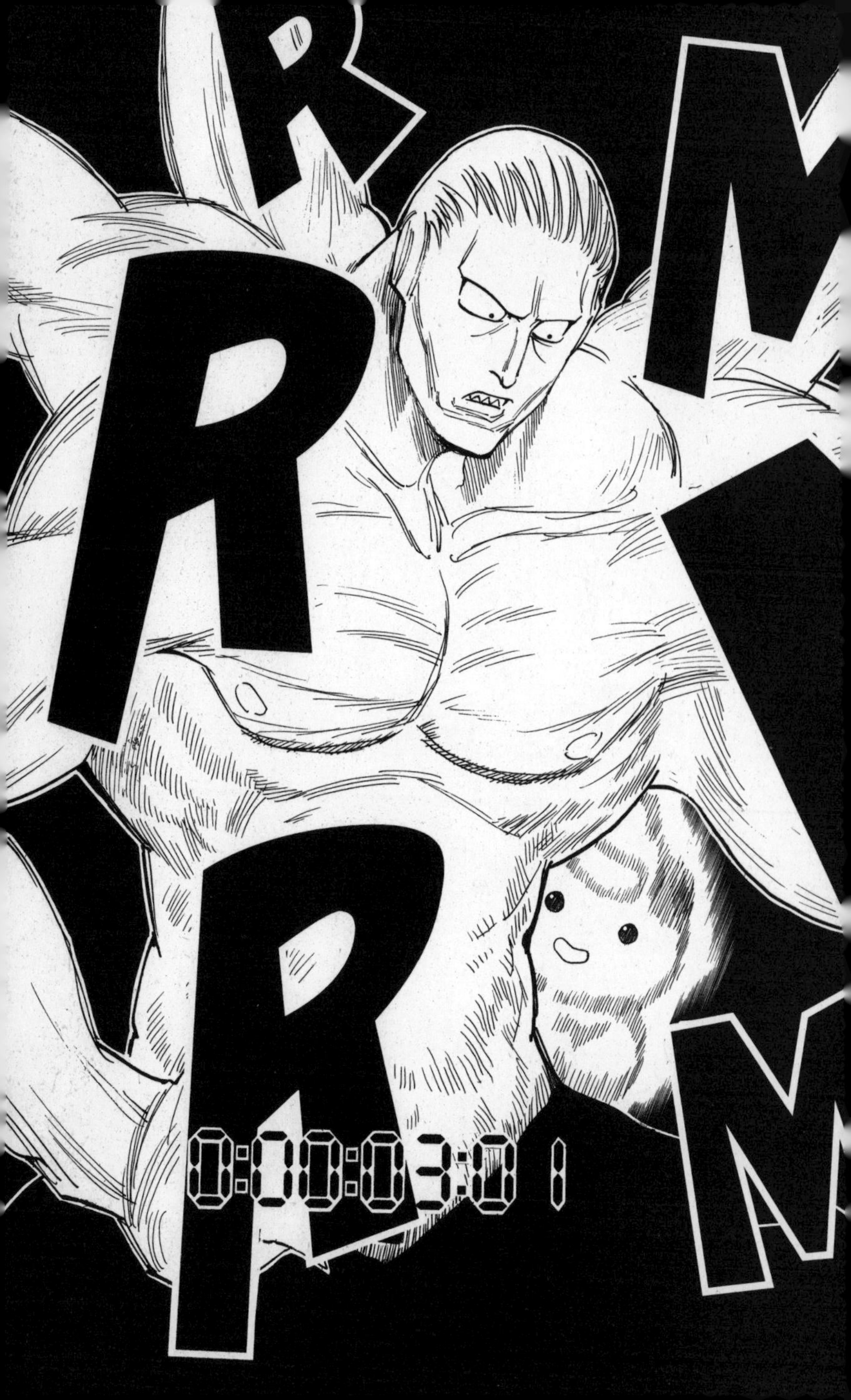
RRRMMM
0:00:03:01

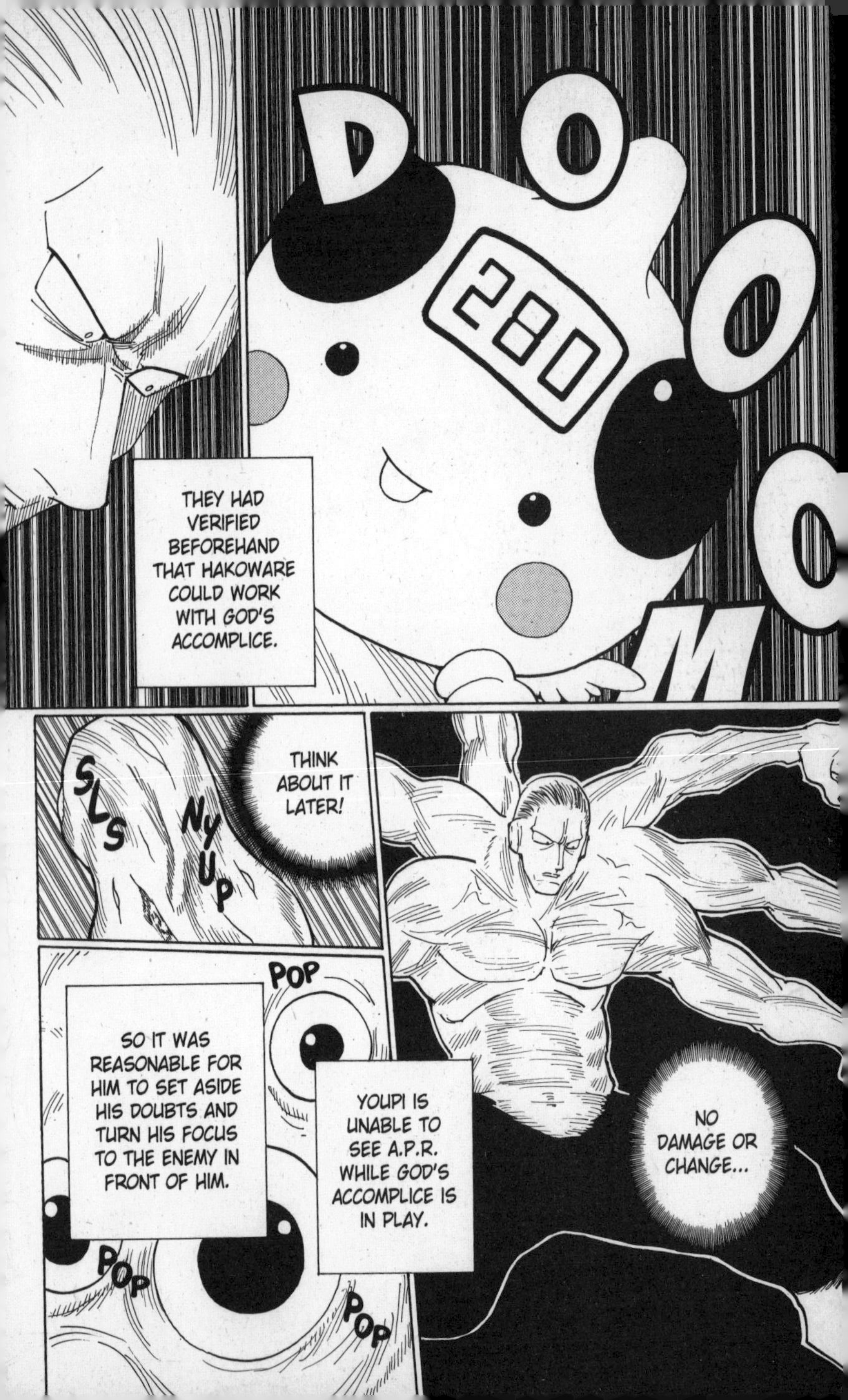
DOOOM
280
THEY HAD VERIFIED BEFOREHAND THAT HAKOWARE COULD WORK WITH GOD'S ACCOMPLICE.
NO DAMAGE OR CHANGE...
YOUPI IS UNABLE TO SEE A.P.R. WHILE GOD'S ACCOMPLICE IS IN PLAY.
THINK ABOUT IT LATER!
SLS
NYUP
POP
SO IT WAS REASONABLE FOR HIM TO SET ASIDE HIS DOUBTS AND TURN HIS FOCUS TO THE ENEMY IN FRONT OF HIM.
POP
POP

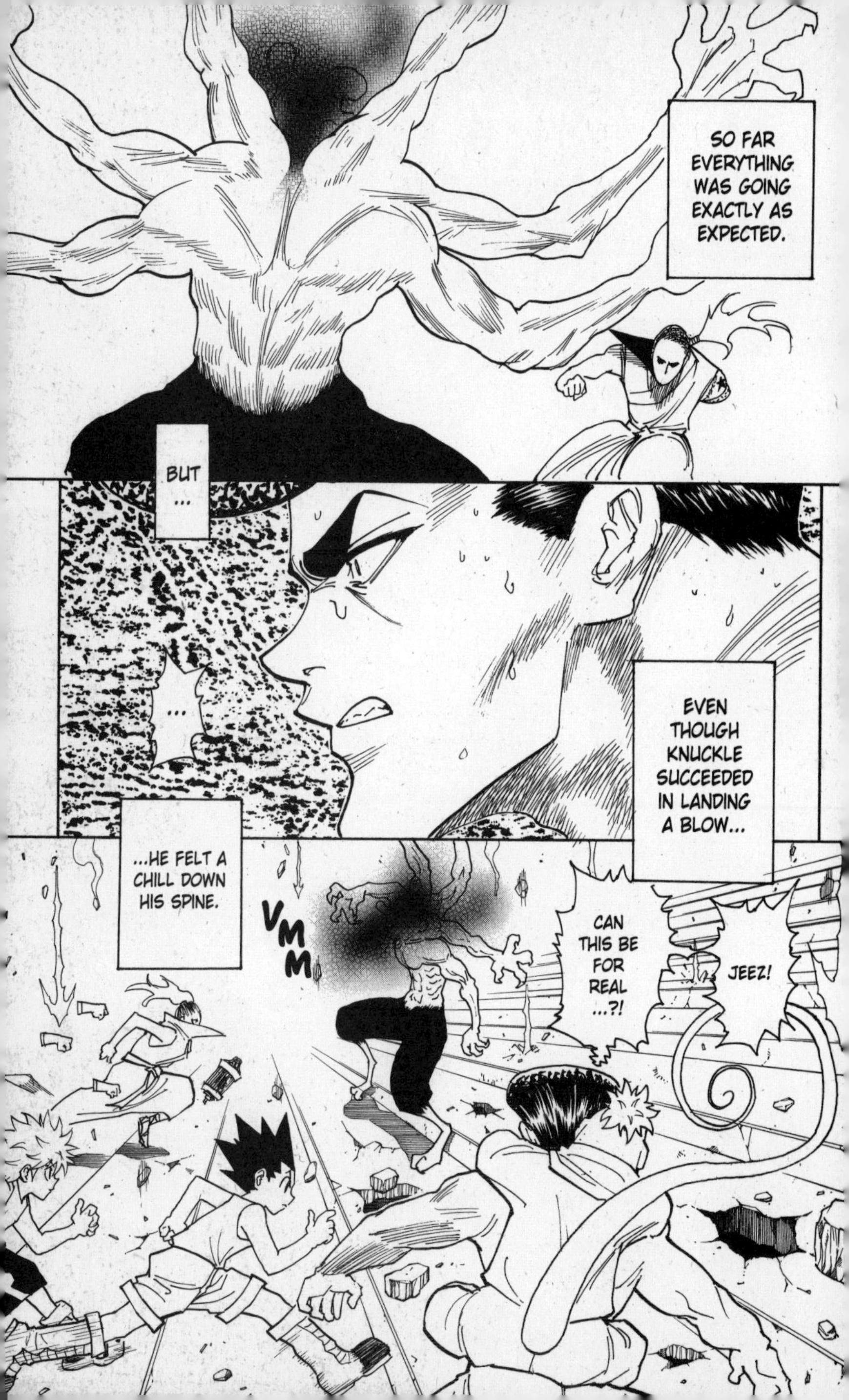

SO FAR EVERYTHING WAS GOING EXACTLY AS EXPECTED.
BUT ...
EVEN THOUGH KNUCKLE SUCCEEDED IN LANDING A BLOW...
...
...HE FELT A CHILL DOWN HIS SPINE.
JEEZ!
CAN THIS BE FOR REAL ...?!
VMM

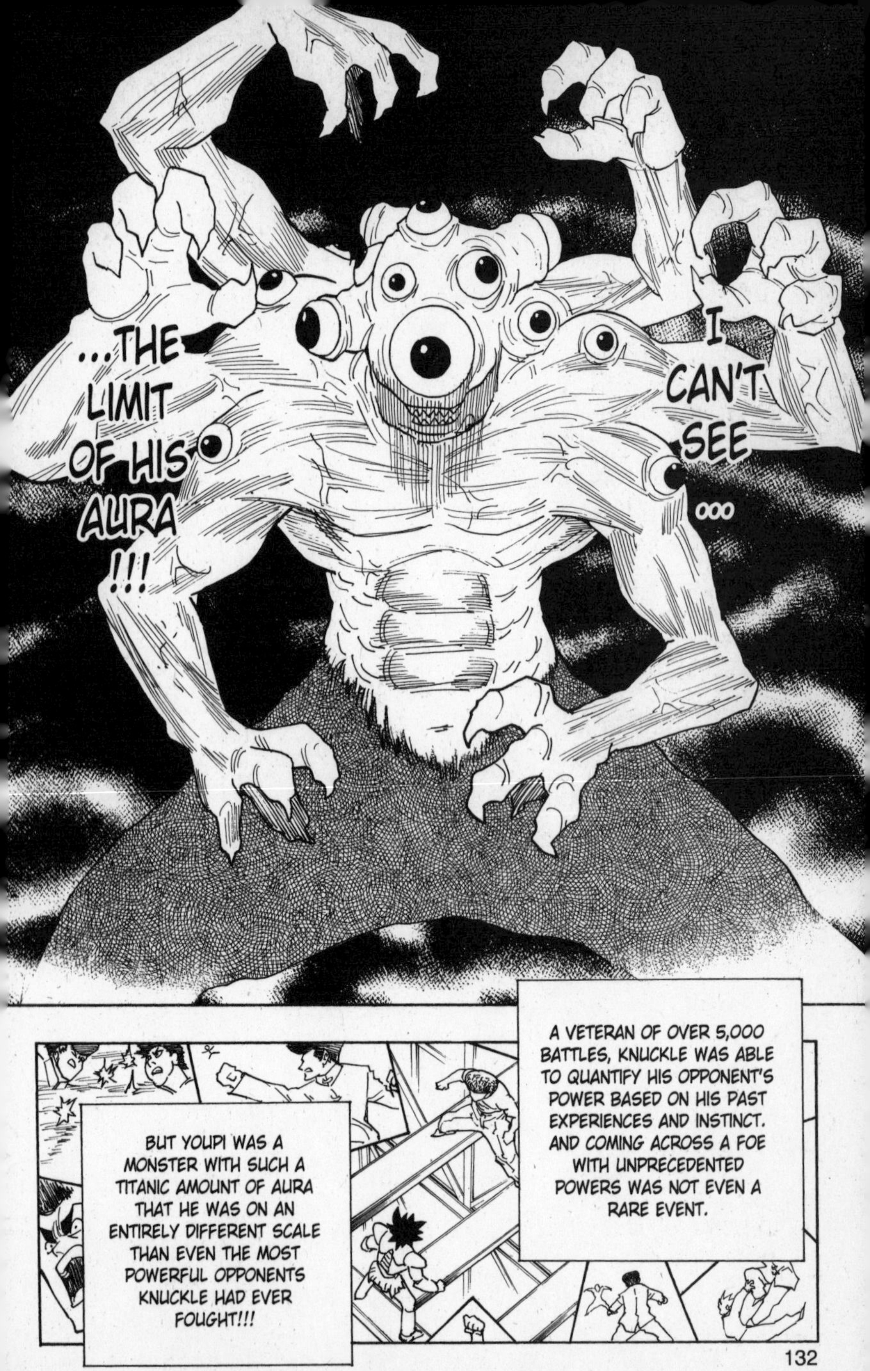
I CAN'T SEE...
...THE LIMIT OF HIS AURA!!!
A VETERAN OF OVER 5,000 BATTLES, KNUCKLE WAS ABLE TO QUANTIFY HIS OPPONENT'S POWER BASED ON HIS PAST EXPERIENCES AND INSTINCT. AND COMING ACROSS A FOE WITH UNPRECEDENTED POWERS WAS NOT EVEN A RARE EVENT.
BUT YOUPI WAS A MONSTER WITH SUCH A TITANIC AMOUNT OF AURA THAT HE WAS ON AN ENTIRELY DIFFERENT SCALE THAN EVEN THE MOST POWERFUL OPPONENTS KNUCKLE HAD EVER FOUGHT!!!

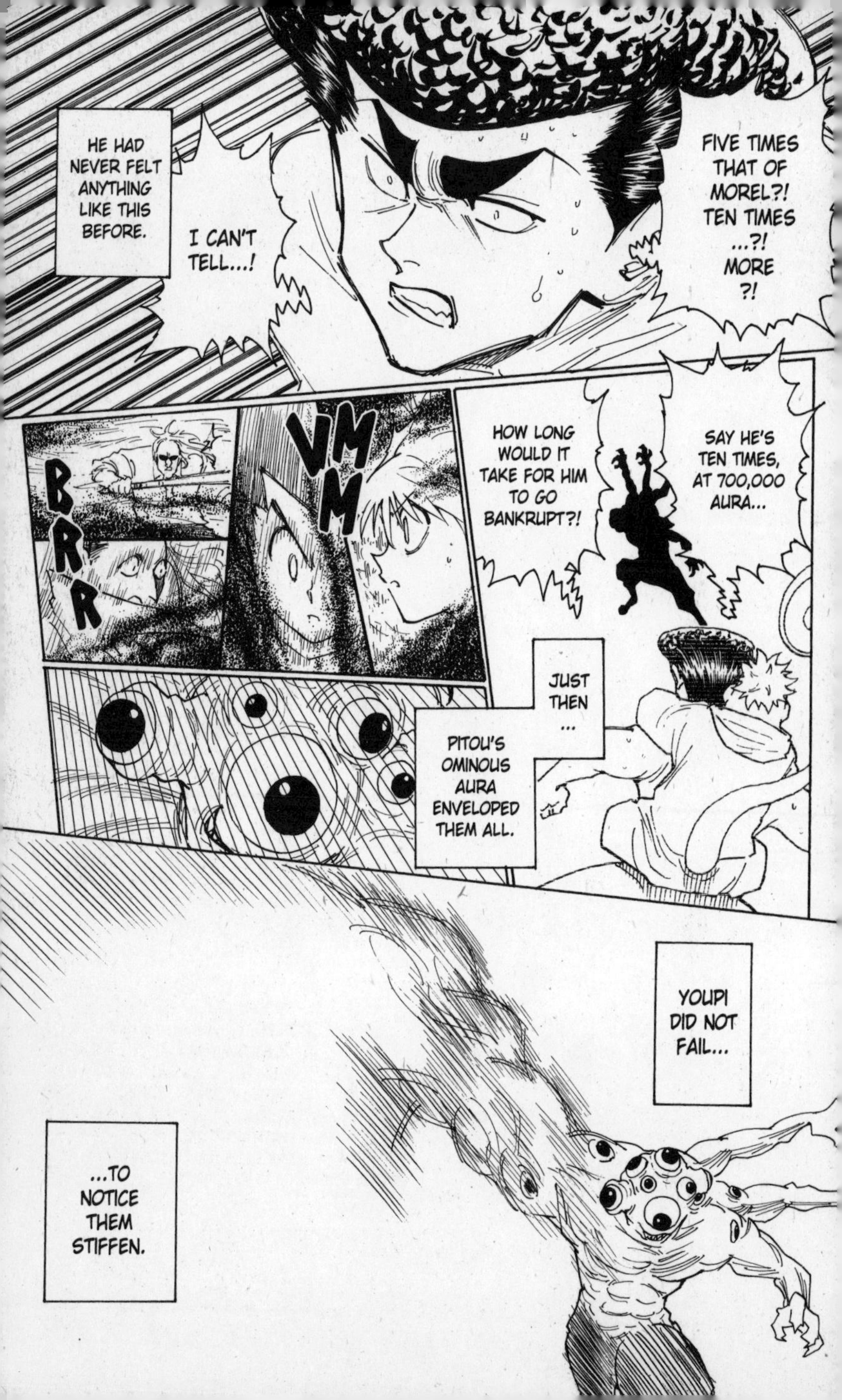
FIVE TIMES THAT OF MOREL?! TEN TIMES ...?! MORE ?!
I CAN'T TELL...!
HE HAD NEVER FELT ANYTHING LIKE THIS BEFORE.
SAY HE'S TEN TIMES, AT 700,000 AURA...
HOW LONG WOULD IT TAKE FOR HIM TO GO BANKRUPT?!
VMM
BRRR
JUST THEN ...
PITOU'S OMINOUS AURA ENVELOPED THEM ALL.
YOUPI DID NOT FAIL...
...TO NOTICE THEM STIFFEN.

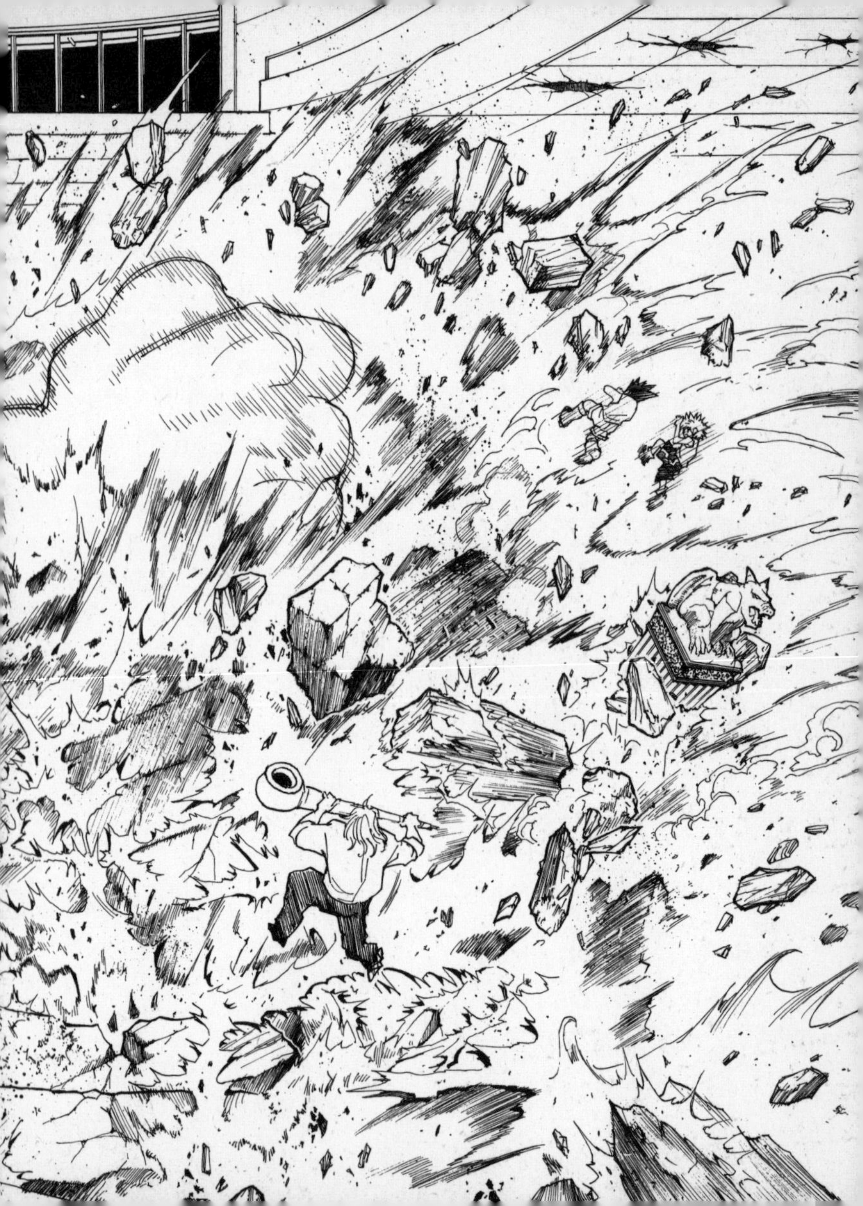

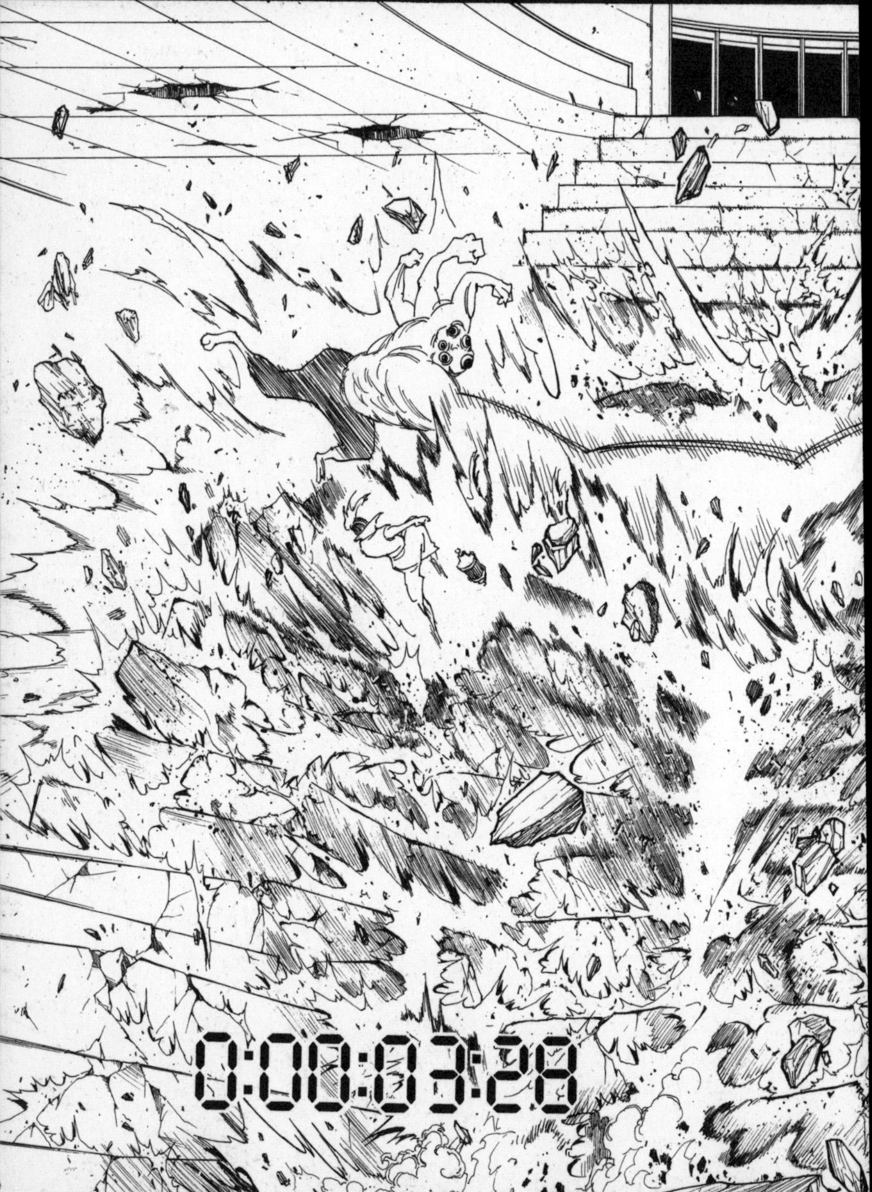
0:00:03:28

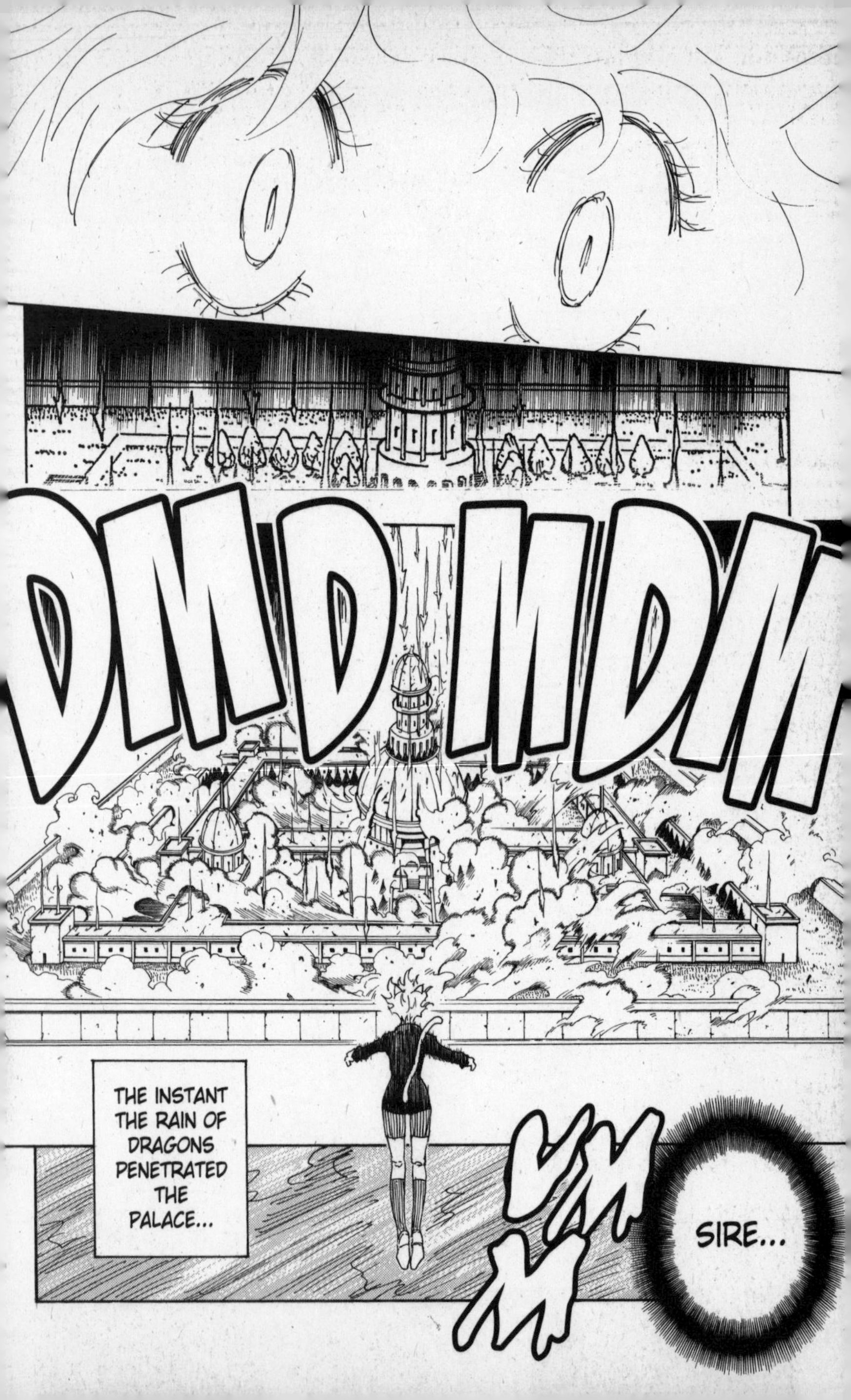

DMD MDM
THE INSTANT THE RAIN OF DRAGONS PENETRATED THE PALACE...
SIRE...

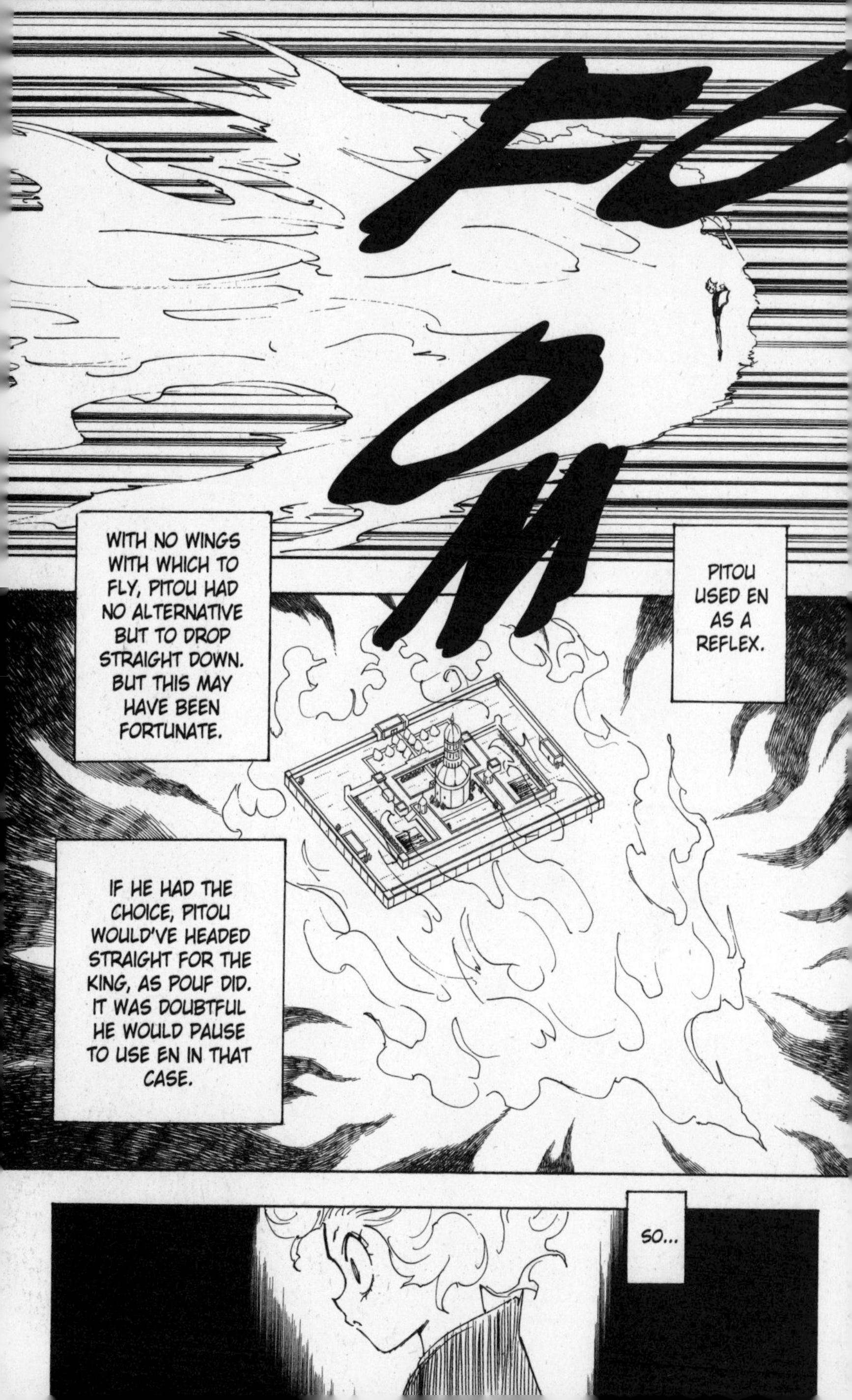
FOOM
PITOU USED EN AS A REFLEX.
WITH NO WINGS WITH WHICH TO FLY, PITOU HAD NO ALTERNATIVE BUT TO DROP STRAIGHT DOWN. BUT THIS MAY HAVE BEEN FORTUNATE.
IF HE HAD THE CHOICE, PITOU WOULD'VE HEADED STRAIGHT FOR THE KING, AS POUF DID. IT WAS DOUBTFUL HE WOULD PAUSE TO USE EN IN THAT CASE.
SO...

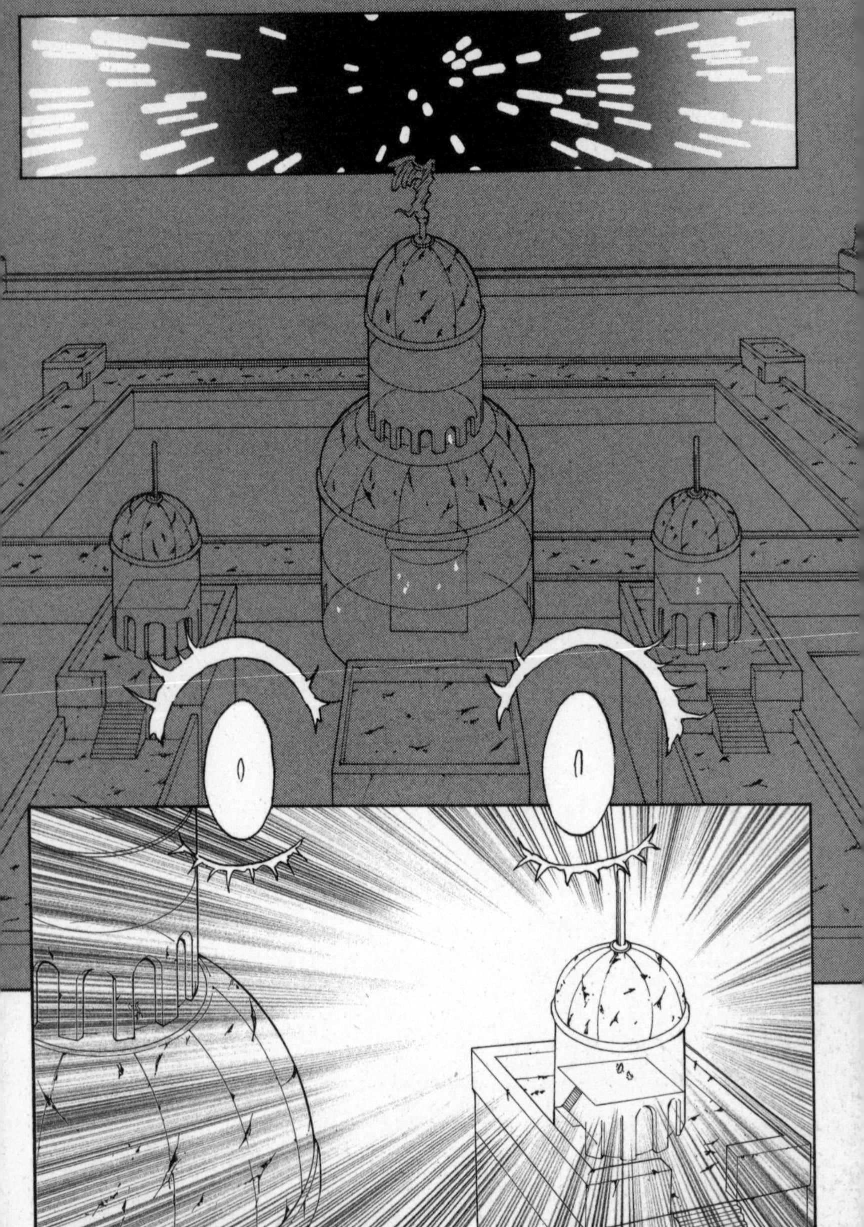

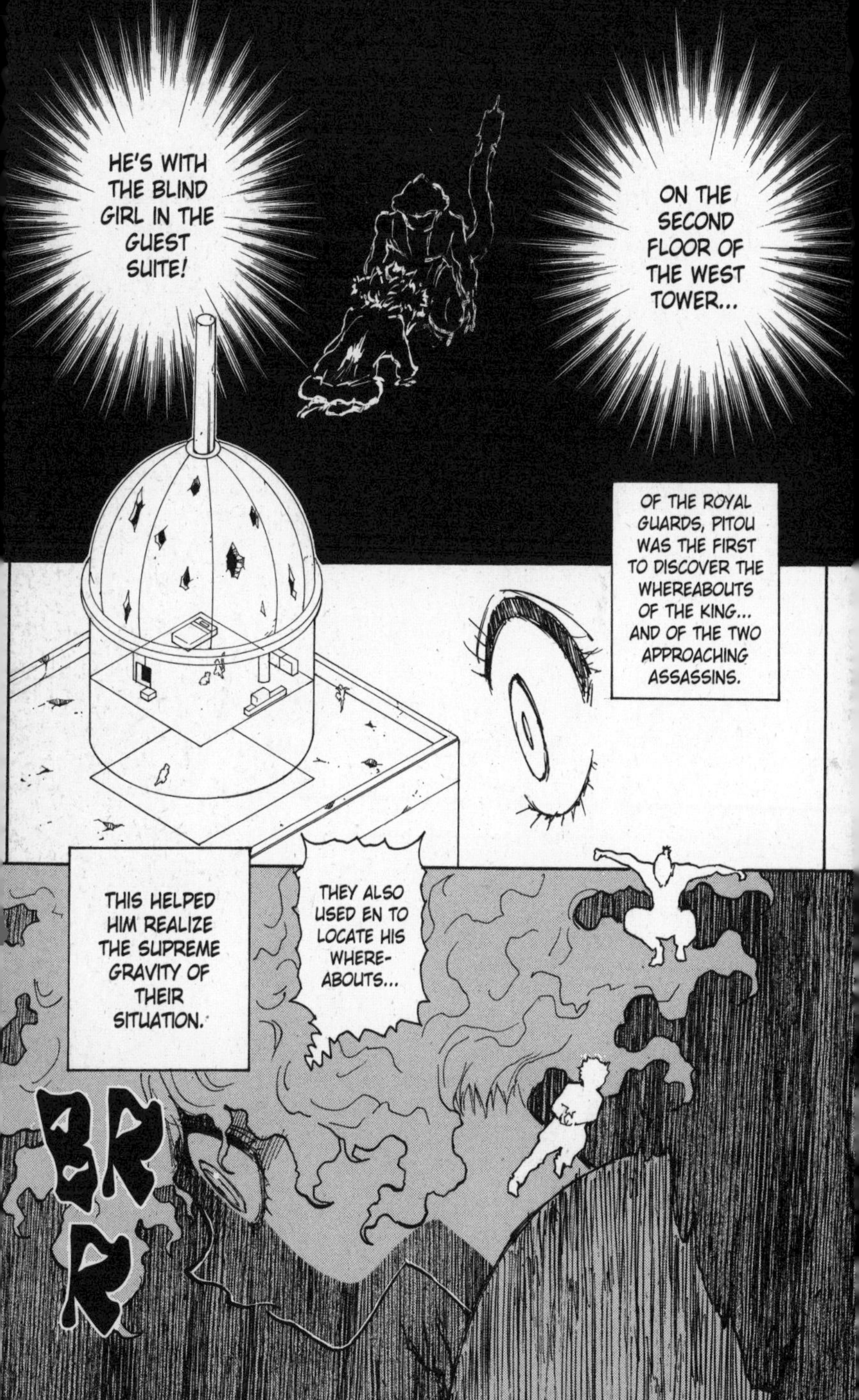
ON THE SECOND FLOOR OF THE WEST TOWER...
HE'S WITH THE BLIND GIRL IN THE GUEST SUITE!
OF THE ROYAL GUARDS, PITOU WAS THE FIRST TO DISCOVER THE WHEREABOUTS OF THE KING... AND OF THE TWO APPROACHING ASSASSINS.
THEY ALSO USED EN TO LOCATE HIS WHERE-ABOUTS...
THIS HELPED HIM REALIZE THE SUPREME GRAVITY OF THEIR SITUATION.
BRR

PITOU CURLED UP LIKE HIS FOUR-FOOTED ANCESTORS...

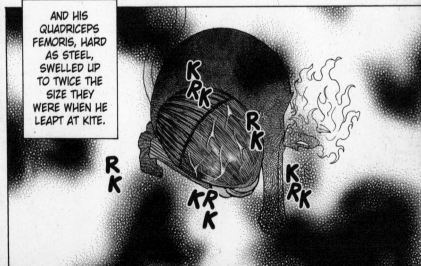

AND HIS QUADRICEPS FEMORIS, HARD AS STEEL, SWELLED UP TO TWICE THE SIZE THEY WERE WHEN HE LEAPT AT KITE.

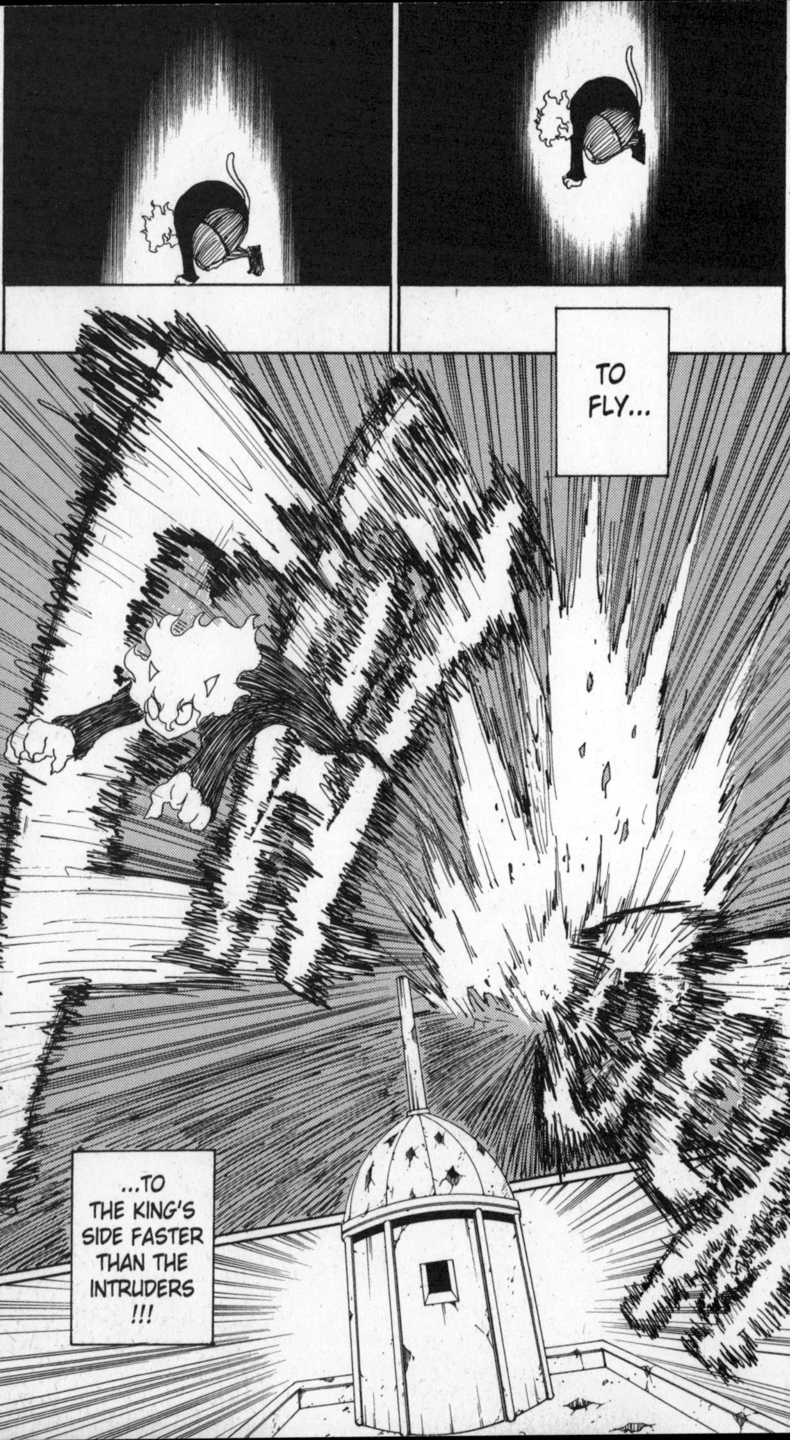
TO FLY...
...TO THE KING'S SIDE FASTER THAN THE INTRUDERS!!!

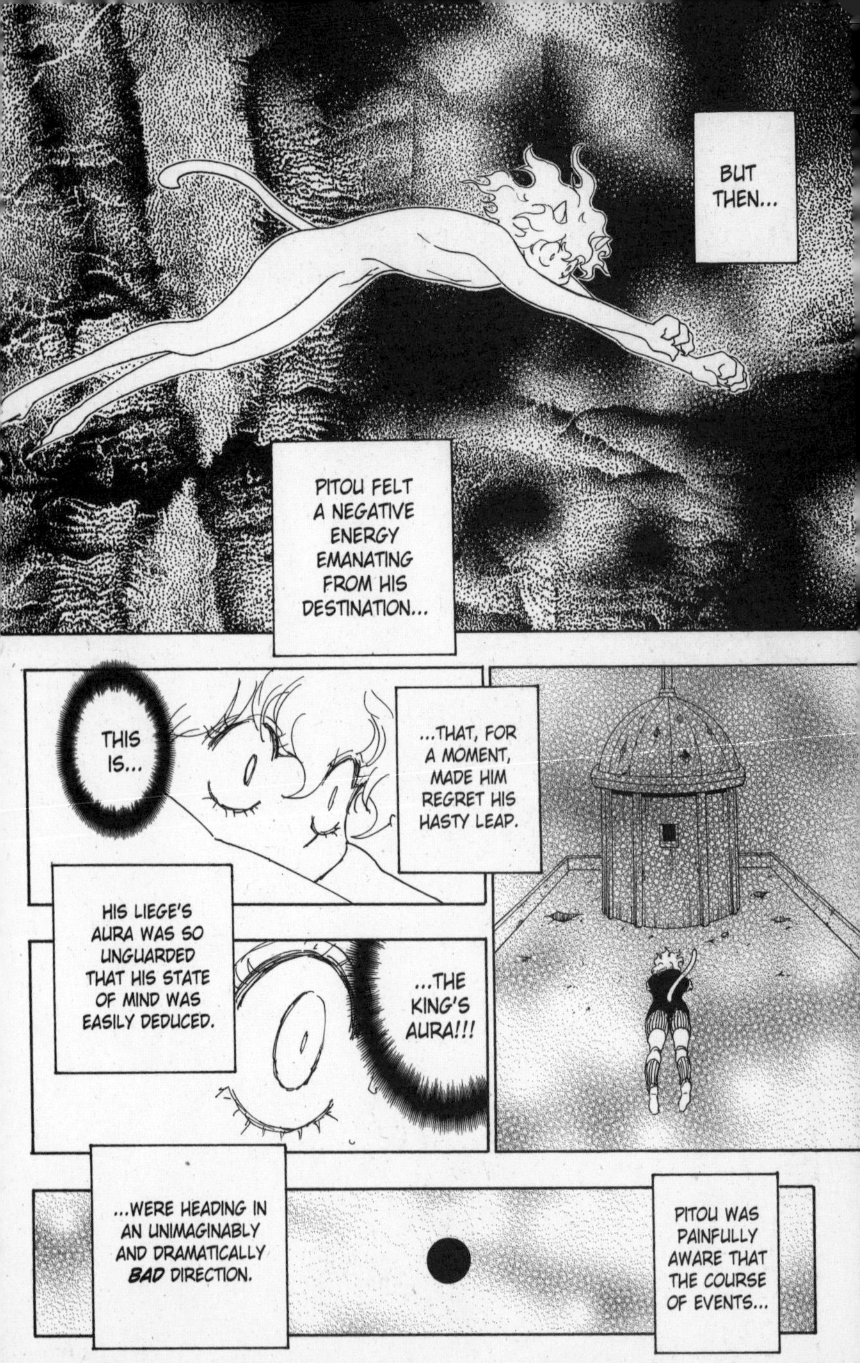
BUT THEN...
PITOU FELT A NEGATIVE ENERGY EMANATING FROM HIS DESTINATION...
...THAT, FOR A MOMENT, MADE HIM REGRET HIS HASTY LEAP.
THIS IS...
...THE KING'S AURA!!!
HIS LIEGE'S AURA WAS SO UNGUARDED THAT HIS STATE OF MIND WAS EASILY DEDUCED.
PITOU WAS PAINFULLY AWARE THAT THE COURSE OF EVENTS...
...WERE HEADING IN AN UNIMAGINABLY AND DRAMATICALLY ***BAD*** DIRECTION.

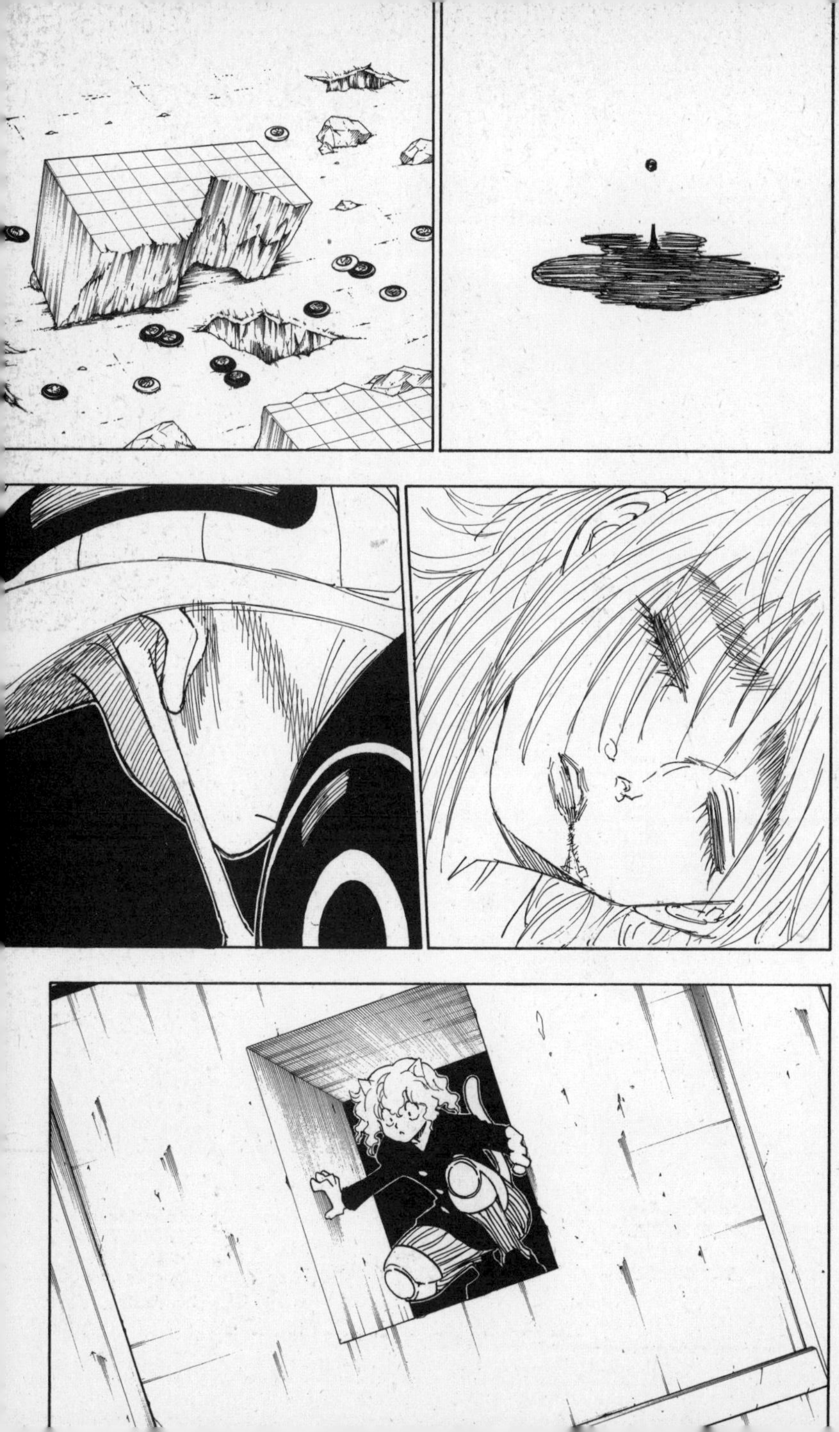

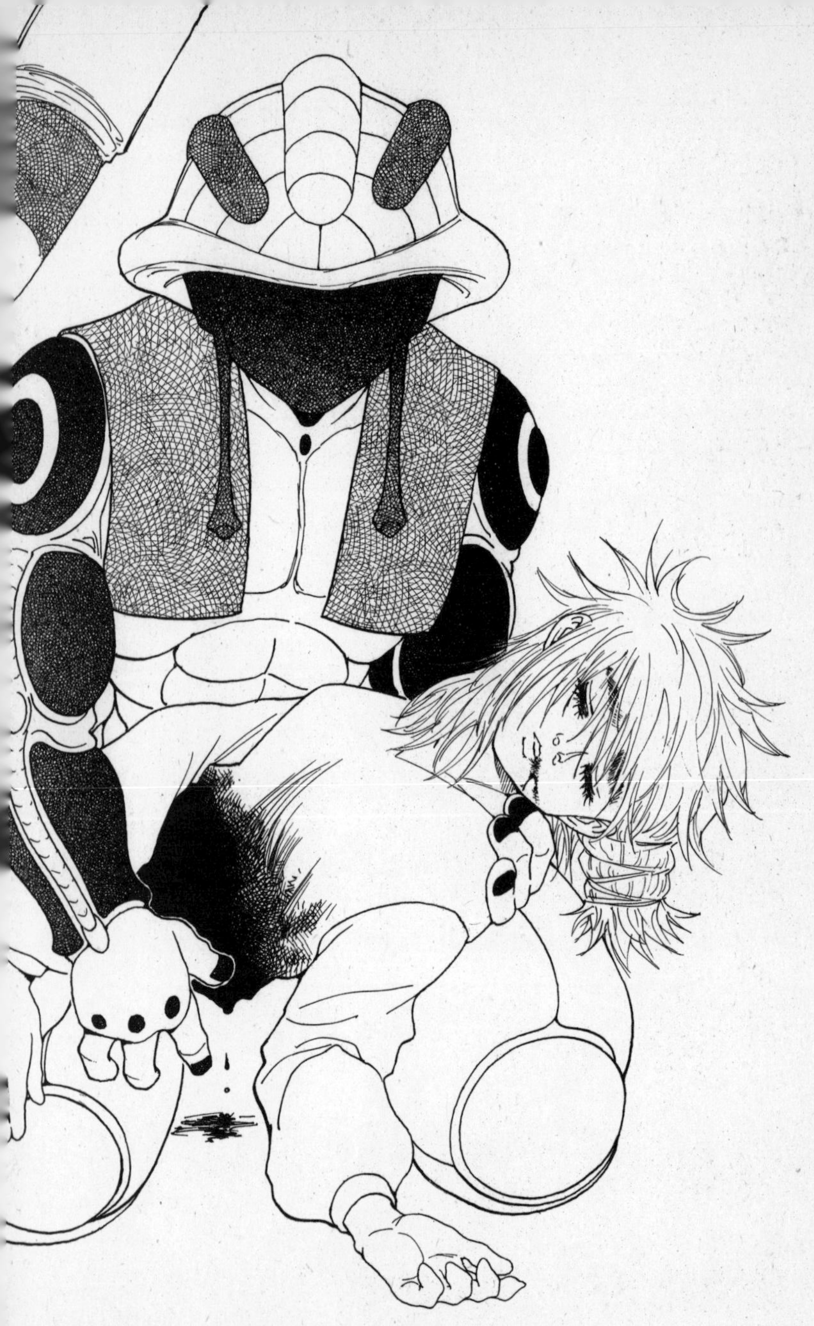

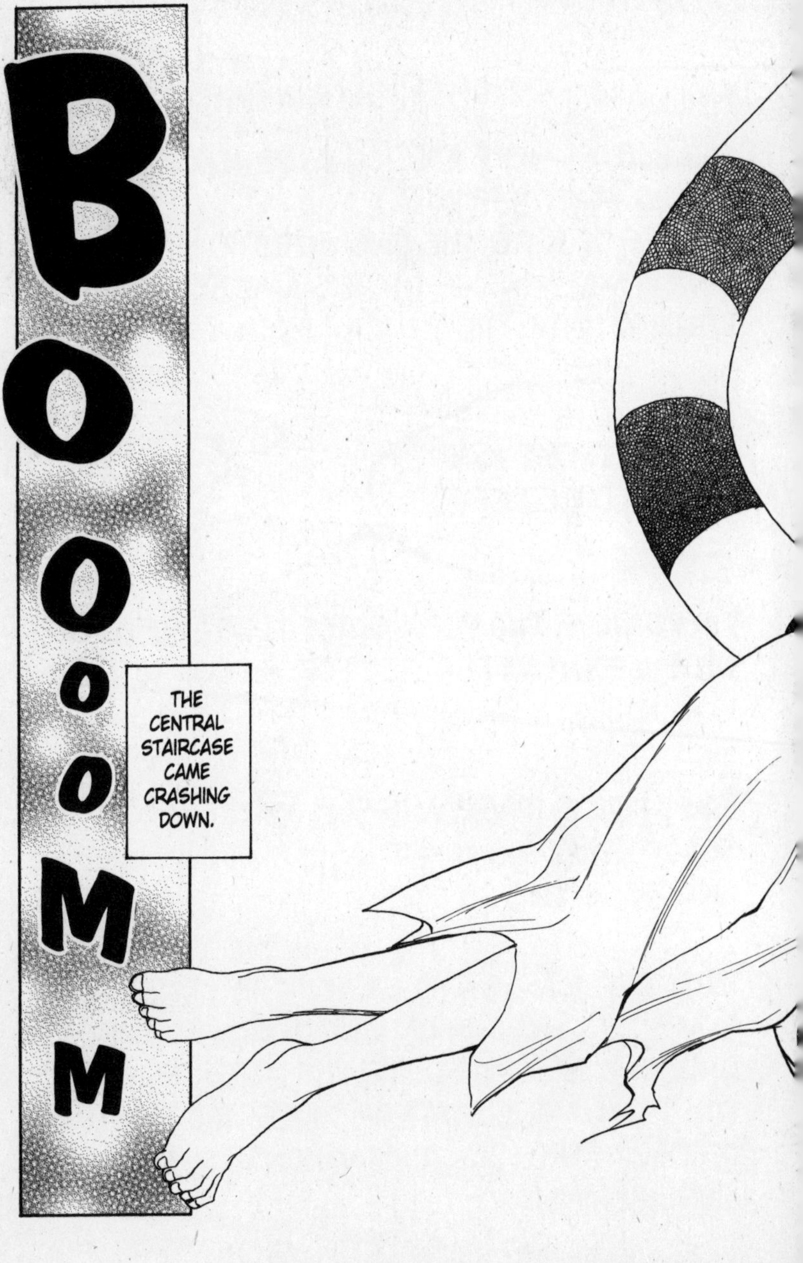
BOOOOMM
THE CENTRAL STAIRCASE CAME CRASHING DOWN.

ROUND SIX: KNUCKLE POWER

TWO PEOPLE FACE OFF, WITH ONLY ONE ADVANCING.

THE SCORES WERE TALLIED BY POWER STAT +
TIMING STAT + DIE ROLL.
IN CASE OF A TIE, THE ONE WITH THE HIGHER
POWER STAT WINS. IF THERE'S ANOTHER TIE, I KEEP
ROLLING UNTIL THE TIE IS BROKEN.

NOW THERE ARE
126 PEOPLE LEFT...

THERE WERE TWO PEOPLE TIED FOR FIRST PLACE
WITH 16 POINTS. FOUR TIED FOR SECOND WITH
15 POINTS.

FIRST PLACE: HIROKI AND SUPI
SECOND PLACE: UMAHIKO, ASUKA, CROW BLOOD
AND SESAMIN

○ MOST APPLICANTS WHO LASTED THIS LONG HAD
STATS THAT WERE BALANCED OVERALL. THERE WAS
ONLY ONE SPECIALIST WHO PUT MORE THAN 7
POINTS INTO ONE STAT!! OF THOSE WHO HAD SOME
OF THEIR STATS SET TO FRACTIONS LESS THAN ONE,
NONE REMAINED.

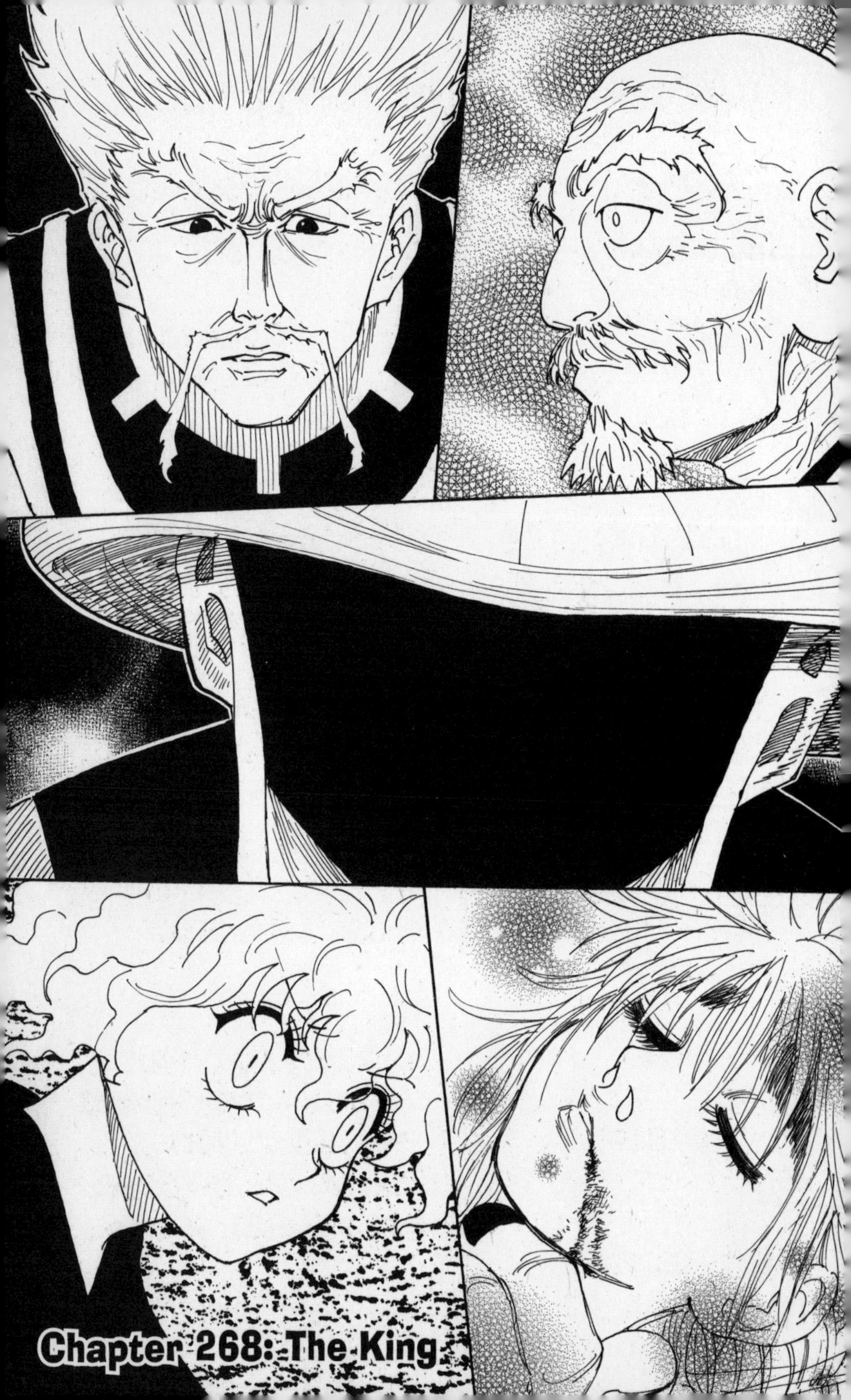
Chapter 268: The King

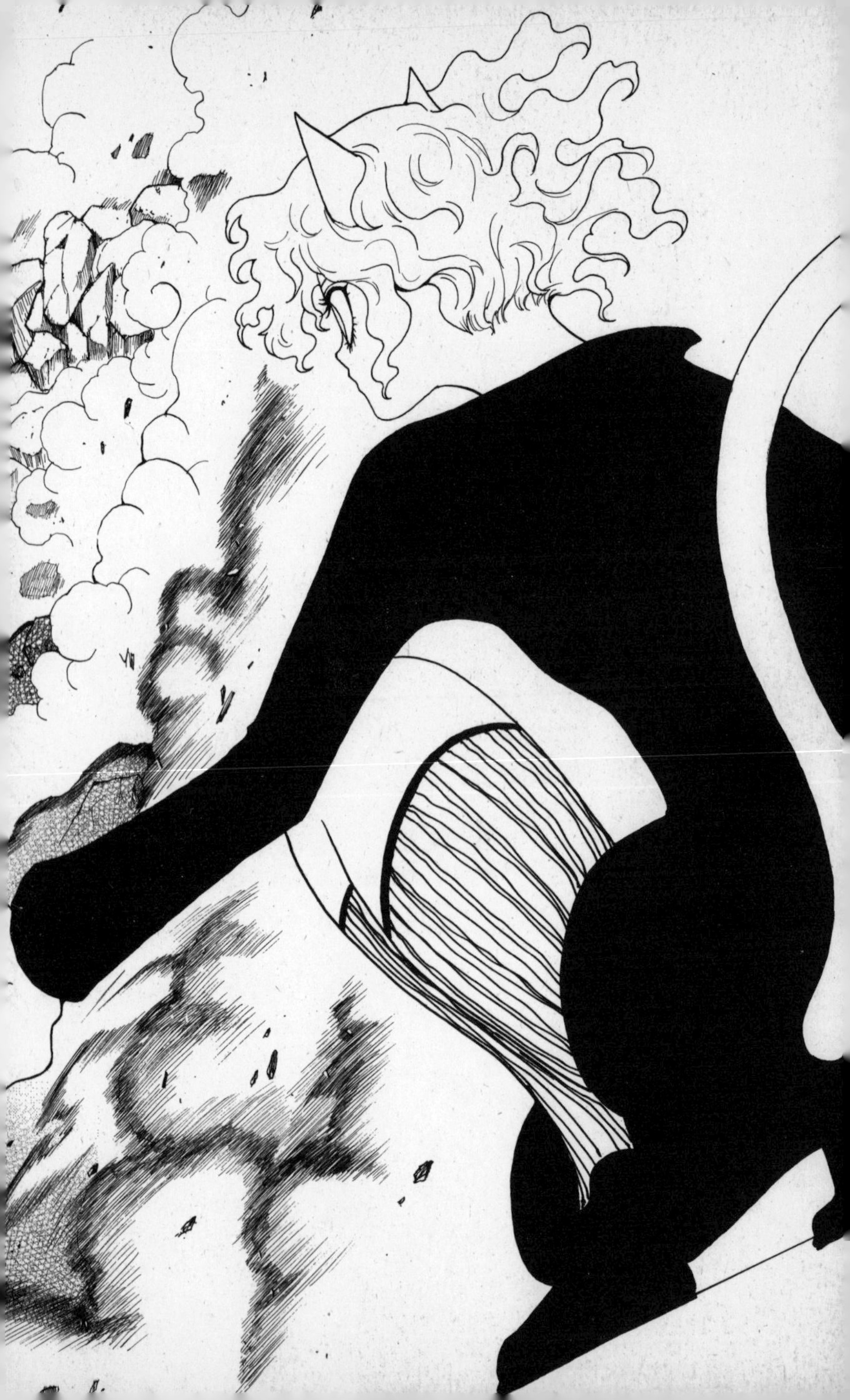

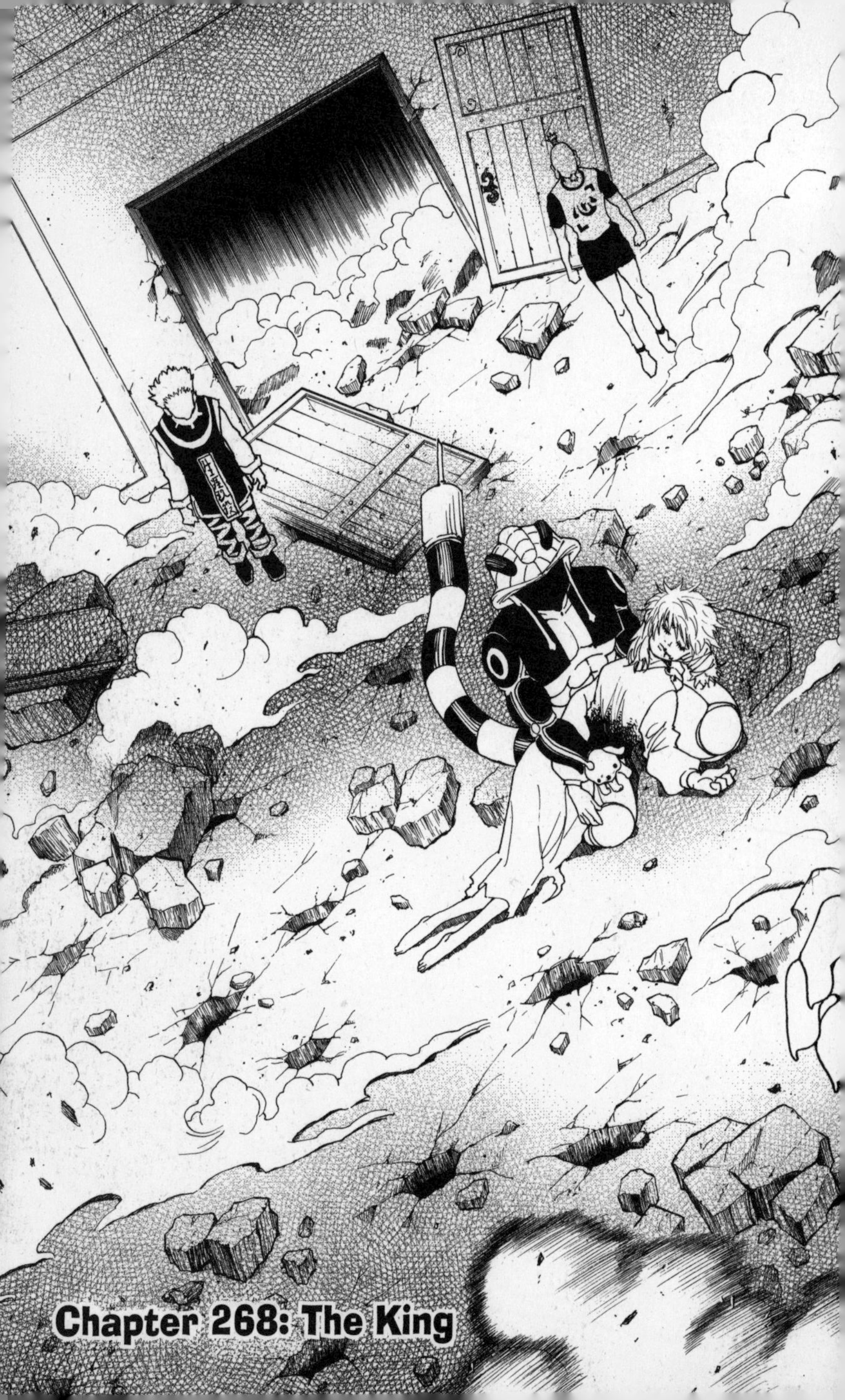
Chapter 268: The King

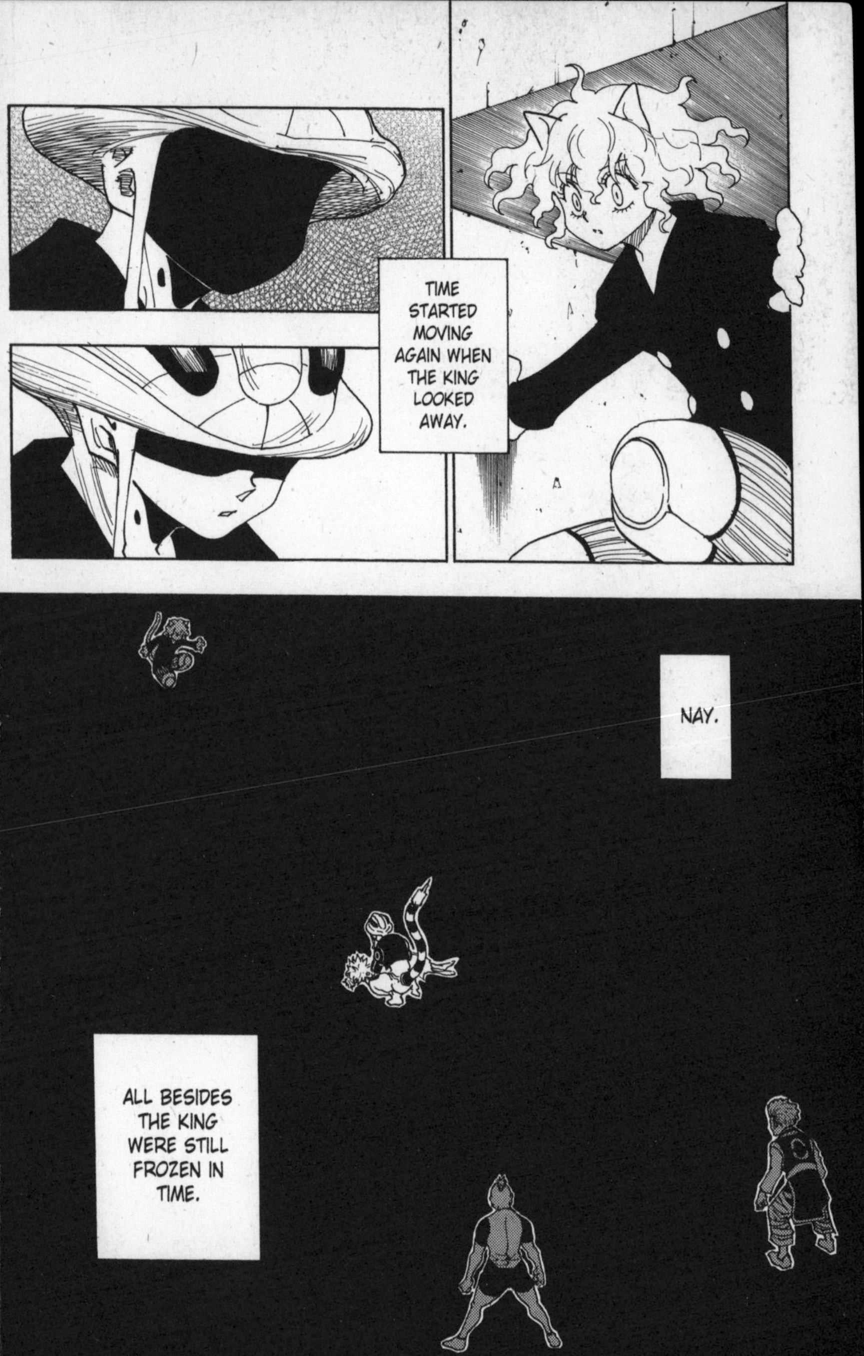
TIME STARTED MOVING AGAIN WHEN THE KING LOOKED AWAY.
NAY.
ALL BESIDES THE KING WERE STILL FROZEN IN TIME.

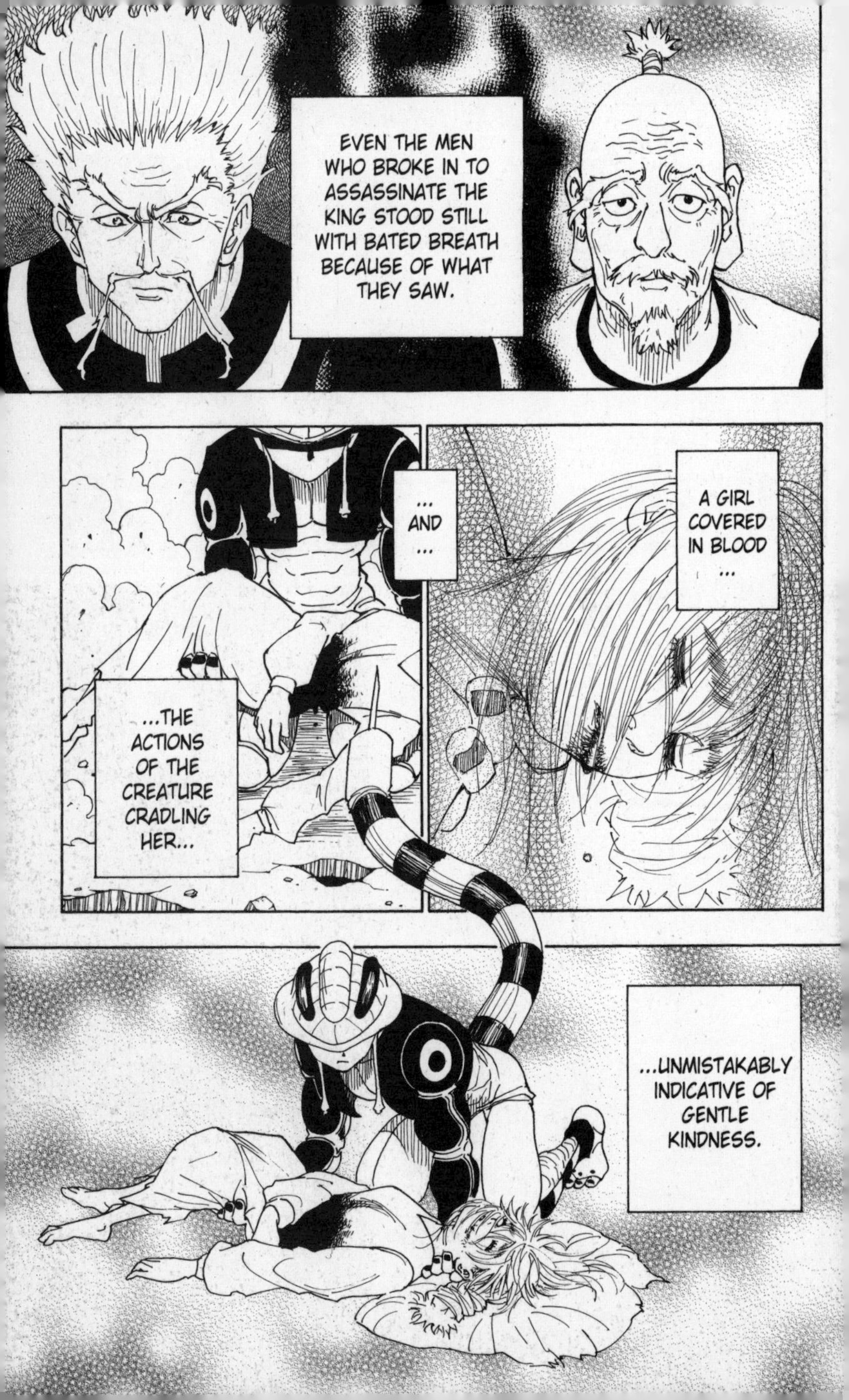
EVEN THE MEN WHO BROKE IN TO ASSASSINATE THE KING STOOD STILL WITH BATED BREATH BECAUSE OF WHAT THEY SAW.
A GIRL COVERED IN BLOOD ...
... AND ...
...THE ACTIONS OF THE CREATURE CRADLING HER...
...UNMISTAKABLY INDICATIVE OF GENTLE KINDNESS.

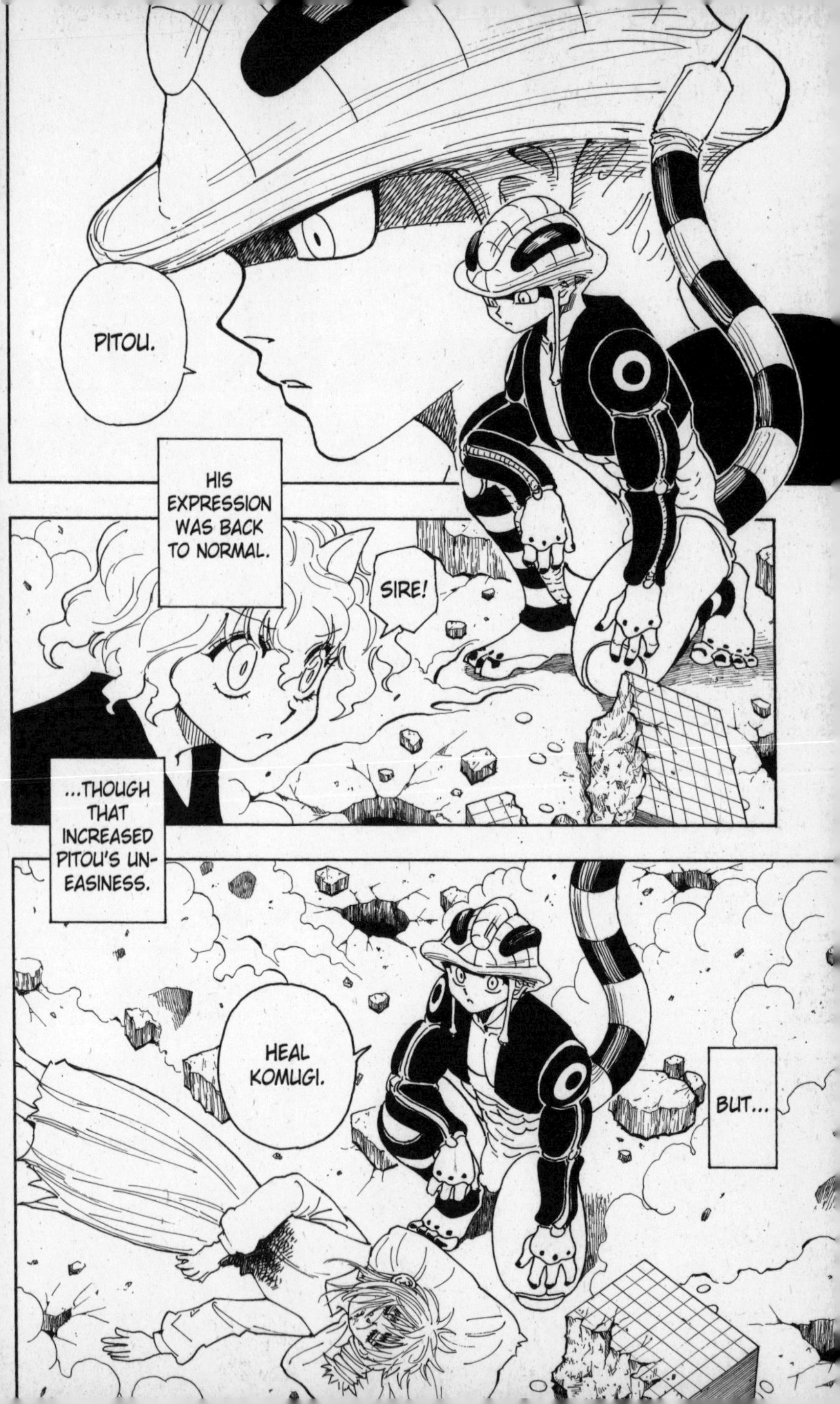
PITOU.
HIS EXPRESSION WAS BACK TO NORMAL.
SIRE!
...THOUGH THAT INCREASED PITOU'S UN-EASINESS.
HEAL KOMUGI.
BUT...

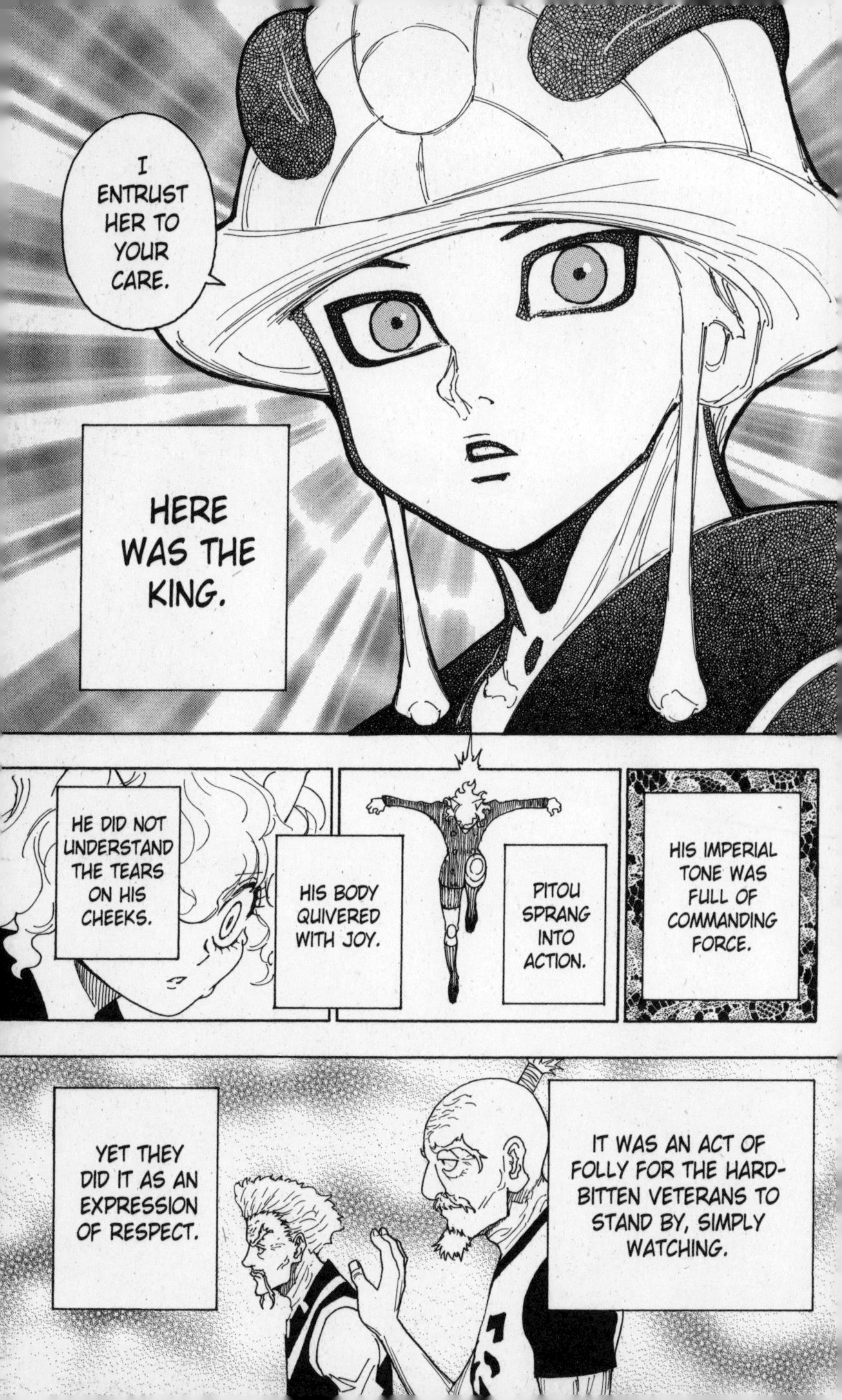
I ENTRUST HER TO YOUR CARE.
HERE WAS THE KING.
HIS IMPERIAL TONE WAS FULL OF COMMANDING FORCE.
PITOU SPRANG INTO ACTION.
HIS BODY QUIVERED WITH JOY.
HE DID NOT UNDERSTAND THE TEARS ON HIS CHEEKS.
IT WAS AN ACT OF FOLLY FOR THE HARD-BITTEN VETERANS TO STAND BY, SIMPLY WATCHING.
YET THEY DID IT AS AN EXPRESSION OF RESPECT.

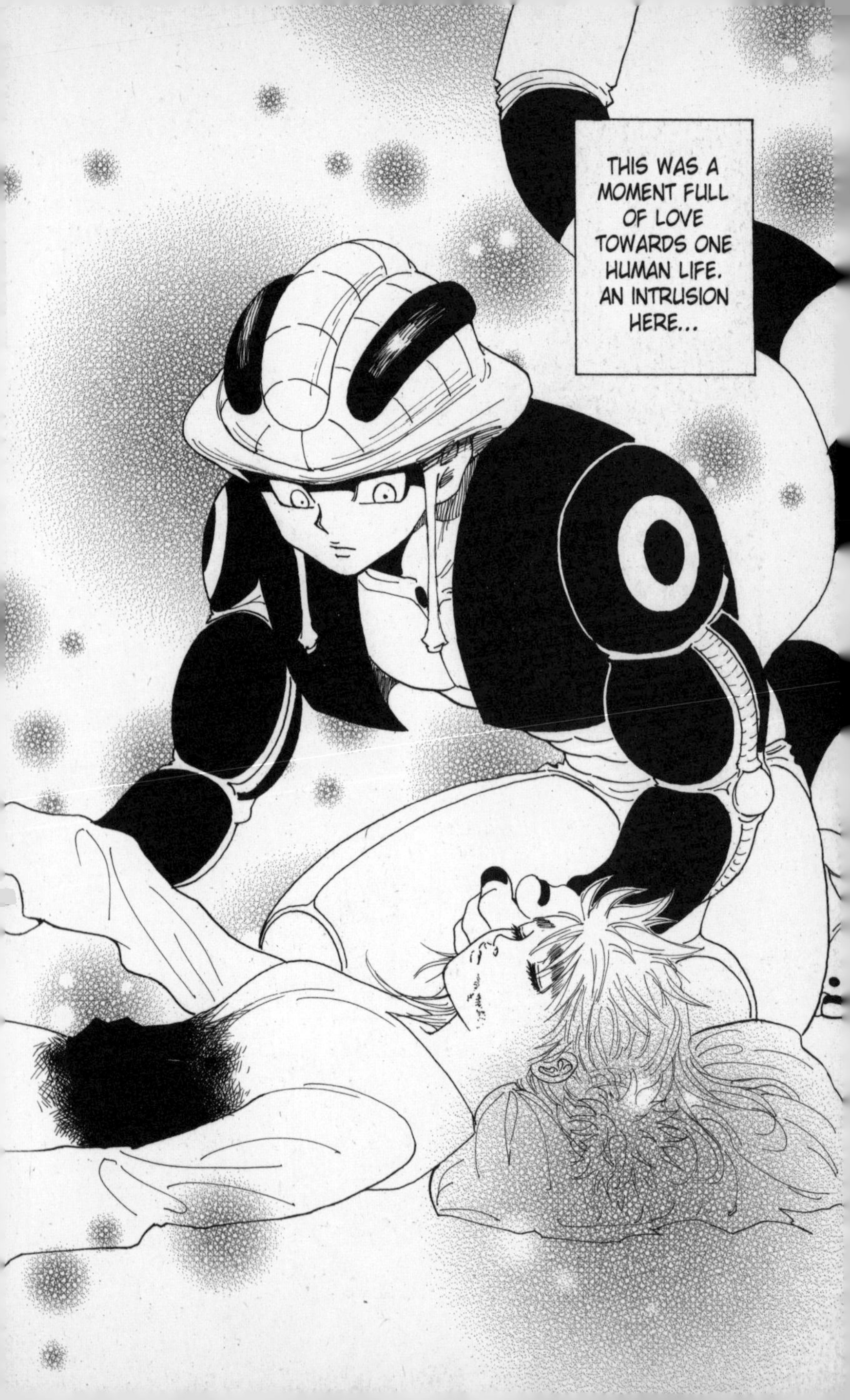
THIS WAS A MOMENT FULL OF LOVE TOWARDS ONE HUMAN LIFE. AN INTRUSION HERE...

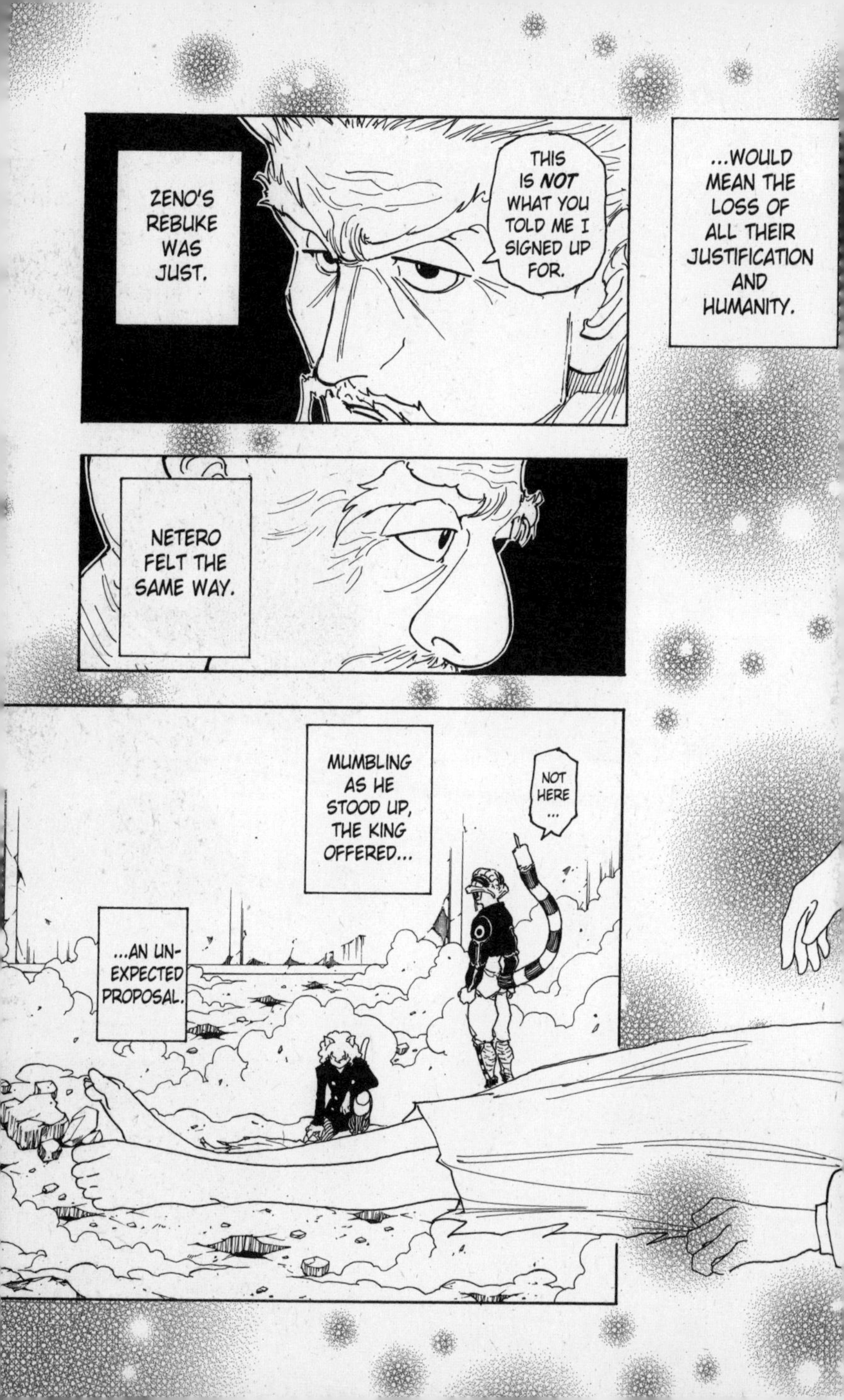
...WOULD MEAN THE LOSS OF ALL THEIR JUSTIFICATION AND HUMANITY.
THIS IS ***NOT*** WHAT YOU TOLD ME I SIGNED UP FOR.
ZENO'S REBUKE WAS JUST.
NETERO FELT THE SAME WAY.
NOT HERE...
MUMBLING AS HE STOOD UP, THE KING OFFERED...
...AN UN-EXPECTED PROPOSAL.

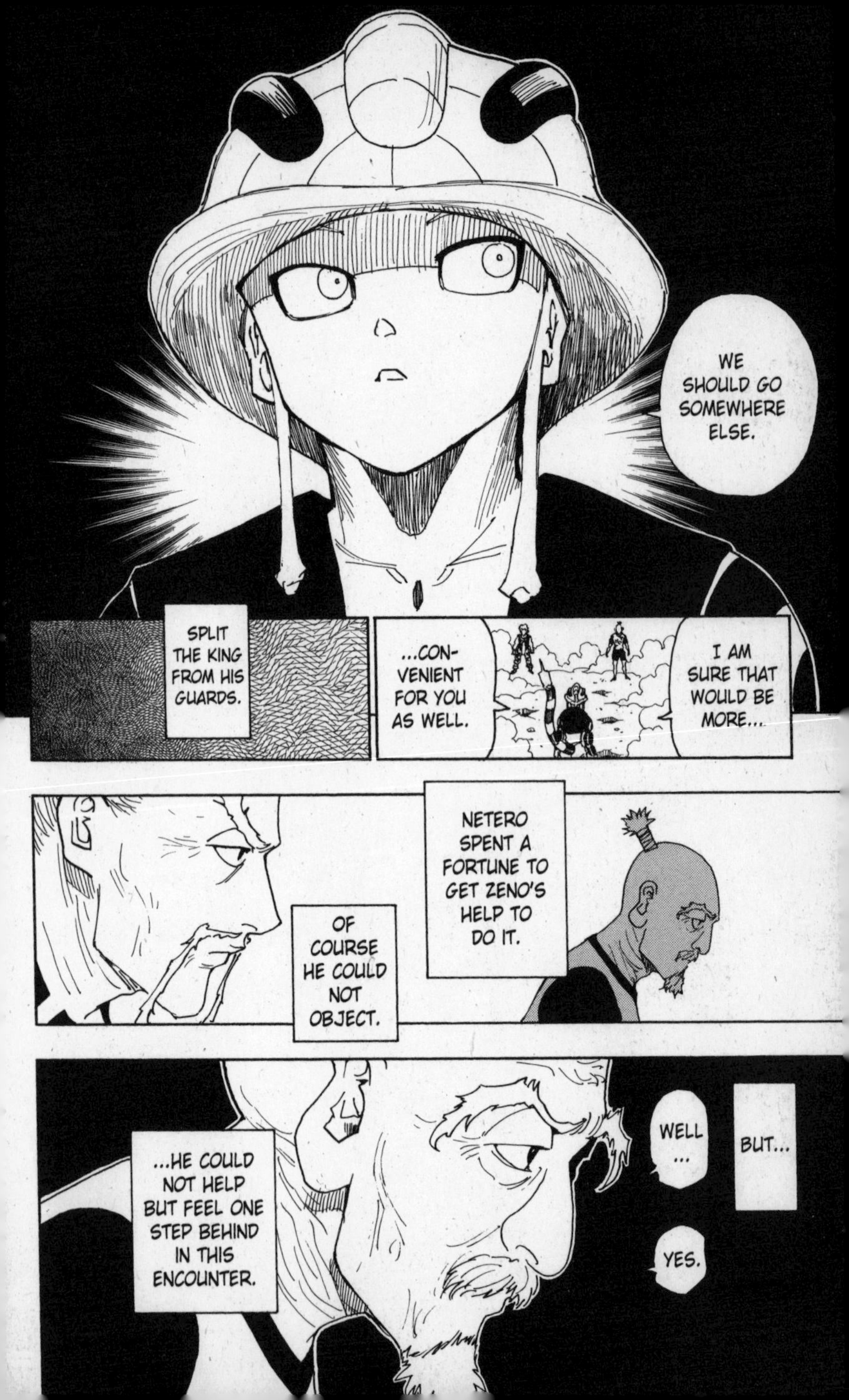
WE SHOULD GO SOMEWHERE ELSE.
I AM SURE THAT WOULD BE MORE...
...CON-VENIENT FOR YOU AS WELL.
SPLIT THE KING FROM HIS GUARDS.
NETERO SPENT A FORTUNE TO GET ZENO'S HELP TO DO IT.
OF COURSE HE COULD NOT OBJECT.
BUT...
WELL...
YES.
...HE COULD NOT HELP BUT FEEL ONE STEP BEHIND IN THIS ENCOUNTER.

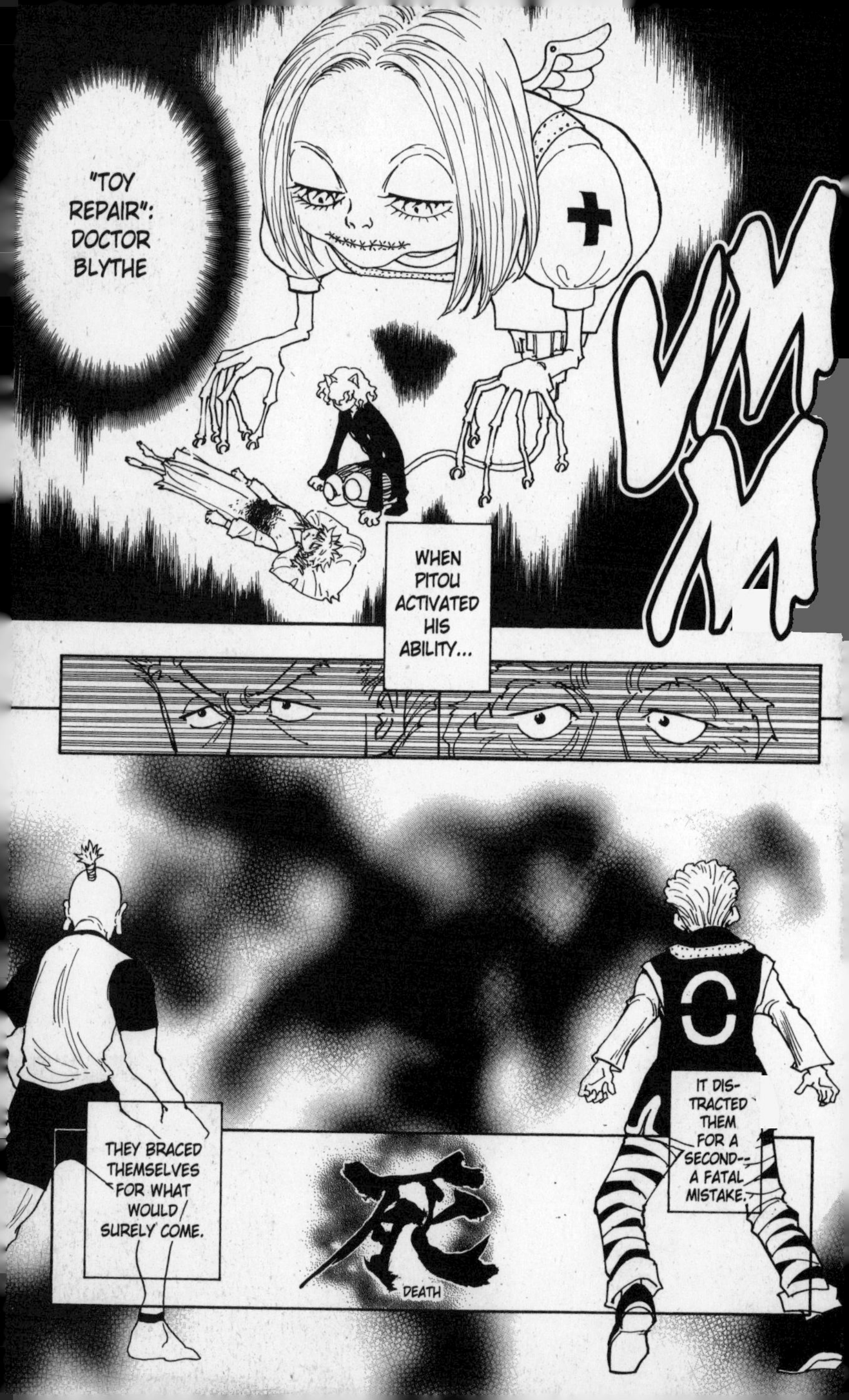
"TOY REPAIR": DOCTOR BLYTHE
WHEN PITOU ACTIVATED HIS ABILITY...
IT DISTRACTED THEM FOR A SECOND-- A FATAL MISTAKE.
死
DEATH
THEY BRACED THEMSELVES FOR WHAT WOULD SURELY COME.

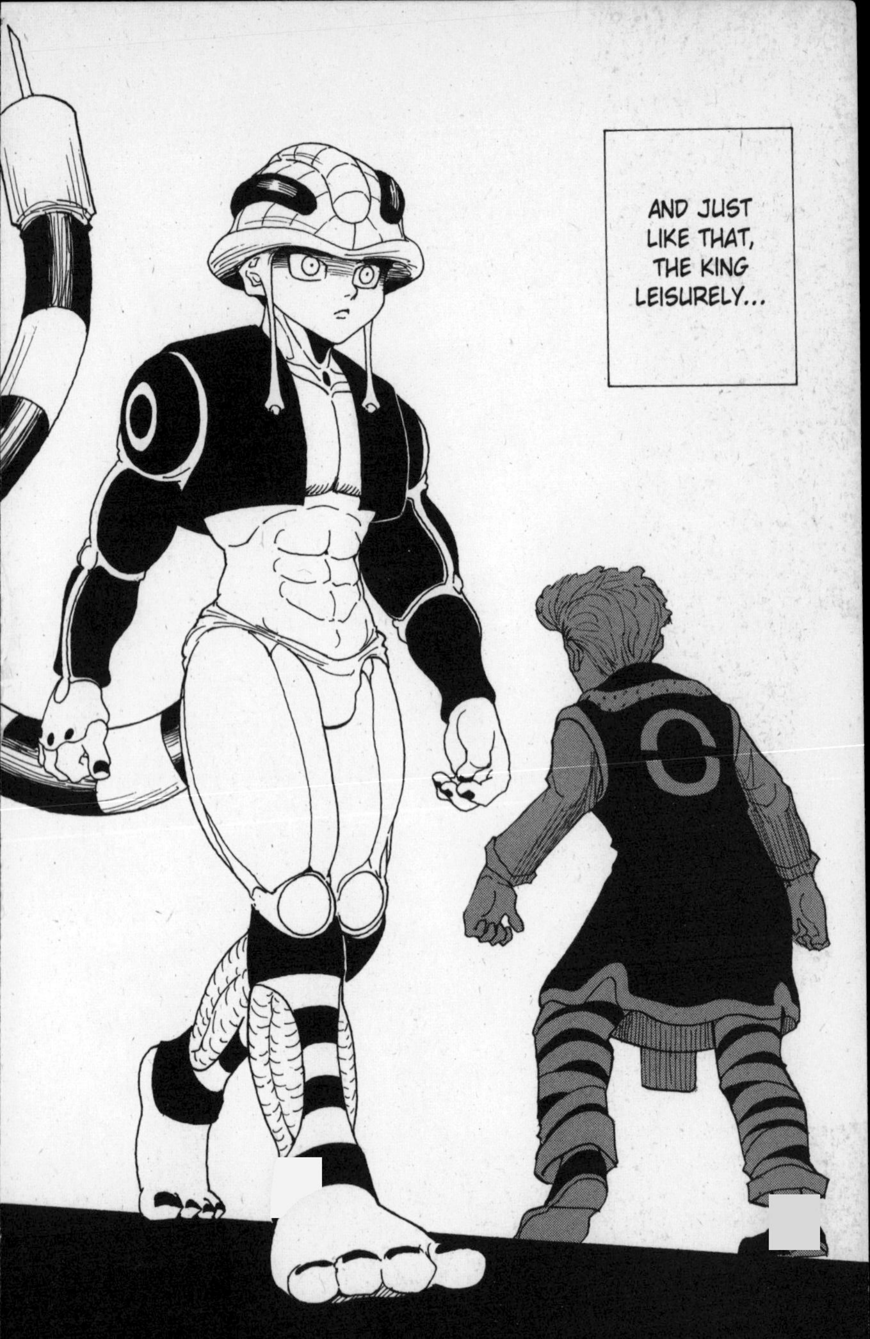
AND JUST LIKE THAT, THE KING LEISURELY...

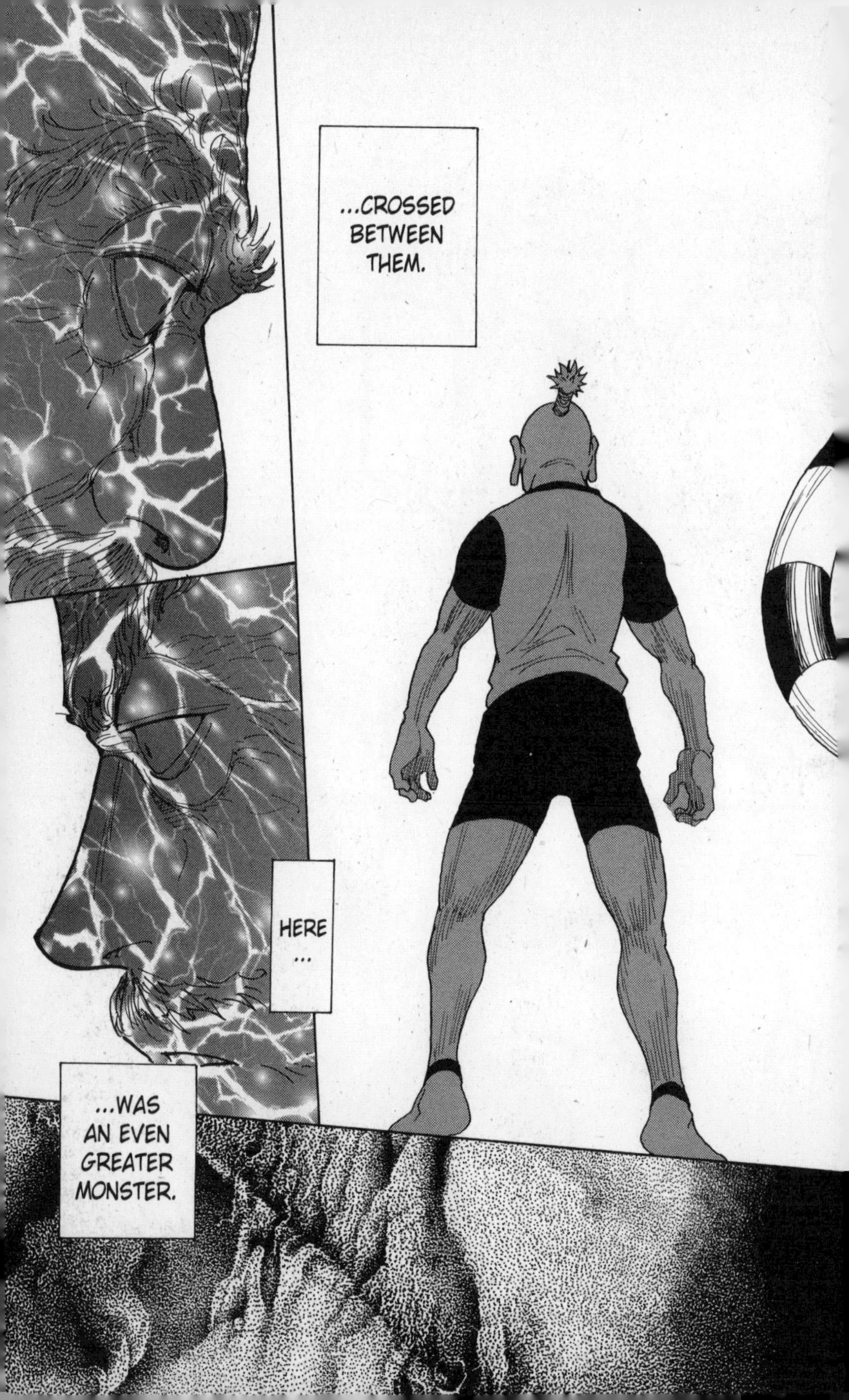
...CROSSED BETWEEN THEM.
HERE ...
...WAS AN EVEN GREATER MONSTER.

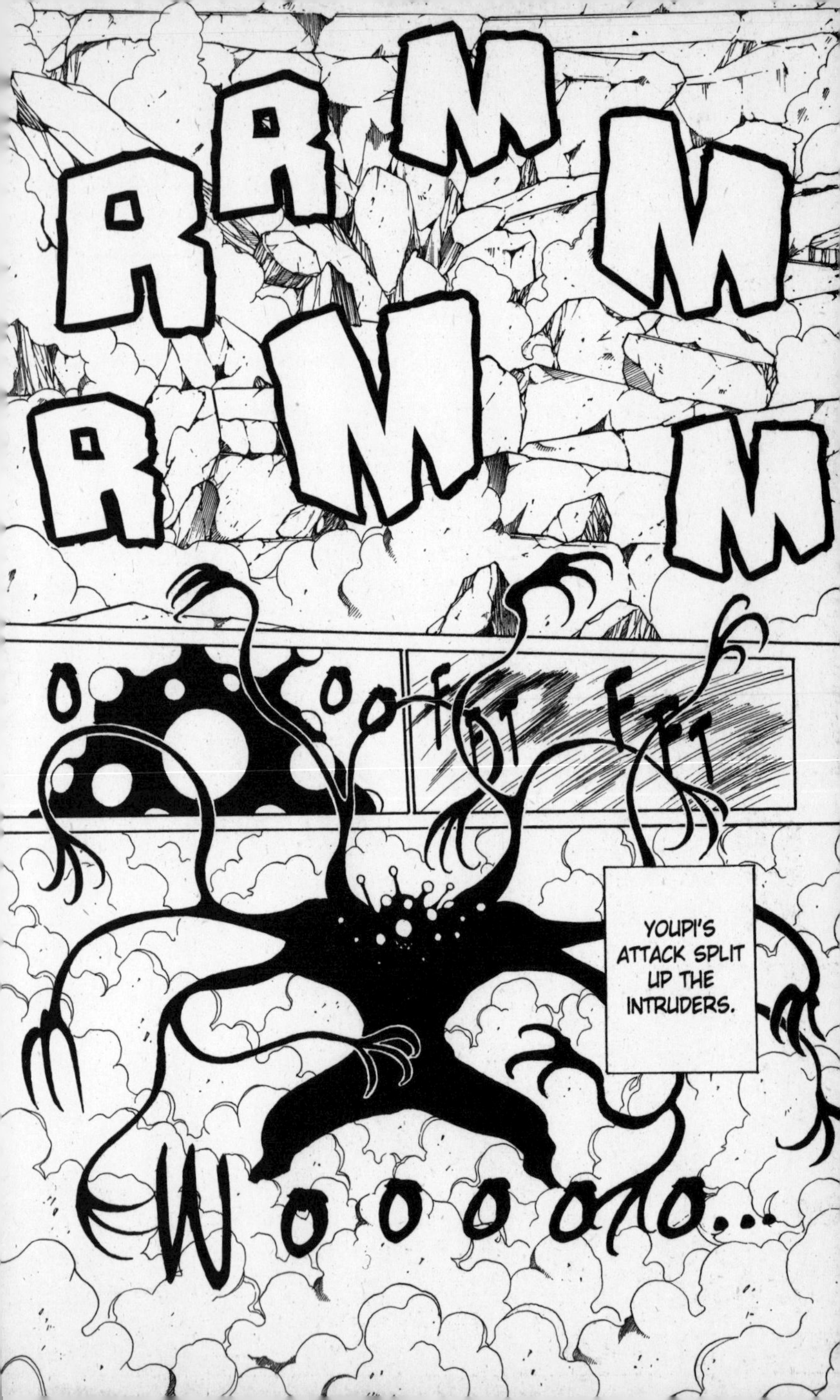
RRMM
RMM
OOOOF
FFT FFT
YOUPI'S ATTACK SPLIT UP THE INTRUDERS.
WOOOOOO...

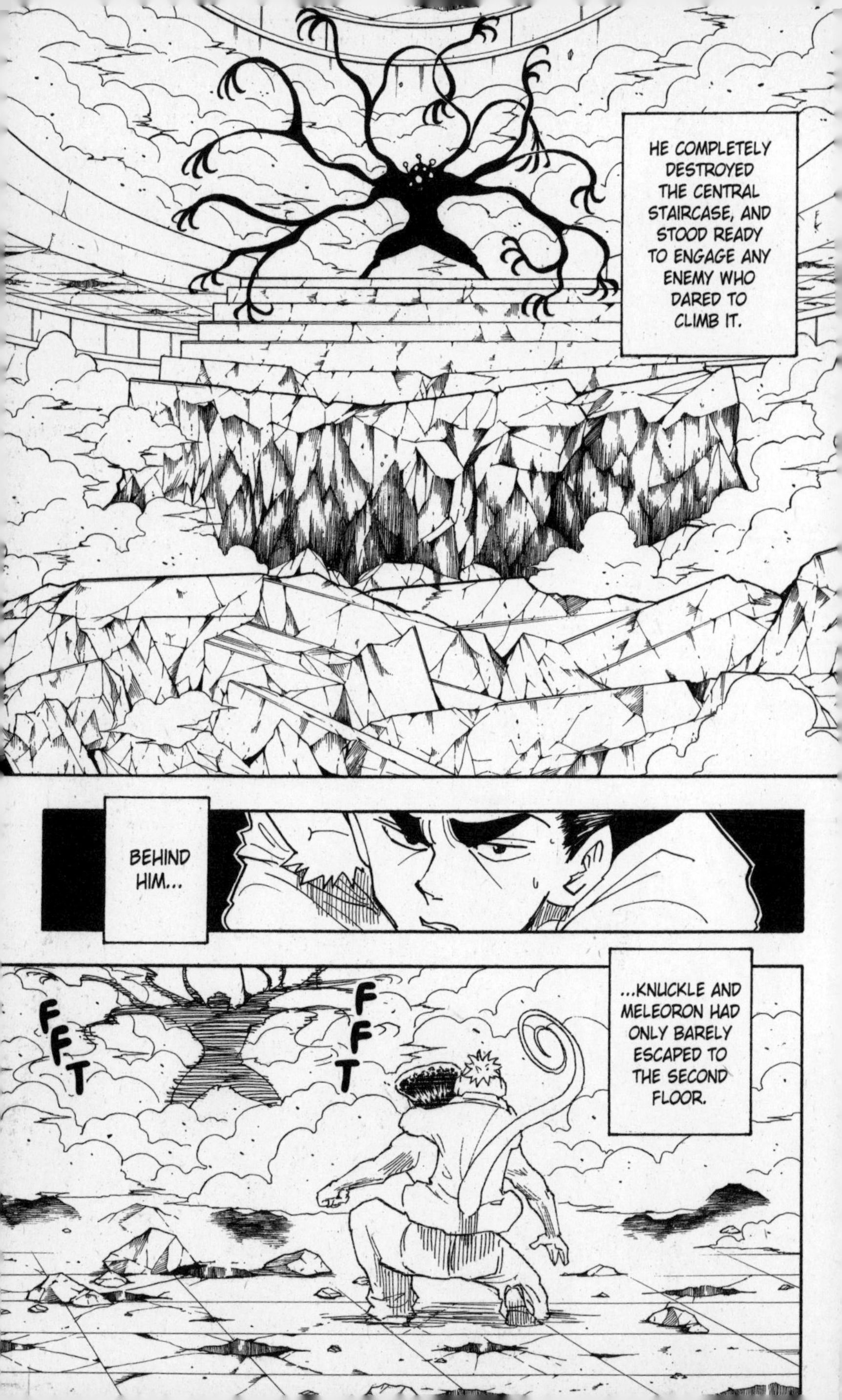
HE COMPLETELY DESTROYED THE CENTRAL STAIRCASE, AND STOOD READY TO ENGAGE ANY ENEMY WHO DARED TO CLIMB IT.
BEHIND HIM...
...KNUCKLE AND MELEORON HAD ONLY BARELY ESCAPED TO THE SECOND FLOOR.
FFT
FFT

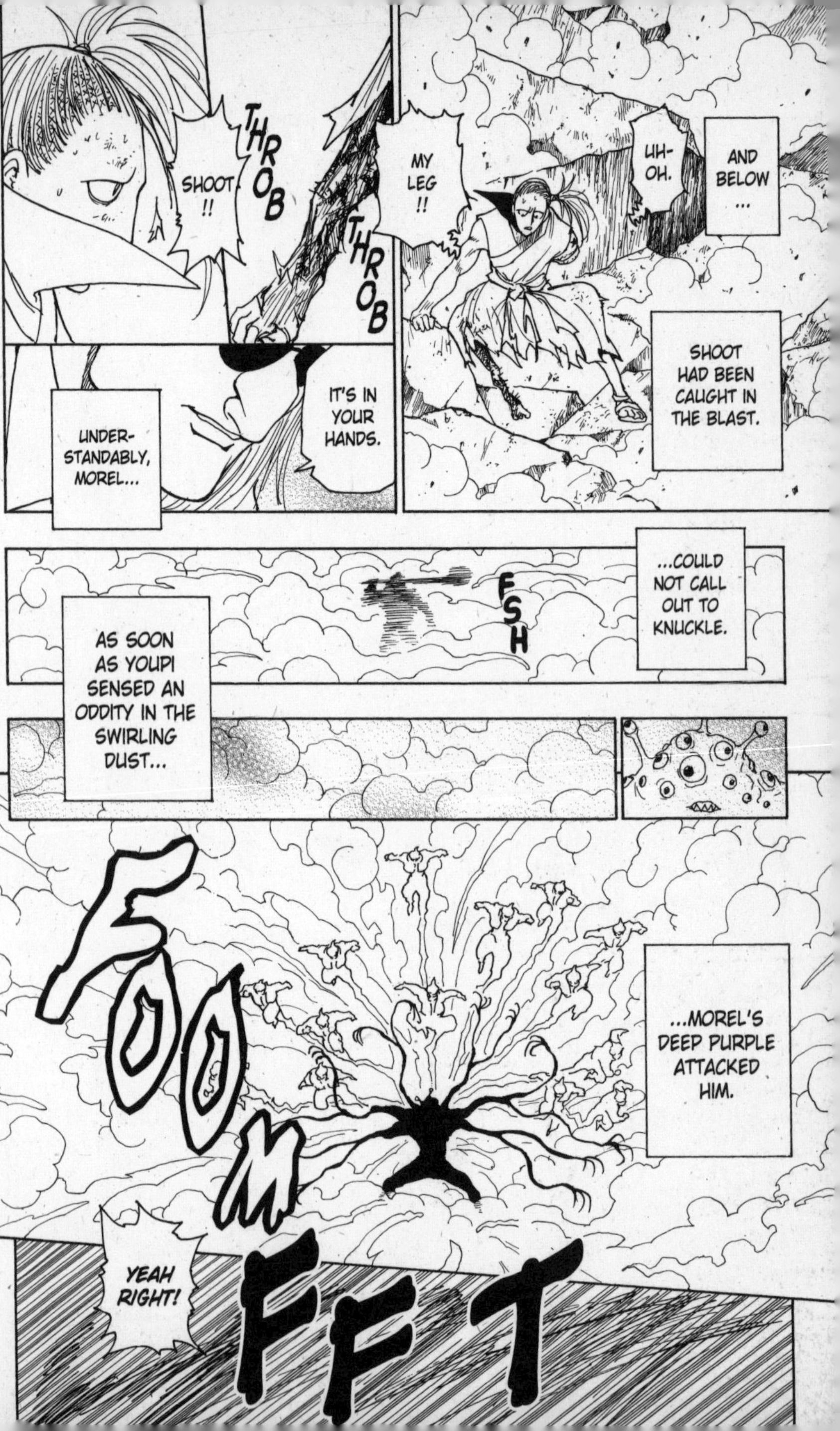
AND BELOW ...
UH-OH.
MY LEG !!
SHOOT HAD BEEN CAUGHT IN THE BLAST.
THROB
SHOOT !!
THROB
IT'S IN YOUR HANDS.
UNDER-STANDABLY, MOREL...
...COULD NOT CALL OUT TO KNUCKLE.
FSH
AS SOON AS YOUPI SENSED AN ODDITY IN THE SWIRLING DUST...
...MOREL'S DEEP PURPLE ATTACKED HIM.
FOOOM
YEAH RIGHT!
FFT

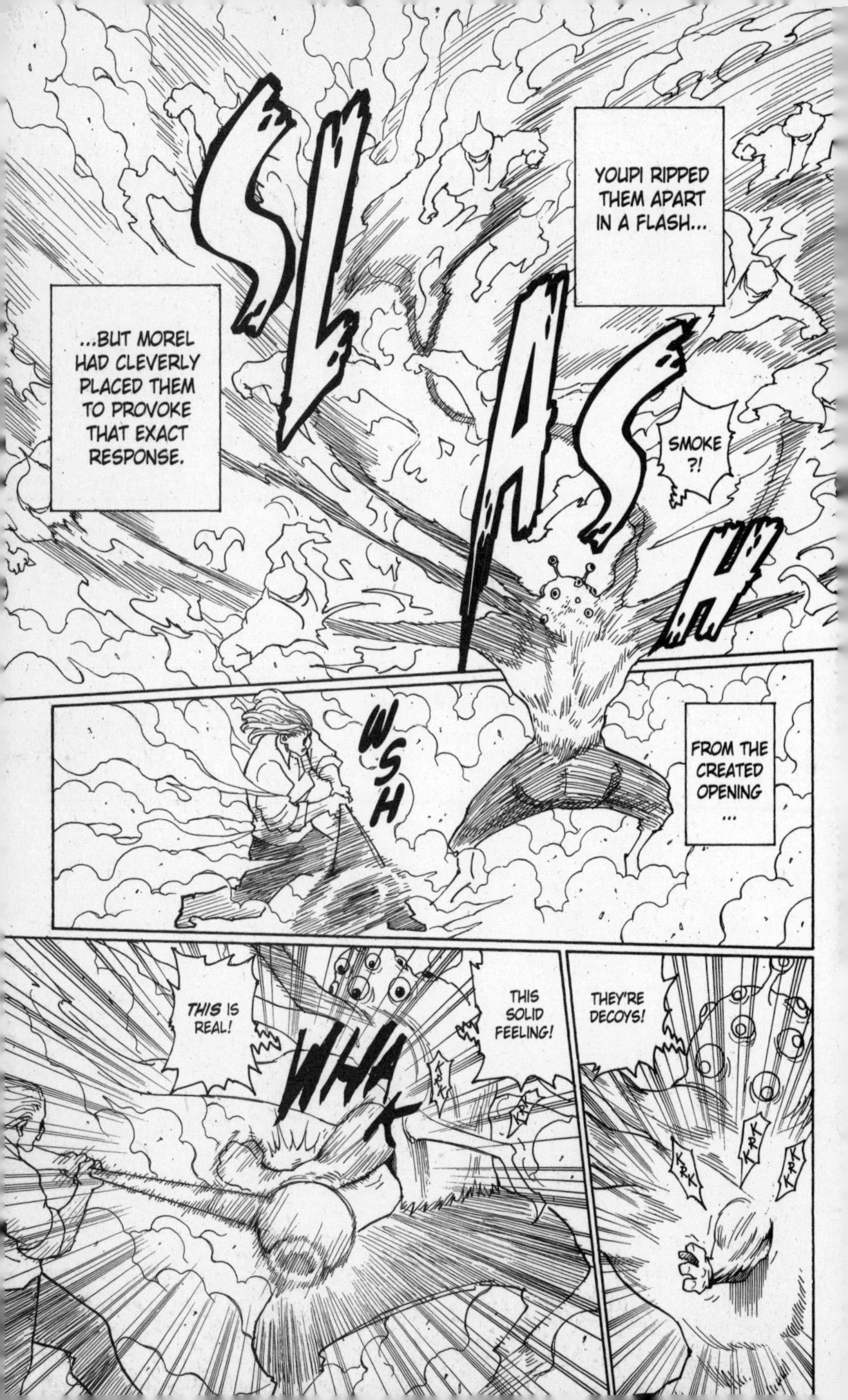
YOUPI RIPPED THEM APART IN A FLASH...
SLASH
SMOKE ?!
...BUT MOREL HAD CLEVERLY PLACED THEM TO PROVOKE THAT EXACT RESPONSE.
FROM THE CREATED OPENING ...
WSH
THEY'RE DECOYS!
KRK
KRK
KRK
THIS SOLID FEELING!
KRK
THIS IS REAL!
WHAK
KRK

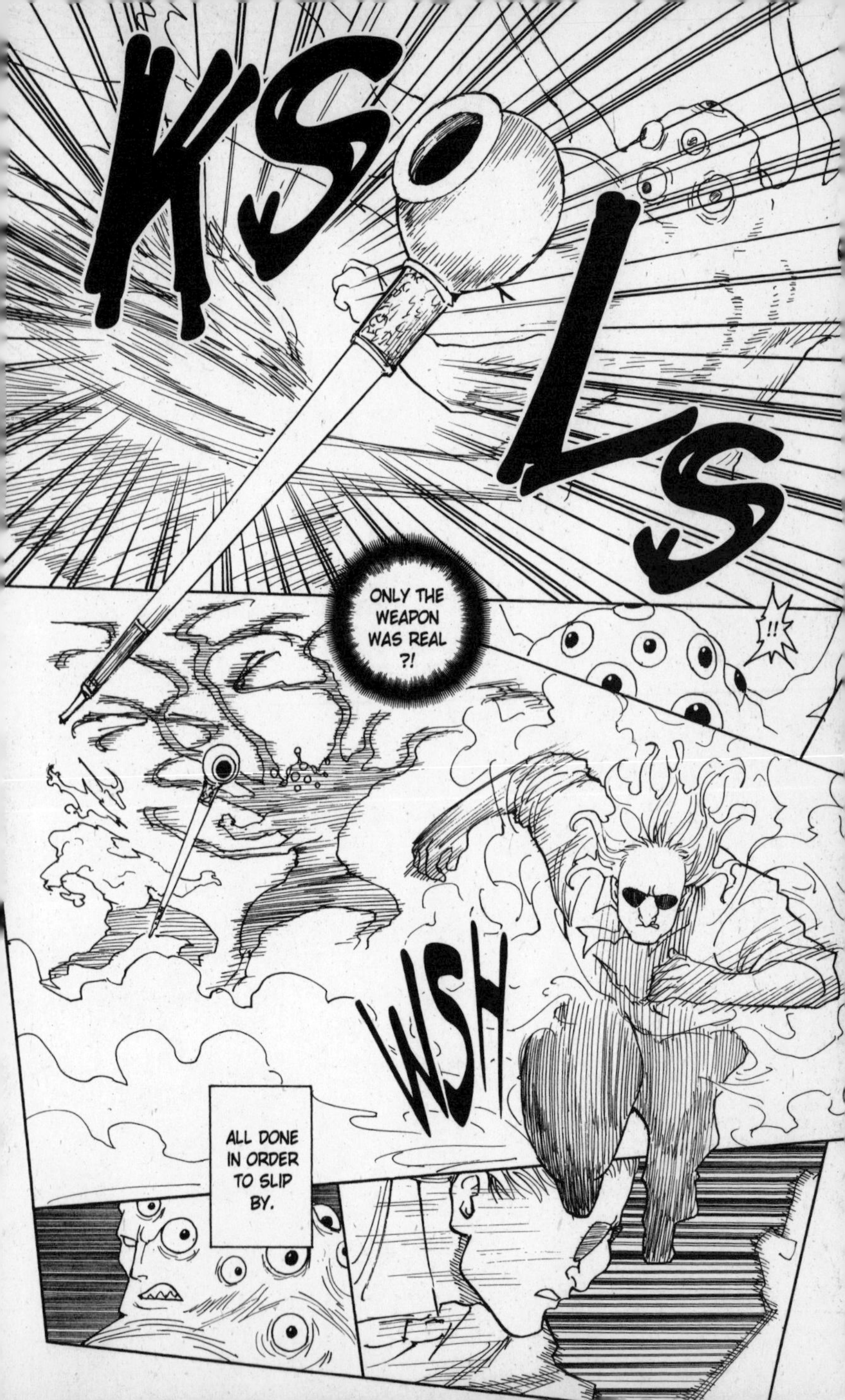
KSO
LS
!!
ONLY THE WEAPON WAS REAL ?!
WSH
ALL DONE IN ORDER TO SLIP BY.

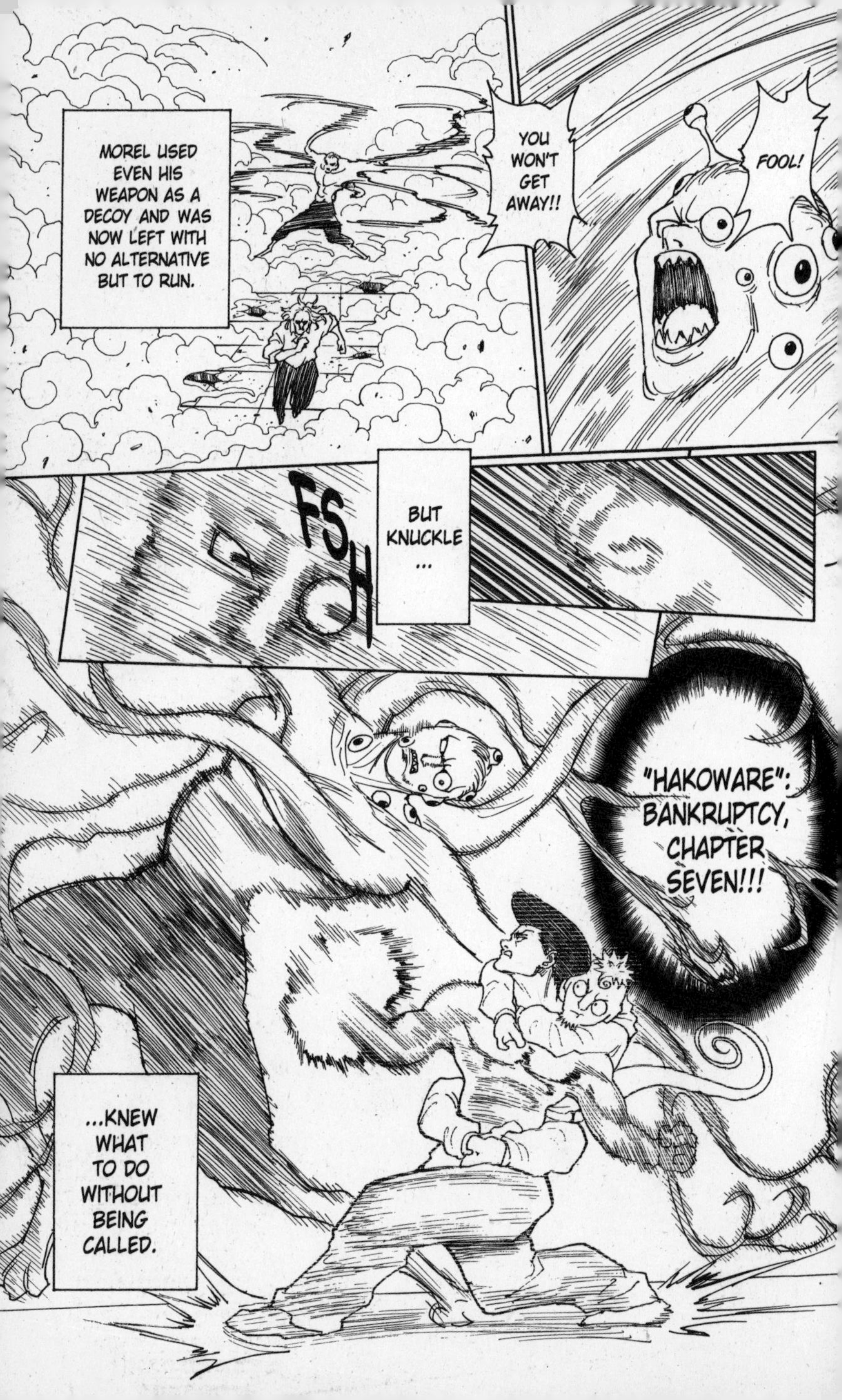
FOOL!
YOU WON'T GET AWAY!!
MOREL USED EVEN HIS WEAPON AS A DECOY AND WAS NOW LEFT WITH NO ALTERNATIVE BUT TO RUN.
BUT KNUCKLE ...
FSH
"HAKOWARE": BANKRUPTCY, CHAPTER SEVEN!!!
...KNEW WHAT TO DO WITHOUT BEING CALLED.

ROUND SEVEN: SURVIVAL RACE

○ THREE TO A GROUP, WITH ONLY ONE ADVANCING TO THE NEXT ROUND. (PLUS, TWO ELIMINATED PLAYERS GET A SECOND CHANCE.)

A TWO-LAP RACE AROUND A 20-SQUARE TRACK. EACH TURN, PEOPLE ADVANCE BY THE NUMBER OF SQUARES TALLIED BY SPEED STAT + DIE ROLL. EACH LAP, THE SLOWEST ONE IS ELIMINATED. IF MULTIPLE PEOPLE PASS THE FINISH LINE IN THE SAME TURN, THE ONE WHO'S MOST AHEAD REMAINS. IF THEY'RE IN THE SAME SQUARE, THE TIE IS BROKEN BY THEIR TIMING STATS. IF THERE'S STILL A TIE, THEY GO ANOTHER LAP.

HERE ARE THE 44 FINALISTS!!!!

FINALISTS:

SUPER NINJA WOLF, HIROKI, RIO, ATRALPU, NUO, KIBBLEWHITE, BONKICHI, AKIHIRO, SHINOBI, SAEKIPUON, KADAYA, UCCHI, TEN-TEN, NAMELESS, MA, K-WAFFLE, TOBIAH, L, HIRO-PON, DANDA-DANDA, ROULETTE BUTLER, HIROSHI, MIHO KUBOTA, SATOSHI, GUSSURA, ATSUSHI, SUPI, AGEHA, MASHIKA, JAM AJI, UMAHIKO, SID, CROW BLOOD, CHEETU BAZOOKA, KIKYO, Y.T., MOOK, SYLVIAN, NEYUS, DEEP IMPACT, TOSHI, YUKITO YÛRAKU, TAIKI PAULOWNIA AND KANA

CONGRATULATIONS!!

Chapter 269: Adversity Is a Good Thing

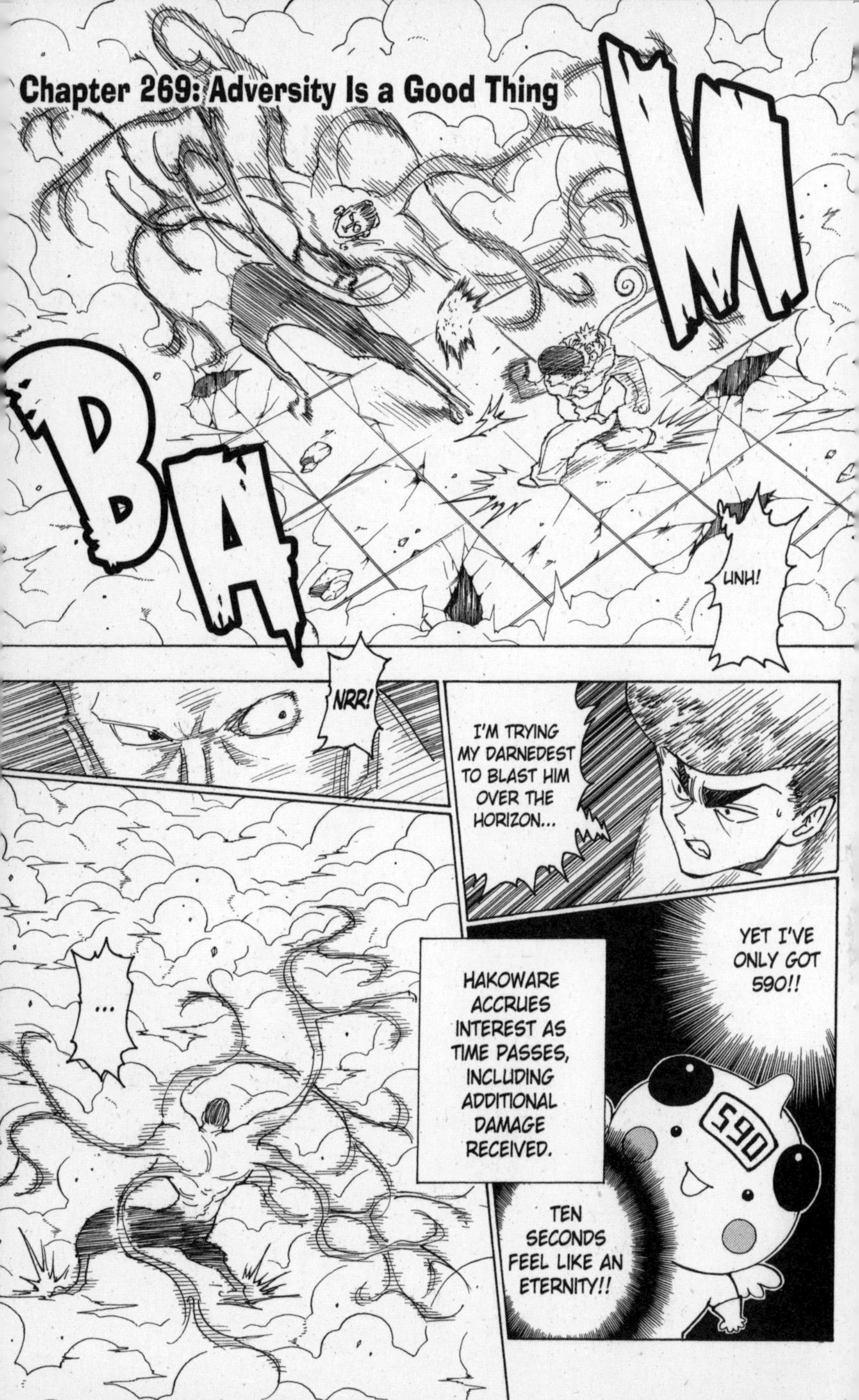

BAM
UNH!
I'M TRYING MY DARNEDEST TO BLAST HIM OVER THE HORIZON...
NRR!
YET I'VE ONLY GOT 590!!
HAKOWARE ACCRUES INTEREST AS TIME PASSES, INCLUDING ADDITIONAL DAMAGE RECEIVED.
590
TEN SECONDS FEEL LIKE AN ETERNITY!!
...

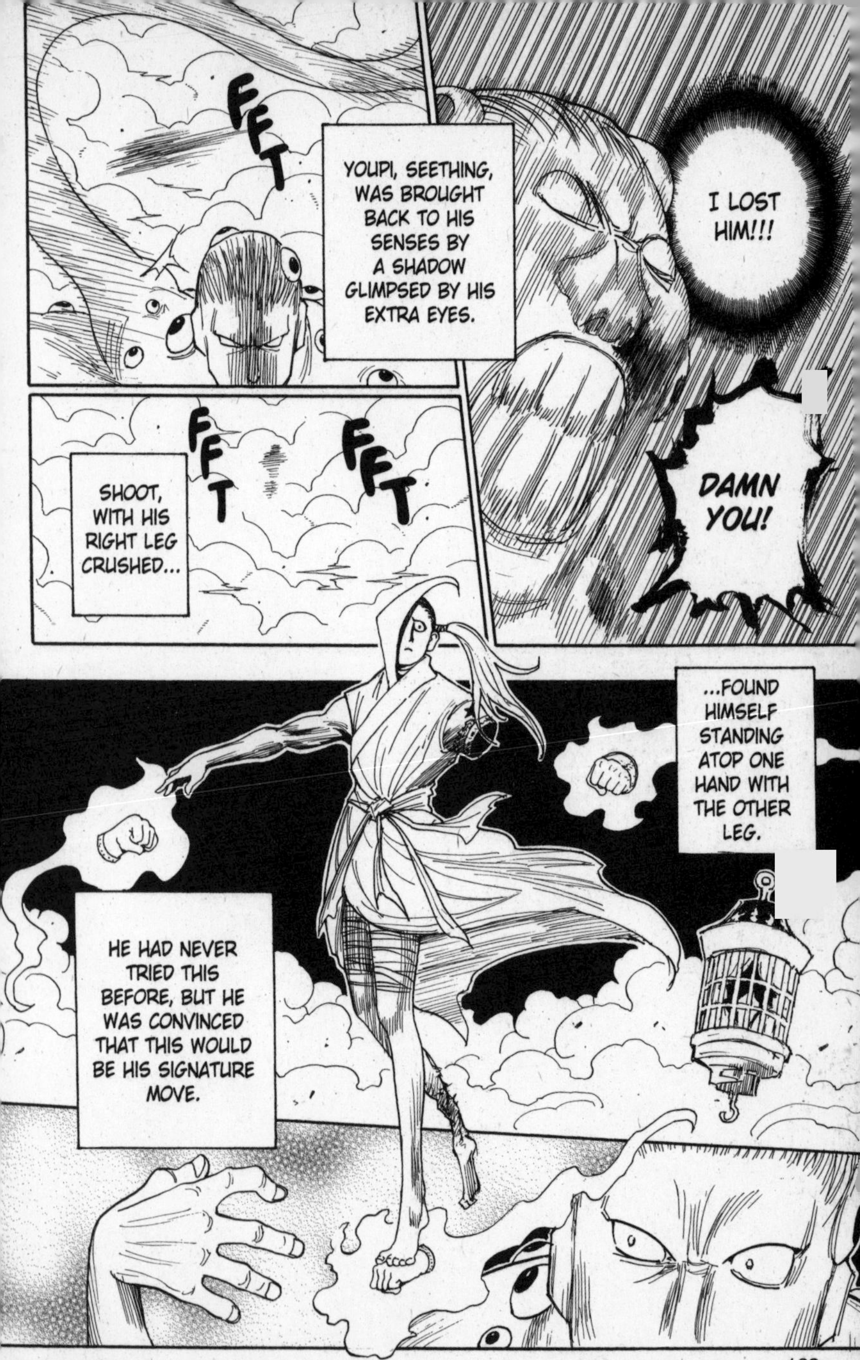
I LOST HIM!!!
DAMN YOU!
FFT
YOUPI, SEETHING, WAS BROUGHT BACK TO HIS SENSES BY A SHADOW GLIMPSED BY HIS EXTRA EYES.
FFT
FFT
SHOOT, WITH HIS RIGHT LEG CRUSHED...
...FOUND HIMSELF STANDING ATOP ONE HAND WITH THE OTHER LEG.
HE HAD NEVER TRIED THIS BEFORE, BUT HE WAS CONVINCED THAT THIS WOULD BE HIS SIGNATURE MOVE.

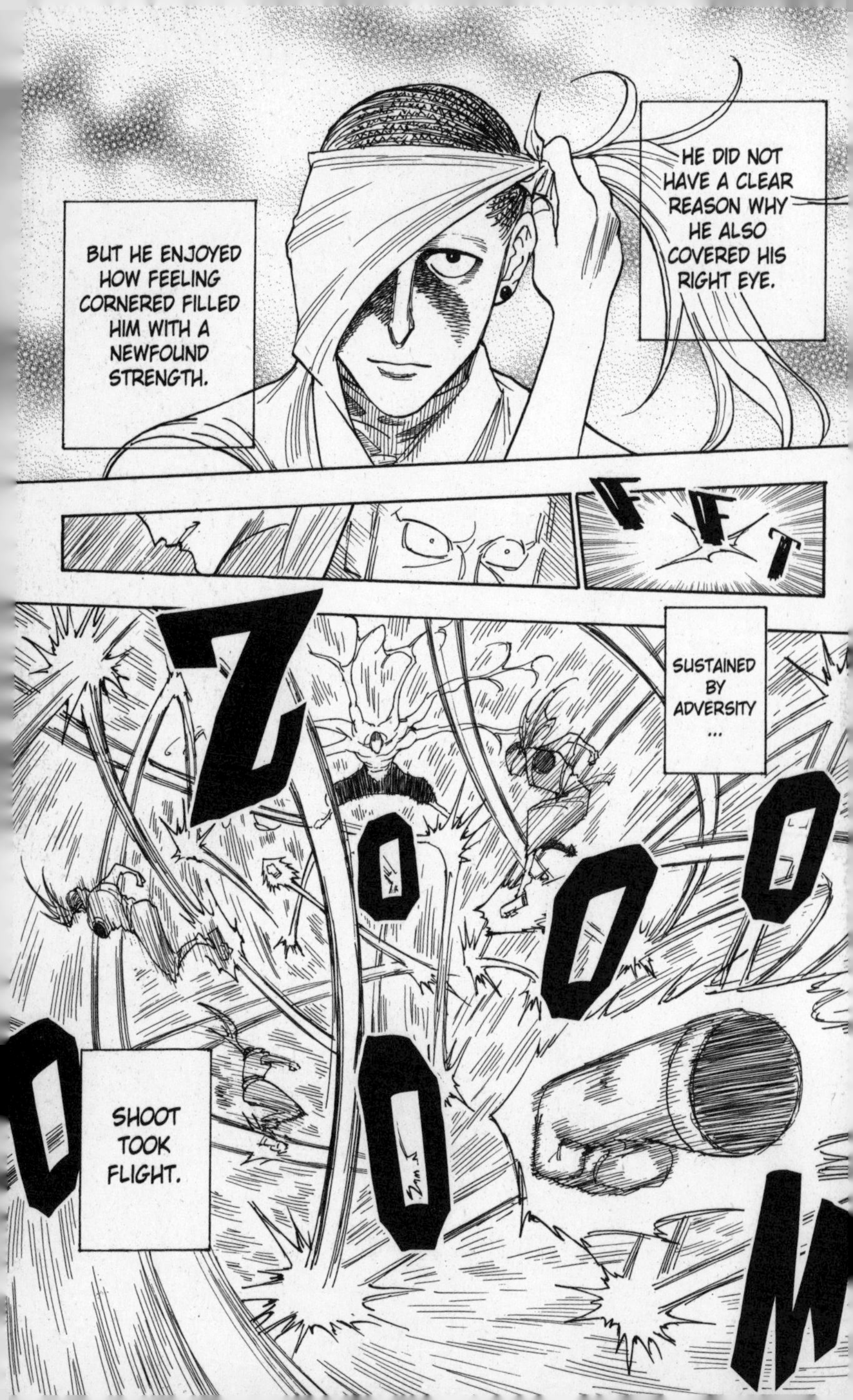
HE DID NOT HAVE A CLEAR REASON WHY HE ALSO COVERED HIS RIGHT EYE.
BUT HE ENJOYED HOW FEELING CORNERED FILLED HIM WITH A NEWFOUND STRENGTH.
FFT
SUSTAINED BY ADVERSITY ...
ZOOOOOM
SHOOT TOOK FLIGHT.

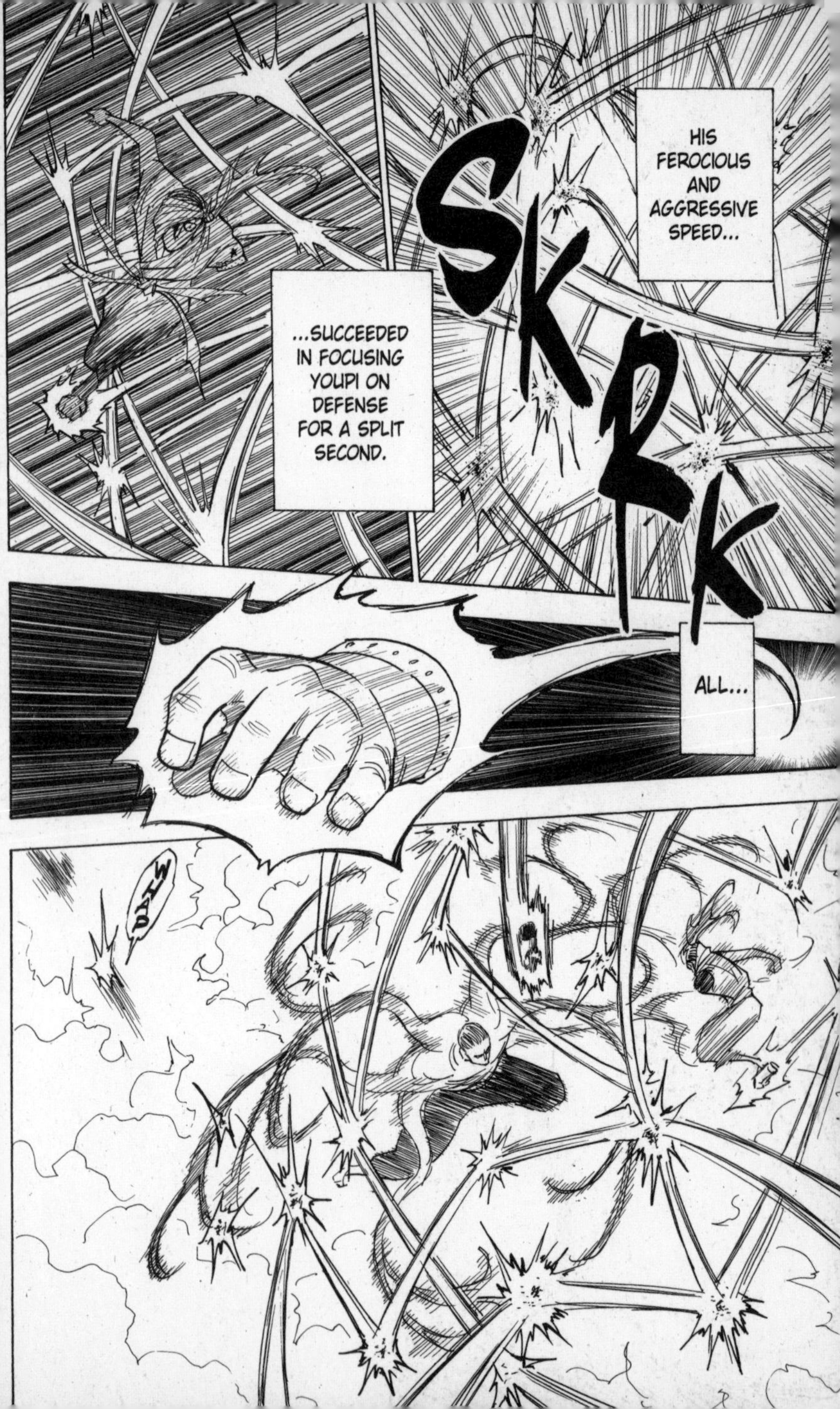
HIS FEROCIOUS AND AGGRESSIVE SPEED...
SKRK
...SUCCEEDED IN FOCUSING YOUPI ON DEFENSE FOR A SPLIT SECOND.
ALL...
WHAM

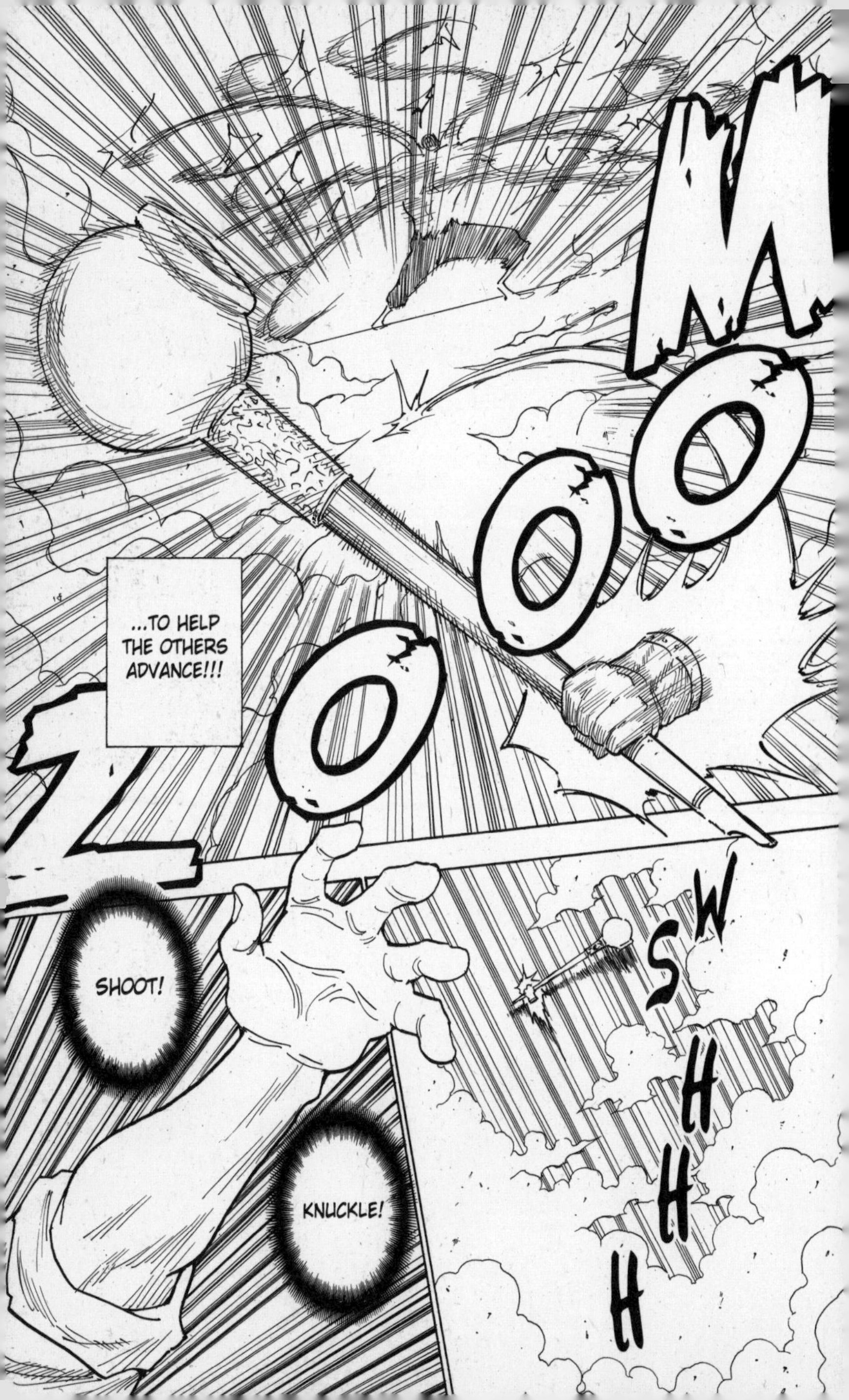
ZOOOM
SWHHH
...TO HELP THE OTHERS ADVANCE!!!
SHOOT!
KNUCKLE!

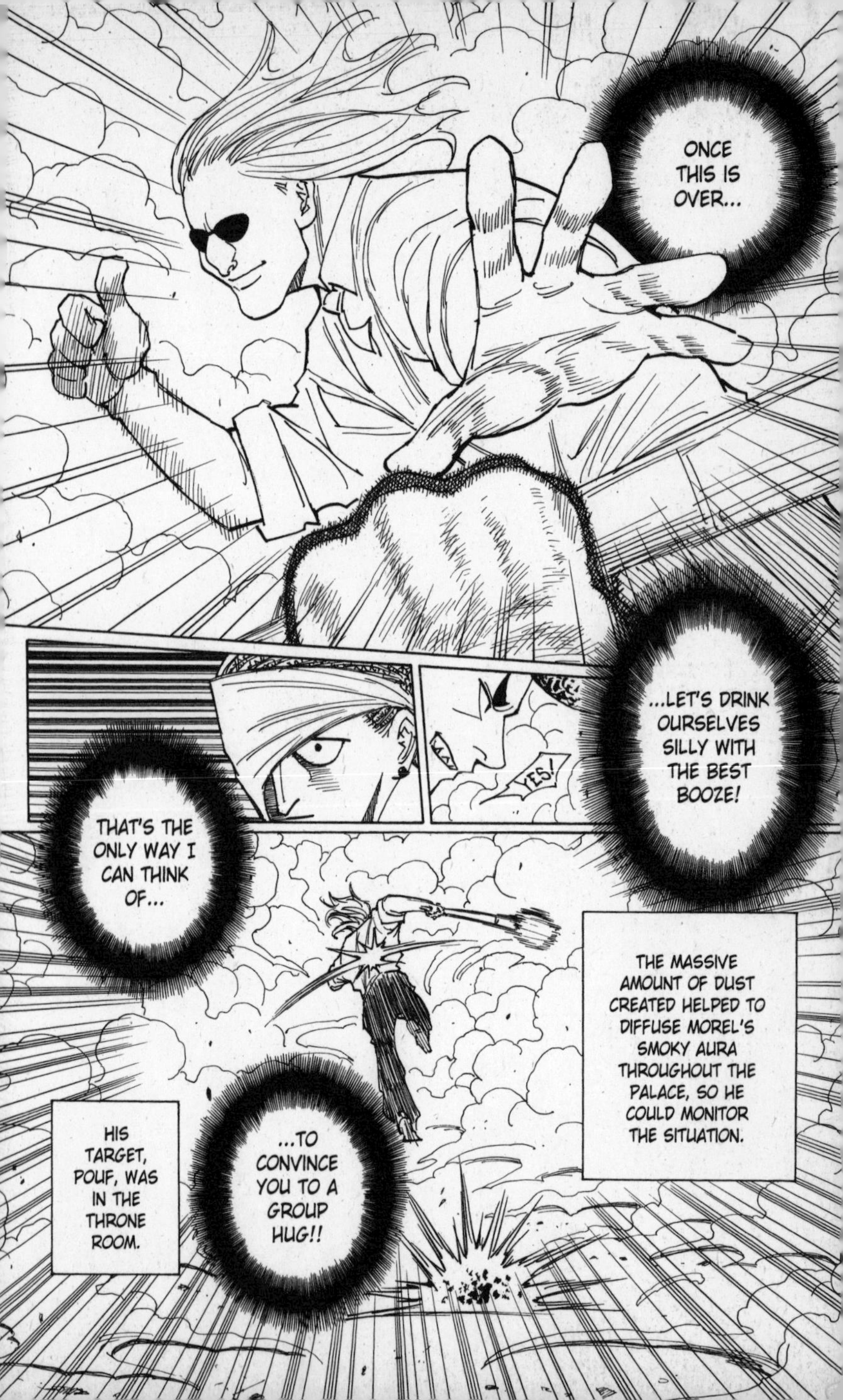
ONCE THIS IS OVER...
...LET'S DRINK OURSELVES SILLY WITH THE BEST BOOZE!
YES!
THAT'S THE ONLY WAY I CAN THINK OF...
THE MASSIVE AMOUNT OF DUST CREATED HELPED TO DIFFUSE MOREL'S SMOKY AURA THROUGHOUT THE PALACE, SO HE COULD MONITOR THE SITUATION.
...TO CONVINCE YOU TO A GROUP HUG!!
HIS TARGET, POUF, WAS IN THE THRONE ROOM.

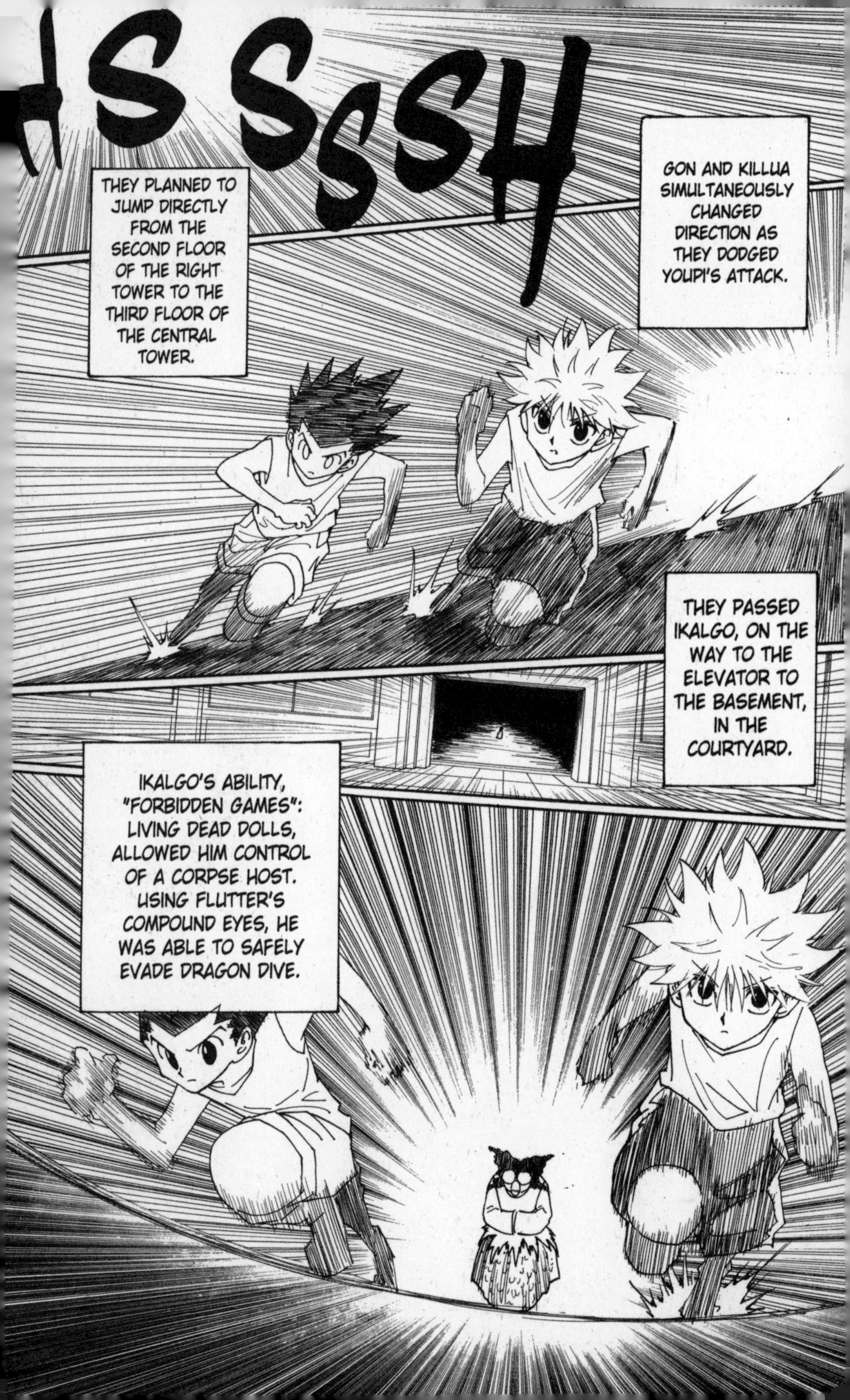
HSSSSH
GON AND KILLUA SIMULTANEOUSLY CHANGED DIRECTION AS THEY DODGED YOUPI'S ATTACK.
THEY PLANNED TO JUMP DIRECTLY FROM THE SECOND FLOOR OF THE RIGHT TOWER TO THE THIRD FLOOR OF THE CENTRAL TOWER.
THEY PASSED IKALGO, ON THE WAY TO THE ELEVATOR TO THE BASEMENT, IN THE COURTYARD.
IKALGO'S ABILITY, "FORBIDDEN GAMES": LIVING DEAD DOLLS, ALLOWED HIM CONTROL OF A CORPSE HOST. USING FLUTTER'S COMPOUND EYES, HE WAS ABLE TO SAFELY EVADE DRAGON DIVE.

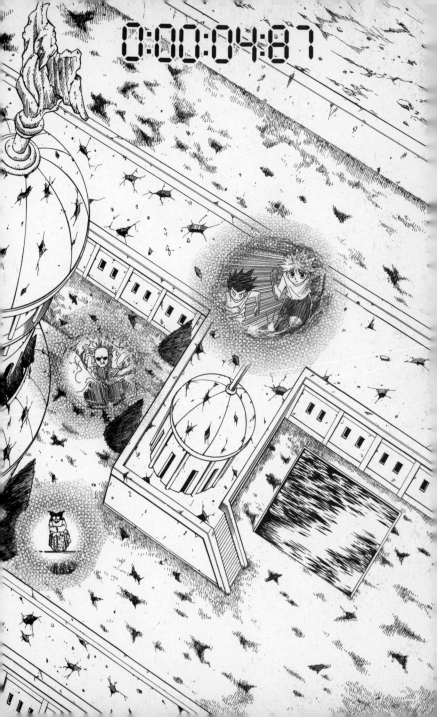

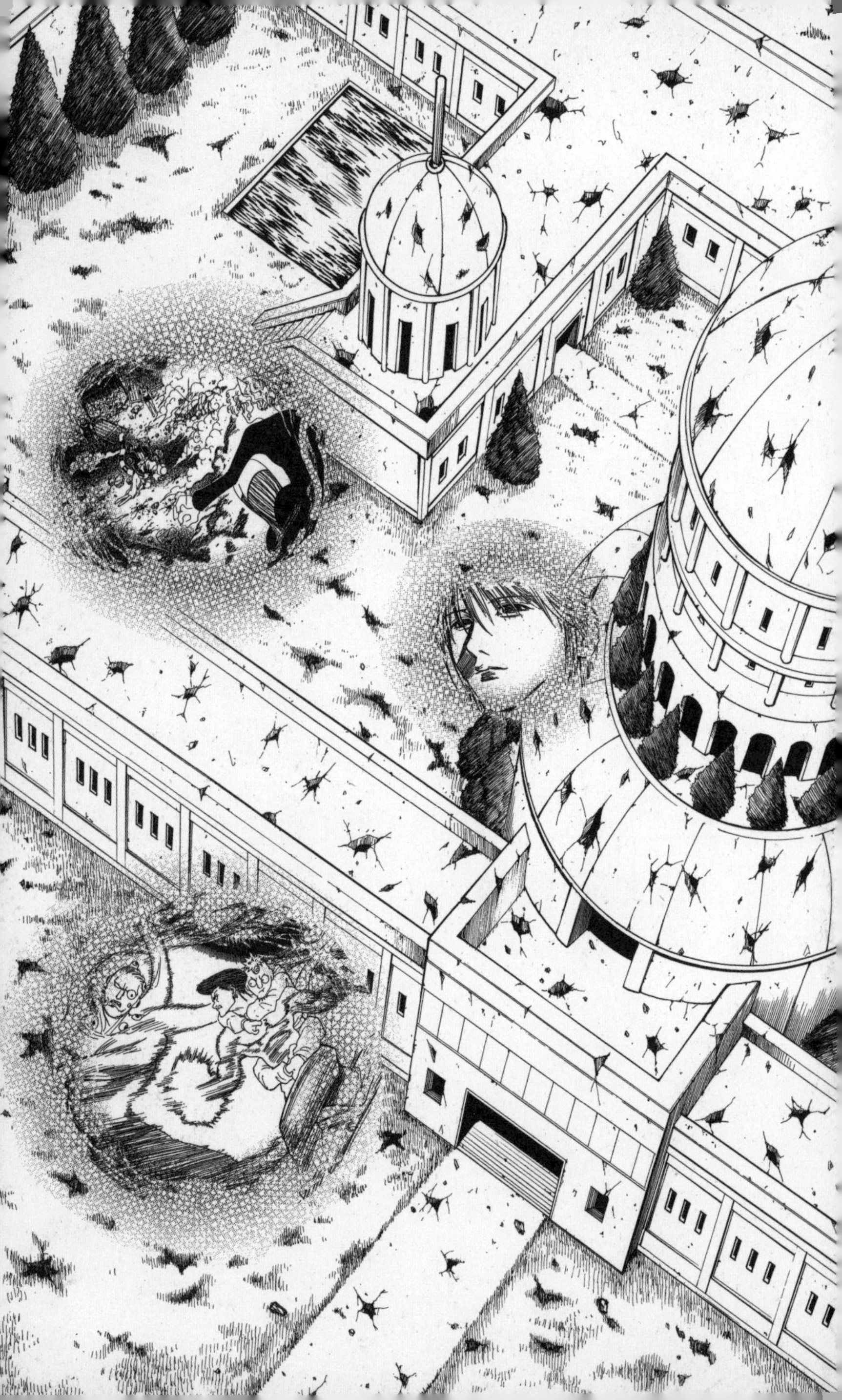

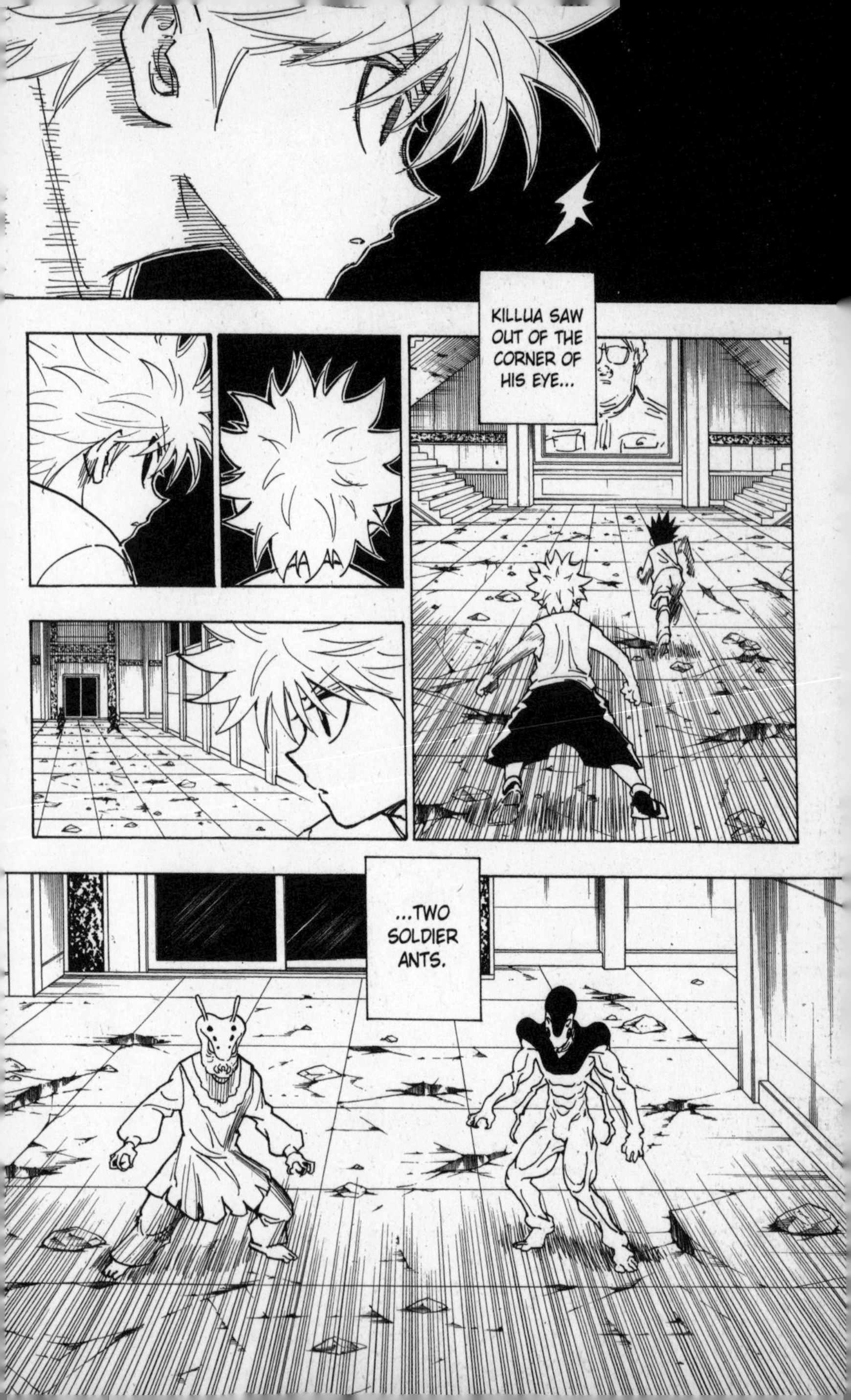
KILLUA SAW OUT OF THE CORNER OF HIS EYE...
...TWO SOLDIER ANTS.

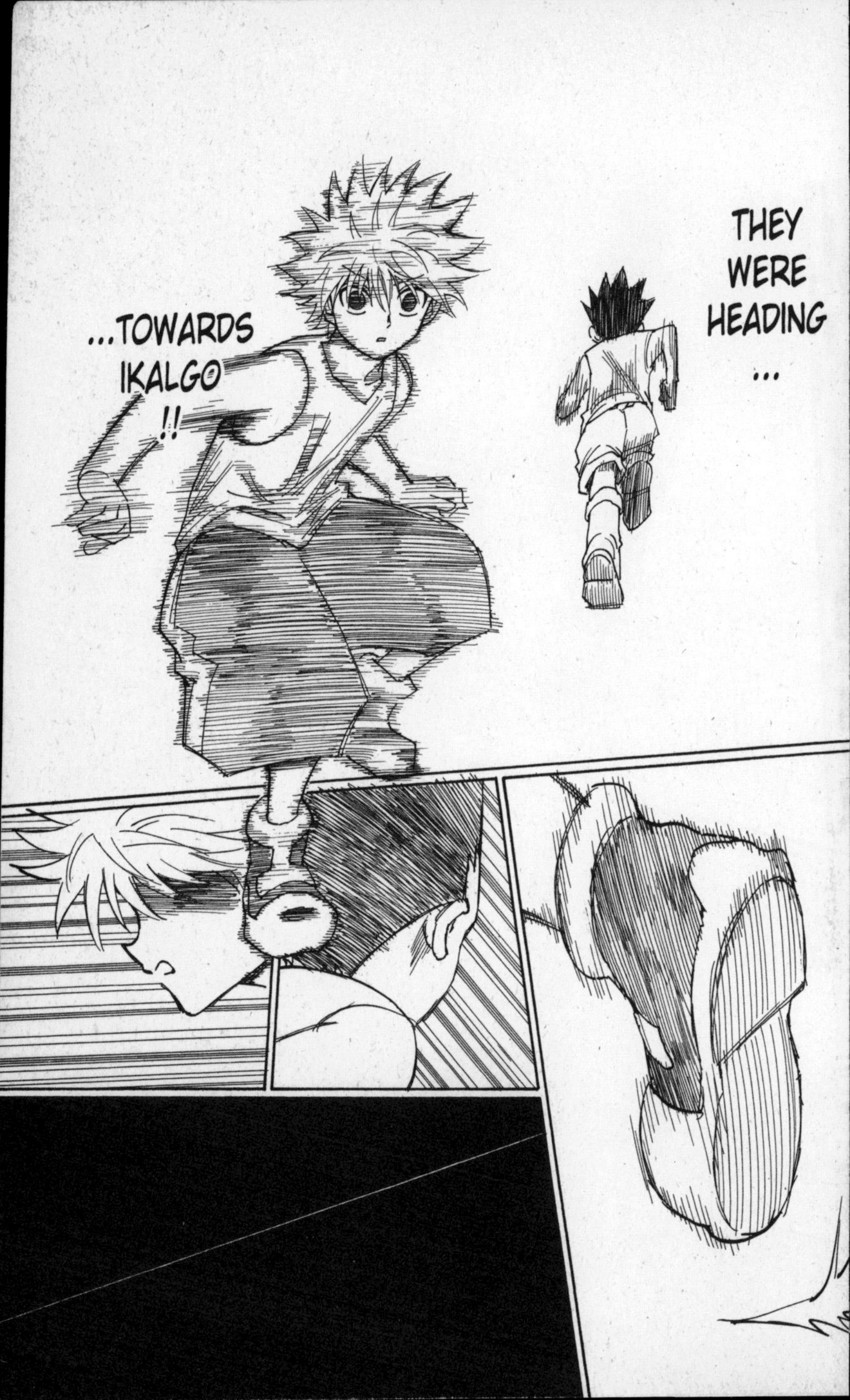
THEY WERE HEADING ...
...TOWARDS IKALGO !!

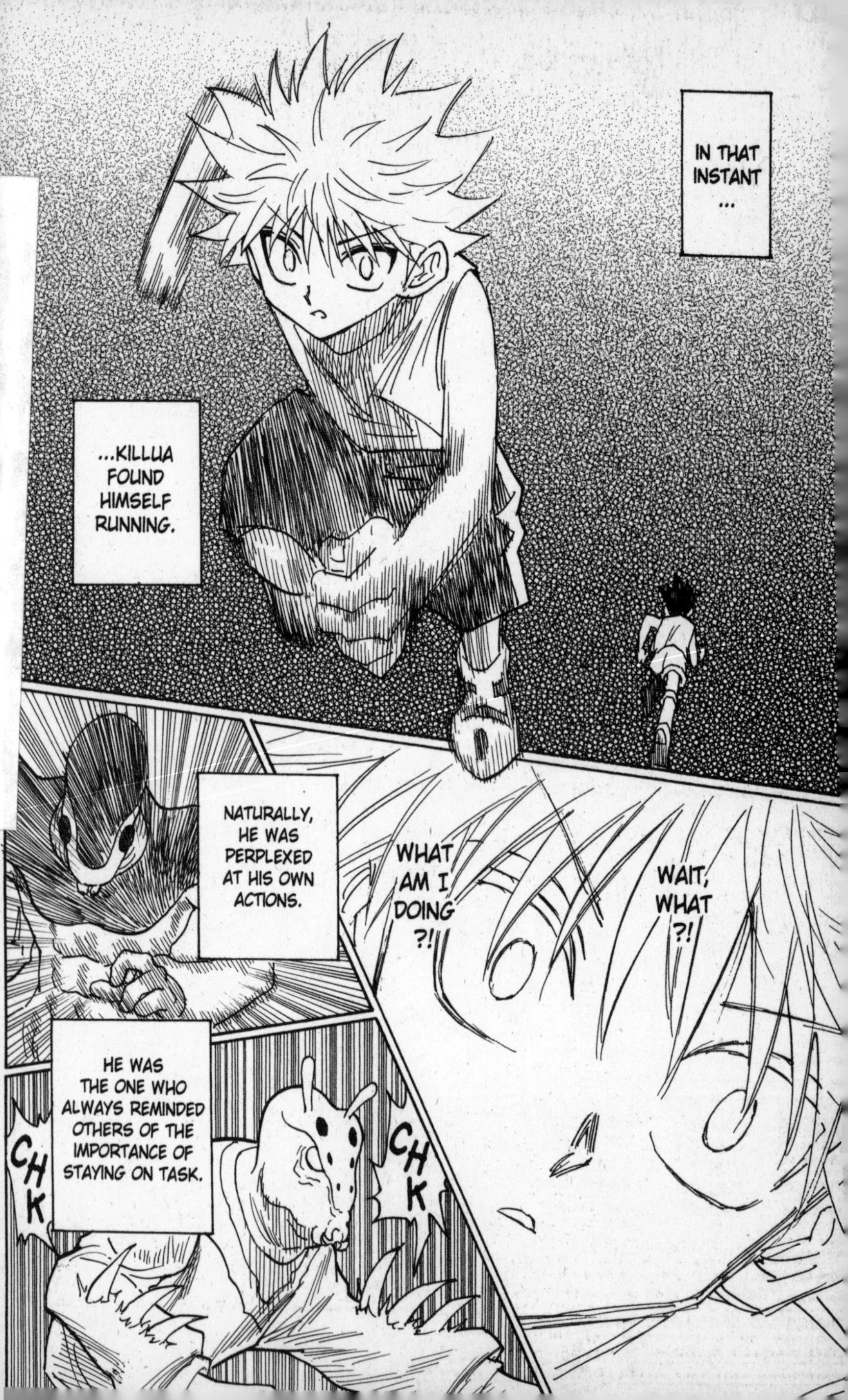
IN THAT INSTANT ...
...KILLUA FOUND HIMSELF RUNNING.
WAIT, WHAT ?!
WHAT AM I DOING ?!
NATURALLY, HE WAS PERPLEXED AT HIS OWN ACTIONS.
HE WAS THE ONE WHO ALWAYS REMINDED OTHERS OF THE IMPORTANCE OF STAYING ON TASK.
CHK
CHK

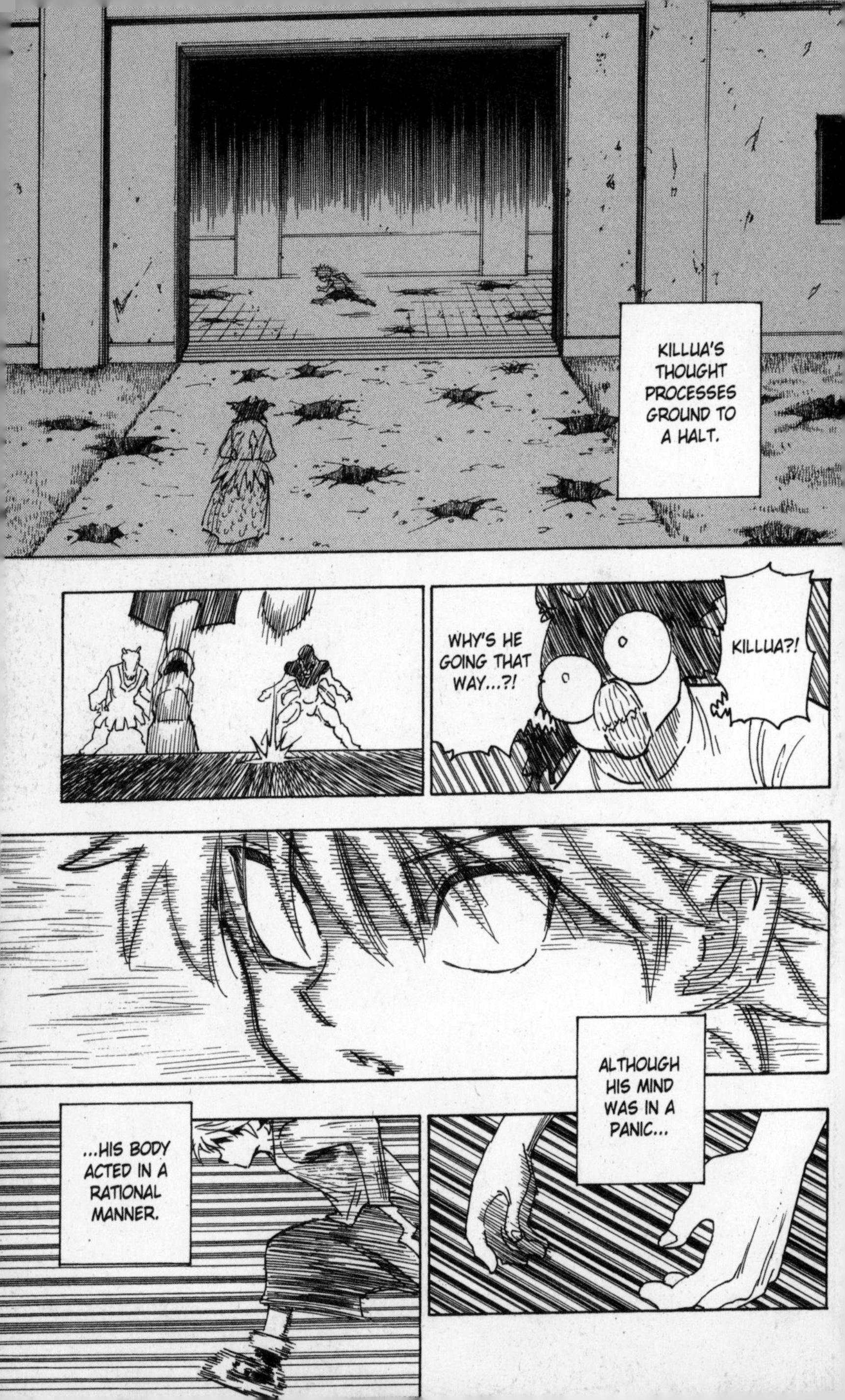
KILLUA'S THOUGHT PROCESSES GROUND TO A HALT.
KILLUA?!
WHY'S HE GOING THAT WAY...?!
ALTHOUGH HIS MIND WAS IN A PANIC...
...HIS BODY ACTED IN A RATIONAL MANNER.

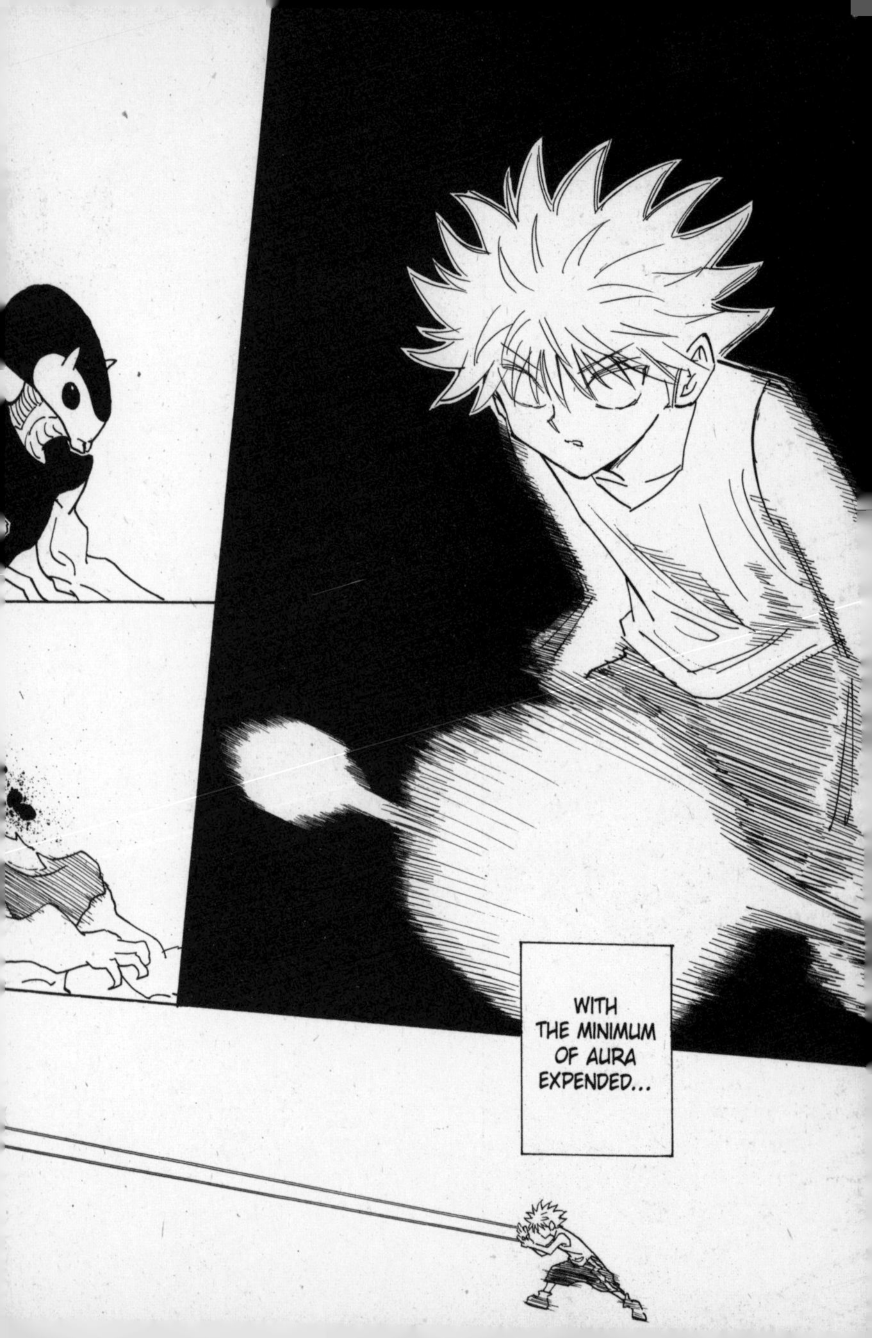
WITH THE MINIMUM OF AURA EXPENDED...

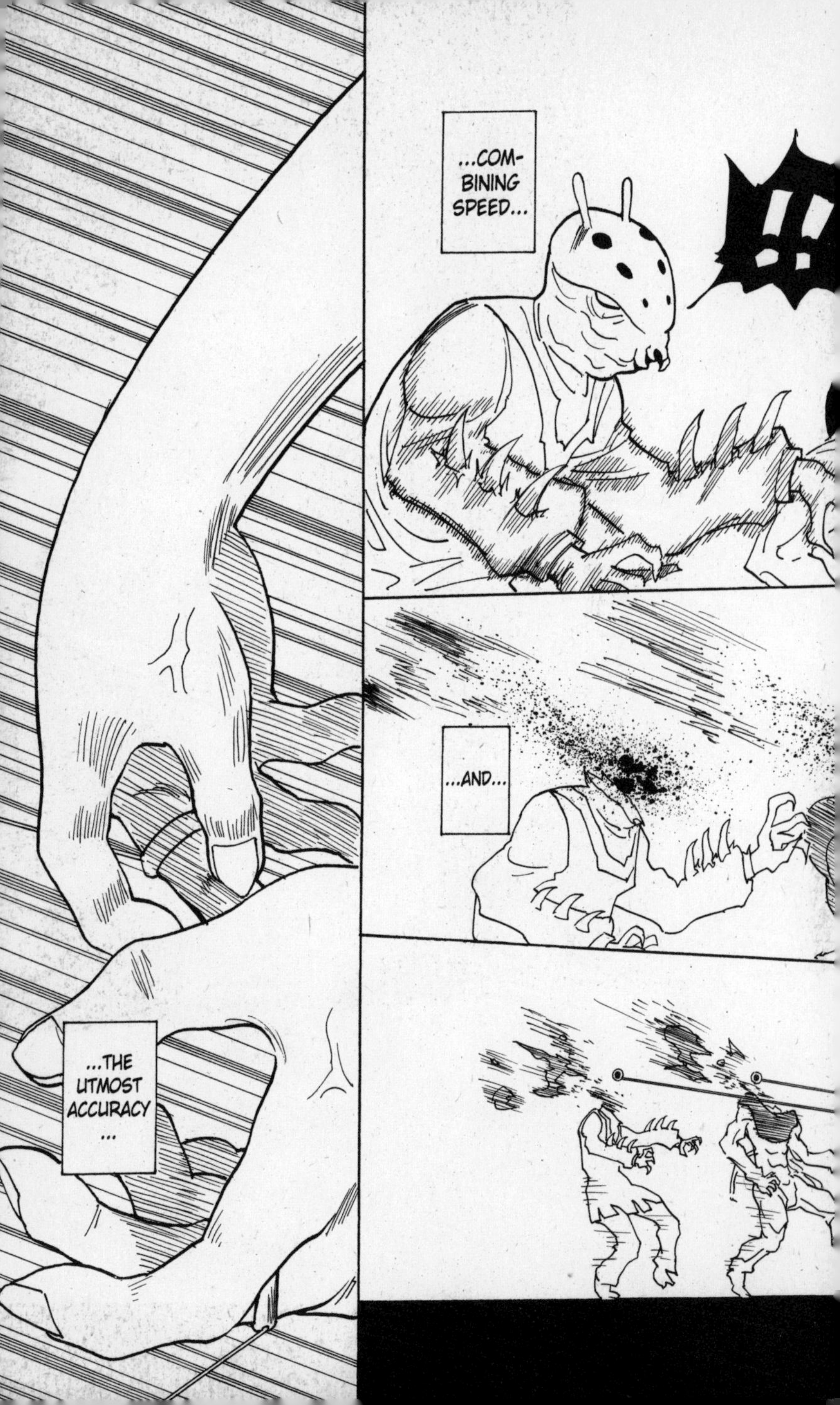
...COM-
BINING
SPEED...
!!
...AND...
...THE
UTMOST
ACCURACY
...

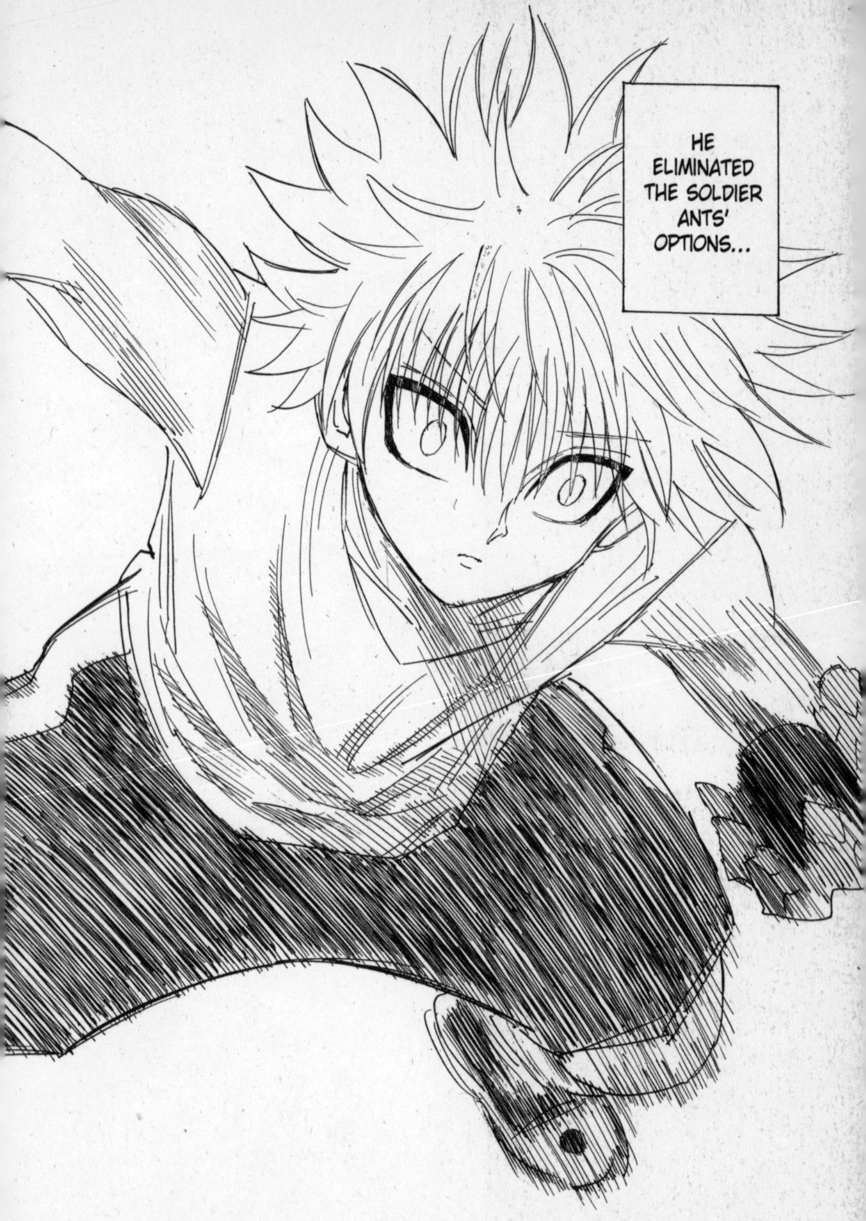
HE ELIMINATED THE SOLDIER ANTS' OPTIONS...

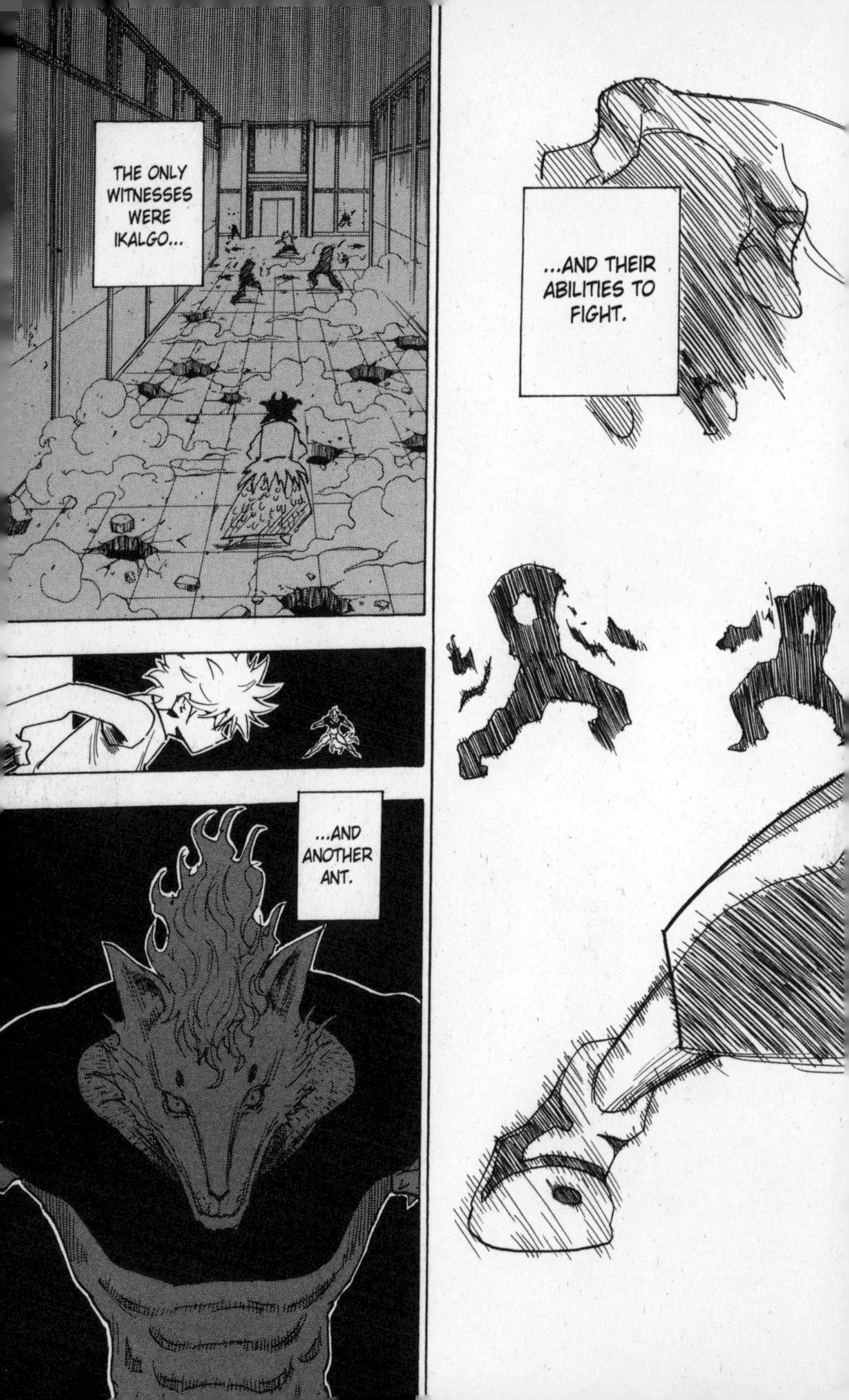
...AND THEIR ABILITIES TO FIGHT.
THE ONLY WITNESSES WERE IKALGO...
...AND ANOTHER ANT.

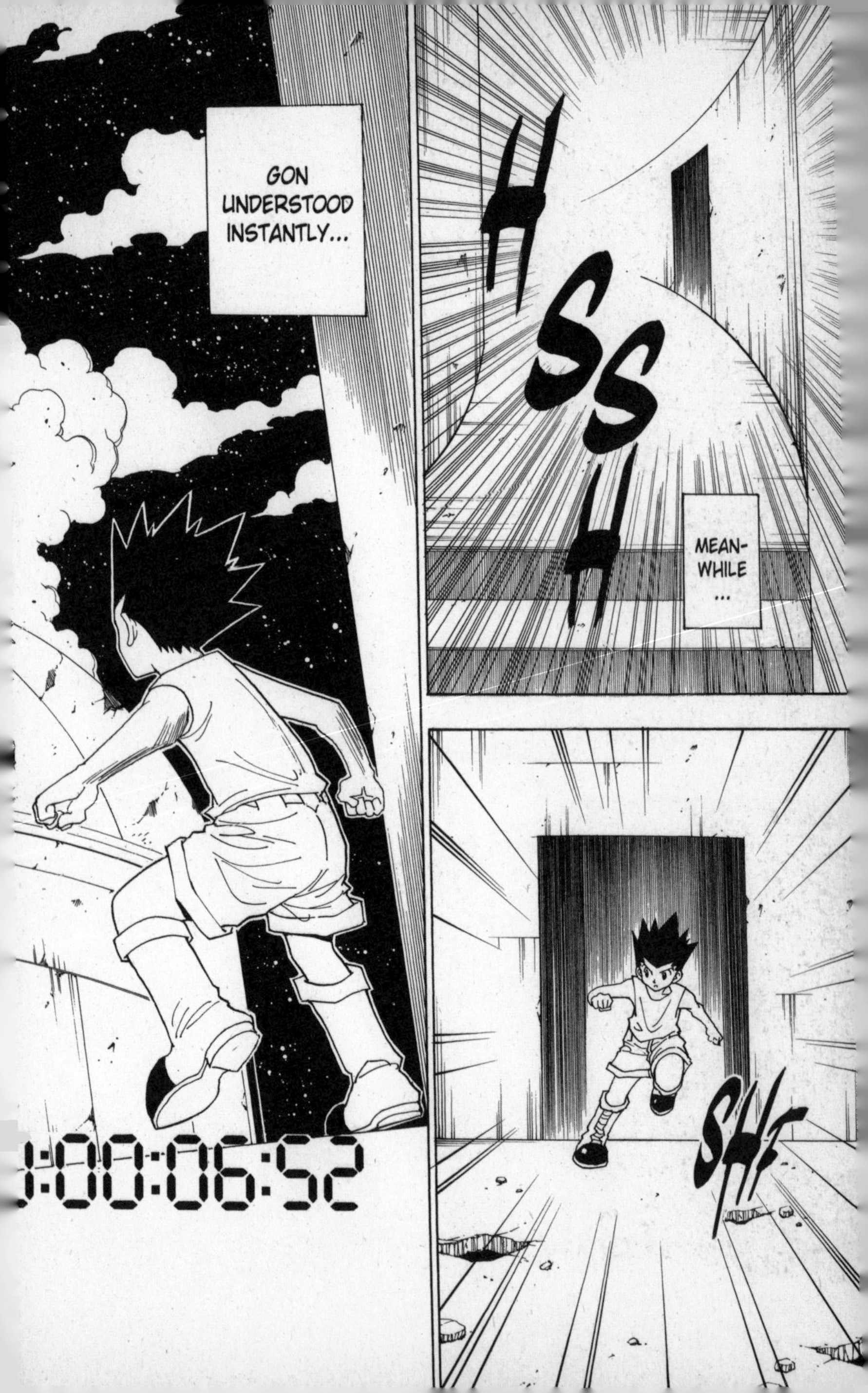
HSSH
MEAN-WHILE...
SHF
GON UNDERSTOOD INSTANTLY...
00:06:52

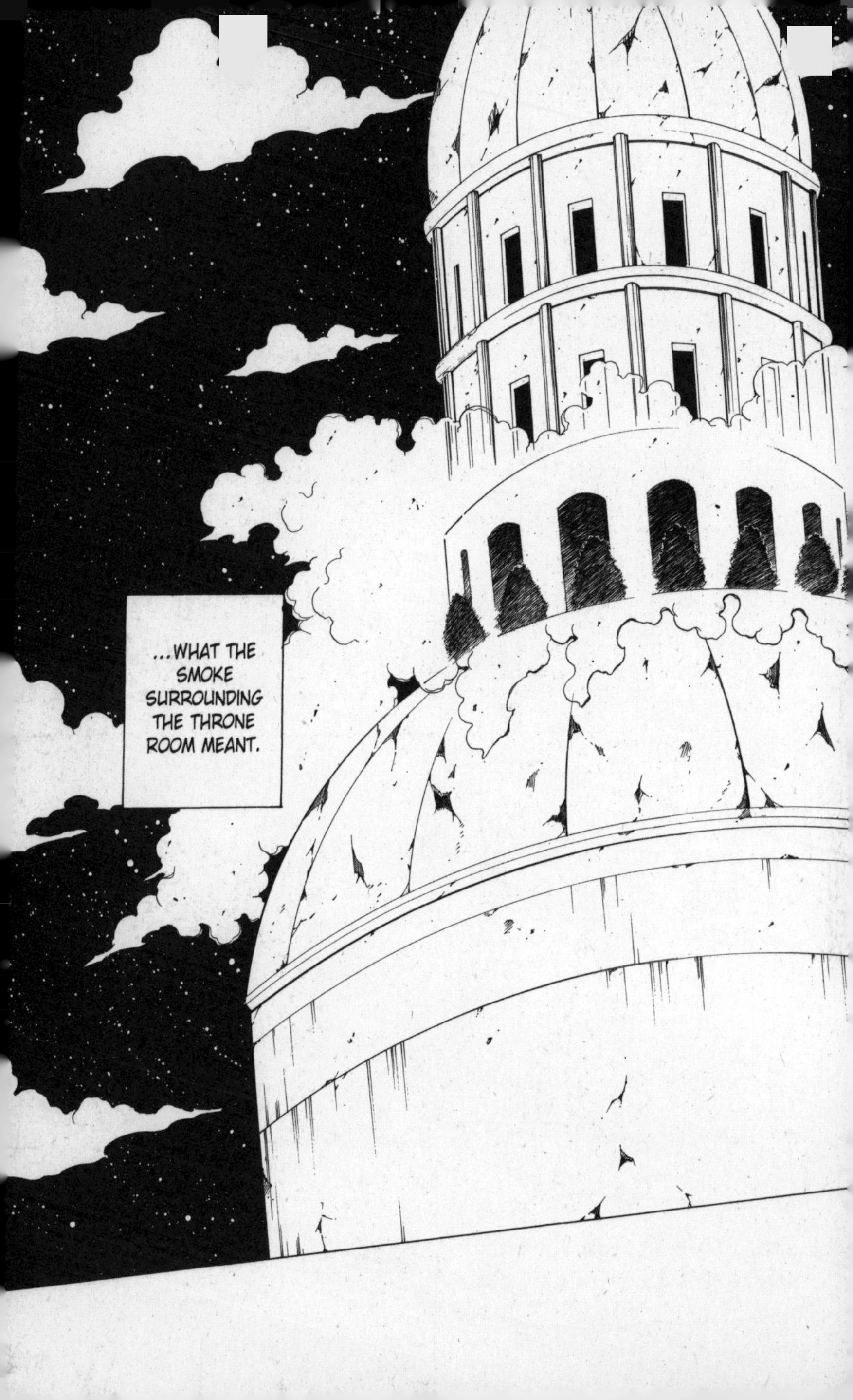
...WHAT THE SMOKE SURROUNDING THE THRONE ROOM MEANT.

FINAL EVENT: TRIPLE MUSCLE

○ FOUR TO A GROUP, WITH ONLY ONE PLAYER WINNING. EACH PLAYER WAS PAIRED IN A SHOWDOWN WITH EACH OTHER PLAYER IN THE GROUP.
SCORES WERE TALLIED BY POWER STAT + SPEED STAT + JUMP STAT + DIE ROLL. WINNING WAS WORTH 3 POINTS, WITH A TIE WORTH 1 POINT. THE HIGHEST NUMBER OF POINTS WINS THE GROUP AND PASSES THE HUNTER EXAM. IF THERE'S A TIE IN THE GROUP, THE ONE WITH THE HIGHEST COMBINED TOTAL OF ALL THREE OF THEIR ROLLS WINS. THE MATCH-UP IS IN THE ORDER OF THE PREVIOUS EXAM PAGE.

	Super Ninja Wolf	Hiroki	Rio	Atralpu
Super Ninja Wolf		O 17	O 16	O 17
Hiroki	X 11		X 12	O 16
Rio	X 15	O 15		O 15
Atralpu	X 14	X 11	X 12	

Super Ninja Wolf (9pts)

	Nuo	Kibble-white	Bonkichi	Akihiro
Nuo		X 12	X 15	O 16
Kibble-white	O 14		X 13	X 14
Bonkichi	O 17	O 12		O 17
Akihiro	X 14	O 18	X 15	

Bonkichi (6pts/roll:46)

	Shinobi	Saekipuon	Kadaya	Ucchi
Shinobi		X 15	△ 14	X 13
Saekipuon	O 17		O 16	O 16
Kadaya	△ 14	X 15		X 15
Ucchi	O 17	X 15	O 17	

Saekipuon (9pts)

	Ten-Ten	Nameless	Ma	K-Waffle
Ten-Ten		X 14	X 15	O 17
Nameless	O 16		O 15	O 15
Ma	O 16	X 13		O 16
K-Waffle	X 12	X 17	X 13	

Nameless (6pts/roll:46)

	Tobiah	L	Hiro-pon	Danda-Danda
Tobiah		O 17	△ 14	O 18
L	X 11		X 12	X 15
Hiro-pon	△ 14	O 14		O 16
Danda-Danda	X 15	O 16	X 13	

Tobiah (7pts/roll:49)

	Roulette Butler	Hiroshi	Miko Kubota	Satoshi
Roulette Butler		O 14	O 13	X 12
Hiroshi	X 13		X 14	O 15
Miko Kubota	X 17	O 17		O 15
Satoshi	O 19	X 15	O 16	

Satoshi (6pts/roll:50)

	Gussura	Atsushi	Supi	Ageha
Gussura		X 13	X 11	X 13
Atsushi	O 16		O 15	O 17
Supi	O 13	X 12		O 15
Ageha	O 18	X 14	△	

Atsushi (9pts)

	Mashika	Jam Aji	Umahiko	Sid
Mashika		X 11	X 11	X 11
Jam Aji	O 17		X 16	X 15
Umahiko	O 14	O 17		X 13
Sid	O 16	O 17	O 17	

Sid (9pts)

	Crow Blood	Cheetu Bazooka	Kikyo	Y.T.
Crow Blood		O 18	O 18	O 14
Cheetu Bazooka	X 12		△ 15	O 16
Kikyo	X 16	△ 15		△ 16
Y.T.	X 12	X 13	△ 16	

Crow Blood (9pts)

	Mook	Sylvian	Nexus	Deep Impact
Mook		X 15	O 15	O 15
Sylvian	O 18		X 14	O 16
Nexus	X 13	O 16		O 17
Deep Impact	X 13	X 13	X 14	

Mook (6pts/roll:50)

	Toshi	Yukito Yuraku	Taiki Paulownia	Kana
Toshi		X 13	X 14	O 18
Yukito Yuraku	O 15		O 17	O 15
Taiki Paulownia	X 13	X 15		O 17
Kana	X 15	X 12	X 12	

Taiki Paulownia (9pts)

THE STATS OF THE WINNERS ARE ON THE LAST BONUS PAGE!

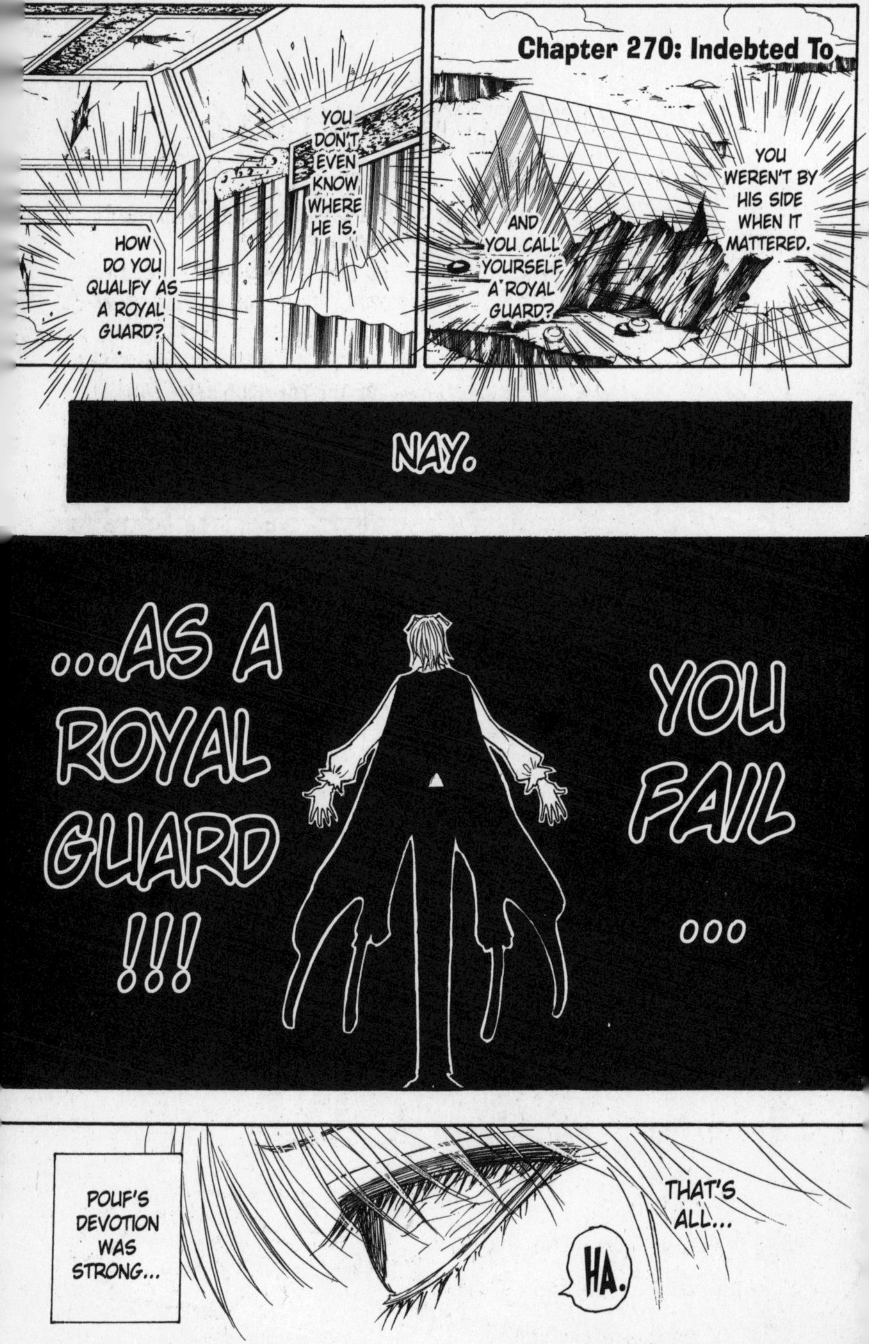
Chapter 270: Indebted To
YOU WEREN'T BY HIS SIDE WHEN IT MATTERED.
AND YOU CALL YOURSELF A ROYAL GUARD?
YOU DON'T EVEN KNOW WHERE HE IS.
HOW DO YOU QUALIFY AS A ROYAL GUARD?
NAY.
YOU FAIL...
...AS A ROYAL GUARD!!!
THAT'S ALL...
HA.
POUF'S DEVOTION WAS STRONG...

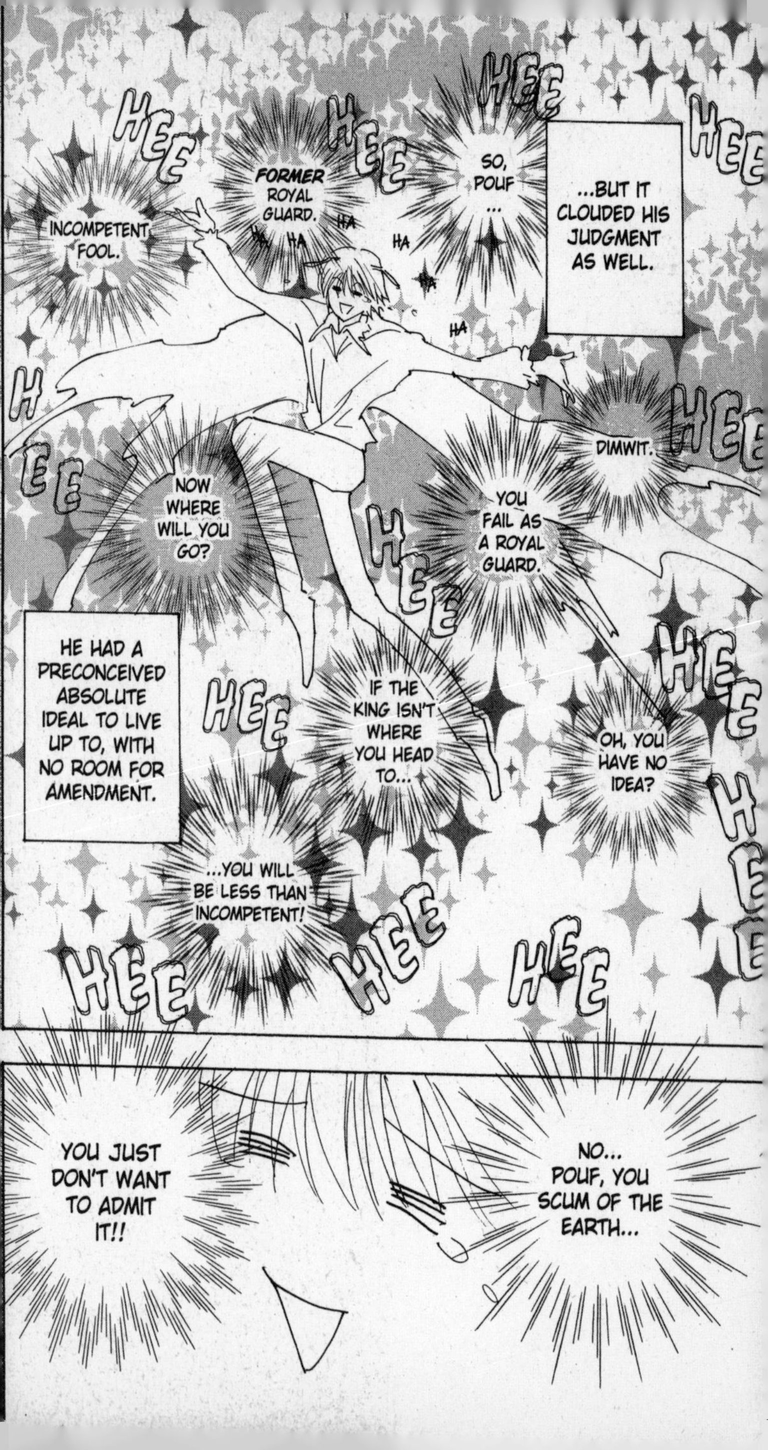
...BUT IT CLOUDED HIS JUDGMENT AS WELL.
HEE
HEE
SO, POUF...
HEE
FORMER ROYAL GUARD.
HA HA HA HA HA HA
HEE
INCOMPETENT FOOL.
HEE
DIMWIT.
H EE
YOU FAIL AS A ROYAL GUARD.
HEE
NOW WHERE WILL YOU GO?
HEE
HEE
HEE
OH, YOU HAVE NO IDEA?
IF THE KING ISN'T WHERE YOU HEAD TO...
HEE
HE HAD A PRECONCEIVED ABSOLUTE IDEAL TO LIVE UP TO, WITH NO ROOM FOR AMENDMENT.
...YOU WILL BE LESS THAN INCOMPETENT!
HEE
HEE
HEE
NO... POUF, YOU SCUM OF THE EARTH...
YOU JUST DON'T WANT TO ADMIT IT!!

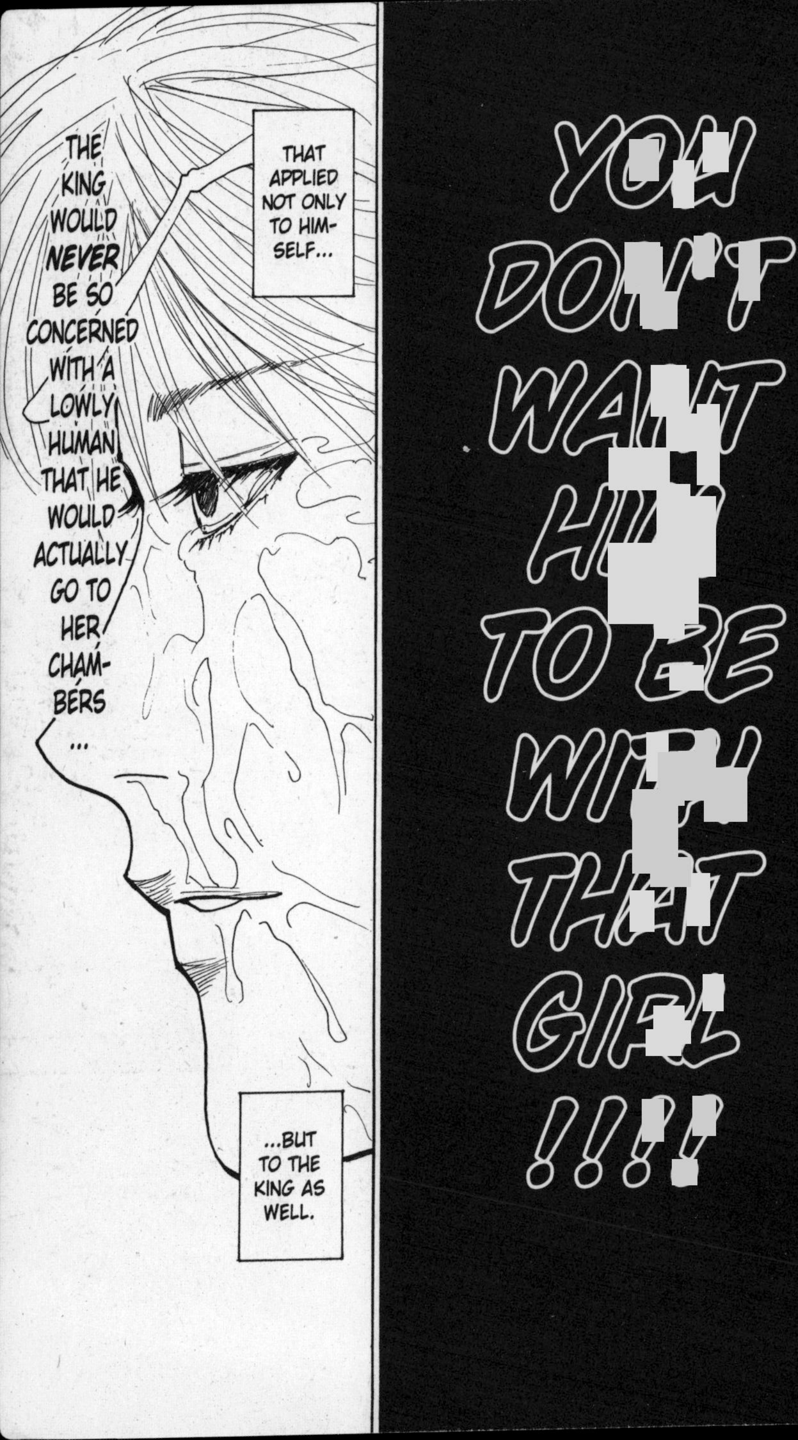
YOU DON'T WANT HIM TO BE WITH THAT GIRL!!!!
THAT APPLIED NOT ONLY TO HIMSELF...
THE KING WOULD NEVER BE SO CONCERNED WITH A LOWLY HUMAN THAT HE WOULD ACTUALLY GO TO HER CHAMBERS...
...BUT TO THE KING AS WELL.

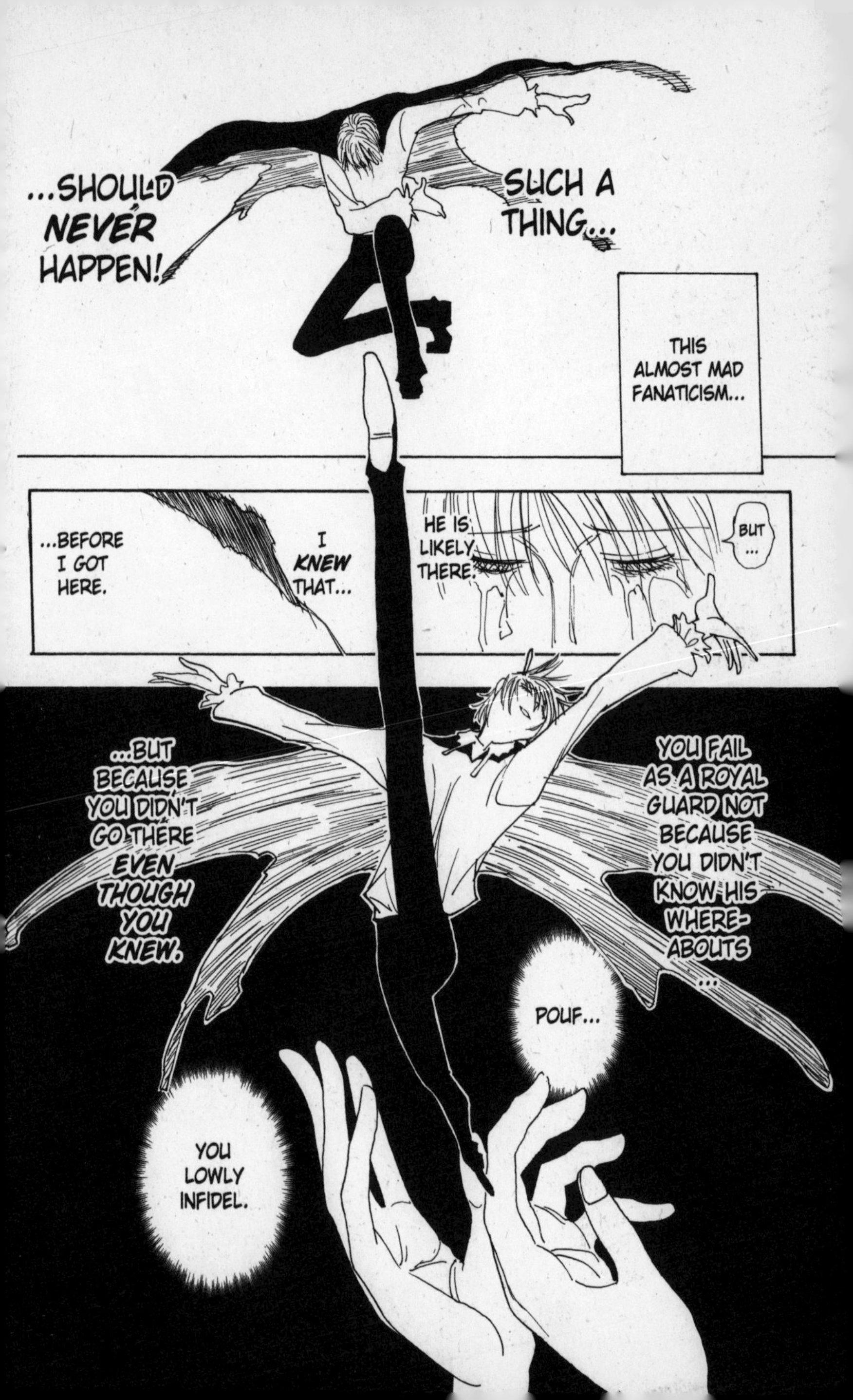

SUCH A THING...
...SHOULD NEVER HAPPEN!
THIS ALMOST MAD FANATICISM...
BUT ...
HE IS LIKELY THERE.
I KNEW THAT...
...BEFORE I GOT HERE.
YOU FAIL AS A ROYAL GUARD NOT BECAUSE YOU DIDN'T KNOW HIS WHERE-ABOUTS ...
...BUT BECAUSE YOU DIDN'T GO THERE EVEN THOUGH YOU KNEW.
POUF...
YOU LOWLY INFIDEL.

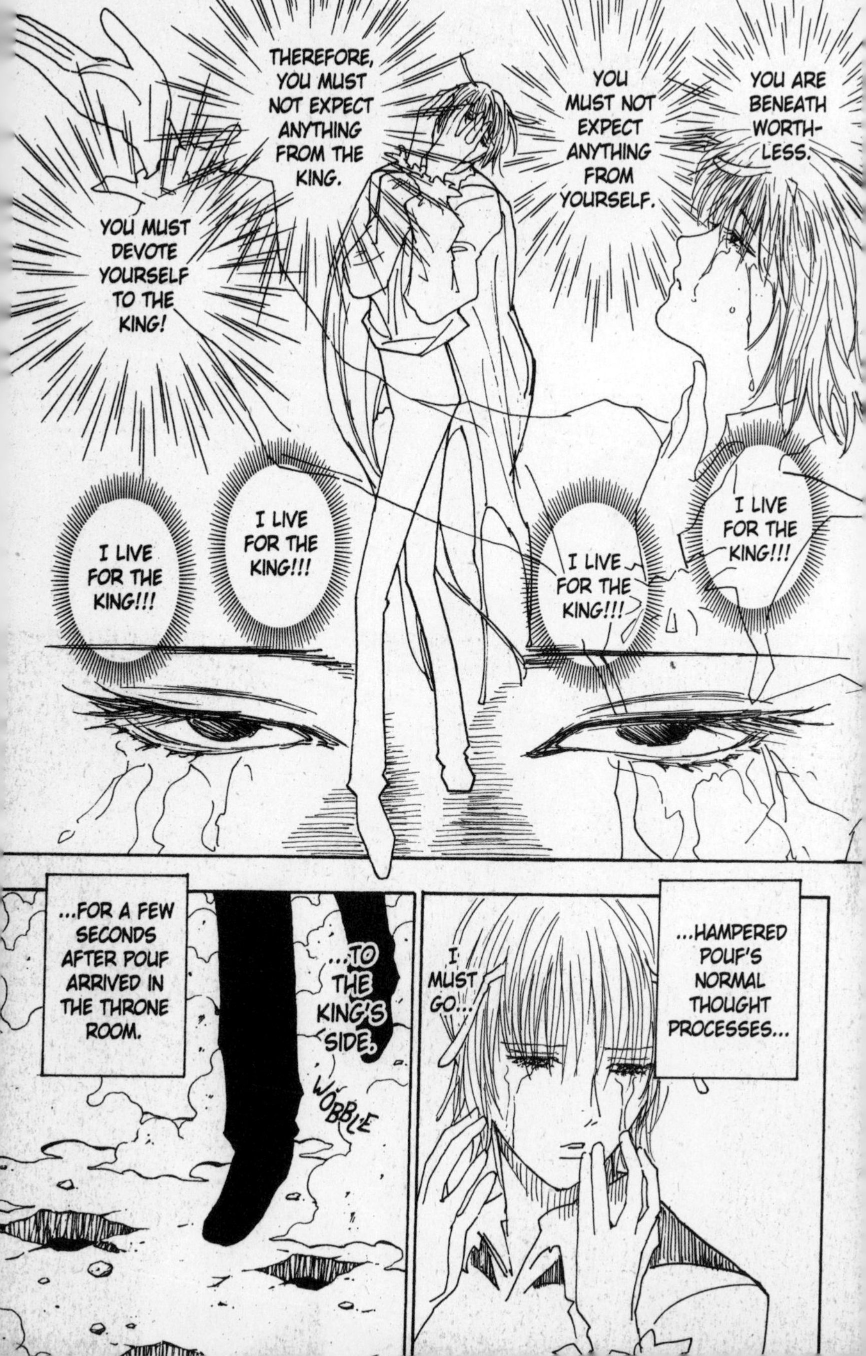
YOU ARE BENEATH WORTHLESS.
YOU MUST NOT EXPECT ANYTHING FROM YOURSELF.
THEREFORE, YOU MUST NOT EXPECT ANYTHING FROM THE KING.
YOU MUST DEVOTE YOURSELF TO THE KING!
I LIVE FOR THE KING!!!
I LIVE FOR THE KING!!!
I LIVE FOR THE KING!!!
I LIVE FOR THE KING!!!
...HAMPERED POUF'S NORMAL THOUGHT PROCESSES...
I MUST GO...
...TO THE KING'S SIDE.
WOBBLE
...FOR A FEW SECONDS AFTER POUF ARRIVED IN THE THRONE ROOM.

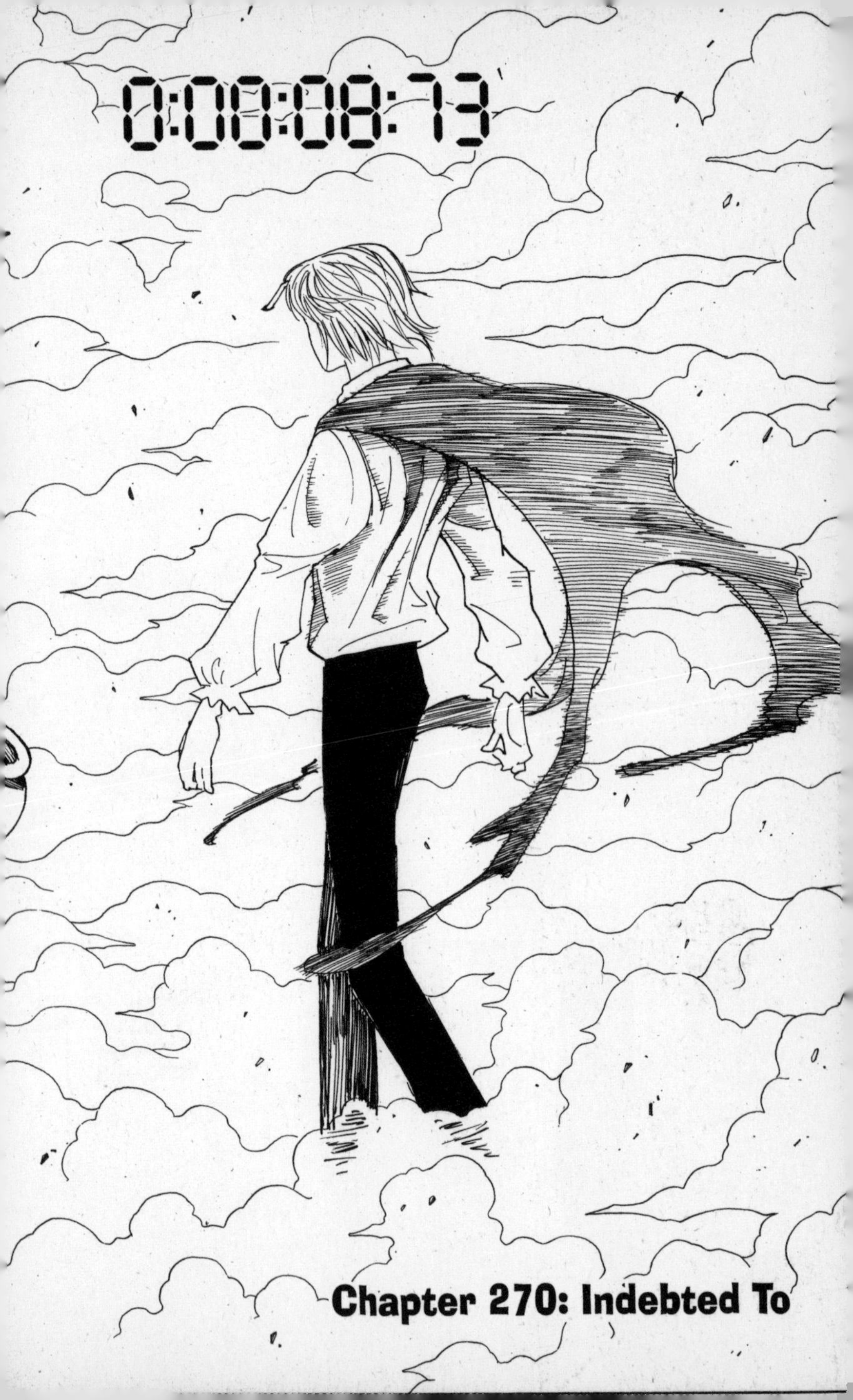
0:08:08:73

Chapter 270: Indebted To

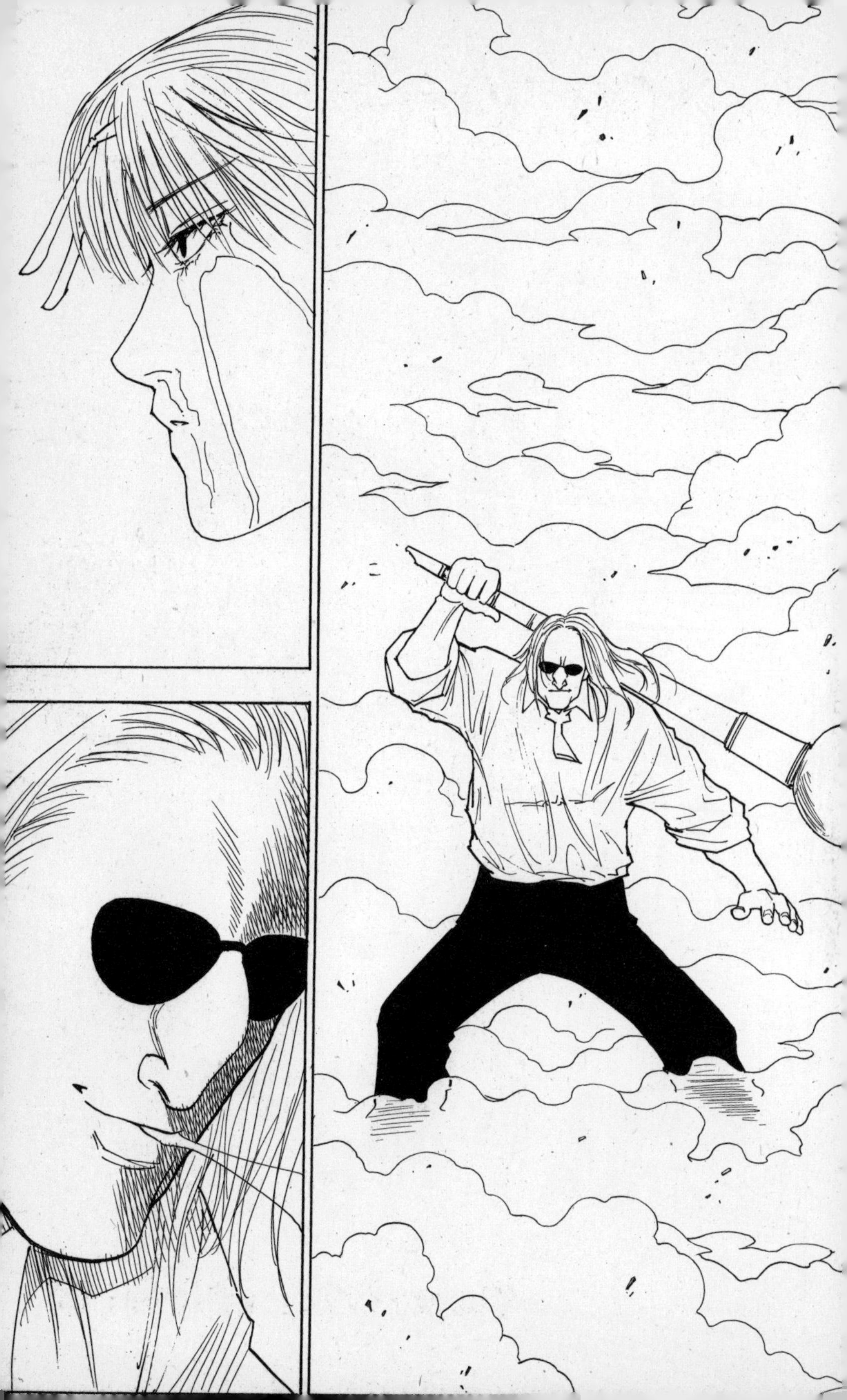

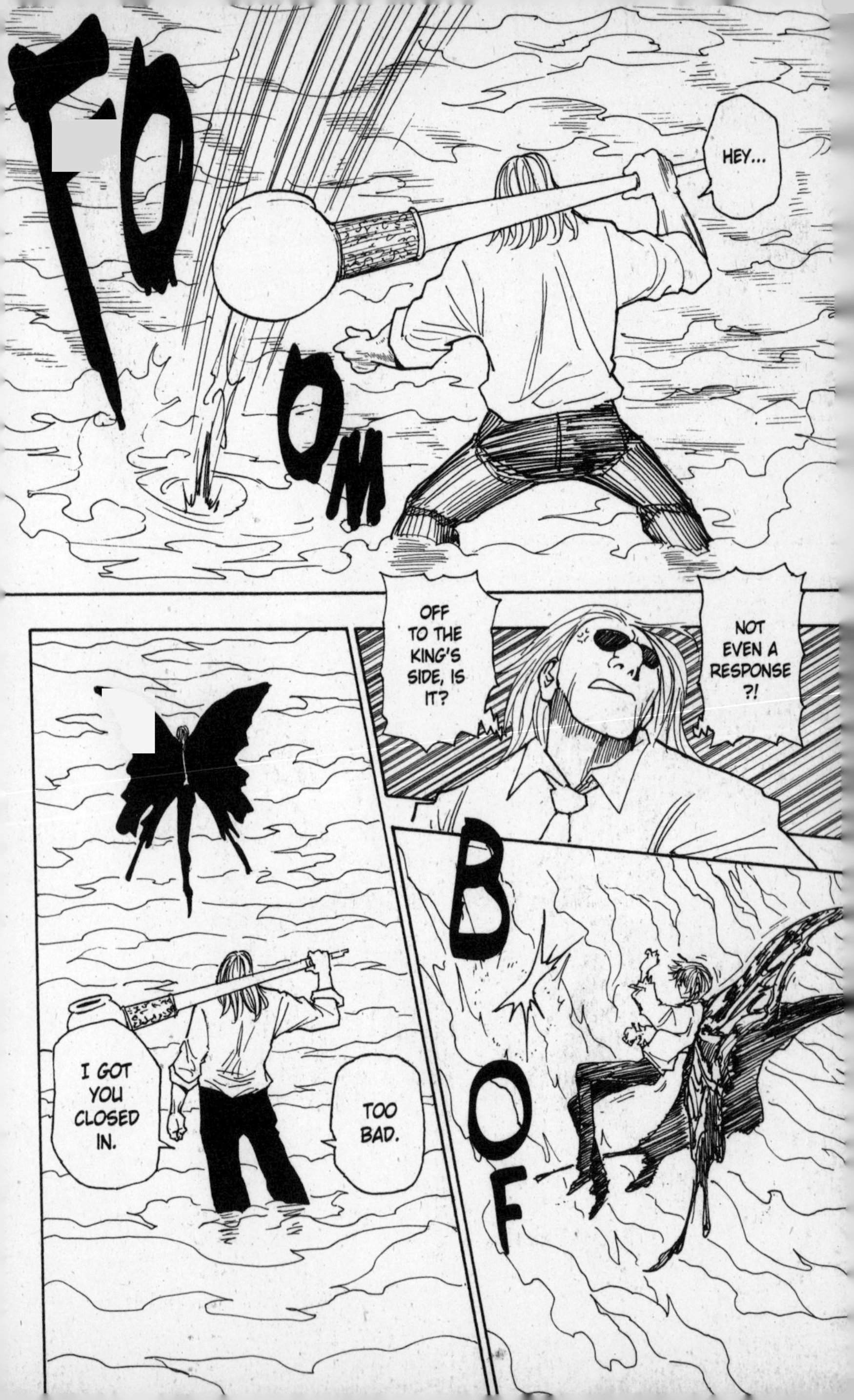
HEY...
FOOM
NOT EVEN A RESPONSE ?!
OFF TO THE KING'S SIDE, IS IT?
BOOF
TOO BAD.
I GOT YOU CLOSED IN.

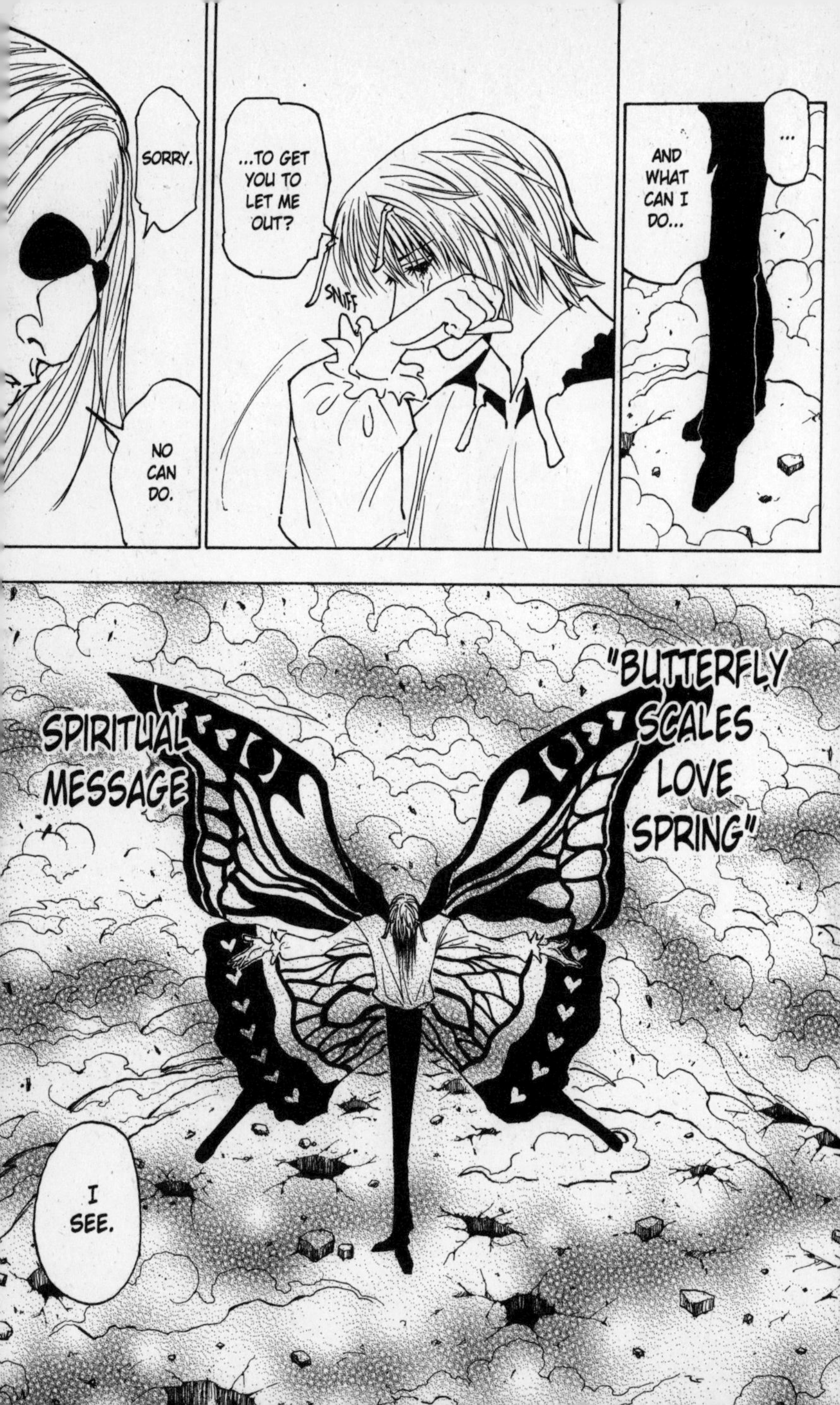
...
AND WHAT CAN I DO...
...TO GET YOU TO LET ME OUT?
SNIFF
SORRY.
NO CAN DO.
"BUTTERFLY SCALES LOVE SPRING"
SPIRITUAL MESSAGE
I SEE.

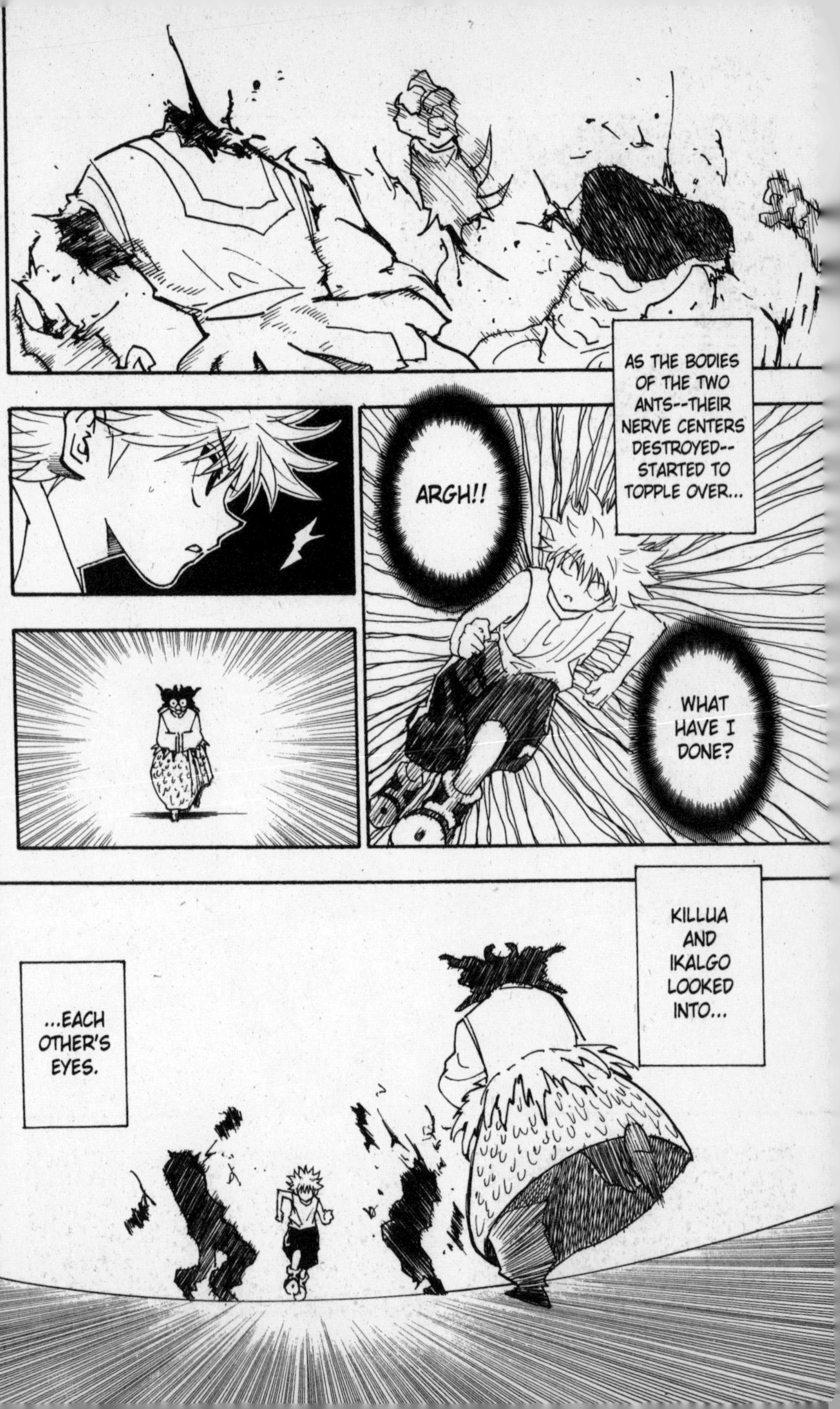
AS THE BODIES OF THE TWO ANTS--THEIR NERVE CENTERS DESTROYED--STARTED TO TOPPLE OVER...
ARGH!!
WHAT HAVE I DONE?
KILLUA AND IKALGO LOOKED INTO...
...EACH OTHER'S EYES.

READ THIS WAY

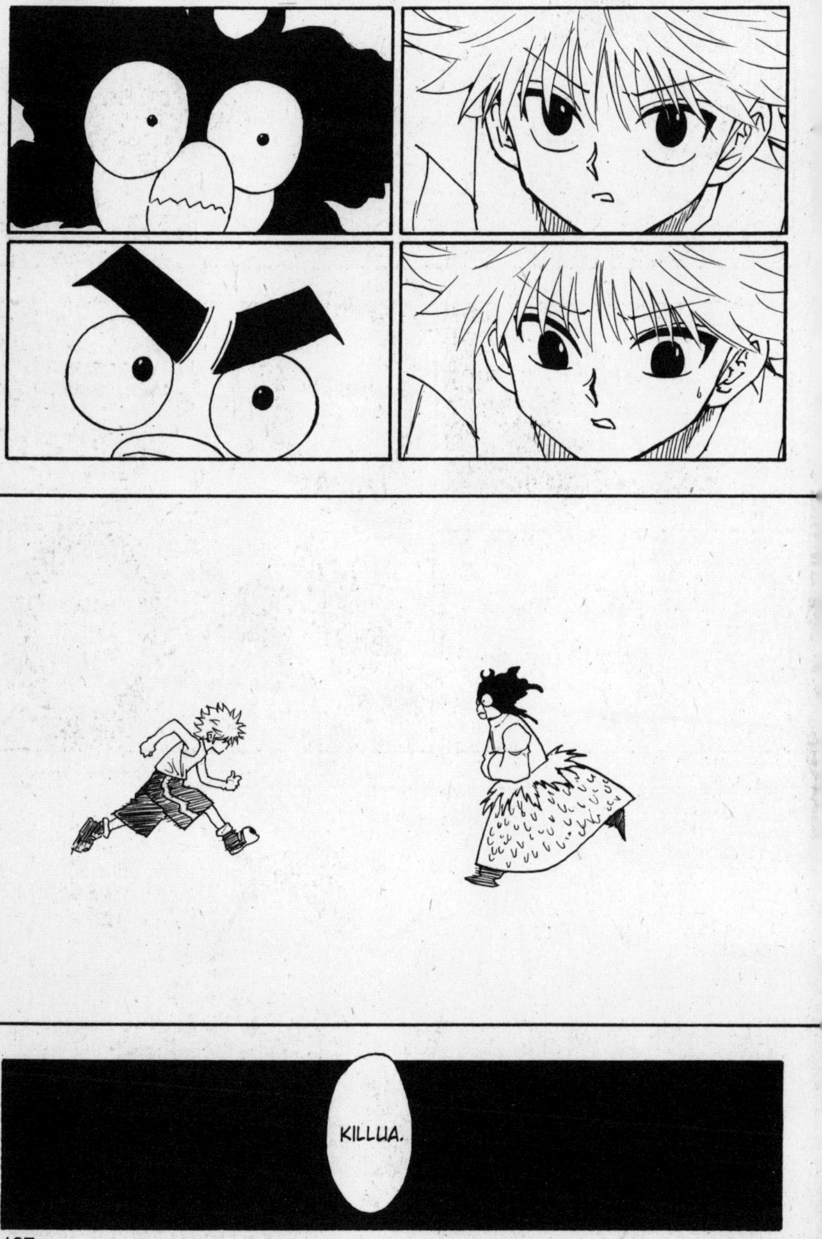
KILLUA.

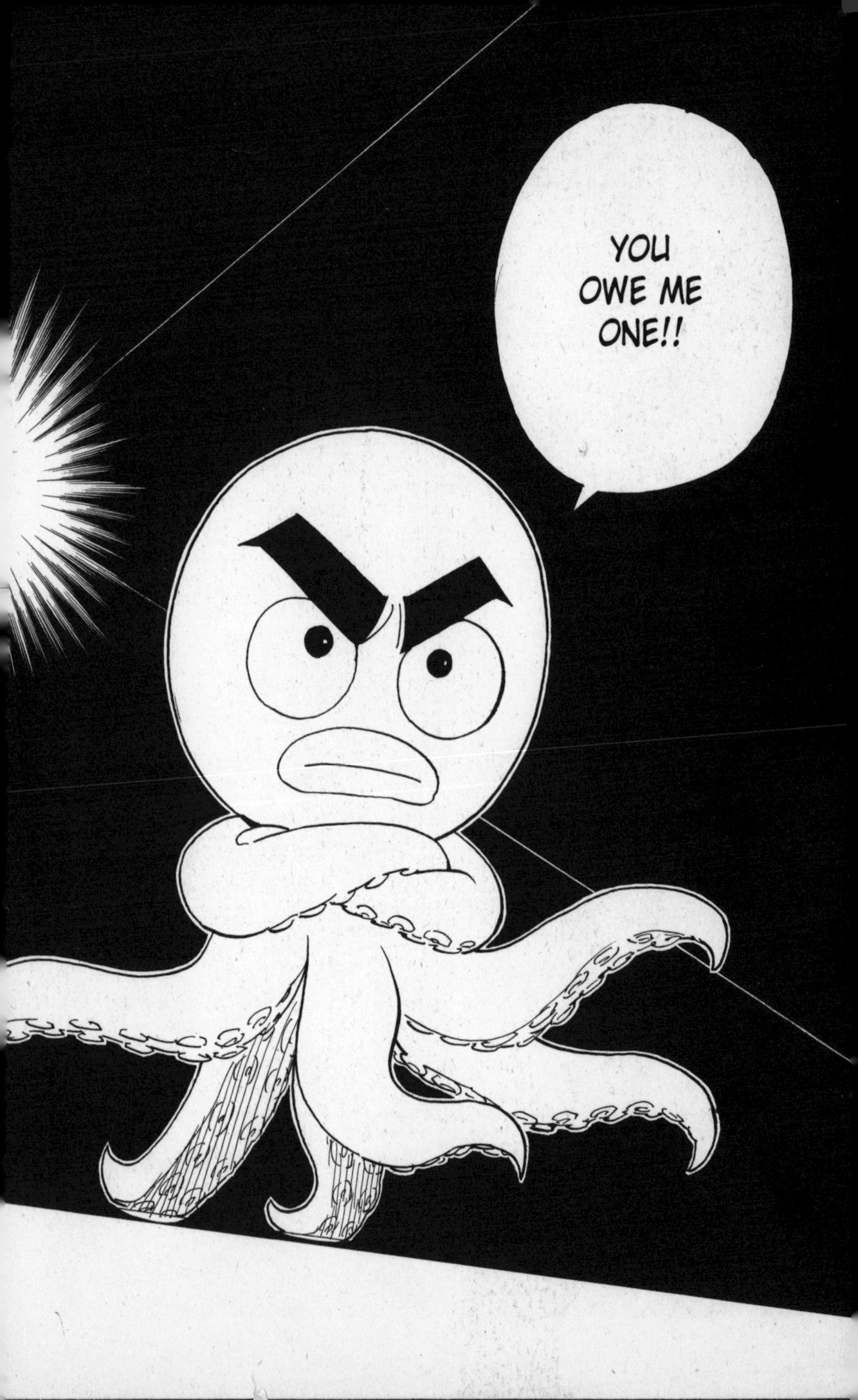
YOU OWE ME ONE!!

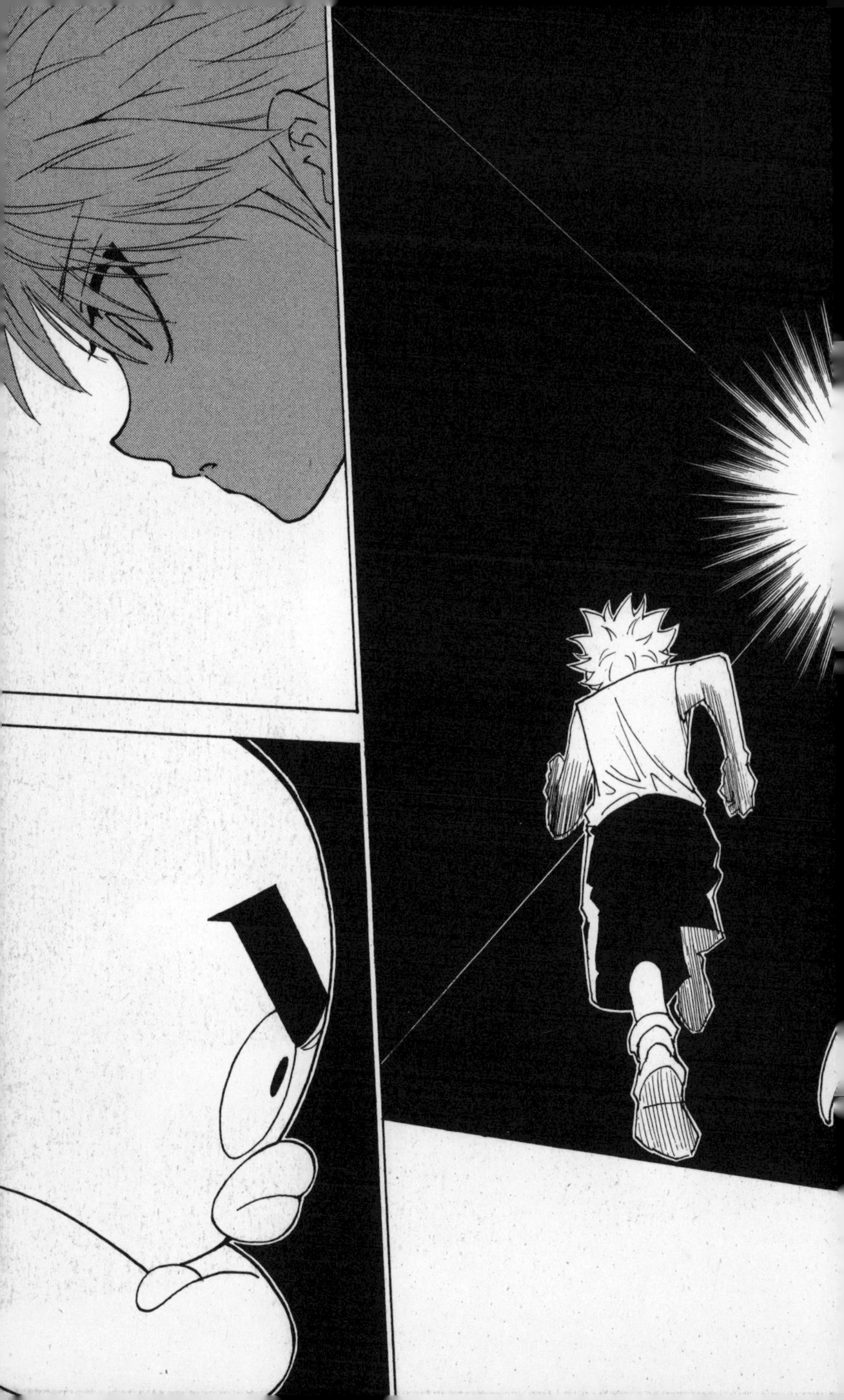

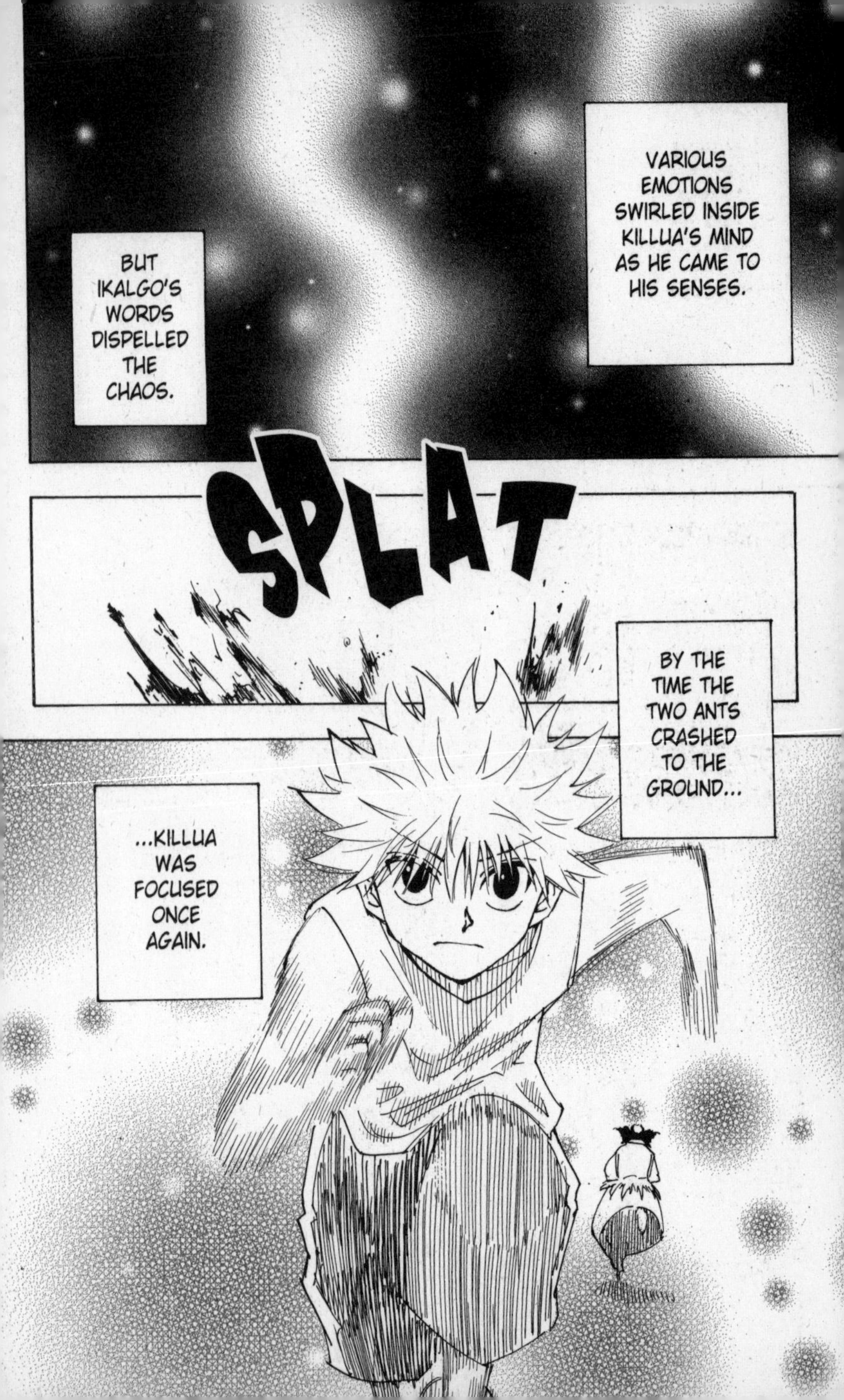
VARIOUS EMOTIONS SWIRLED INSIDE KILLUA'S MIND AS HE CAME TO HIS SENSES.
BUT IKALGO'S WORDS DISPELLED THE CHAOS.
SPLAT
BY THE TIME THE TWO ANTS CRASHED TO THE GROUND...
...KILLUA WAS FOCUSED ONCE AGAIN.

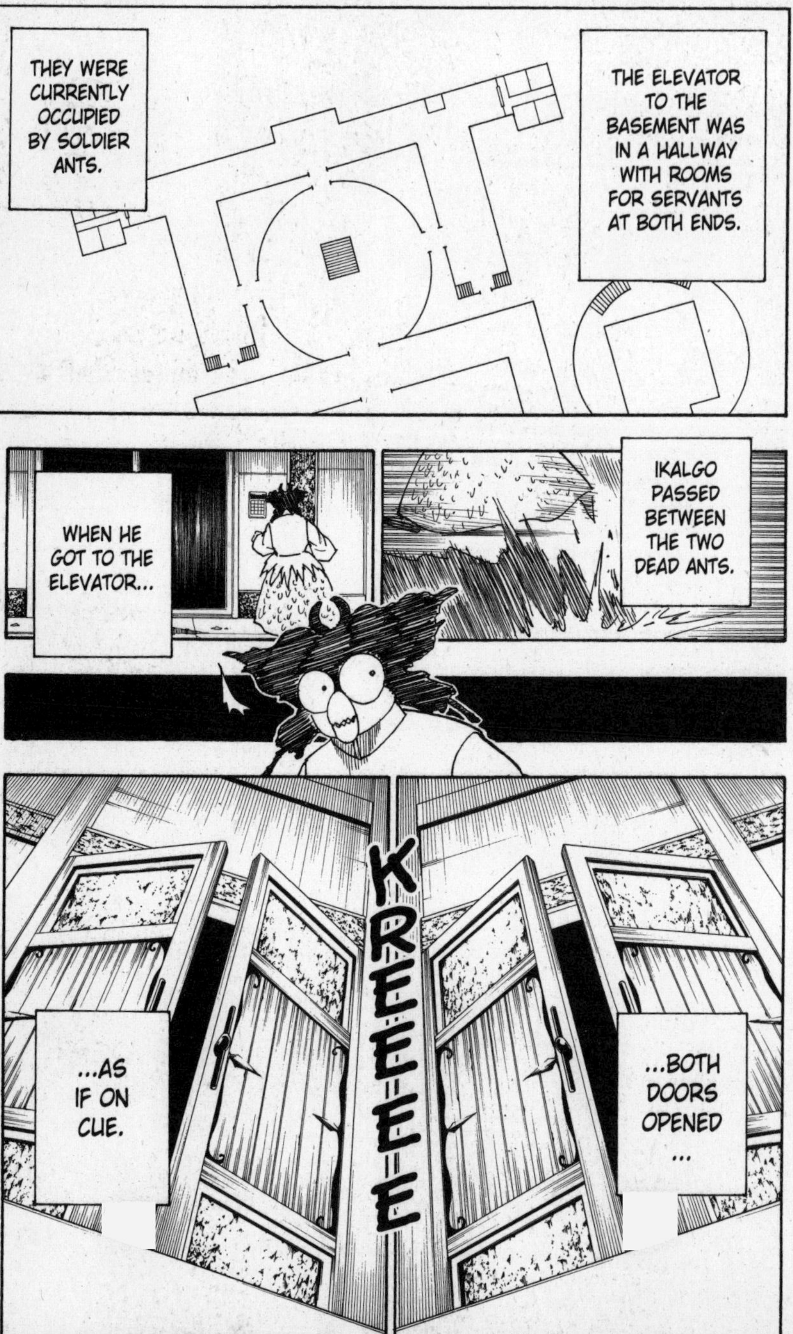
THE ELEVATOR TO THE BASEMENT WAS IN A HALLWAY WITH ROOMS FOR SERVANTS AT BOTH ENDS.
THEY WERE CURRENTLY OCCUPIED BY SOLDIER ANTS.
IKALGO PASSED BETWEEN THE TWO DEAD ANTS.
WHEN HE GOT TO THE ELEVATOR...
...BOTH DOORS OPENED ...
KREEEEE
...AS IF ON CUE.

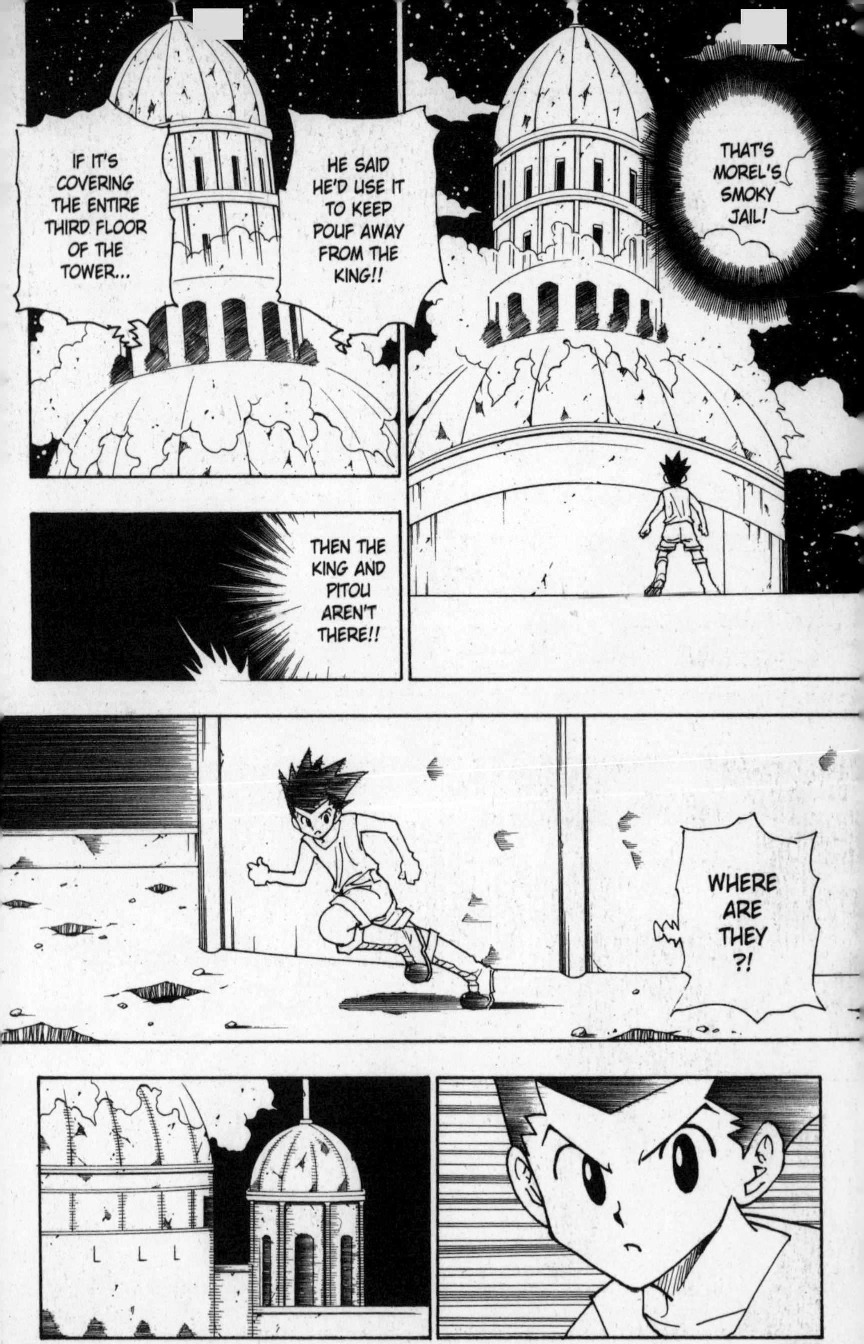
THAT'S MOREL'S SMOKY JAIL!
HE SAID HE'D USE IT TO KEEP POUF AWAY FROM THE KING!!
IF IT'S COVERING THE ENTIRE THIRD FLOOR OF THE TOWER...
THEN THE KING AND PITOU AREN'T THERE!!
WHERE ARE THEY ?!

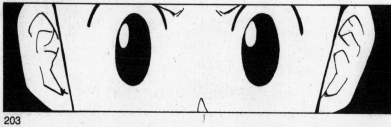

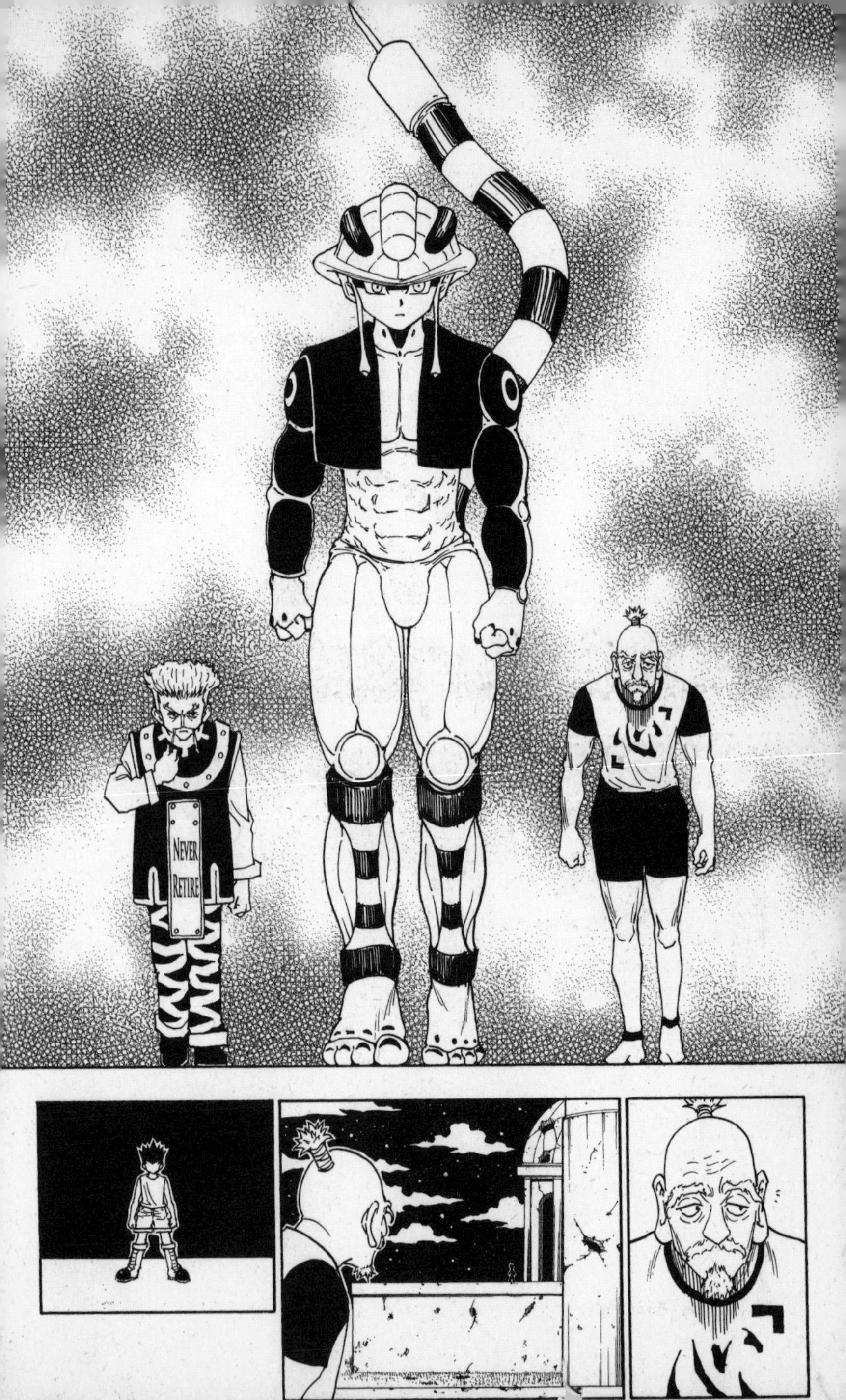
NEVER RETIRE

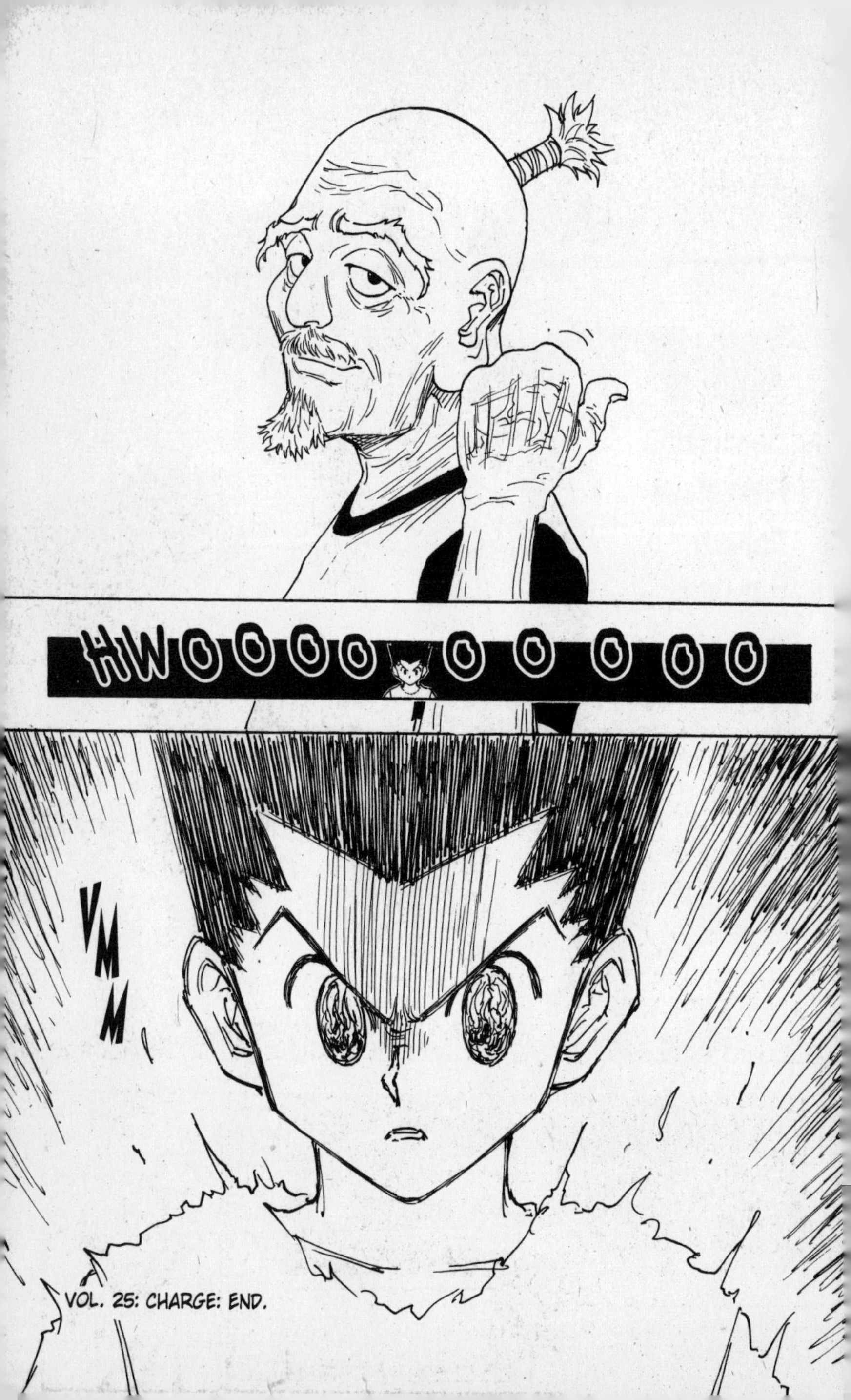
HWOOOO OOOOO
VMM
VOL. 25: CHARGE: END.

THESE ARE THE STATS OF THE WINNERS!!

Name	Power	Speed	Jump	Timing
Super Ninja Wolf	4	5	3	3
Bonkichi	3	5	3	4
Saekipuon	4	5	3	3
Nameless	3	5	2	5
Tobiah	4	5	4	2
Satoshi	6	6	1	2
Atsushi	4	6	3	2
Sid	4	4	4	3
Crow Blood	6	4	2	3
Mook	4	5	3	3
Taiki Paulownia	5	5	2	3

NOW YOU CAN
CALL YOURSELVES
HUNTERS!!

Coming Next Volume...

The Hunters are thrown for a loop when nothing goes according to plan for their big showdown with the Ants! Chairman Netero's grand entrance not only surprises the enemy, but the Hunters are distracted too! With no room for error, the Hunters find themselves overwhelmed by the Royal Guards, but Gon has another problem when Neferpitou doesn't even put up a fight!

Available in January 2010!

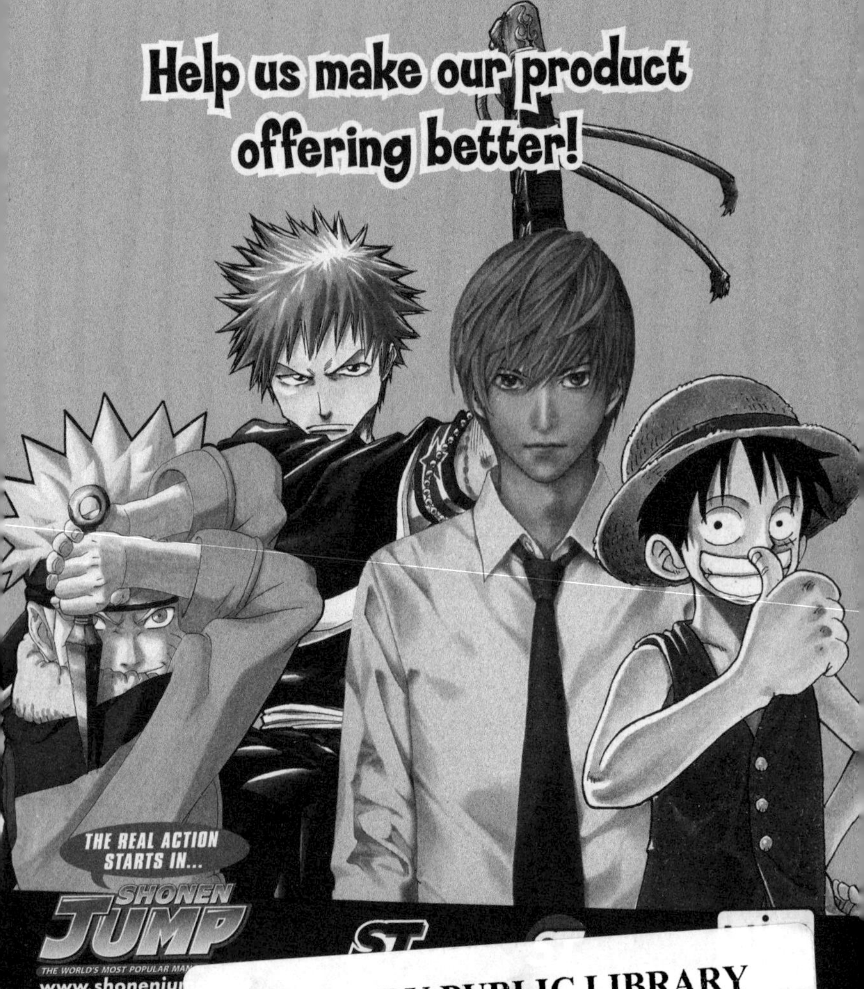

THE REAL ACTION STARTS IN...
SHONEN JUMP
THE WORLD'S MOST POPULAR MAN
www.shonenju
DEATH NOT